DEATH COMES TO BRUTON,

a market town in Somerset c.1400-c.1900

By

P.W. Randell

Grosvenor House
Publishing Limited

This book is published by
Grosvenor House Publishing Ltd
28-30 High Street, Guildford, Surrey, GU1 3EL.
www.grosvenorhousepublishing.co.uk

A CIP record for this book
is available from the British Library

ISBN 978-1-78148-702-0

Com'st thou to gaze upon my tomb
And leave a fruitless sign
Or com'st thou in youth's purple bloom
To learn that thou must die
Death may be hov'ring o're thine head
Awake believe and pray
The Saviour who on Calvary bled
To wash my sins away.

(On the gravestone in Pitcombe Churchyard of John Cook who died on 14th November 1827 aged 57.)

Sic sum, et sic eris tu.
(Thus I am, and thus you will be)

(On the brass memorial plate in the nave of Brewham Church of Francis Lynewraye, who died on 30th September 1598.)

CONTENTS

Books by the same Author   ix
Acknowledgements   x
Tables and Illustrations   xi
Explanation of Terms   xiii
Introduction   1

1. Setting the Scene   9

2. Causes of Death   15
   a) Epidemics   17
   b) Other diseases and illnesses   30
   c) Living and working conditions   40
   d) Childbirth   47
   e) Weather-related factors   52
   f) Violence   60
     i)   Murder   60
     ii) Manslaughter   63
     iii) Infanticide   64
     iv) Violence unknown   66
     v)   Suicide   67
     vi) In War   75
   g) Accidental Death   78
     i)   Deaths involving animals and vehicles 79
     ii) Machinery   83
     iii) Fire   84
     iv) Drowning   86
     v)   Miscellaneous accidents   88

3. Death for Young and Old 94
   a) The Young 94
   b) The Elderly 99

4. Attitudes to Death 105
   a) Medieval attitudes 107
      i) Gifts to the Church 108
      ii) Call upon Saints 110
      iii) Mass, prayers and remembrance 111
      iv) Free from debt 122
      v) Prayers of the poor 123
      vi) Acts of Charity 124
   b) The Reformation 131
   c) Seventeenth century attitudes to death 139
   d) Eighteenth century attitudes to death 143
   e) Nineteenth century attitudes to death 145

5. The Role of the Parish Church and the Churchyard 154
   a) The Parish Church 154
   b) The Churchyard 158

6. Burial of the dead: general 169

7. Burial of the wealthy 190
   a) Medieval 190
   b) Post Reformation 195
   c) 1700 and beyond 200

8. Burial of the poor 204
   a) Help from the Parish 205
   b) The poor of Sexey's Hospital 210
   c) The role of Friendly Societies 214

9. Burial of children 217

10. Burial of Non-Conformists 223

11. Burial of the Dead: Miscellaneous   227

12. Prosperity in Death   230
     a) Medieval   232
     b) Post Reformation and seventeenth century   235
     c) Eighteenth and nineteenth centuries   243
     d) Wealthy females   249

13. The Worldly Consequences of Death: Wills   256
     a) Alternatives to Wills   256
     b) Wills: General considerations   263
        i)   Executors and Overseers   263
        ii) Witnessed   267
        iii) Timing   273
        iv) Administrative matters   278
     c) Wills: Bequests of the deceased to family   282
        i)   Bequests to a wife   283
        ii) Bequests to children   290
        iii) Bequests to other relatives   298
        iv) Bequests of animals   309
     d) Wills: Bequests to the Church   313
     e) Wills: Bequests to the Poor   316
     f) Wills: Bequests to Servants   322
     g) Wills: The Issue of Debts   329
     h) Wills: Specific Items   335
     i) Wills: The Unusual   341

14. The Worldly Consequences of Death: Human   353
     a) Widows and Widowers   358
     b) Children   369
        i)   for the wealthy   370
        ii) for the poor   373
15. The Worldly Consequences of Death: Mourning   378
16. The Worldly Consequences of Death: Monuments   384
17. Conclusion.   395
18. And finally ..... or not?   399

Appendices   404
Appendix 1   Relative value of money   404
Appendix 2   List of Wills consulted   405
Appendix 3   Causes of death in Wincanton Sanitary
                District 1878-1897   415
Appendix 4   Monuments and Memorials   417
Appendix 5   Inventories   425
Appendix 6a   Epitaphs from Bruton Churchyard   434
        6b   Epitaphs and Memorials from local
                churches and churchyards   439
Appendix 7a   Victorian Hymns   449
        7b   Victorian Popular Songs   452
Appendix 8   Dialect Poetry   456
Appendix 9   Principal members of the Berkeley
                Family from 1545 to 1773   458

Notes and References   459

BOOKS BY THE SAME AUTHOR

Stones We Cannot Eat: Poverty, the Poor Law, Philanthropy and Self-help in Bruton, Somerset, c1500-c1900. Pen Press, 2009.

Life in a Rural Workhouse: Wincanton Workhouse, Somerset, 1834-1900. Pen Press, 2010.

Crime, Law and Order in a Somersetshire Market Town: Bruton, c1500-c1900. Pen Press, 2011.

Alcohol, Violence, Feasts and Fairs: Leisure Pursuits in Bruton, Somersetshire, c1500-c1900. Pen Press, 2012.

ACKNOWLEDGEMENTS

As always I am indebted to the staff of the Somerset Heritage Centre for the time and care which they have taken pursuing my many requests. Similarly the staff of both the Wiltshire and Dorset Heritage Centres have also played their part. The monument of John 1st Lord Berkeley of Stratton was originally located in the Chancel of Twickenham Parish Church but has been moved and is now some twelve feet above the ground in the space below the Tower. I wish to thank Diana Wells, the Hon. Archivist of the Church, for providing me with photographs of this monument, though how she managed it I have no idea! Above all I am grateful to my wife Anne who has patiently endured my journey through this topic. Death of course has the potential to be a very depressing subject and I am sure that at times when I was deeply immersed in writing an air of gloom could be present. On the other hand, having spent so many years researching and teaching History it was worth remembering that in all that time the vast majority of the events were well in the past and that the characters with whom I dealt were already dead.

Once again Anne helped with proof-reading but no matter how many times we read passages errors still seem to creep through!

TABLES

1. Average age of death in Bruton 1854-1914   12
2. Population totals 1801-1901   13
3. Years with 75 or more burials 1554-1900   14
4. Burials in Bruton 1666-1676   21
5. Poor Law Expenditure in Bruton 1665-1676   22
6. Child Deaths in relation to the total number of deaths in Bruton 1590-1919   94
7. Months of most child deaths as a %   98
8. Percentages of men and women aged 60 and over   101
9. Number and % of deaths in Bruton 1784-1800   103
10. Average age of death in Bruton 1784-1914   104
11. Value of personal and household goods 1584-1736   236
12. Short time between a Will made and burial in Bruton 1554-1754   274
13. Longer time between a Will made and burial in Bruton 1554-1754   275

EXPLANATION OF TERMS

1/4d	a farthing
2 farthings =	1/2d, halfpenny
4 farthings or 2 halfpennies =	1d, one penny
12 pennies =	1s, one shilling (equivalent to 5p)
20 shillings =	£1
21 shillings =	One Guinea

In the earlier period the £ sign was often written as li and followed the figure and many of the figures themselves were written in Roman numerals with the last small i written as a j to indicate the end of the figure, for example

v li = £5
vj li = £6
xjs viijd = 11s 8d

A Groat was a silver coin worth 4d.
A Noble was originally worth 6s 8d but increased in value to 8s 4d in 1464.
One Mark was 13s 4d.

A Quart	2 pints
4 quarts	1 gallon
Hogshead	54 gallons
Ton/tun	252 gallons.

Virgate	Measure of land, often about 30 acres.
Carucate	As much land as a plough-team could plough in a year and a day, usually up to about 100 acres.
Hide	Amount of land needed to support a free family, often 60-120 acres.
Messuage	A dwelling house with outbuildings and adjacent land such as a garden or orchard.
Tenement	Usually a house or cottage leased to tenants which may include lands or rights but occasionally just a piece of land.
Cauldron	A large pot, metal or earthenware, with lid and handles, often used for boiling over an open fire.
Crock	An earthenware pot or jar, sometimes two or three feet tall.
Platter	A large flat dish or plate, usually round or oval, used for serving food.
Whittle	A long knife, often used for butchering meat.
Maser	A silver-bound drinking vessel.
Potynger/podinger	A shallow cup or bowl with a handle.
Sawcers/saucers	A condiment dish.
Flock beds	A bed with a mattress stuffed with flock, that is coarse wool or cloth cut into small pieces.
Truckle bed	A servant's or apprentice's low bed which could be pushed under another bed.
Coverlet/Keverynge	A cover for a bed, a bedspread or quilt.
Tester	A canopy over a bed
Kercher/Kerchief	A woman's square scarf, often worn as a head covering.

Kirtle	A long gown or dress worn by a woman.
Neckerchief	A scarf worn around the neck.
Heriot	A tribute due under English law to the Lord of the Manor on the death of a tenant.
Kyne	Cows
Rother	Cattle or black cattle

Will and Testament (originally)

a) Will	Directions written in legal form for the distribution of a person's real property such as a house, land, money, goods etc.
b) Testament	A declaration of belief, often with soul given back to God, the hope of salvation, a wish to be buried in consecrated ground, a bequest to the Church.
Testator	A person who made a Will
Codicil	An addition or modification to an existing Will.
Obit	A memorial service.
Dirige	The service or office of Matins for the dead, of which 'Dirige' is the first word.
Placebo	The service or office of Vespers for the dead, of which 'Placebo' is the first word.
Missal	A book containing prayers, rites etc. for celebrating Mass for a whole year.
Pax-brede	A carved and decorated plaque with a handle, kissed by celebrant during Mass and then brought to each congregation member in turn at the altar rail.
Cruett	A small vessel for holy water or wine used in the celebration of the Eucharist.
Rack	A framework with bars.

INTRODUCTION

In the twenty-first century images of death are all too familiar. Modern technologies enable such pictures whether of death on the battlefield, through natural disasters, famine or terrorist atrocities, to be instantly accessible. Yet at the same time many individuals do not wish to contemplate or make the necessary arrangements for their own death, as witness, for example, the number of people in this country who die intestate as they have not written a Will. There remains the belief that it can always be done tomorrow.

In generations gone by the situation was often very different as death was a constant companion, one which could strike at any moment without warning and decimate entire families and whole communities. The lack of any organised welfare system, except the Poor Law after 1601, in the period under consideration, meant that the death of the main breadwinner could reduce the rest of the family to destitution.

Death was usually portrayed as a figure in literature and above all in paintings. Many medieval churches contained wall paintings where death featured and provided a constant reminder for parishioners of the transitory nature of life. The walls of St Mary's Church in Bruton undoubtedly displayed such paintings, probably then either destroyed or more likely painted over at the time of the Reformation. For some three hundred years the plaster on these walls was repeatedly whitewashed until finally chipped off by the Victorians who did not realise what was there.

In a rural county such as Somerset a wide array of superstitions became associated with death. At one extreme there were the curious beliefs about what would lead to death and included the idea that to turn a mattress on Good Friday, the day of the Crucifixion, would result in the death of the head of the household. There was also the belief that every last remnant of Christmas decoration had to be cleared out of the Church before Candlemas day (2nd February) or there would be a death in the family that occupied the pew in which as little as one leaf or berry was left.

At the other extreme there were many superstitions about practices which had to be performed once death had occurred. In some cottages black ribbon or crape was tied around any plants in pots so that they could mourn or they would die. More importantly, on the death of their master it was believed that cows and sheep had to be told immediately or they too would die. The same went for bees in a hive or they would swarm and their owner's spirit would never leave the earth.

When a miller died all the blades in the arms of the windmill were removed and as the funeral procession made its way to the church with the bell tolling, the arms were turned in unison. When another member of the miller's family died a smaller number of blades were removed such as nineteen for his wife and thirteen for a child.

A more unusual belief was that it was necessary to bury a shepherd with a small piece of sheep's wool in his hand. Because of the nature of his work, often miles from anywhere and with the need to tend constantly his sheep, he was often unable to worship regularly in church on Sundays. The piece of wool was designed to remind God on the Day of Judgement why this man had been absent.

How far these and similar superstitions were prevalent in Bruton and the surrounding area is now lost in time.

Certainly ringing bells was and is much associated with death as not only was a church bell rung near, at and after the death of a parishioner during the medieval period but also the practice continued in modified form after the Reformation. In addition bells were rung on other days such as All Hallows' Eve (31st October), All Saints' Day (1st November) and All Souls' Day (2nd November), on which occasions it was felt that it would provide comfort to all Christian souls. Despite attempts by Henry VIII, Edward VI and Queen Elizabeth I to ban the practice, it continued in many rural areas. Bells were also rung extensively on Holy Innocents' Day (28th December) to bring similar comfort to the souls of the children slaughtered by King Herod.

This study on death in Bruton and its immediate neighbourhood has concentrated on four main areas: the first is the causes of death which were many and varied, and some of which remained constant throughout the period such as accidents, while others declined dramatically, particularly those related to illnesses such as plague and smallpox. Secondly, attitudes to death are examined and these show a marked variation through the centuries from a belief in the importance of assistance for the Soul by the living in the medieval period, to the concept of a heavenly home beloved by the Victorians. The third area focuses on burials themselves, including the role of the parish church and the churchyard. It soon becomes clear that in death, as in life, there was a vast gulf between the wealthy and the poor.

Finally the worldly consequences of death are examined in some detail, beginning with the mass of fascinating information provided by Wills, although sadly most of these derive from the wealthier in the community as they had something of value to leave and so give a very one-sided view. There are also the human consequences for those left behind to grieve: widows, widowers and children. For the wealthier in the community no matter what the depth of their grief, there was often material security but for the poor it was another matter. As the centuries passed by memorials of various types became more prevalent as did an array of epitaphs.

As the churchyard of St Mary's did not originally include the land to the east of the Chancel, it was a relatively small burial area. It must have become very crowded, especially with the rapid rise in the population in the eighteenth and nineteenth centuries, as it was in use for over a thousand years. The Burial Registers from 1554 to 1900 indicate that there were over 14,000 interments there. This figure for deaths, however, is misleading for three main reasons.

In the first place it assumes that the Registers were kept accurately. At various times in Bruton this was clearly not the case as so much depended upon the competence, dedication and ability of the Parish Clerk or possibly a curate. It is in fact quite rare to find a whole month when there were no burials yet between 11th February 1577 and 29th July 1578 there were none. Similarly no burials at all were recorded between March 1581 and September 1582, a period of some eighteen months but by comparison in the previous eighteen months there had been twelve burials and in the same period following eleven. There are a number of other smaller gaps, such as between 17th July and 12th October 1585, 13th February and 7th June 1599. In the seventeenth century there were no burials recorded between 26th May and 21st August 1606, 17th August and 11th October 1607, 25th December 1607 and 14th March 1608, 26th February and 17th June 1616. As the century advances the record keeping seems to improve but there were difficult periods in the eighteenth century, for example between 28th February and 21st July 1743 and 18th November 1744 and 9th January 1745. There was another gap between 11th May and 3rd August 1767 and then a Memorandum was added in the Burial Register, "Note that John Biggs, late Clerk, have neglected registering the Funeralls from November ye 6th 1767 to this time, June ye 3rd 1768." Clearly at times all was not well.

These examples represent readily identifiable gaps in the Burial Registers and cover in total nearly six years but how far individual burials were omitted in particular months is impossible to determine. With the introduction of the Registration Act in 1836 and a Registrar appointed based upon each Poor Law Union greater accuracy was achieved. (1)

Second, there were a number of categories that were excluded from a Christian burial in consecrated ground. Anyone who died while excommunicated was buried beyond the boundary of the churchyard and references to a small number of these appear in the Registers. For centuries suicides were often denied a final resting place in a churchyard, although as an act of charity a burial could take place but at night and without the presence of a Minister so no record was kept. Those judged guilty of treason were also excluded, an unlikely category in Bruton.

Third, a much larger group was the stillborn and un-baptised infants. While it was often the practice, especially in the later part of the period, to bury them in churchyards, generally on the north side, their interment was by the Sexton without a Minister. Such actions, which were still taking place in St Mary's in the early twentieth century, were not recorded in the Burial Registers.

How many bodies were interred without a record being made is impossible to determine but it must have reached many hundreds through the centuries.

There were, of course, many others who died in Bruton but made a deliberate decision to be interred elsewhere. For some it was within the church in the parish where they had been born or where there was a pronounced family connection and possibly even a vault. For others it was a choice as a result of their religious beliefs: a small number of Catholics in the post-Reformation period may have been buried elsewhere; a few Quakers requested burial in their own burial grounds; and a limited number of Congregationalists took advantage of their own burial plot in Wincanton.

The community in the small market town of Bruton faced the same problems and issues as the rest of the country. The inhabitants knew that death was an ever-present threat and reality and in many respects they approached it in the same way as it was confronted elsewhere. This was particularly the case when dealing with its causes, the varying and developing attitudes towards death as well as the rites and methods of burial. National statistics are useful in that they provide a general picture, an indication of specific trends. Sometimes the statistics from Bruton conformed closely; at other times they did not as a result of local circumstances.

When local men and women who had something to leave drew up their last Will and Testament they did so using the formats and formulae common elsewhere. But every Will was very individual and almost unique in that it not only reflected particular circumstances but also gave an indication of those other people and material goods which were important to the testator in this world at that moment.

All the bereaved in this country experienced a common grief but in the last analysis every individual's reaction was unique, from the relatively comfortable surroundings of the wealthy to the stark reality of life without a breadwinner experienced by the poor. The latter often had to rely upon the charity of their neighbours in their community and later the Poor Law which could be less than generous in its payments.

At first sight a study of death is a morbid topic but it is one with which every community and family in the country had and has to deal. While in the centuries studied death nearly always brought forth grief, sorrow and sometimes physical suffering, it also demonstrated the resilience of the human spirit and above all the concepts of faith and hope.

> Better by far you should forget and smile
> Than that you should remember and be sad.
> *Remember* by Christina Rossetti.

1

SETTING THE SCENE

For much of its existence Bruton was a small market town that grew from an Anglo-Saxon settlement where a Royal Mint had operated before the Norman Conquest in 1066. The overwhelming majority of its medieval inhabitants lived on the sloping northern side of the River Brue as the southern side was occupied by at least one church and an Augustinian Priory, raised in 1510 to the status of an Abbey. Some visitors to the town wrote flattering descriptions: "The situation of the town is very pleasing, it standing in a fine rich warm vale open only to the south, and being almost surrounded by fine swelling hills.... with beautiful sequestred hollow glens and winding valleys intermixt, in a style unusually picturesque and delightful." (1)

As the town was situated so close to a river there was an increased possibility of water-borne diseases such as malaria being more prevalent and a cause of death. A Reply to the Society of Antiquaries in the mid 1750s, however, indicated that that was not in fact the case. "The nature of the air seems rather dry than moist, tho the Parish lies low it is not subject to Fogs; nor noxious Vapours arising from swampy ground, there is not a Rush to be seen in the whole Vale above or below the Town; it is pure and healthy, neither the subject to Agues or Fevers, the people live to a good old age, to four score, ninety." (2)

During the period under consideration agriculture remained an important activity with many inhabitants leasing land in the two Open Fields and later in the enclosed fields, often referred to as 'Closes'. Some labourers found their employment on this land that was predominantly used for pastoral purposes, although a significant acreage was arable. A Survey in 1798 indicated that in the Manor of Bruton just under 50% was pasture, 11% meadow, 20% arable, 17% coppice and the remainder occupied by houses, gardens and orchards.

Rural industry also flourished and as early as 1542 John Leland noted that the town was "much occupied with making of clothe." The Accounts of John Smythe, a Bristol merchant, revealed that he received substantial amounts of woollen cloth in the 1540s from John Yerbury of Bruton. By the middle of the eighteenth century there were "manufactures of Broad Cloth, Serges and knit Stockings." Production remained in the hands of leading families such as the Yerburys, Whiteheads and Goldesbroughs, sometimes for generations.

The decline of the West Country woollen industry in the eighteenth century led to the silk industry dominated by the Ward family becoming a major employer from the 1770s. By 1823 John Sharrer Ward estimated that he employed, "From eight to nine hundred, or perhaps to one thousand, the children often working at their own houses with their parents." Faced with foreign competition it too declined and was replaced by other smaller industries such as horsehair seating with the Boyds and the Whites. (3)

Throughout the centuries there was also a wide range of other occupations associated with the countryside from brewing to tanning to slaughtering to edgetool making. In the absence of any considerations of safety and health all of the industries cited included processes which had the potential to cause sickness, injuries and even death. Report after Report, especially in the nineteenth century, highlighted the way in which their waste products flowed through the streets and bartons and polluted the water supply.

Needless to say as both agriculture and industry flourished the town prospered and attracted a multitude of merchants, traders and craftsmen, such as Gabriel Felling the goldsmith. Their prosperity allowed them to improve, develop or rebuild their properties, often with fashionable facades. In the early nineteenth century Edward Dyne purchased the former Bell Inn on the south side of the High Street and between December 1807 and December 1808 his Account Book indicates that he spent over £300 converting it to a private dwelling, now called Priory House and formerly Berkeley House. Some men were able to build, extend or develop detached houses, just a short distance from the mass of inhabitants: Coombe Villa, Coombe Lodge, Tolbury House, Berkeley Villa and Plox House. In 1805 Coombe Farm was demolished and rebuilt as a gentleman's residence by Dyne. These houses were one step removed from the potential pollution and its consequences. (4)

For many of the inhabitants of Bruton through the centuries life was a constant struggle, both economically and physically. Poverty, disease, ill-health and death were common place. It is accepted by historians that nationally by 1640 life expectancy was thirty-two years and that between a quarter and a third of all children would be dead before their fifteenth birthday. An analysis of the Burial Registers for Bruton suggests that at times the situation there was even worse. The statistics are of necessity from later years as the first full year in which the age at death was recorded was 1784. In that year the average age of death in the town was 27.5 years, declining to 24.4 years a decade later. While there were significant annual fluctuations, generally in the first half of the nineteenth century, it rose to the mid thirties, slightly lower than the national average of forty years, and then continued its upward trend. (5)

TABLE 1 Average age of death in Bruton 1854-1914

	Average age in years
1854	34.4
1864	35.3
1874	41.6
1884	45.3
1894	53.3
1904	52.4
1914	59.2

Whatever its problems Bruton remained the largest centre of population compared with all the surrounding villages and hamlets. Prior to the compilation of Census figures in the nineteenth century population totals are generally estimates but nevertheless give an indication of its development, although it is far from being a picture of uniform increase. At the time of the Domesday Survey in 1086 it was considered as having about 250 inhabitants and then steadily increased until the fourteenth century. A combination of a decline in the grain yield with particularly bad harvests between 1315 and 1317, along with the appearance of the Black Death in 1347-1348 decimated the population nationally. In 1300 it had been estimated at between four and six million but by 1477 was three million and continued falling to two and a half million in the 1520s after which a slow recovery began. How far Bruton was affected is impossible to determine but a study for neighbouring Wiltshire found a significant decline in terms of both the peasantry and the lords of the manor. (6)

A Subsidy Roll for 1547 suggested a population in Bruton of about 890 while another for 1576 indicated a similar total of about 900. It may have reached 1,156 in 1631 when a Report from Justices of the Peace Henry Berkeley and James Farewell found that there were that many buyers for 168 bushels of wheat in the town. The rise was once again checked by the Plague in the late 1660s so that the Hearth Tax of 1678 suggested just over 1100. In 1791 Collinson estimated a population of 1,600 which was close to the first official Census total a decade later. (Table 2) (7)

TABLE 2 Population totals 1801-1901

Census Year	Population
1801	1631
1811	1746
1821	2076
1831	2223
1841	2074
1851	2109
1861	2232
1871	1905
1881	1849
1891	1788
1901	1776

In some years the mortality rates rose significantly as a result of a national epidemic such as influenza in 1558 and in 1666 at the time of the Great Plague. In some years it appears to have been more localized epidemics such as smallpox between 1727 and 1729. (See Table 3) Occasionally Bruton managed to avoid the worst impact of epidemics such as the plague in 1592 when there were only thirty-one deaths and in those of 1602 and 1603 when there were just twenty-two and thirty-eight deaths respectively. Nevertheless these killer diseases which in some years, such as 1558, 1728 and 1741 killed nearly 10% of the population of the town, were a serious blow to the inhabitants. This is particularly the case when it is considered that these outbreaks incapacitated as many people as they killed and left behind a large number of widows with children, and orphans. The increase in poverty which resulted was significant for some families. The economic disruption, especially to the labour force, was manifest, for example it was reported that in 1737 in Bruton 443 people caught smallpox and that thirty-four died from it.

TABLE 3 Years with 75 or more burials, 1554-1900

Year	Number of burials, 75 or more	Number of burials in preceding year	Number of burials in succeeding year
1558	78	48	28
1588	91	22	18
1597	82	38	32
1651	82	18	39
1666	83	29	46
1668	78	46	43
1686	87	45	36
1721	81	43	30
1728	102	62	85
1729	85	102	81
1730	81	85	53
1737	75	21	55
1741	128	38	67

Nationally death rates rose to thirty three per 1000 in the late sixteenth century and could be much higher in specific years of mortality such as those indicated above but towards the end of the nineteenth century improvements in public health, more and better food, increased medical and scientific understanding and higher wages were among a wide range of factors which led to an increase in life expectancy. In the last two decades of that century the Annual Reports of the Medical Officer of Health of the Wincanton Poor Law Union, which included Bruton, revealed an average death rate per 1000 of the population of 16.2, peaking at 19 in 1883 and then generally declining to 10.9 at the end of the 1890s. (8)

2

CAUSES OF DEATH

Death was so common in the later medieval period and beyond that every family experienced it on an almost regular basis: losing parents, spouse, children, friends, employer or employee. The Parish Registers for Bruton contain many burial entries for the same family in relatively short periods of time, such as in 1559 on January 16th Thomas Walter, on January 26th John Walter and three days later Frances Walter; in 1591 on 22nd January Robert Penny, the next day Jane Penny, on 25th April John Penny, 6th June William Penny, 12th June Edith Penny and two days later Margaret Penny, all of Discove. In 1623 Walter Griffen was interred on 29th July and on 2nd August Margaret Griffen, both of Bickwick. On 4th February 1660 Elliot Beasly was buried and on 4th March John and Thomas Beasly "both together". In 1734 John Jacob buried his wife, Grace, on 1st July and his son Emanuel on 30th August. Nearly one hundred years later a local newspaper reported the death of Jacob Browne of Shepton Montague, "Severe calamity has visited his family. He had followed to the grave within a few weeks four of his children, three of whom, only a fortnight previous to his own dissolution, were buried on the same day."

The causes of such deaths were many and varied, although given the level of medical knowledge some of the diagnoses were very imprecise. A lengthy illness gave the medical man some chance of coming to an appropriate diagnosis but a rapid death, possibly involving a fever, did not. In addition, of course, a relatively minor infection could lead to a person succumbing after years of poor diet, exposure to harsh working conditions and other periodic illnesses, which had together significantly weakened the immune system. For a minority there was a violent or unnatural or sudden death which was a cause of much concern, especially in the earlier part of the period.

In these cases it was expected that a Coroner, aided by a jury of local male inhabitants, would determine the cause of death. The office of Coroner itself was ancient, being established in England just after the Norman Conquest. Initially their function had been to protect the interests, especially financial, of the monarch in any criminal proceedings. As such it was rare for anyone appointed a Coroner to be below the rank of a knight, but through the centuries the role developed as did the social rank of the men appointed. Increasingly their primary function was to take an inquisition upon any corpse which was found within their district. There is evidence from some parts of Somerset that parish officials were not always too keen to inform the Coroner of a suspicious death, mainly as a result of the costs incurred and their dislike of what was perceived as outside interference.

By the eighteenth century when a Coroner's post fell vacant there could be fiercely contested elections as in September 1789 for East Somerset, the area which included Bruton. There were three candidates and it was reported that, "The contest was a very warm one." The election of Mr Ashford of Castle Cary to the post in March 1828 led to widespread celebrations: his carriage was met by a troop of yeomanry four miles from the town and as it travelled nearer the horses were removed from the carriage and it was pulled by local inhabitants, thousands of whom were reported to have turned out. Every house and cottage was decorated with branches of laurel, flags and ribbons; ladies displayed blue ribbons and waved handkerchiefs. "The bells rung a merry peal and the cheerful strains of an excellent band of music exhilarated the hearts of the joyous multitude." (1)

a) Epidemics

Epidemics were intermittent: the one that appeared on various occasions through several centuries was bubonic plague. It was a most dreadful disease that was generally a rodent disease but was transmitted to human beings by infected fleas. If a flea could not find another living rat, having just killed its host rat, then it moved to a human being instead. Along with a high temperature of 104° F there were a range of symptoms such as pain, vomiting, headaches, delirium and usually a final coma. Its most characteristic features were swelling of glands, usually in the groin, in the neck and under the armpits, and haemorrhages under the skin which created black patches which could become gangrenous. It frequently killed some 50% of its victims within a period of about eight days, but during severe outbreaks this could rise to up to two thirds.

The most devastating outbreak of the disease arrived on the Dorset coast in 1348 and "Travelling all over the south country, it wretchedly killed innumerable people in Dorset, Devon and Somerset." Initially the Bishop of Bath and Wells, Ralph of Shrewsbury, writing from the safety of Evercreech, advised processions, abasement and devout prayers so that God will "turn away from his people this pestilence." By January of the following year he recognised the seriousness of the situation, especially as there was no longer a sufficient number of priests to administer the Sacraments of the Church, particularly to the dying which was a major concern given the beliefs of that time. He issued therefore a remarkable order that if the sick "are on the point of death and cannot secure the services of a priest, then they should make confession to each other....whether to a layman or if no man is present, then even to a woman." (2)

It has been estimated that up to 45% of all priests and monks perished along with the ordinary people. How far Bruton was affected is impossible to determine but the scenario of whole families wiped out, of cottages lying empty and of land uncultivated, was a very real one. As the Augustinians were not an enclosed Order they would have had considerable contact with local people and may well therefore have suffered greatly. This of course is based on the assumption that they remained at the Priory and continued to minister to the people rather than seeking refuge in remoter areas as happened, for example, at Winchester. Certainly the Prior, Robert Coker, survived as he was to die in October 1361, possibly during a subsequent outbreak. One interesting document concerning the Priory's lands in Horsley in Gloucestershire indicates that some eighty oxen and cows were received "for mortuaries and heriots in the time of the plague, to the value of ten pounds." This situation came to light when the Priory's representative there, Henry de Lyle, sold them without authorization. (3)

There were at least five other outbreaks of plague in the remainder of the fourteenth century, although less severe, and then more intermittently in the fifteenth century. It has been argued that the outbreak in the 1340s was so devastating as this was the first occasion that it had infected Europe and consequently there was little immunity. As many of the survivors were immune gradually resistance built up.

Nevertheless London was rarely free from plague in the Elizabethan and early Stuart periods and it has been suggested that it was not uncommon for plague to visit other towns every ten years or so. The evidence indicates that in some years when the plague was in London, the number of burials in Bruton also rose dramatically which suggests that it had spread. In 1597 for example London suffered a severe outbreak and in that year the number of interments in Bruton rose from thirty-eight in 1596 to eighty-two in 1597 and then fell back to thirty-two in 1598. During the reign of Queen Elizabeth it has been estimated that it killed about a quarter of a million people which represented about one eighth of the population of the country.

The plague struck indiscriminately as poet Thomas Nash wrote in 1600:

> In Time of Plague.
> Rich men, trust not in wealth,
> Gold cannot buy you health;
> Physic himself must fade;
> All things to end are made;
> The Plague full swift goes by;
> I am sick, I must die.
> > Lord have mercy on us.

Plague struck in London again in 1609, causing over 4,200 deaths and it had certainly spread to Somerset by August 1610 when Sir Maurice Berkeley of Bruton Abbey, as one of the Deputy Lieutenants of the County, requested that the planned musters of troops be delayed until the spring of the following year "as for that diverse partes of this countrey have of late bin visited and are yet infected with the plague." In fact the position became even worse the following year because "of the great contagion of the plague dangerously dispersed in diverse parts of the countrey" which Berkeley reported and he was concerned that troop movements "may endaunger other places not yet infected." The Burial Register for Bruton suggests that plague probably visited the town as in the five years before 1610 the average number of burials each year was twenty-six but in that year rose dramatically to forty-eight, and then thirty-one and thirty-six in the next two years.

So serious was an outbreak in the locality in 1646 to 1647 that the inhabitants of Maiden Bradley in Wiltshire were "debarred from markets, or having any commerce with our neighbours, and being in such sad condition, were inforced... to crave relief from our neighbouring parishes." By this period the actions taken in the event of an outbreak of plague had become severe as it was not unusual for the house of a plague victim to be boarded up with all the family inside and there they remained until all were dead or found to be still alive after six weeks. Bruton may have escaped this outbreak as there was no significant change in burial numbers, although some 20% of burials for 1646 did occur in October. (4)

The last major outbreak of this disease struck London in 1665 and reached Bruton in the spring of 1666. It marked the beginning of a decade or more of death and disturbance for the town. As Bruton was such an important centre for the woollen trade and as a result had strong links with London, it was perhaps surprising that the Plague took so long to reach the town, peaking in the months of August, September and October 1666 with forty-one deaths and occasionally three burials a day. Given the prevailing attitude towards attending a body after death and accompanying it to the Church and the grave, it does help to explain the ease with which the disease spread. No matter what the risks involved, the disfigurement or stench of the dying and dead, the rituals had to be continued.

TABLE 4 Burials in Bruton 1666-1676.

Year	Total Number of burials	Child burials Number	% of total	Peak month(s)	Number
1666	80	Not specified		October	16
1667	41	Not specified		October	9
1668	79	Not specified		August	12
1669	51	18	35.3	March	9
1670	67	20	29.9	September	10
1671	44	10	22.7	February	7
1672	57	22	38.6	December	9
1673	53	19	35.8	December	7
1674	51	16	31.4	January/October	8
1675	64	24	37.5	May	12
1676	57	15	26.3	December	10

In the five years from 1661-1665 the average number of burials was thirty-four a year. From 1668 the word 'child' was included but no age range was specified. It may well be that the Plague lingered or reappeared until about 1670 when the change in the month of maximum deaths suggests diseases of a more respiratory kind, as well as the appearance of smallpox in 1674 and 1675. Evidence for any subsequent visitations of the Plague in Bruton has not yet emerged.

One example of the economic consequences of death through the Plague may be seen in the Accounts of Sexey's Hospital for this period. In 1666-7 the income the Visitors derived from all their estates was some £578 which declined to £482 the following year and £472 in 1668-9, a reduction of over 18%. Much of their income came from heriots when a tenant died and fines when they issued a new lease, often for twenty-one years. The number of these rose significantly: in 1666-7 there were eight heriots and fines, in 1667-8 nine, 1668-9 fourteen, 1669-70 thirty-two and 1670-1 twenty-four. Clearly many of their lessees were dead and new tenants had to be found.

The consequences for the families of plague victims are difficult to imagine: the death of the breadwinner reduced some to poverty; widows had to struggle to make ends meet; and orphans had to fall back on the generosity of other relatives or, if none were available or willing, became parish children. Some inhabitants who survived may have been seriously weakened and either could not work or became susceptible to other diseases and their passing has left no traceable evidence to link it to the Plague. Certainly many more of the poorer members of the community were forced to seek help from the Poor Rates and expenditure increased significantly, placing a much greater strain on the ratepayers. In the ten years up to 1664 the average annual expenditure by the Overseers of the Poor was just over £92 a year.

TABLE 5 Poor Law Expenditure in Bruton 1665-1676.

Year	£	s	d
1665	155	13	3
1666	150	11	10
1667	124	3	11
1668	170	16	9
1669	168	17	2
1670	167	15	9
1671	151	6	2
1672	157	15	8
1673	142	12	3
1674	164	8	7
1675	183	9	4
1676	160	10	6

[*A guide to converting these figures to present day values may be found in Appendix 1*]
In the twelve years covered in Table 5 the average expenditure had increased to over £158 a year, a rise of some 71.7%, which must have left a number of the ratepayers struggling as well.

Many of the payments were granted to those "in sickness" and were often very small such as 9d a week, a deliberate attempt to prevent dependence on the poor rates. There were also a large number of grants towards the cost of burial. (5)

After the late seventeenth century bubonic plague does not seem to have occurred in Bruton but in its place came the next dreaded killer: smallpox. This disease only appears nationally very infrequently before 1600 but for 150 years after 1650 was a significant killer. It was a disease which was spread by personal contact and for those who survived such as Queen Elizabeth I, there could be permanent and distressing disfigurement.

The illness started with sudden shivering followed by a fever in which the temperature could rise to 104°F. This decreased on the third day only to rise higher by the eighth or ninth day. Its symptoms also included thirst, headache, vomiting, constipation and pain, usually in the back. On the third day spots appeared on the face which by the eighth or ninth day became pustules which stank, especially when they burst. These pustules then began to dry up so that their scabs fell off leaving permanent scars.

Smallpox struck down both the rich and the poor as in 1682 Charles, 2nd Lord Berkeley of Stratton died aged twenty when he contracted the disease on board his ship, 'The Tyger', of which he was the commander. His body was brought to Twickenham Parish Church and buried in the family vault on 21st September.

Year after year smallpox made its presence felt in Bruton. Payments by the Overseers of the Poor to those suffering from the disease and the occasional inclusion of 'SP' alongside the name of the deceased in the Burial Register, indicate that it was present in the town in at least seven years between 1675 and 1693 and in some twenty-three years between 1721 and 1785.

(6) In twenty-one out of these thirty years the number of burials was significantly above the average with peaks of seventy-four in 1690, eighty-one in 1721, one hundred and two in 1728 and eighty-five in 1729, although of course not all the deaths were directly attributable to smallpox. It was claimed that in 1737 some "443 persons had the smallpox and 34 died of it."

As the disease was transmitted by contact it spread rapidly through families with children as may be seen from entries in the Accounts of the Overseers:

"1675 April 23 To Wm Nichols' wife, widdow Slade,
Hen Ames in want,

	theire children being sick of the Small Pox	0	4	0
May 2	To James Bartlett his Children being Sick in the Smallpox	0	1	0
1682	To Widd Seymore children in the Pox	0	1	0
1737 June	To Amy Lumber's ffamily in the Small Pox	0	1	6
1753 April	To Wm Ridwood fam sick in the smallpox	0	1	0"

As with so many payments from the Poor Rates these were small sums, designed to help overcome a temporary problem and avoid the danger of longer-term dependence.

Occasionally the sums granted were for a specific person such as

"1728 July	ffrances Darke to attend Absaloms wife in ye Smallpox	0	4	0
1736 May	To Mathew Heggins in the Small Pox	0	2	6"

Sometimes payments were made for items designed to ease the disease:

"1737 April	Saffron & Dough ffiggs for Clavey's Boy in the Small Pox	0	0	3
1753 June	Shugar Apples & other things for the Children in the Sm Pox this week	0	1	0"

The children referred to were the parish orphans in the town's Poorhouse and this entry perhaps reflects one of the dangers of close confinement in an institution. On 14th July another 4s 41/2d was spent on "Extraord: of all sorts for the children."

Given the length of time which smallpox lasted some families were dependent upon repeated payments, for example, "Richard Boole in ye Smallpox" was paid 8s 0d in April 1729 and a further 5s 0d in May. In May, June and July 1736 the Higgins family received several payments of 2s 0d, two of 2s 6d as well as £1 10s 0d specifically for a nurse to attend Eliza Higgins.

For some the inevitable consequence of infection was death and entries in the Overseers' Accounts paint a vivid picture:

"1742 June	To Anne Hill in the Small Pox	0	1	0
	Laying out Anne Hill & Soap to wash her Cloths	0	0	10
	A Coffin Shroud and burying Anne Hill	0	11	0
1764 Nov.	ffrancis Hills wife in small pox	0	2	6
	Gave Francis Hill in Distress at various times	0	3	0
	Gave in laying out Francis Hills wife	0	1	0"

The attempts made to help a family will have been very welcome but the distress caused in the end must have been overwhelming:

"1770 Nov.	Cornelius Hawkins' Family in Sickness	1	2	0
	Burial of Cornelius Hawkins wife 10 6 Burial of his 2 Children 14 6	1	5	0
Dec.	To Harry Hawkins' Wife for taking care of Corn Hawkins Wife & Family in the Small Pox	0	2	6
1784 May	Shores family in the Smallpox	0	13	0
	Grace Shores Two Childrens Funerals	0	11	0"

The dangers of spreading smallpox by contact were obviously not fully understood as laying out still occurred and sometimes a victim was carried to a neighbouring town for burial. On 29th September 1768 Revd. James Woodforde recorded, "I buried Thos Roach of Bruton, who died in the Small Pox there, a poor wild creature he has been, this afternoon at C. Cary." Woodforde's Diary for 7th March 1765 also indicated the way in which there could be complications in a weakened body: " Master Shorte one of Mr Clarkes Patients died this Morning about 12 o' clock in the Small-Pox. He had a Complication of Disorders, Wormes, Ague, etc."

Because of the concern for a decent burial, an idea which was centuries old, care was also taken to inter not only local inhabitants but also outsiders:

| "1690 June 30 | Expenses on a woman sick in ye Small pox at ye Bull and for burying one of her Children and other necessaries | 0 | 14 | 9" |

Once again this was a disease that caused significant disruption to the community; many widows with children and orphans requiring support. In addition it was also a disease which left a permanent reminder through the often deep pockmarks, especially on the face. Such was the fear of the disease that it threatened to disrupt normal activities. In April 1757 one Justice of the Peace from Ditcheat expressed concern about attending the Quarter Sessions in Bruton, "I am afraid to come to Brewton for fear of the Smallpox." (7)

Attempts were made to try and limit the disease and gradually over a long period of time these began to have the desired effect. In the mid-1760s Revd. Woodforde's brother-in-law, Dr. Clarke of Castle Cary was inoculating on an extensive scale and in 1778 the Bruton Vestry agreed to pay Dr Michell £11 0s 0d to inoculate the poor as smallpox was in the area. The problem was, however, that this particular process, which had been introduced into England in the early eighteenth century, involved the inoculation of the smallpox virus into the body. While this seems to have been fairly successful in those so inoculated, it soon became clear that they could infect those who had not been inoculated. At the end of the century Edward Jenner made the discovery that the inoculation of cowpox acted as a preventative method. By the early nineteenth century the Bruton Vestry was acting decisively:

"1805 Oct 27 Special Vestry....that the Poor in this parish should be Inoculated for the Small-Pox and the Expense to be paid out of the Poors rates and that Mr Saunders and Mr Knight to be the Two Surgeons to Inoculate them at the Price of four shilling p Head, the Number to be Equally Divided between them."

When a death from smallpox occurred in the Wincanton Union Workhouse in January 1840 the Board of Guardians immediately ordered their Medical Officer to vaccinate "all the young men, women and children in the house to prevent, if possible, any other cases terminating fatally." They appear to have extended this policy to the whole of the Union as in September of the same year a local newspaper congratulated them on "The most prompt and energetic measures....to secure the immediate, complete, and successful vaccination of all persons in the Union who have not been vaccinated."

By October 1853 the Vaccination Act, which made such vaccination compulsory, was in force in the Union and in the first three years of its operation John Crouch, who was the Medical Officer of Health for the Bruton District, vaccinated 271 people, mainly infants, with only two reported failures. In the last thirty years of the nineteenth century his successors as Medical Officer vaccinated on average seventy local inhabitants a year, once again the overwhelming majority being infants.

In this way the scourge of smallpox was eventually eradicated, although it still managed to appear in Bruton and its neighbourhood on odd occasions, such as in 1856 when five out of nineteen deaths were reported to be from smallpox "which has been very general in the town of late." Thirteen years later in 1869 Dr. Heginbothom was granted an additional £10 by the Board of Guardians "for his extra services during the past year in consequence of having a great many cases of Small-pox under his care." When smallpox broke out in North and South Brewham three years later it was said to have been brought from Bristol by a servant-girl and one labourer who died left a widow and eight children.

The third epidemic disease centred on those illnesses which induced a rapid fever, the commonest of which was influenza. The symptoms of this remain familiar today: chills, fever, headaches, aching limbs and tiredness, usually with a sore throat and cough.

Nationally there was a serious outbreak between 1557 and 1559 when some 150,000 men, women and children died: this represented about 1 in 12 of the total population. Bruton was clearly affected and this seems to be substantiated by the Burial Register. In the three years from January 1557 to December 1559 some 160 burials were recorded, an average of fifty-three a year, compared with seventy-six, or an average of twenty-five a year, between 1560 and 1562. The disease appeared to have been particularly severe during the winter months of 1558 to 1559 as forty-two interments occurred between November and March. Men seemed to have been more susceptible to this disease as of the 160 deaths some 95 (59%) were of males, including one Knight of the Realm, Sir John Divall who was buried on 8th October 1559. These statistics for Bruton would seem to be particularly alarming as they represented the death of about 1 in 6 of the local population at that time.

Unfortunately this type of illness was virtually never specifically identified in the documentary evidence for Bruton. One of the reasons for this was that the onset followed by death was so rapid that the medical men were never given long enough to make a diagnosis. In addition there was a tendency for influenza to lead to other illnesses which may have caused the actual death, for example, in his Report for 1891 the Medical Officer of Health for the Wincanton Union noted that, "At the commencement of the year.....a visitation of Influenza – 10 deaths are attributed to this cause directly." Yet in his statistics none are given but rather the deaths were blamed upon pneumonia and bronchitis. The following year, however, one death was attributed to influenza itself. [8] It was to remain a deadly killer in the twentieth century as the period immediately after the First World War was to show. In 1919 for example there were thirty-three burials in Bruton compared with sixteen in 1918 and thirteen in 1920.

b) Other diseases and illnesses

There was a range of other diseases and illnesses which led directly or indirectly to death. Unfortunately very little detailed evidence has survived for Bruton and that which does remain is predominantly for the nineteenth century. There is no doubt however that considerable amounts of disease and illness had existed for centuries but was often covered by the general words "in sickness" when grants were made by the Overseers of the Poor and few attempts were made to specify the exact nature. In the late nineteenth century the Wincanton Rural Sanitary Authority, which covered the same thirty-nine parishes that made up the Poor Law Union, received a wealth of statistical data in the Annual Reports of its Medical Officer of Health and this does give some indication of the extent and scope of the diseases prevalent in the Bruton area.

In the medieval period and well into the seventeenth century, in the event of illness the first action taken was often to pray for divine assistance. If death followed it would be ascribed to the Will of God and no precise medical diagnosis given. In addition in villages and rural areas many of the sick were treated by older women who had acquired some knowledge through an oral tradition or by experience of the benefits of a range of natural remedies, often involving plants. If they failed the exact cause of death was never specified, although in extreme cases allegations of witchcraft could follow.

For men who had studied older texts on medicine, the predominant theory still rested on the four humours: earth, air, fire and water. If a person was ill it was believed that it was because these humours were not balanced and so action needed to be taken to re-balance them. One method which was frequently used was blood-letting which sometimes had the effect of weakening still further an already very sick person. What finally killed the patient would in many cases be impossible to determine. Finally as medical knowledge in previous centuries was much more limited it was often the case that in some instances a local doctor might not be sure of the exact cause of death, especially if it was rapid as the result of the onset of a fever.

In a market town such as Bruton it was not unusual to find different types of practitioners, sometimes with over-lapping functions. There was the occasional physician who had received a theoretical training but much more common were apothecaries who dispensed drugs and medicines and gave unofficial medical advice. Surgeons could be relied upon to let blood, draw teeth, set broken bones and, if all else failed, amputate a limb. There were also no antibiotics to deal with infectious diseases such as cholera and typhus, so the use of plants and herbs remained extensive. Finally, of course, the weekly markets and annual fairs attracted a range of notorious quack doctors who always seemed to find buyers for their fraudulent pills and potions.

The most that many doctors could do was to relieve pain through the use of opium-based drugs or provide moral support for the family. They did however have their successes, for example in 1750 the Earl of Ilchester told his brother that the local surgeon and apothecary, Thomas Clarke, had saved his son's life at Redlynch "by puting on him blisters on his back, and plaisters on his feet." Clarke continued to practice until his death in June 1762. There developed in many cases a strong psychological bond with practitioners held in high regard by significant numbers of local people. The Ilchester family was said to have had "a great opinion" of Thomas Sampson who succeeded Clarke as their doctor in Bruton, while their governess, Agnes Porter, believed that he was "a very well-informed, intelligent person."

When Dr. Saunders retired through ill-health in October 1863 it was reported that "a very gratifying testimonial was privately presented to him, accompanied by a well-filled purse of sovereigns subscribed by nearly all the respectable inhabitants of the town and neighbourhood." The same newspaper reported the funeral of Dr. Heginbothom in 1879, which involved a large procession, and commented, "that deceased hastened his end in administering to the sufferings and afflictions of his fellow creatures, though, as the result proved, sadly in need of that rest which he so often recommended."

As the failure rate was so high it was remarkable how much faith was placed in medicine and surgery through the centuries. It is also very noticeable, especially in the earlier part of the period, although everybody knew that death was inevitable and so much emphasis was placed upon preparing for it and for eternal life, that there was a widespread determination to stay alive, even if that meant undergoing the most dreadful treatments.

There were, however, those who were more sceptical: "The longer one lives the less one can place faith in the doctors I think – theirs at best is a science of guesswork." Some older inhabitants simply refused, for whatever reason, to see a doctor: one such example was John Groves aged 77 of South Brewham who was taken ill in March 1887 with stomach pains and shortness of breath. After three days he felt such better and "he went downstairs, sat in a chair, and died almost instantly." A verdict of "Death from natural causes" was returned.

In some instances the concerns were justified as in 1889 after the County Coroner criticised Dr Wybrants for failing to attend a child in Wincanton Workhouse, the Local Government Board had no hesitation in holding an Inquiry and the Board of Guardians resolved "that the conduct of Dr Wybrants has for a series of years been so unsatisfactory that the Guardians present are therefore unanimously of opinion that he should no longer have the medical care of the

Poor." As a result of the Inspector's Report the Local Government Board required Dr Wybrants to resign, which he did a week later. This episode was a sad reflection on the attitude of the Guardians towards the poor under their care. Their concerns about the doctor's conduct had existed for years but they had taken no action and only did so when the Coroner was critical. (9)

In the late eighteenth and nineteenth centuries as a result of limited information a common verdict returned by the Coroner's Jury was "Died by the Visitation of God." While this may have some similarities with a modern-day verdict of "Natural Causes", it covered a much wider area and was not always substantiated by medical opinion. The following examples illustrate the sort of cases which were included: this was the verdict returned on William Baker in 1753 when he was found dead in a lane at Hadspen; on an unnamed elderly woman found dead in her dwelling house in August 1810; on Charles Newman when he was returning home to Sturminster Newton from Bruton Fair "whilst in the act of paying to toll at the turnpike-gate, fell back in his gig, and instantly expired"; on Robert Ridout who died while shaving in November 1852. Earlier in the year Henry Hiam died while preparing his supper in the kitchen of the Old Bull Inn and the same verdict was recorded even though "The poor man has for many years past at times been afflicted with sudden illness, depriving him of speech and unable to move." When Maria Thorn "for many years letter carrier for this town" died suddenly in February 1867 it was the same verdict.

There was some criticism of these juries for returning such verdicts without medical information, for example, after the Inquest on Mary Parsons, aged forty-seven who was found dead in bed by her husband the morning after she had "complained slightly of a pain in her chest," in July 1858, one newspaper commented, "We cannot refrain from observing that we think Inquests without direct medical testimony, little better than a mockery, and that a post mortem examination ought to be made in every case unless the medical attendant can confidently state the cause of death." (10)

Post mortem examinations were much more common in the latter part of the nineteenth century and duly influenced verdicts. In September 1885 Dr. Stockwell performed a post-mortem on James Sutcliffe, a Glass and China Dealer, who died after a fall on the stairs at his house and he "found the base of the skull fractured from the fall, and a clot of blood deep in the substance of the brain. This clot had caused a fit, and in the fit he had fallen.....The jury returned a verdict accordingly." Three years later Dr. Stockwell performed another post-mortem this time on a six year old girl, Emma Jane Hopkins and he "found traces of chronic inflammation and ulceration of the intestines; also a slight patch of pleurisy on the right lung." The jury gave as their verdict that she "died from natural causes – to wit, exhaustion supervening chronic peritonitis." (11)

There were of course many diseases and illnesses causing death, some of which particularly affected children under five years of age and others those over five. Statistics prepared for the Medical Officer of Health for the Wincanton Rural Sanitary Authority at the end of the nineteenth century show that deaths of children under five years of age were caused especially by measles, scarlet fever, usually called scarlatina at that time and often the result of drinking infected milk, whooping cough and diarrhoea or dysentery. These diseases were also to be found in children over five and it has been suggested that they actually increased in this age-group after 1880 as school attendance became compulsory and infections spread more rapidly.

For those over five years of age diphtheria, typhoid, diarrhoea or dysentery were present but were far surpassed by heart disease and above all respiratory diseases such as consumption, bronchitis, pneumonia and pleurisy. These were the diseases specifically requested for the statistics but there were many others as well as for children under five 60.3% of all deaths and 60.9% for those over five were recorded as "Other Diseases." (see Appendix 3) As such diseases existed at this period it is reasonable to assume their presence in generations before that. With the development of modern medicines and vaccinations it is too easy to forget that what are now relatively harmless illnesses were killers. In the Overseers' Accounts for 1752, for example, was the entry that they paid 3d "for Shugar for Eliza Hore's Children in the Measell." In February 1885 the Coronor attributed the death of six-year old Walter Henry Field of Milton Clevedon to an attack of measles.

Pleurisy was certainly present in previous centuries as it killed John, 3rd Lord Berkeley of Stratton. He was a nephew of Sir Charles Berkeley of Bruton Abbey and had pursued a career at sea, with varying degrees of success but he did rise to the rank of Admiral after just three years' service as an officer. While on leave he contracted pleurisy and died on 27th February 1699, being buried six days later on 5th March. (For the relationship between the principal members of the Berkeley family see Appendix 9).

Recording a death from heart disease was common, for example, in November 1843 James Borley, who was born near Bruton, died in Bristol aged 18 where he "got his livelihood by singing about the streets," was taken ill and died on a doorstep within a few minutes even after "a quarter of a noggin of rum was given to him." Heart disease was also the verdict on J.R. White, the factory owner in March 1874, on Mrs Shepherd at the Bell Inn in July 1876 and on Mr F. Mogford who dropped dead in April 1881. A decade later the same verdict was returned on Mrs Saxon of Berkeley Villa, aged 72, even though she had never complained of heart problems. In her case she was at Cole Station intending to catch a train to Bath. As she crossed the rails to reach the up platform she felt a sharp pain and put her hand on her left side. "She fell, and was lifted off the rails by Dr. Stockwell, who happened to be close behind her. She never spoke, and death was almost instantaneous."

After Philip Park of Lamyatt had eaten and drunk a pint of beer in the Old Bull Inn in Bruton, he set off one evening in February 1885 up the road to Creech Hill to tend his sheep but at the top collapsed and was not found for some five hours. He died the next morning and his death was attributed to heart disease, although cold and exposure may also have played a part. At Shepton Montague Martha Sims' death in December 1888, when she was lacing up her boots, was also believed to relate to heart disease, especially as she had suffered from rheumatic fever which Dr. Stockwell felt had affected her heart. The same doctor had been more surprised by the death of Charles Buggler aged 13, also of Shepton Montague, five years earlier. While the boy had been reported to have been "weakly from birth", the post mortem revealed that he died from "fatty degeneration of the heart", which the doctor stated was unusual for someone of that age.

The verdict on William Beer in July 1889 was rather more vague. He was the sixty-seven year old head keeper of the Earl of Ilchester at Redlynch, a position which he had held for many years according to an inscription on his gravestone in Shepton Montague Churchyard. He was found dead early one morning in a field where he had gone shooting and his gun was found beside him. It was stressed at the Inquest that there were no signs of a struggle, as clearly there were suspicions about the presence of poachers. Although Beer had complained of a pain in his chest for some two years and particularly in the few days before his death, Dr. Stockwell stated that he had treated him only for indigestion. The jury decided death was from natural causes, "to wit, probably failure of the heart's action."

Other verdicts centred on aortic aneurisms but in previous centuries the terminology was slightly different, for example, in August 1862 a hawker, John Welch, "Ruptured a blood vessel in the chest." In January 1866 Joseph Singer died in his bed after his wife "heard a gurgling in his throat" and the verdict was "Death caused by rupturing a blood vessel." Mary Ann Coward was dead in January 1876 before Dr. Heginbothom could reach her house: "Died from a rupture of a blood vessel in the abdomen."

Over one hundred years before in 1769 a Coroner's jury returned a verdict that the death of Elizabeth Palmer "was entirely caused by the mortification of an old rupture." This decision was vitally important for two men as for several weeks it had been alleged that she had "been very ill-used by two tradesmen on the road between Yeovil and Bruton", when she was being given a ride in their cart. A correspondent from Bruton claimed in the 'Bath Chronicle' that one of the men had "treated her in an infamous manner… by throwing her out of the cart, and inhumanly abusing her." Two surgeons gave evidence on the cause of her death and that "she had received no injury from them." The result was that "the men so unjustly accused were honourably acquitted." In this instance too many people including the local press had jumped to the wrong conclusion. Betty Palmer, who was about sixty years of age, was interred in Bruton churchyard on 3rd March 1769.

Ann Thompson was particularly unlucky in the summer of 1873 as in an accident she fractured and dislocated her elbow joint. As her arm did not get better Dr. Heginbothom decided to operate using chloroform and within two minutes of it being administered she was dead. The jury returned a verdict that she "died from the effects of chloroform" but added that no blame was attached to the doctor.

Some diseases were virtually never mentioned, one being cancer. Yet by a strange coincidence the deaths were reported in the press in May 1875 of two elderly women who were buried on the same Sunday. One was Mrs K. Weeks aged eighty-one and the other Mrs Bateman aged ninety-two, "Both died from the same cause, viz, cancer." There were those who offered "Cures for Cancers without Incision", such as Mrs Plunkett Edgecumbe. In an advertisement in 1787 she claimed that one of her successes was a Mrs Stocker of Bruton who was "cured of a Cancer on the Side of her Neck."

Another rarely recorded disease was dropsy, which was excessive retention and accumulation of water in the body. On 13th February 1843 Henry Newman Cann was reported to have died of dropsy when he was only seven years old. In addition on just one occasion does it appear in the Overseers' Accounts when in 'September 1708 they paid 8s "for ye Wid Dartis Cofin dying of a Dropsey." (12)

To die from an apoplectic fit, which was most likely a stroke, or sometimes just referred to as a fit, was much more common. On 12th June 1668 Sir Charles Berkeley of Bruton Abbey died "of a short apoplecticall distemper" at Whitehall in London where he served Charles II after the Restoration as first Controller and then Treasurer of the Royal Household. His youngest brother met a similar end. John, 1st Lord Berkeley of Stratton was a staunch Royalist commander during the Civil War, accompanied the Royal Family into exile in the 1650s and returned with Charles II in 1660 to become a prominent courtier and diplomat. In October 1675 he was appointed Ambassador to France but on the 27th of that month he had an apoplectic fit at the Council Table in Whitehall. After various doctors had treated him with remedies such as hot fire-pans, spirit of amber on his head, and cupped him on the shoulder, he recovered sufficiently to undertake his mission, even though he was impaired physically and his memory sometimes failed.

Berkeley himself felt that there was definite improvement as early in December 1675 he wrote, "I thank God I recovered much of my strength in my iorny, and eat and drink and sleepe as well as I ever did." He clearly remained unwell, however, especially through the winter of 1677 to 1678 as Dr. Edward Lake, later Bishop of Rochester, noted in his diary for 23rd December 1677, "I administered the Sacrament to the Lord John Barclay (being not well)." He deteriorated slowly and returned to England on 31st July 1678, died on 26th August and was buried in a vault in Twickenham Parish Church on 5th September.

This particular cause of death does seem to have been prevalent in the Berkeley family as nearly one hundred years later in 1773 the last holder of the Stratton title was to die in Bruton Abbey "of a paralytic disorder."

In June 1790 George Ward, the silk manufacturer, died "in an apoplectic fit." He was referred to as "an affectionate husband, a tender parent, and an honest man." The Vicar of Bruton the Rev Stephen Hyde Cassan died of apoplexy in July 1841 aged 51, although he had become so mentally ill from 1839 that his duties were being performed by other local clergy, as may be seen from the Parish Registers. One month later Robert Ellis died when he fell down stairs in "apoplexy". Charles Mitchell aged 66 of Whaddon House lingered unconscious for three days after he "was seized by apoplexy" on 17th May 1854 and Isaac Golledge, the landlord of the Royal Oak, died when "he was seized with apoplectic fit" in December of the same year just outside of Bruton as he was returning from Frome market. In October 1862 a servant discovered coal merchant Philip Stephens "at the side of his bed quite insensible, from an apoplectic seizure." It was reported that he had eaten "a hearty dinner" the evening before. While Walter Stuckey, the former manager of Stuckey's Bank in Yeovil was visiting his sister in Lamyatt in October 1871 he "was seized with an apoplectic fit and death shortly resulted."

The death of the Earl of Ilchester nearly a century before in October 1776 may well have been a stroke although the description given was very general: "His Lordship was suddenly seized with the Disorder which occasioned his Death." An indication of the nature of the 'Disorder' may be found in the words which were added, "and never spoke afterwards." (13)

Fits carried off a number of other inhabitants such as in December 1812 Mrs George, the widow of a local clothier, who was "cheerfully enjoying the company of a friend, when she fell out of her chair in a fit, and instantly expired." The twenty-year-old son of the landlord of the Crown Inn did the same in April 1864. The death of a child was sometimes attributed to a fit, such as the infant daughter of Charlotte Lugg in October 1865 and the illegitimate baby of Kate Lumber in April 1882. In some instances the fits may well have been related to epilepsy, such as that of Frank Cook in June 1867 as it was reported by his father that he was prone to fits and had been treated by Dr Heginbothom. The same was said at the Inquest on the death of Ann Lumber in April 1874 as she had had a similar fit three months earlier. (14)

c) Living and working conditions

A number of the diseases and illnesses considered so far which caused deaths along with several others were the direct result of the dreadful living and working conditions of so many of Bruton's inhabitants. Report after Report in the last quarter of the nineteenth century condemned the town's public health conditions. While these undoubtedly grew worse as the population rose, they had been similar for generations before that. In the late eighteenth century the juries in the Manorial Courts criticized the nuisances caused by filth:

"1788 October 24....that William Dunn shall remove his nuisance by Patwell in ten days" or face a fine of £2. He was clearly a repeat offender as, for example, he received a similar order to remove a dung heap from there in October 1797.

"1795 Nov 3
We also present the Dung and other filth in Elliotts barton to be a very great nuisance."

"1800 May 26
We also present the Dung heaps in and belonging to the Occupiers of the Backway.....to be nuisances & to be removed forthwith."

An outbreak of typhoid fever in 1871 prompted a letter of complaint to the Sanitary Commissioners from the Headmaster of King's School, A.D. Gill, who drew attention to the sewage which was allowed to accumulate in the mill stream in Lower Backway, the presence of two slaughter houses in the centre of the town which caused "frequent and extensive annoyance and the keeping of pigs by inhabitants in their yards." Not all the ratepayers were so concerned and on behalf of the Vestry, Henry Dyne, a Churchwarden, wrote to the Secretary of the Local Government Board that "they believe that on the whole this Town is better drained than other Towns in this, or indeed any other neighbourhood...... Bruton until the recent outbreak of typhoid fever has been for many years remarkably free from any epidemics that could be attributed to local causes."

A Subcommittee was established however to investigate and in January 1872 it produced a damning Report. Its members found that there was a drastic lack of toilet accommodation with up to seven tenements sharing "one stinking, tumbledown, insecure privy" which was "enough to account for the deposits of human excrement that disgrace nearly every alley and byeway of the Town." They also found that most of the wells were polluted to some degree.

Their Report was substantiated by that of Dr Homes who investigated on behalf of the Local Government Board as he found no proper sewage or water supply arrangements and discovered that many of the poorer inhabitants obtained their drinking water from public wells such as Patwell which was close to the River Brue and often flooded by it. "As house drains conveying excremental matter open into the Brue a few yards above the well thus exposed to be flooded, the alternative choice of the people of Bruton for water would seem to be a poor one." Nearly one hundred years earlier, however, this source of water had been praised, "In Patwell Street is a spring of very fine water which supplies most of the inhabitants."

Although as a result of this pressure the Vestry initiated discussions and started to draw up plans for sewage disposal and a pure water supply, two Reports by Dr. Airy in 1885 and Dr. Parsons in 1886 found that virtually nothing had actually been done. In fact, apart from covering the mill-stream, little was achieved before the twentieth century. A failure to accept reality, inertia and cost were largely to blame. (15)

The presence of excrement in the streets, dung heaps in the backways and bartons, pigs and their sties in the centre of the town, along with the seeping contents of cesspools, the waste products of local agricultural industries such as tanning, meant that fly-borne diseases such as endemic diarrhoea, dysentery, typhoid and cholera, which was also spread by polluted food and water, could easily take hold and become serious. Dysentery developed rapidly with pain in the abdomen followed by diarrhoea which contained a lot of blood. There was also usually fever, shivering and nausea. Typhoid was much slower in developing with headache, tiredness, feverishness and gradual increase in temperature in the first week and diarrhoea and spots in the second.

The problems associated with poor living and working conditions became more widely recognised in the nineteenth century. In a lecture in March 1853 local factory owner J.R. White stressed the "ill-effects which ill-built, badly ventilated, and inefficiently drained dwellings have upon the health, strength, comfort, and happiness of the labouring classes." He went on to cite the way in which cholera had broken out in the same streets, houses and rooms in 1848 as it had done in 1832. He might not, however, have agreed completely with one local newspaper editorial which alleged that, "Cleanliness, temperance, and moderation in diet, are great safeguards against the attack of Cholera."

At times when cholera was prevalent nationally the number of deaths recorded in Bruton's Burial Register increased significantly. In 1832, for example, there were fifty burials of which twenty were for children, compared with thirty-five burials the year before, forty-four in 1833 and thirty-three in 1834.

During his investigation Dr. Homes discovered that in total ninety-two people in Bruton had contracted typhoid from September 1871 to February 1872, twenty of whom lived on Tolbury in seven out of the fourteen cottages, and that there were seven deaths. He had no doubt whatsoever but that, "The general condition of the town in regard to pollution by excremental and other offensive matters, fully accounts here for the presence of enteric fever." Although actual deaths from typhoid remained very small, the disease kept recurring, for example, it broke out in July 1877 and lasted until December. This outbreak was perceived to be of a mild type for while it infected thirty-four people there was only one death. (16)

Contaminated water remained a potentially lethal problem. It appears that at Durslade Farm, Dorothy, Franklin and Stuart, three of the children of Josiah Jackson, may have died as a result of drinking polluted water. At the time when Dorothy was on her deathbed in March 1895 at least three other members of the household were ill. Dr. Stockwell visited the farm and "I let him have a bottle of the water out of the well in the court." The doctor was obviously suspicious about the water supply and on the day after Dorothy's death "Dr Stockwell came & had a look at Well, Court, & Drain and recommended some improvement to be done." Jackson took the recommendations seriously and in early May purchased 2,400 bricks to build a reservoir in Mary Mead. Sadly, by the time that the work was complete in late May with pipes laid to the house both Franklin and Stuart were also dead. (17)

As the population of Bruton had increased, especially in the eighteenth and early nineteenth centuries, many small cottages had been built on each side of the narrow bartons, further up Cats Lane and in the courtyards behind the large houses which fronted the main streets, principally the High Street as there was available access to them from Higher and Lower Backway. Many of these cottages were very small and so easily became overcrowded. In the 1861 Census for example there were twenty-six cottages listed as occupied in Cats Lane and Tolpenny or Tolbury, excluding Tolbury House. Fifteen of these cottages had five or more occupants with a third of these having more than eight, and the greatest number in one cottage being ten.

The cottages were often cheaply built, with little sanitation, poor ventilation and tended to be damp. If a member of the family was sick they usually had to lie in the same room with the rest of the family. In 1844 Dr Crouch, the Medical Officer of Health for Bruton expressed his "opinion that Charles Perry will remain ill and disabled a long time if he continues to live in his present dwelling. In the corner of the room in which all the family sit is a common necessary and during the winter months there has been a great deal of sickness in the family." In addition, of course, many of the inhabitants of these cottages had the poorest paid jobs and frequently worked outside in all weathers without adequate protective clothing.

It was no wonder therefore that a series of other diseases which could lead to death were ever present. In 1878 Dr. Heginbothom noted, "Defective or insufficient cottage accommodation for the poor......Overcrowding in damp, badly ventilated rooms is a sure cause of Phthsis." Deaths from this, bronchitis, pneumonia and pleurisy were common, as may be seen from Appendix 3.

It was, however, not only the poor who suffered from these diseases as it was bronchitis which killed Daniel Morgan, the landlord of the Blue Ball and Wellington Inns, in April 1853 when he was aged forty-eight, and twelve years later the Earl of Ilchester, aged 70. In April 1884 Frances Cannon, the fourteen month old daughter of a publican in North Brewham, succumbed to pneumonia. In her case she was found by Dr. Stockwell to be well cared for and well nourished but interestingly she was not at home but "was put out to nurse". As she deteriorated linseed poultices were applied to her back and chest but without any success.

The overcrowded conditions in so many cottages meant that in the winter months typhus was much more prevalent and led to deaths. At that time of year in cold, damp cottages families had a greater tendency to huddle together for warmth. This situation was ideal for body lice which spread this disease, usually identified by pain in the back and limbs, fever and rash.

Outside, working in the fields, especially low-lying ones, there was always the greater danger of malaria, although the mosquitoes which spread the disease also bred in the stagnant pools of dirty water around the town itself. It usually became manifest a week or two after a bite and generally took the form of uncontrollable shivering followed by a high temperature and sweating. It could in fact be so common that it was regarded as a part of normal life so victims just carried on. For some there was a tertian fever, that is it recurred every three days, for some a quartian fever as it recurred every four days, and, worst of all, quotidian fever, as it recurred every day. While it had been lethal when it first arrived in England, by the late eighteenth century it tended to lead to severe exhaustion rather than death on any significant scale. It was often referred to as the ague and was certainly in the Bruton area in the seventeenth century as the Overseers of the Poor were granting some aid:

"1671   Item to relieve Henry Ames and his   0   1   6
           family he being sick of an ague and
           fever

1674   Mar 4 To Phillip Smith being sick of   0   1   0
           an ague and having 4 small children

1685   To Em Lumber being sick of an Ague   0   2   6"

After that date mention of it does not seem to appear in the surviving documentary evidence.

The same lack of evidence surrounds tuberculosis or consumption as it was generally called. It has been claimed that nationally it killed more people than smallpox and cholera combined. Yet its name rarely seems to appear in Bruton's records, except on odd occasions such as, for example, the reported death from consumption at Gant's Mill in April 1856 of a visiting relative. In June 1841 Sophia Melin aged twenty-seven died "of rapid consumption" at Henley Grove, as did John Charles Donne in January 1857. It was easily spread through coughing and sneezing and so flourished in overcrowded accommodation. It was a dreadful, debilitating disease which led to blood being coughed up, yet it was often romanticized, especially in Victorian fiction as it was used to demonstrate Christian fortitude in the face of suffering. (18)

d) Childbirth

A further cause of death was childbirth or its immediate consequences, particularly puerperal fever. In the sixteenth century the death rate in childbirth was 1 in 50 but, although it has been argued that in general pregnancy and childbirth were roughly 150 times more dangerous before the mid-eighteenth century than in the late twentieth century, it is important to remember that the vast majority of females did survive childbirth. Deaths were, however, more likely to occur if there were complications.

On the other hand, infant mortality rates remained high and were still at about 150 per 1000 throughout the whole of the nineteenth century. It has been suggested that one reason they stayed so high was that many women from the labouring classes were forced to go back to work immediately after giving birth as a result of economic pressure. The babies were left at home and fed, usually by grandmothers or siblings, with the aid of bottles with corks and long rubber tubes, and although these bottles were notoriously unhygienic as they were a breeding ground for bacteria they remained popular before 1900.

As there was so much fear associated with childbirth before the Reformation, the Roman Catholic Church did attempt to offer as much comfort as possible to pregnant women. They were encouraged to clutch religious relics or symbols and Bruton Abbey possessed its own: "oure Lades gyrdell of Bruton, rede silke, wiche is a solemne reliquie sent to women travelyng, wiche shall not miscarie in partu." When in labour women were encouraged to call upon St Margaret, the Virgin

Mary or any locally used supernatural helpers. The Catholic Church also offered masses "on behalf of women labouring with child" and prayers to the Virgin Mary, "the benign assister of women in travail."

At the time of the Reformation scepticism was apparent and in 1538 Bishop Shaxton of Salisbury attempted to ban the use in his diocese of "any girdles, purses, measures of our Lady, or such other superstitious things to be occupied about the woman while she laboureth, to make her believe to have the better speed of it." In rural areas it is doubtful if he achieved much success, especially amongst those families which continued to lean towards the Catholic faith.

As there was so much concern, especially in the medieval period, about the consequences of failure to baptise before death, baptism tended to occur very quickly after birth particularly if the health of the infant was judged to be poor. Before 1784 Bruton's Baptism Registers rarely included ages but there was an exception between 1654 and 1659 during the Commonwealth period. This clearly shows that some 10% of children were still christened on the day of birth and the most of the rest within about one month. In 1784 and the years immediately following the tendency was for the majority to be baptised within a few days of birth, often when a baby was two days old, but after 1795 baptism was delayed sometimes into the third and fourth weeks of life, possibly reflecting a changing attitude to religion. (19)

The Overseers of the Poor could be called upon to arrange for assistance at the time of birth, for example, there were a number of payments in the 1760s to Mrs Thridgould who acted as a midwife for a standard fee of 2s 6d:

"1765   Pd Mrs Thridgould for Delivering   0   2   6."
         Jn Paskalls wife

She was replaced by Jane Jackson who delivered the children of the poor for the same payment during the 1770s and 1780s.

"1784 Aug. Pd Jane Jackson for delivering Francis Hill's wife." (20)

These women had no training and adhered to no particular codes of practice. It has been suggested however that in many respects they were preferable to doctors as this was the only function which they performed and so had adequate time to attend a woman, stay with her and deliver the baby. If the comments of Dr. John Crouch are to be believed when he was defending himself against allegations that he failed to attend two women in labour, the standard of some of these midwives left a great deal to be desired. He referred to one nurse as "an old, deaf, feeble, sickly, and incompetent midwife."

If there were likely to be complications at a birth then a doctor could attend and after the formation of the Wincanton Poor Law Union the District doctors were paid 10s for each midwifery case. It was two of these that Crouch failed to attend and while one passed off satisfactorily, the other did not and the mother, Jennie Shean of Hadspen, died. Crouch had in fact sent his brother, who was a surgeon in the Militia but whose qualifications did not meet the Poor Law Board's requirements. To compound the matter he actually visited Jemima Shean not Jennie. Crouch was required to resign. (21)

The Overseers also arranged for the burial of poor mothers who died in childbirth, such as Martha Batt who had an illegitimate child, died in childbirth and was buried on 26th July 1739 for the cost of 10s 3d. Thereafter the Overseers paid Frances Wake 2s a week to care for the child until he too died and was buried in February 1741 at a cost of 4s. Other cases were more straightforward such as

"1766   Sept Burial of Joan Flower & Child   0   6   0."

The wealthy could be just as vulnerable as the poor in childbirth, for example, Lady Frances Berkeley, the wife of William, 4th Lord Berkeley of Stratton, who subsequently resided in Bruton Abbey, died in 1707 while giving birth after just a few years of marriage. Berkeley himself was to remain a widower for another thirty-four years. He was to suffer a further bereavement when Ann his youngest daughter, who was married to James Cocks, also died in childbirth in February 1739 in Burlington Street in London while giving birth to a son, James. Similarly medical knowledge was sometimes no help as in February 1853 surgeon John Crouch, junior, buried his infant son aged just three weeks.

In fact in the later Victorian period it was not unusual for wealthier families to announce a stillborn child in a local newspaper. A stillborn son was recorded for J.P. Fitz-Gerald of Discove in March 1865 and one for John Grove Cox of Wyke Champflower in June 1873. More unfortunate was the wife of William Clark of Brewham as he died on the 21st January 1873 and the following morning his "widow was delivered of a dead child." In March 1879 the unnamed wife of a labourer gave birth to twins: the first was stillborn "with its head shattered" but the second survived (22)

The Burial Registers contain many examples of mother and child dying in childbirth or one of them surviving for just a short time afterwards.

"1606	Mar 9	Grace Plympton, w. of Henry Plimton
	Mar 9	A woman child of the same Plimton
1678	Ap 7	Margaret Penny, of Discove.
	Ap 7	Margret Penny, a child.
1693	July 16	Hannah, ye wife of Peter Talley, & Hannah, ye daughter of Peter Talley."

Hannah had given birth to twins who were baptised on 22 May and Peter the other twin survived for nearly two years, being buried on 10 May 1695.

"1743   Dec 25   A Child of John Truemans

           Dec 29   The w. of John Trueman."

Mary Fleetwood aged thirty-three was buried on 28th May 1800, the same day that her daughter Sarah was baptised. The latter survived but was buried on 22nd February 1801.

Mother and baby were usually buried in the same grave and that fact was sometimes recorded as two examples from gravestones which originally stood in Pitcombe churchyard illustrate:

"A loyal loving virtuous wife moste dear,
With her sweet babe doth lie interrred here."

These lines were carved in 1733 and nearly one hundred years later in 1820 came the following:

"This peaceful grave doth now contain
A wife and child together laid."

(The complete epitaphs may be found in Appendix 6b).

In the late nineteenth century cases of puerperal fever still caused deaths within the Wincanton Poor Law Union, such as two each in 1881 and 1884 and one in 1887.

On 23rd May 1901 Annie, the second wife of Josiah Jackson of Durslade Farm gave birth to a daughter. He noted: "A. very ill indeed despaired of her life, Dr Stockwell with her for several hours." In an interesting touch he noted,

"J Rex and G James put sawdust on the road in front of the house to deaden the sounds of wheels & horses &c as they pass." Annie lingered for nearly three weeks but eventually died on 12th June 1901 aged forty-one. It was in many respects a classic Victorian good death: after she was given oxygen "she revived a little and had a little talk. Wished us each good bye and bid us be good and not to think too much of business. We promised her the dear Baby should be taken care of 'which may God help us do and may we all meet her in the heavenly home through Jesus Christ and for his sake'. She fell asleep about 8.10 (evening) after saying Into Thine hands I commit my Spirit." (23)

e) Weather-related factors

The increase in the number of deaths from fly-borne diseases in warmer weather and through respiratory diseases and typhus during the winter months has already been considered. There were a number of other weather-related deaths.

The cold itself was an important factor and it is no coincidence that in the 344 years between 1555 and 1899 for which burials are recorded in the Bruton Parish Registers, on fifty-three occasions January records the highest monthly total and January, February, March and April on 179 occasions.

Late December and January 1564 were particularly cold months and this was the period when observers recorded people walking, practising archery and playing football on the River Thames in London. The Burial Register for Bruton shows that of a total of forty burials for the year some fourteen were in January, February and March. The remainder of the 1560s witnessed cold winters and the increase in the death rate may be clearly seen, for example, out of forty deaths in 1568 some fifteen occurred in the first three months of that year.

The Overseers of the Poor did what they could to help those who were suffering:

"1674   Mar 7   To Susan fforde the weather 0   1   0."
                   being so frostie that her
                   husband could not work

Mary Ames received 1s 6d for the same reason.

"To Priscilla Collins the weather being   0   0   3."
very cold.

While such relief may have helped in some cases it was insufficient as eight deaths were recorded in January and seven in March, compared with an average of 3.6 in the other months of the year, an average itself which may be rather high as there was a possible outbreak of influenza later in the year causing eights deaths in October.

On 22nd January 1715 a Justice of the Peace ordered the Overseers to grant additional relief to the poor "in consideration of the long continuance of cold winter weather." Out of fifty-three deaths in that year twenty-one (40%) occurred in the first three months. These same months in the following year also registered a high total of twenty-seven (44%) out of sixty-one burials.

Worse was to follow later in the century as in 1783 to 1784 there was a volcanic eruption in Iceland. The impact of the vast amount of debris which was thrown into the atmosphere and so affected the power of the sun's rays, was that there was a bitterly cold winter in 1784-5 with heavy snowfalls in October. The number of deaths in Bruton rose from an average of just over forty a year up to 1783 to sixty-five in 1784 and seventy-one in 1785 (an increase of between 60% and 77%) before falling back to the usual average. Of the twenty who were buried between 12th December 1784 and 27th March 1785 twelve were over sixty years of age.

On a cold December day in 1859 William Melhuish of Bruton was found dead near King Alfred's Tower. The Inquest jury decided that he must either have fallen in a fit or sat down from fatigue but whatever happened he froze to death. Similarly in February 1882 Elizabeth Hayward aged fifty-seven went missing while "sticking" in Cogley Wood and her body was discovered two days later in a nearby field. She was prone to fits but the jury once again retuned a verdict of "Died from cold and exposure." Rain and cold could have the same effect as at the end of November 1861 an unknown man was found on the road between Bruton and Castle Cary soaked to the skin. He was taken in a waggon to Castle Cary but before the surgeon could be called he died "from exposure to the inclement weather."

At the other extreme some winters could be exceptionally mild such as 1248-1249 when the chronicler Matthew Paris recorded that trees were sprouting in February and young birds singing. Too much heat could of course also kill as in September 1898 one local newspaper claimed "Another death through the Heat." On this occasion it was George Saxon of Parklands who collapsed in his garden and died without regaining consciousness. He was referred to as "an artist of no mean ability, and has exhibited at the Royal Academy." (24)

Much more serious and far-reaching in its consequences was crop failure caused by bad weather, usually prolonged rain. Heavy rain in the summer and autumn was extensively feared as it significantly upset the often precarious balance between the population and its food supply. Rain caused the crops, especially wheat, to rot in the fields and sheep became prone to foot rot and liver flukes. Before the transport developments of the eighteenth century much grain was grown and consumed locally as it was difficult to carry any distance so crop failure could be more intense in a particular district. In addition the man who farmed just a few acres was left to make the dreadful decision: eat his meagre supplies of grain and so have little or none to sow for the following season or starve.

In previous centuries it was generally considered that one bad summer would lead to price rises and malnutrition; two bad summers meant starvation; and three bad summers meant famine with thousands dying and countless families becoming destitute as they lost everything.

While images of starvation in the last fifty years have become restricted to more Third World countries, scenes of starvation and starvation-related diseases were to be found in England until at least the seventeenth century: weight loss, hair loss, dental problems, bloated stomachs and ultimately death. Those over fifty years of age and young children seemed to have been most at risk, with in the latter a halt to their growth both physical and mental and their lungs attacked by tuberculosis.

Matthew Paris recorded that during the summer and autumn of 1258 the cold and the wet caused the harvest to fail, "the north wind blew without intermission, a continued frost prevailed, accompanied by snow and such unendurable cold, that it bound up the face of the earth, sorely afflicted the poor, suspended all cultivation, and killed the young of the cattle." Historians now attribute this bad season to a massive volcanic eruption somewhere in the tropics but at the time it was seen as a punishment from God and led to a rise in fanatical religious movements across Europe, especially those which practiced self flagellation. Paris observed that, "Owing to the scarcity of wheat, a very large number of poor people died; and dead bodies were found in all directions....In fact famine prevailed in England to such a great extent, that many thousand human beings died of hunger." A mass burial pit from this period found in the Spitalfields area of London contained more than 10,000 skeletons which represented about a third of the usual population of the city. (25)

There was further severe harvest failure in 1315, 1316 and 1317, largely caused by rain, that led to scarcity with very high food prices and it has been estimated that about 10% of the population died. It has also been suggested that as a result of the deprivations that they suffered, many of those who survived or grew up in the famine years were more susceptible to the Black Death in 1348, some thirty years later.

The Tudor and Stuart periods witnessed repeated food crises leading to an increased number of deaths. There was famine in 1587-1588 and this was starkly illustrated from Bruton's Burial Register. In the four years before 1588 the average number of deaths a year was just under twenty, but in 1588 it rose dramatically to 102 and then fell back to an average of twenty-four a year in the succeeding four years. Crop failure at each harvest between 1594 and 1597 as a result of heavy rain led to food prices rising beyond the means of the poor. Widespread famine struck in 1597 and once again the death rate in Bruton rose, repeating the pattern of the previous decade. The average number of deaths in the four years before 1597 was twenty-nine, about 45% above the usual, and in that year reached eighty-one, fell back to forty-four in 1598, of which ten were in January and then in the following years reverted to an average of twenty.

A decade later serious problems re-emerged as in June 1609 Sir Maurice Berkeley referred to "our distressed countrymen, by reason of this yere's great dearth of corne." Once again Bruton's death rate increased: from twenty-four in 1609 to forty in 1610, remaining high at thirty-five in 1611, of which ten were in January and February, and thirty-four in 1612, before declining to the mid-twenties in the following years.

In 1611 as well as plague it was also noted that, "by the unseasonable weather the haie and corne harvest in those partes is exceeding backward."

Respite was short-lived as in 1623 famine caused by harvest failure struck again but this time made worse by a pronounced economic crisis in the woollen trade, on which the Bruton area depended, so that there was little money to purchase the meagre supplies of grain which existed. In 1623 the number of deaths reached forty-five, significantly above the average once again and peaked at fifty-nine the following year and then decreased slightly to fifty in 1625. It was of course the winter months which witnessed the most deaths when resistance was lower, for example, sixteen burials between December 1623 and February 1624 and twenty-two between November 1624 and January 1625.

As the seventeenth century advanced specific famines declined, partly as more and more cattle were slaughtered for food, and partly as grain prices fell as land was converted to arable purposes. There was still, however, harvest failure as a result of bad weather and for a small community the effects could be devastating, although at times the consequences were less pronounced than previously, for example in the period 1647-1649 when Bruton's burials reached forty-one in 1649 it was in that year alone. The Overseers' Accounts do record a payment "To Tho Sweets wife being readie to starve" but while there were other payments in very cold weather there is little suggestion of famine during the latter part of the century.

There was still some harvest failure, however, in the 1690s which had an impact. In the first four years of that decade the average number of burials was forty-three and then rose to fifty-four a year in the next four years before decreasing to an average of forty-six. There was some dislocation caused by seven wet years, starting in 1768 with torrential rain on

September 1ˢᵗ in Bruton which resulted in serious flooding. It is suggested that this poor weather, including cold winters, was caused by the violent eruption of Cotopaxi volcano in Ecuador. On this occasion however the impact on the death rate was not severe as between 1769 and 1773 it averaged forty-eight a year and then fell back to forty-four a year in the next five years. It was to be another twenty years before the crops failed on a large scale again but by this time improvements in transport meant that food could be moved much more easily and while the poor were very badly affected, having to resort to seek aid from the poor rates which rose substantially, the number of deaths fluctuated only slightly, reaching fifty-one in 1794 and 1795 which was just three above the 1793 figure and five above that of 1796.

Deaths from starvation as a result of weather-related harvest failure in the nineteenth century were much rarer, except in Ireland in the 1840s with the Potato Famine and the Great Hunger. The potato crop also failed in Somerset at the same time and its consequences caused misery for many labouring families. By that decade potatoes had become the staple food of many labouring men in the Bruton area and reports in late 1845 indicated that what appeared to be sound potatoes when they were stored, just turned to a rotten, stinking mess. Growers, who had been receiving 9s a sack previously, were forced to sell their diseased crop to farmers with pigs for 1s a sack.

In Bruton market prices rose to 12s a sack for good potatoes which placed them far beyond the resources of most labourers and they were found begging the pig farmers to sell the rotten potatoes to them for 2s 6d a sack. The result was that there was a higher than average number of burials in the period 1845 to 1847, fifty-two as opposed to forty-four just before and thirty-nine just after. How far some of these resulted directly from starvation or as a result of bodies weakened by lack of adequate food and so became susceptible to other illnesses, is impossible to determine.

As more and more markets and territories were opened up and exploited during the course of the nineteenth century, such as the Canadian Prairies, Australia and New Zealand, grain and other foodstuff poured into this country. The days of deaths from weather-related harvest failure were finally over.

There were of course very lucky escapes from the impact of extreme weather, for example, the area was struck by a severe storm on the night of 26-27th November 1703, the effects of which were recorded by Daniel Defoe in 'The Storm' which was published the following year. He received a letter from Hugh Ash of Bruton detailing one man's survival. "At Brewton what was most remarkable was this, that one John Dicer of that town, lay the night as the tempest was, in the barn of one John Seller, the violence of the wind broke down the roof of the barn, but fortunately for him there was a ladder which staid up a rafter, which would have fell upon the said John Dicer; but he narrowly escaping being killed, did slide himself through the broken roof, and so got over the wall without any great hurt."

A labourer named Ingram was less fortunate in July 1845 when he was killed by lightning during what one newspaper described as, "one of the most awful thunder storms ever remembered in that part of the country." On that Thursday with another labourer he was turning a heap of manure in a field near Colinshayes House when the rain started and both men ran to shelter under a crab-apple tree. Ingram was leaning against the trunk of the tree when it was struck by lightning, was badly burnt on the head and back and died instantly. The other labourer, though injured, managed to use a spade as a support to reach the house and raised the alarm. A doctor was sent for and interestingly tried to revive the dead man when he "opened a vein in the arm of the deceased." Ingram was buried on the following Sunday on what would have been his 39th birthday and he left behind a widow and three young children "to lament the loss of an excellent husband and a kind father, thus suddenly taken from them in the prime and vigour of life."

The only other lightning fatality seems to have been James Williams, aged 52, who was struck by lightning at the end of June 1881, although no details were given, and was buried on 1st July. Unsurprisingly through the decades there were a number of reports of animals in the fields being killed by lightning.

The report of one weather-related death in June 1790 probably reflected more the beliefs current at the time than actual reality. The Countess of Ilchester died at Redlynch from "a violent cold and fever" which it was believed had been "caught by walking in the park, and getting wet in her feet." (26)

f) Violence

A violent death was regarded, especially in the earlier part of the period under consideration, as one of the worst forms of death possible as it did not permit all the necessary arrangements to have been made, not only worldly but also spiritually. Violent forms of death occurred in Bruton and its immediate neighbourhood through the centuries but fortunately rarely.

i) Murder.

Only a very small number of murders were recorded mainly because to establish that as the cause of death beyond any doubt, it had to be proved that the action was premeditated. Several examples that appeared to fit into that category occurred in the thirteenth century. In 1225 Reginald le Nappere was accused of causing the death of Gregory the Shepherd but the local jury decided that he was innocent as Gregory had been killed by Gervase the son of Walter who had fled and so was outlawed. In the same year a merchant was murdered in the house of Waldrick de Hunewic and Emma his wife. Although Waldrick fled, the local jury declared that he was not guilty as he was not at home when the incident occurred. They decided that the merchant was murdered by Emma's two brothers, Solomon and Osbert, and that she was complicit. The brothers were arrested, escaped from custody but later after he was recaptured Solomon was executed and Osbert outlawed.

A few years later in 1242 an unknown stranger was found dead in La Sewell between Bruton and Upton Noble. Although there were no wounds on the body and no one was suspected, the jury decided that it was murder. There were also four victims at Shepton Montague, Osbert the chaplain, Robert his brother, Cicely and Isabella whose house was also burgled and although the stolen goods were found in the house of Warin de Harewoode and his wife Isabella they were not suspected and allowed to go free. The jury found Walter Poydras guilty even though he had previously been found not guilty by a county court and he was subsequently hanged.

The 1530s were clearly a turbulent decade in Bruton, possibly fuelled by the religious turmoil of the times. In 1532 William Collys, a mercer, and Roger Stere were charged with helping Nicholas Pynerton to escape after he had been "taken for suspected murder." Unfortunately who Pynerton was suspected of murdering was not recorded. Two years later in 1534 John Whyt was granted a pardon by Henry VIII for the murder of William Nicholas in the town. The latter had attacked Whyt at night in the dark and as he defended himself he struck Nicholas with his sword and he died instantly.

Later in the Tudor period in July 1580 Ralph Penny of Bruton, husbandman, along with three other men, also received a pardon for his part in the murder of Robert Granger of Bruton who was assisting the Sheriff of Dorset restore property in Dorset to Christian Holwall, the widow of Thomas Holwall of Bruton. (27)

Murders appear to have been committed during the Civil War period in the seventeenth century. One account by Fuller relates that in 1647 Robert Bolsham, a clergyman of Shepton Montague, was killed by Cavaliers. This is probably Robert, the son of Henry and Julia Balsam who was born in the village in August 1611. It has been suggested that the subsequent murder of Alexander Randal, another clergyman living in the same village, was a reprisal in 1649. Parliamentary soldiers forced their way into his house and shot him dead, before stealing many of his goods. (28)

On 25th August 1765 a particularly brutal murder occurred in Creech-hill Lane when James Wilson, a packman, was beaten to death. The Coroner's jury had no hesitation in bringing in a verdict of wilful murder by person or persons unknown but no one was ever apprehended. The motive was probably robbery as he was believed to have been carrying valuables. One local newspaper referred to him as "a native of Ireland" but in the Burial Register it was noted "supposed to be a Scotchman, found dead in Creechhill Lane." (29)

When it came to murder the wealthy and influential seemed to have been able to fare much better than the mass of the population. James Fitzjames of Redlynch was implicated in the murder of two members of the Hartgill family. As a result of this on 6th April 1557 he was ordered to pay "the somme of c li of good and lawfull money of England by waie of a fine, and unto the two widowes of the Hartgilles the somme of fiftie poundes, that is to saie xxv li to eche of them......and further do contynue of good behaviour towards the King and Quenes Majesties and their subjectes."

In the following century John, 3rd Lord Berkeley of Stratton, and John Berkeley, gentleman, presumably a relative although not a legitimate son as the former had no male heir, were cited for the murder of Ralph Tonycliffe, gentleman, in Middlesex. Lord John was the nephew of Sir Charles Berkeley of Bruton and it was alleged that in April 1684 he "slew and murdered the said Ralph Tonycliffe by giving him with a rapier a mortal wound in and upon his belly near the navel", and he died nine days later. It is possible that this occurred in a duel between the two men. He was convicted but on 12th May a warrant for a pardon was issued at Windsor, procured by Sidney Godolphin who was related to Berkeley by marriage. (30)

ii) Manslaughter.

The charge of manslaughter was usually brought when death resulted from a spur of the moment action and later in the nineteenth century as the result of recklessness or negligence. Very few such cases have emerged in Bruton.

In October 1767 after a drinking session Robert Francis and John Wilmot quarrelled and started fighting during which Wilmot struck Francis so hard that he died instantly. The Coroner's jury brought in a verdict of manslaughter. The Burial Register very unusually gave the cause of death when Francis was buried on 6th October, "lost his life by fighting with Jno Willmott." Excessive quantities of alcohol were also responsible when John Rich killed Richard Strongman, a shoe-maker of Stoney Stoke in 1790. It was stated at the inquest that Strongman, who was "disguised in liquor", abused Rich, threw alcohol in his face and was about to strike him when Rich pushed him, he fell backwards and fractured his skull "in so terrible a manner that he died instantly." One local newspaper took the opportunity to observe that, "The unhappy cause, to which most of the melancholy events similar to the above are owing, was *inebriety*."

In August 1851 Joseph Coles and Thomas Lawrence also quarrelled, this time over their respective share of wages paid. Lawrence kicked Coles who struck him back on the side of his head which caused Lawrence to fall over and hit his head on a piece of wood. The jury recommended mercy and the judge agreed so as Coles had already been in custody for seven months he was released.

At the Somerset Assizes in August 1865 James Andrews was sentenced to six months imprisonment for the manslaughter of engine-driver Alfred White and stoker Radford Bartlett as the result of an accident at Bruton Station. Their ballast-train with thirteen trucks was diverted into a goods siding through his negligence and crashed into and demolished the buffers and ended up falling into Dropping Lane. Henry Trim aged twenty-four was more fortunate in 1871 when he was charged with the manslaughter of Catherine Shears of Shepton Montague. During a disturbance he had thrown stones, one of which struck her in the chest and she subsequently died. The jury found him not guilty.

Finally in November 1890 James Andrews, a labourer, was sentenced to six months imprisonment with hard labour for the manslaughter of his brother, Richard. This was presumably a different James Andrews to the one who had faced the 1865 charge as no mention was made of a previous conviction. While there was ample evidence of a quarrel as a drunken Richard tried to stay in his brother's house, there was some dispute about whether James struck Richard with a walking stick. The victim had walked away from the house but was later found dead resting against a wall nearby. (31)

iii) Infanticide.

While infantile mortality rates were high in the period covered it is impossible to determine the level of infanticide in Bruton.

Between October 1783 and December 1813 out of 1,319 burials recorded in the Burial Register 221 or 16.8% were for infants aged below one. In the last thirty years of the nineteenth century the figures had decreased but were still high: out of 943 burials 110 or 11.7% were under one. National evidence suggests that infanticide tended to occur only in exceptional circumstances, often related to the disposal of illegitimate children. As so many children died young anyway it was almost impossible to establish if they were aided by a specific action or by pre-determined neglect.

In most instances there was just suspicion such as the case recorded by Revd. Woodforde on 28th September 1765 at Castle Cary, "Dr Clarke's maid, Mary, was this morning found out in concealing a dead child in her box of which she had delivered herself yesterday morning." The Inquest jury two days later decided she was not guilty of murdering the baby.

In 1796 the Overseers of the Poor in Bruton paid £1 12s 91/2d for a Coroner and three Juries "on the body of a Child found in the Backway and for a knife to open the body." For "opening the body" Dr. Grant was paid two guineas. Unfortunately no verdict seems to have survived. When Dr Heginbothom performed a post-mortem on the body of a child discovered in the mill pond in May 1870, "He could not say that the child had a separate existence, but he was sure the injuries were inflicted during life." As a result the jury was only prepared to return a narrative verdict, "Found dead in the Mill Pond."(32)

Sometimes newborn babies were just abandoned, mainly in the hope that they would be found and raised by someone else. That of course did not always happen as in the case of 'Moses' who was buried on 2nd December 1836 having been "found" on Park Lawn. Although no christening is recorded, that he was given a name suggests that he was alive when discovered but did not survive. The name given to the child was no doubt to reflect similarities with the Old Testament account of the early life of the Jewish leader Moses.

iv) Violence unknown

Several other people met violent deaths in and around Bruton and to which there are tantalizing references, usually in the Burial Registers, but no details were given.

> "1613 August 16   John Androes was buried, being slaine the Saterday before.
>
> 1625 June 15   Edward Davidge, killed in Koggly [*Cogley Wood*]
>
> 1644 May 17   Thomas Bolster, Killd.
>
> 1646 September 26   Nicholas Wilton, killd.
>
> 1682 July 30   Thomas Green, a stranger, killd.
>
> 1716 February 15   Two Souldiers yt was shott to death."

Murder, manslaughter, accident - the exact reason may never be known except for the last case which was a firing squad. After this execution in 1716 a local tradition developed in relation to its location. In a lecture in August 1857 J.G. Bord made reference to it: "A stone, taken from the Park Wall, in Plocks, which tradition has handed down as the stone which was pierced by the balls of the soldiers who shot the above, is now exhibited," presumably in the temporary museum in the National Schoolroom.

In addition in 1738 the Overseers of the Poor paid £1 13s 8d in fees to the Coroner and jury "on Acct of John Illing's Son being killed by Jos Ames Son James." The Burial Register recorded that Francis, son of John Illing junior, was buried on 30th August 1738. No other details were included in either source.

Finally, in June 1905 William Viney aged eight was found unconscious and injured in a field at Bruton and died the following day. The Coroner's jury returned a narrative verdict: "That deceased died from fracture of the skull with compression of the brain, the result of extreme violence, but how or under what circumstances the fatal injuries were caused there is no evidence to show." (33)

v) Suicide

Suicide was traditionally regarded as a form of murder. It was seen as usurping the prerogative of God to decide when a life should end and depriving the monarch of one of his or her subjects. In addition it was viewed as ignoring both God's mercy and the promises of future eternal life. The result was that some people were so superstitious that they would not touch the corpse of a suicide: neither cut down a hanging body nor drag one from a river or pond. It was also the usual practice for a suicide's family to be deprived of all his possessions. On 23rd April 1406 the King granted £20 to John Mersshe from the goods of William Batyn of Bruton, a baker, "and pertaining to the king because the said William killed himself at Bruton." Such a situation was very detrimental to any surviving family and so instead juries did tend to return a verdict of "non compos mentis", that is, not of sound mind. In such a case the possessions were not forfeited.

National evidence suggests that during the Reformation and after the law was enforced more rigorously but by 1700 the dislike of the savage penalties increased and so there were more "non compos mentis" verdicts. On the other hand there may well have been some people who contemplated suicide but who were deterred by these harsh penalties that would be imposed on their families. Others along with Shakespeare's Hamlet may well have feared the unknown:

"Who would bear the burdens of a weary life,
But that the dread of something after death,
The undiscover'd country from whose bown
No traveller returns, puzzles the will,
And makes us rather bear those ills we have,
Than fly to others that we know not of."

Through much of this earlier period, including after 1700, suicides were often buried at cross roads or beside highways without any Christian service. The legal prescription required burial of suicides "in or near to the highways with a stake thrust through their bodies, to terrify all passengers, by that so infamous and reproachful a burial, not to make such their final passage out of this present world." This prescription remained in force until 1821.

Different reasons were advanced to explain burial at cross roads, such as to diffuse the evil in as many different directions as possible and to tread the poor corpse well and truly underfoot. The stake was designed to prevent the body or the ghost from rising again. A more charitable explanation was that as crosses were often erected at junctions, it would allow the body that had been denied all holy rites at least to be near something consecrated.

In 1762 after an argument with his wife a journeyman-weaver hanged himself in Bruton. Following an inquest verdict of suicide, (*felo de se*, that is felon of himself) "his body was buried in the Cross Road." Unfortunately there was no indication of which one, that may of course in itself suggest that there was a well-known location at that time.

In the late nineteenth century there was a post at a cross roads between Bruton and Galhampton with the inscription:

"Oh, Reader, pause – may this unhallowed sod
Remind thee of thy duty to thy God –
Thou shalt do no murder,"

It was put up in memory of William Coles who committed suicide aged eighty in the spring of 1805 and was buried at that spot. Just before his death he had received several pounds and spent it on alcohol.

There was a decided lack of Christian charity in the remarks of one local newspaper when it reported in 1815 the burial of nineteen-year-old Peggy Miles of Frome at a cross roads near the town. "It is much to be wished that the sentence of the law will operate as a useful warning to many weak and depraved females." (34)

In 1821 the law was finally changed to permit burial in a churchyard for a suicide, between nine and twelve o'clock at night without the presence of a minister. The side of the churchyard most frequently allocated for such burials was the northern shaded side, sometimes referred to as the devil's side. The forfeiture of property finally ended in 1870, although by that time so many juries had disapproved of the penalties that for decades they had tended to return verdicts of temporary insanity so that the law would not apply. This practice did not meet with universal approval as in September 1884 'The Lancet' claimed, "scarcely one in a hundred of the so-called cases of 'temporary insanity' are correctly so described." In the following month it went further, "it is not their physical but their moral condition which is at fault. They want to flee from the trials and troubles of life." (35)

Through the centuries a number of cases of suicide emerge from Bruton. Death by hanging was the method chosen by several men in the eighteenth century so that in February 1703 the Overseers paid 3s to summon the Coroner "on Jerome Sweet that hanged himself" and a further 10s 3d "To guard watching him all night and 4 more men to bring him to buryall and Expenses on them." In 1732-3 the Overseer spent 17s 6d on the Coroner "when Williams's son hanged himself." No record of their burials appears in the Burial Register so they too may have been interred at a crossroads. In November 1772 a local newspaper reported the sad case of Mr. M. of Bruton, the name was not specified, who "hanged himself last Wednesday at an inn at Warminster." The newspaper went on to speculate as to motive, "This melancholy action is said to be owing to his having had so many losses lately, particularly by the failure of Mr Fordyce the banker." Finally in May 1800 there was the simple report that an inquest had taken place "on an old man who hung himself at Bruton."

There were also nineteenth century examples from neigh-bouring villages, such as for example in July 1822 David Hoare hung himself in a cow-house at Snagg Farm in Lamyatt which led to a verdict of "Lunacy". In November 1857 the wife of Thomas Dowding of Shepton Montague was found hanged and as it was reported, "she having been for some time previous in a very low state of mind", a verdict of "Temporary insanity" was returned. The motivation of retired farmer Joseph White, of Lamyatt aged 72, was explored more fully after he was found hanged from a beam in his bedroom. He was said to have "been in depressed spirits for some few months past in consequence of the marriage of a young woman to whom he had been much attached, and had also complained of feeling very lonely." It was added for good measure that one of his relatives had died in a Lunatic Asylum. Once again a verdict of "Temporary Insanity" was returned.

A couple of suicides cut their own throats, not an easy task, but at least the appropriate razors were readily available. On 3rd April 1898 Josiah Jackson simply recorded in his Diary, "Mr Macken cut his throat & Killed himself today." A very tragic case was that of Frances Young aged forty-one who cut her throat on 26th November 1905, three days after her husband's death. The Inquest returned a verdict of temporary insanity but at least "Deceased and her husband were buried together on November 29th."

Only two suicides by shooting have emerged which is surprising given the prevalence of guns in a rural area but it is likely that a number of other cases were attributed to accidents. In 1845 an employee of the Earl of Ilchester went into the summer house attached to the garden of Redlynch House, laid down on his back, placed the muzzle of a gun in his mouth and managed to pull the trigger with his foot so that he died instantly as his skull shattered. It was reported that, "the poor man had of late suffered great depression of spirits, and had often shown symptoms of derangement of mind." A verdict of temporary insanity was returned and although he was not named in newspaper reports this was probably William Moor aged forty-five who was buried in Bruton churchyard on 25th June 1845 and referred to as a suicide. Secondly, in December 1904 Ernest John Plantagenet Cassan, aged seventy, shot himself in Bath. He was the son of a former vicar of Bruton and had been educated at King's School, from where he won an Exhibition to Magdalan Hall, Oxford. In his youth he had been a talented fast bowler in cricket and was reckoned to be one of the fastest amateur bowlers in England even though he had "a very peculiar delivery, with much screw from an old gun-shot wound." (36)

Two other methods of suicide seem to have been more prevalent: one was taking a poison of some kind. When Hannah Baltch aged thirty-seven, was buried on 3rd September

1786 a note was added in the Register "poisoned herself." If this burial was in the churchyard it showed a very enlightened or charitable approach at that period. In January 1840 an Inquest found that Edward Bradford of Pitcombe had taken poison while in "Lunacy". In November 1862 a travelling hawker, named Bell, drank a quantity of spirits of vitrol, "He lingered in the greatest agony for two hours and expired." It appeared that he had neglected his wife and six children and dreaded being arrested. He did not find a resting place in Bruton churchyard.

A very sad case occurred in Wyke Champflower in the spring of 1858 when Mrs Everett who occupied a small farm poisoned herself. It was clearly carefully planned and executed as a few days before she took her life she sent a boy to Hill the chemist in Bruton with a note to buy sixpenny worth of laudanum, stating that it was to be used on her cattle and then one or two days later she obtained a similar quantity. Together these constituted the fatal dose, even though a doctor was sent for and he used a stomach-pump on her. A reason for her actions soon emerged as her nephew and niece lived with her and had undertaken "For sometime past an improper and unnatural intimacy…the result of which was the birth of a child about three weeks ago." The shame and possibly guilt was too much for Mrs Everett. In the end "She was buried unattended by any Clergyman or any Service, near Midnight, on Monday, in the churchyard" at Wyke." (37)

The second common method of suicide was drowning and various locations were used. In June 1887 John Hockey aged fifty-six was found dead, face down in two feet of water in Colman's Bay. He appeared to have been worried about money as the result of a contract he had at Cogley and had been drinking. "Labouring under temporary insanity" was the verdict. In March 1900 James Crocker aged seventy-eight who was an inmate of Sexey's Hospital drowned himself in a pond in Daydon Lane and the same temporary insanity verdict was returned after the Master of the Hospital, J.W. Parfitt, had given evidence that although Crocker suffered from 'melancholy', he had no reason to suspect that he would drown himself. Both of these men were granted Christian burial.

Batt's Hole was the other usual location and it was here that Alexander Thorne aged forty-three was found in shallow water in 1861. He had recently lost his job and there had been a domestic quarrel. He left "a wife and three children quite unprovided for." Less than a year later the body of John George Indermaur aged forty-five was recovered from the same spot. For many years he had been the station-master at Bruton Station but had left this employment six months before as a result of depression. Despite being carefully monitored he managed to slip out of his house unobserved. In spite of all the evidence the jury returned a narrative verdict of "Found drowned", no doubt to help his widow and six children retain his property. Both were buried in Bruton Churchyard. (38)

For some suicides there was no specific information, for example, in July 1687 the Constable paid 1s 8d on a jury as "A woman at Woolston destroyed herself."

Even the attempt at or threat of suicide was taken very seriously. When Robert Humphreys, a Bristol chapman, was detained by Bruton's tythingmen in 1656 he was immediately taken in front of a Justice of the Peace as one tythingman gave evidence that, "He told me he did not care of his life, and he should now be brought to hanginge, and he will poison himself." In September 1871 there were two attempted suicides, each by cutting the throat. An inmate of Sexey's Hospital had his allowance stopped as a result of drunkenness that led him to cut his arm and throat. He survived but the Visitors were so appalled that he was expelled from the Hospital. Shortly afterwards a woman named Hillier cut her throat after she was sent home from work when she had been drinking. She too survived and when she appeared before magistrates she was dispatched to Wincanton Union Workhouse.

Early in 1873 local druggist and postmaster John Robinson had attempted suicide by swallowing various chemicals after he was arrested for stealing £6 from an account at the Post Office.William Hughes of South Brewham attempted to cut his throat in 1889 as a result of pain from a growth on his neck. He too was sent to the Workhouse to recover from "the effects of his rash act" before being brought before the Magistrates. In Court he was advised by the Chairman of the Bench, "to take a more cheerful view of life."

Occasionally an attempt at suicide could evoke some sympathy as in the case of an unnamed young lady from South Brewham in August 1868. She jumped into the mill pond there but had been seen going in that direction by her mother who was suspicious of her intentions. She was pulled out unharmed by her brother, the miller and two other men. The local newspaper report added, "The young lady has been for some time subject to fits, and is supposed to have been labouring under delusions at the time. General sympathy is felt for the young lady and her family"

The most intriguing case, however, occurred in the eighteenth century and once again may indicate the different standards that existed for the wealthy and the poor. In 1765 Charles Berkeley was found dead in a pond, presumably one of the ornamental ponds in the grounds of Bruton Abbey to the east of the road to Wincanton. The official version of his death appeared in publications such as 'The Annual Register' which reported the death of "Hon Charles Berkeley, Esq, of Bruton, in Somersetshire. As he was fishing in his own pond, the boat in which he was, overset, and he was unfortunately drowned." Local gossip, however, was less charitable and attributed his death to suicide. These rumours were recorded by Revd. John Wesley when he was in the area two months later. "In the evening I preached at Shaftesbury, and on Tuesday at Wincanton. Riding homeward we saw the pond in which a great man, a few weeks since, put an end to a wretched life. And is death more welcome than life, even to a man what wallows in gold and silver?" (39)

vi) In War

Death in battle always came as a shock to the family as once again there was often the un-preparedness. It has been estimated that nationally about 25% of those who went to fight against the French in the late eighteenth and early nineteenth centuries died compared with up to 74% of those who were fighting abroad in the 1620s. In the same context the impact of the First World War was devastating as not only were larger numbers of men killed far from home but also many had no known grave at which relatives could mourn.

Ordinary men from Bruton had joined various regiments and militia through the centuries but as these were predominantly the poor they have left virtually no trace. Those who were killed have disappeared completely but some did survive to be discharged, often with a small pension. In 1631, for example, Walter Cleeves of Bruton, mason, petitioned the Quarter Sessions for a pension as a result of his service as a soldier under Captain Henry Bewtely.

Lord Fitzharding in 1665 had his own particular view on the reason for bravery on the battlefield as well as the reaction of men when they finally faced death there. He was convinced that many men acted bravely in battle as they were "more apt to think they shall escape than another man in fight" but that in the end when they faced death they were "as much troubled and apprehensive of it as any man else."

Fitzharding himself was the second son of Sir Charles Berkeley of Bruton Abbey, and a staunch Royalist who at the Restoration of Charles II in 1660 was showered with rewards and titles, including Lord Fitzharding and later the Earl of Falmouth. Thomas Salisbury commented, "Lord Fitz-hardingge grows daily more potent, opulent, and I had almost said, formidable in the Court. For he hath lately been regaled with new titles and £3000 per annum land to maintain them." Such power and influence meant that he was not universally popular and on one occasion Samuel Pepys recorded in his Diary that he was called "pimp to the King", and that he was "A witty man.... but of no good nature." He certainly fell foul of Lord Clarendon, particularly after his involvement with his daughter Anne. He commented that he was "A young man of a dissolute life, and prone to all wickedness in the judgment of all sober men.... of an insatiable ambition."

One Victorian historian believed that he was "a gallant and handsome profligate, whose society was as agreeable as his principles were indifferent." Bishop Burnett, however, was more charitable for he believed that "if he had outlived the lewdness of that time, and come to a more sedate course of life, he would have put the King on great and noble designs." He did remain loyal to his master, the Duke of York, the future James II, and volunteered to go to sea with him to fight against the Dutch. Even Pepys reported that "he is confessed to have been a man of great honour, that did show it in this his going with the Duke, the most that ever any man did."

In the Battle of Texel or Southwold Bay on 3rd June 1665 he was killed standing beside the Duke, who was the Lord High Admiral, by the same cannon shot that took off the head of Richard Boyle and also killed Lord Muskerry: "their blood and brains flying in the Duke's face; and the head of Mr Boyle striking down the Duke, as some say." In a letter the Duke simply related that, "Poor Lord Falmouth is killed." The King, however, was severely affected, "He was lamented by the King with floods of tears." In fact Clarendon went so far as to say that "those who knew his Majesty best, and had seen how unshaken he had stood in other very terrible assaults, were amazed at the flood of tears he shed upon this occasion." Later in the month the Earl of Sandwich commented that his "generosity cannot enough be valued." His death even elicited a short couplet in a poem:

"Though Falmouth, Portland, noble blood did spill,
They have their Honour, we our Sandwich still."

He was buried with fitting honours in Westminster Abbey on 22nd June.

His critics however were less charitable as one of them speculated that he may have attended the Duke simply in the hope of advancing his political career, possibly with a Dukedom, and that the cannon ball that had so injured his head "gave the first last proof, that he had Brains." (40)

Fitzharding's younger brother, Sir William Berkeley, a Vice Admiral, was also involved in this war against the Dutch and he too was killed. Immediately after Fitzharding's death a scandalous rumour circulated that Sir William, who had been chasing nine Dutch men o'war with a squadron of six ships, suddenly became over-cautious and possibly cowardly as he though it

"Not good
To venture more of Royal Harding's Blood:
To be immortal he was not of Age.....
And judg'd it safe and decent, cost what cost,

To lose the Day, since his dear Brother's loss.
With his whole Squadron straight away he bore,
And like good Boy, promis'd to fight no more."

In June 1666, however, when his ship, 'The Swiftsure' was cut off from the main fleet, he refused to surrender. In the battle he was shot in the throat with a musket ball and died on the table in his cabin. His ship was captured and his body taken to Holland but later returned and, like that of his brother, buried in Westminster Abbey. Even his final action, however, was not enough to stem some of the criticism:

"And if the thing were true, yet paint it not,
How Berkeley (as he long deserved) was shot,
Though others that survey'd the corpse so clear
Say he was only petrified with fear." (41)

g) Accidental death

Accidents and the injuries sustained from them constituted a significant cause of death in the Bruton area. Unfortunately detailed information only becomes available with the spread of local newspapers from the middle of the eighteenth century but it is unlikely to be incorrect to speculate that the same sort of accidents had been occurring for many generations before. In fact as early as 1242 a jury recorded that Robert Weland died instantly when a branch fell on him. This particular presentment did lead the jury to be in mercy as it was subsequently found that their information was incorrect as he had not died instantly but had lingered for three days.

The exact nature of many of the accidents will remain lost as, for example, the statistics collected by the Medical Officer of Health for the Wincanton Poor Law Union in the last decade of the nineteenth century used the all encompassing word "Injuries" [See Appendix 3]. How many of these men, women and children could have been saved with modern medical techniques and the use of antibiotics is impossible to determine.

It is possible to examine the accidental deaths in several broad categories:

i) Deaths involving animals and vehicles.

By the sixteenth century about one in ten of all fatal accidents involved animals, with horses as the prime culprits. As horses were the commonest means of transport for many men above the level of the poor, and were a significant source of power for labour, it was inevitable that accidents would occur. While the majority led only to some injury, a number were fatal and it has been estimated that more than a third of all 'animal' accidents resulted from falls from horses.

Nicholas Keates of Brewham died the day after he fell from his horse in April 1774. William Clarke, a builder and surveyor from Shepton Mallet was particularly unfortunate in August 1810 as he was returning home from Bruton. While riding over Milton Bridge his horse threw him and he must have been stunned or knocked unconscious as he drowned in the river. Henry Snell of Combe near Bruton was returning home in April 1815 when his horse fell over a heap of stones "which, to the great discredit of an individual in the neighbourhood, had been carelessly placed in the middle of the road", and he was thrown and killed. In October 1849 Joseph Farley, who was employed by a baker in South Brewham was thrown from a horse, "when his spine was so seriously injured that he died on the following morning." In 1869 Mr Beale of Henley Grove fell from his horse and "immediately expired".

Horses could be dangerous in other ways, particularly in kicking, trampling, biting or dragging and led to nearly a third of all 'animal' deaths. When the five year old son of Joseph Crees followed his father to feed several colts in January 1859, one of them kicked him on the back of the head "which caused almost instantaneous death." A similar fate some twenty years later awaited farmer John Ashford, aged thirty-five of Wyke Champflower, whose horse kicked him in the abdomen as he removed the halter. He lingered in great pain for six days until "death put an end to his suffering."

In July 1765 Revd. Woodforde recorded "A terrible Accident" that occurred while he was at dinner with some friends at Babcary. "A poor Boy was dragged and killed by a Horse about half a Mile from us on the Ilchester road. The boy was about 14 Years old – I hope to God the Poor Boy is happy." Needless to say Woodforde and his friends went to view the scene and they were surprised to discover that, "There was no bone broken neither was his Skull fractured – but he is dead."

Some accidents were clearly the result of the carelessness or recklessness of the rider, as in the case of Samuel Howell, who was about ten years old. He was reported to have been riding a horse in Pitcombe "at full speed.....and flogging the animal every step he went." Unfortunately for the boy "the horse turning a corner rather quick, he was thrown off and killed." (42)

Wagons of all kinds proved to be dangerous as well. Jane Smith, a child aged six, was killed in September 1823 as the result of "a waggon passing over her on the bridge, in consequence of the horses taking fright." The bridge may well be the one over the River Brue by the church which at this time had not been widened and so was still very narrow. Another child, Caroline Winter, aged three, was killed seven years later when she "fell from a cart, and was so injured that she died the following day." She was referred to as "an interesting child."

In September 1839 an Inquest on John Warr of Pitcombe found that he had been "killed by a wagon" although exactly how was not specified. A similar fate befell fourteen-year-old Henry Davidge in May 1857 when he was discovered on the road between Bruton and Wincanton with his head protruding from underneath a donkey cart. He had delivered his load of hurdles and was returning home when the accident occurred. There were no witnesses but it was speculated that, "he must have been driving too fast and on reaching the four turnings, the wheel of the cart must have struck against a spur stone, and caused it to upset." The death of John Tanner between Lamyatt and Creech Hill in April 1878 led to speculation that he had either been run over by the wagon he was driving or by a trap that had passed the wagon. There does not appear to have been any serious investigation into the latter which might have led to a charge of manslaughter.

The death of John Baker in August 1852 may also have been partly his own fault. He was driving a wagon loaded with nearly five tons of goods from Bruton to Shepton Montague when he came to Shooter's Hill, referred to as 'Strouter's Hill' in the newspaper report, and he appears to have "neglected to drag down the hill." The wheels of the wagon ran over his chest "crushing him very much." The verdict, as in so many of these examples, was 'Accidental death'. As many as one in eight of all fatal accidents involving carts took place on downward slopes.

The same verdict was returned on twelve-year-old Peter Hix of Lamyatt in July 1859, although the circumstances were very different. He was driving a cart laden with calves to Castle Cary Station for his father. Somehow one of the calves managed to knock him off his seat at the front of the cart and he was thrown head first onto the road and he died shortly afterwards.

Once again alcohol played a part in deaths as in May 1861, for example, after driving his father to Bruton Railway Station,

Charles Creed's eldest son went into the town and began drinking with his father's bailiff. "On leaving for home they drove off at a furious pace" and the cart turned over killing the young man almost instantly. In March 1872 Charles Butt was killed when the horses pulling the wagon he was driving were startled near Redlynch Gate and he was thrown from the wagon which then ran over his chest. A labourer, named Sims, had been similarly crushed by a wheel passing over him some ten years earlier. On this occasion he was at Bruton Station loading goods onto the wagon when a whistle from a train caused the horse to start and he tried to stop it. In November 1900 Maria Maidment died from a "hemorrhage of the brain" after she was knocked down by a pony and trap near Sexey's School. Finally in the same month carter George Benger aged thirty-six was killed when he was thrown from a trap. (43)

As technology advanced the railways were built and they opened up another potentially lethal vehicle. Fortunately few railway-related deaths were recorded in the Bruton area. A dreadful accident occurred in 1858, two years after the celebrations at the opening of the railway, when just as a man named Baker and his daughter were crossing the line "the up-express train came and literally knocked him to pieces.... The engine-driver saw the deceased on the line, and blew the whistle, but to no purpose, as the poor fellow seemed to be paralysed with fright." His daughter survived.

In December 1899 the body of Walter Bergman of Castle Cary, and formerly of Colinshayes House, aged 44, was discovered on the railway line near the level crossing at Gant's Mill. His body was so mutilated that it was unrecognisable and he was identified by documents he was carrying. He had had the misfortune to have been struck by a fast goods train travelling to London. The inquest was informed that during the evening he had frequented the Blue Ball Hotel and intended to catch the last train back to Castle Cary but it was running late and so, being a keen walker, he may have decided to walk. The foreman of the jury stated that joining the railway line at the level crossing in the small lane which linked the top of Plox to Lusty and following the track reduced the distance to be walked considerably. After Dr. Stockwell gave evidence that Bergman suffered from epileptic fits and may have had one if startled by the noise of the approach of a train and so would have been unable to get out of the way, the jury reached a verdict of 'Accidental Death'.

The most serious railway accident had occurred in 1865 and led to a Board of Trade Inquiry. The railway policeman on duty, James Andrewes, had arranged for a truck loaded with flour to be pushed into the sidings to allow a ballast train to go through the station as there was only a single track at that time. Unfortunately he forgot to reset the points and the train went into the sidings as well, through a goods shed, pushed the flour truck in front of it into the buffers and all crashed down some twenty-five feet onto the Wincanton road, killing the engine driver, Alfred White, and fireman, Radford Bartlett. Andrewes was subsequently found guilty of manslaughter and sentenced to six months imprisonment. (44)

ii) Machinery.

Any machinery that was operated by a power source had the potential to create a danger. In September 1851 miller Chaffins' daughter was oiling the cogs of a water-wheel in their mill when her dress caught in the machinery and she was dragged in. Despite medical assistance, including amputating her leg, she died shortly afterward. "The calamity is all the more distressing since she was the chief stay of the family, her father being insane, and the business entirely devolved on her." Some thirty years later Simon Veasey was killed when he was run over by a threshing machine drawn by a traction engine. Exactly what happened at his Inquest was not specified but "The extraordinary behaviour of Mr C Balch, Solicitor, was carried to such an extent during the enquiry that the Coroner ordered his removal from the court, and threatened to commit him for contempt." (45)

iii) Fire.

As so many of the houses, cottages and outbuildings were thatched, especially prior to the nineteenth century, it was no wonder that fire was a constant threat. On more than one occasion during hot summer weather the Constable ordered that buckets of water should be placed near inhabitants' front doors and that they must not carry lighted coals between houses. Although fires occurred remarkably few deaths were ever recorded.

As early as 1242 a man and several members of his family had died when their house was destroyed by fire at Honeywick, "Reginald Patewyn, Alice his wife, William his son, Margaret his daughter, and Eva his servant, were burned in Reginald's house at Hornwyte by misadventure. John son of Reginald, who first found them, comes and is not suspected, nor is anyone else."

Various Inquests and newspaper reports recorded the death of a number of individuals as a result of being burnt, and sadly several of these were children, such as in October 1824 William Bishop, referred to as "a child", whose clothes caught fire "in the absence of a woman to whose care he was entrusted." In January 1834 Mary Ann Hunt aged three and in December of the same year Frederick Partingale aged two were "accidently burned". In February 1843 Eliza Hyatt, aged two, died within a hour after her clothes caught fire when her mother "incautiously left her two children at home, locked in a room where there was a fire, while she went, according to custom, to gather firewood." In December 1851 an unnamed mother in

Pitcombe left her ten-year old daughter alone at home and somehow her clothes caught fire.

In South Brewham two children were left alone in a cottage by their parents and a fire broke out. It was spotted by blacksmith Henry Hill and he managed to rescue a four-year old boy but his five-year old sister, Clara Jones, died from her burns. At the subsequent inquest in November 1873 various witnesses testified that the mother was a very careful woman and fond of her children. Eleven years later in March 1884 Jane Jefferies left her two-year old granddaughter, Annie Louisa eating in front of a fire while she went upstairs. Somehow the child's pinafore caught fire and she died the following day.

One noticeable similarity in a number of these examples is that one or more children were left alone in a cottage. It may well be that in some cases a mother was normally at home but went out to undertake some household chore but in others the impression created is that the children were left for longer periods, possibly as a result of the mother having to undertake some paid employment to supplement the family's income as it was only in the late nineteenth century that wages in agricultural areas began to show an appreciable rise. For some families they were fortunate that there was a suitable relative close at hand to help with children or they were able to make use of a carer, but even then the consequences of the family's decisions and actions in some cases was clearly tragic.

In a few instances ages were not stated such as for Rebecca Vigar in April 1838. The age of Jane Eaton was not mentioned at her Inquest in October 1843 but on the 23rd of that month a girl with the same name aged seven was buried in Bruton Churchyard. Over twenty years later in February 1867 Elizabeth Maby aged eighty-four suffered the same fate.

So serious were the injuries sustained that on three occasions death resulted from scalding water, in these instances it was children and young people who were involved. In June 1838 Jonathan Sutcliffe was accidentally scalded, although no details were given, and his age was recorded as fifteen when he was buried on June 22nd. Thirteen years later in May 1851 "a fine boy, about five years of age, named Williams" was playing with his sister in their home when he upset a kettle of boiling water which was on the fire, "by which he became dreadfully scalded" and died four days later. There is no record of his burial in Bruton churchyard. A similarly tragic accident occurred at Milton Clevedon six years later when the wife of John Welch was about to bathe her infant son aged eighteen months. A servant had partly filled a bath with boiling water and as Mrs Welch was waiting for her to bring cold water the child accidentally fell into the bath. Despite rapid medical aid he died the following day. (46)

iv) Drowning.

By far the commonest cause of accidental death was drowning. A significant reason explaining this fact was that many of the clothes worn throughout the period under consideration were made of wool or linen and when these materials became waterlogged they were extremely heavy so that swimming was almost impossible. The earliest recorded case appeared in the Burial Register for 13th October 1629 when alongside the name of Umphrie Meeler is the word "drowned". In 1738-9 the Overseers of the Poor paid 14s 4 for "the Coroners Fee & Warrant touching a Child drowned at the Workhouse." Once again however no details were given so the first for which there is more information related to a Miss Hunt of Pitcombe who went to fetch water from a stream at the bottom of her garden, fell in and drowned. On finding the body her sister went into convulsions on the bank.

"Accidentally drowned" were the verdicts returned on Charles Rex aged eighteen months in September 1837 and John Bracey in May 1838. When Leah Clarke aged thirty-three was drowned in December 1841 the word "Lunacy" was added which may suggest that this one was not an accident. In the Burial Register alongside the name of John Hill aged fifty-seven on 4th April 1848 are the words "found drowned." Just over a year later an inquest was held on the body of a boy who was discovered in a mill-stream adjoining Bruton. He was not named but it was reported that, "It is supposed that the boy, who was of weak intellect, fell in while playing near the water."

On 1st August 1861 Edward Norman aged nine "was drowned while bathing in a dangerous place called 'Batt's hole'." His friends told him not to go into the water but he ignored them and as this was not the first death at that spot, it was reported, "that it is to be enclosed with iron-spiked railings." Another swimmer who drowned was George Williamson aged about forty-two, who was a packer on the Great Western Railway. In July 1876 he swam into the River Brue near Cole, turned on his back and sank. Although there were three other men with him at the time none of them could swim. In his Diary for 23rd May 1895 Josiah Jackson noted that, "A Joseph Young (of Bruton) drowned in (Batts Hole) river." This entry may possibly be a reference to Joel Young aged seventy-nine, an inmate of Sexey's Hospital, who was buried on 25th May. Clearly that location on the edge of Bruton remained a very dangerous place, despite attempts to prevent swimming there.

In a similar way in December 1859 William Day, a carter, was found dead in a ditch near Discove Farm. He had been in the Old Bull Inn in Patwell Street the previous evening and left there at midnight, "it is supposed he fell into the ditch and was suffocated." This was probably yet another case where alcohol played a part in the death. Over ninety years before in 1767 the same mode of death in a ditch led to a tragic train of events. The son of Thomas Haynes was missing and as he searched for the boy, who was about eleven years old, he met a man who told him that his son had been found drowned in a ditch, "on hearing of which, the father dropt down dead, and so soon as the melancholy news reached the mother, she was seized with fits, and it's supposed she cannot live out the night."

Finally in October 1896 Ann Tanner, aged sixty of Wyke Champflower, drowned not in a ditch but in a four-foot deep pond, or "pool of water" as it was called, some fifty yards from her cottage. She had set out at about 10 o'clock on a Saturday evening as usual to do her shopping in Bruton. Her husband was described as "a general labourer" and would have been paid his weekly wages late on Saturdays so it was the custom for shopping to take place very late on that day and some shops remained open until midnight. Her husband went to bed and as he did not wake he did not miss her until the morning. Although a verdict of "Accidentally drowned" was returned it was also stated that, "Deceased must have died without a struggle, as a basket of groceries was found on her arm", which suggests that there may have been some medical reason. (47)

v) Miscellaneous accidents

Through the decades there was a miscellaneous collection of accidents which led to deaths. In December 1859 John Bacon, aged ninety and an inmate of Sexey's Hospital, fell down three steps and died a few hours later. James Curtis of Pitcombe had a much greater fall a decade later when the rope by which he was being lowered down into a deep well broke and he was killed instantly.

A fall from a wall in Hadspen was enough to break the neck of a man named Wheeler in January 1766 and he died instantly.

Charles Huish aged forty was also very unlucky in September 1862 as a wall, against which mud was being thrown from a mill-pond at White and Bord's factory, collapsed and killed him. The Coroner was in Bruton for another Inquest so he reconvened the same jury that returned a verdict of "Accidental Death".

The same verdict had been returned on John Gapper who was just ten years old when he was killed in June 1822. Like so many boys he was already labouring to help support the family and on the fateful day was working on the roof of the Wellington Inn. The actual cause of his death was attributed to "the negligence of a collier who had left his cart and horse in the street (which has been a common practice with them), and the animal teazed by the flies, pushed the cart under the ladder upon which the boy was, and threw it down." The boy's skull was fractured.

There were of course the slightly more unusual and rarer causes of death from accidents, for example, Mr C. Bacon, a brick manufacturer who lived at Brick Kiln, choked to death on a piece of meat in August 1872 and Uriah Penny of Yarlington died two years later after drinking stream water following an energetic game of barn-ball. In one instance alcohol was directly blamed for a death. Under the heading "Death by drinking Spirits" a local newspaper reported that in November 1828 Peter Parfitt, a farmer from Nunney, had spent the evening in a Bruton tavern with some friends. At the end of the evening he "called for a pint of gin, which he drank off in its raw state" and then went to bed. There he died or as the newspaper expressed it, "but in a very short time afterwards was a corpse."

When thirty-two year old William Balch of Brewham was found dead in a ditch in November 1870 after drinking in the Bull Inn, the landlord was careful to point out in his evidence that when the deceased left the inn about ten o'clock in the evening he was sober. There was speculation that he may have had a fit, fallen into the ditch and died from exposure. When James White of Lamyatt was found dead in a ditch in September 1821 there was just the straightforward verdict of "Accidental death". Another death which resulted from a fall was that of William Shearn of Pitcombe aged 57 in February 1864. In his case he had fallen into a quarry when he was walking to work in the dark. Surprise was expressed that he was walking too far on the left hand side of a route despite having used it for twenty years. No blame was of course attached to the landowner, Henry Hobhouse of Hadspen, although the jury did suggest, "that the quarry should be railed in."

Another unusual accident which led to death occurred in Shepton Montague in March 1858 when the father of four year old John Bond threw a piece of iron which was used as a poker out of doors with such force that it struck the boy so hard on the head that he died a few hours later. The effects of age may well have played a part in the death of retired farmer John Fowler aged 88 of South Brewham in January 1885, as he appears to have fallen out of a first floor window "which it is supposed he mistook for the door."

As guns were prevalent in rural areas for hunting purposes, it was not surprising that there were occasional accidents with them that led to death. In February 1819 as the Earl of Ilchester's game-keeper at Redlynch was setting a spring-gun, he accidentally trod upon the trip wire, the gun went off and he was struck by the contents, which was usually lead shot. While his death was very unfortunate it was an example of the barbaric methods which landowners had no hesitation in using against poachers at that period. This particular weapon, along with man-traps, had been legalised by an Act of Parliament in 1816.

Violent deaths from guns happened to a number of young people, in two instances when they were related. When a servant girl saw a wood pigeon at the kitchen widow of the house in which she worked, she asked the young master to shoot it. By the time that he had loaded his gun it had flown away but he left the gun in the kitchen. Later the girl picked up the gun and pointed it at her sister who was sitting by the window working. For some unexplained reason she pulled the trigger and shot her sister in the head. In November 1873 two brothers, William and George Day, went into the cottage of Mrs Cox near the National School. William, the elder brother aged twelve, found a gun which had been left there, pointed it at his brother aged nine and it went off, hitting George in the neck and chest so that he died instantly.

In August 1896 Clement Squibb, the twenty-year-old son of the tenant of Greenscombe Farm, had been out on the farmland with his double-barrelled gun but had not shot anything. On his return he had successfully removed one of the cartridges but the other jammed, possibly, he considered, as a result of water entering the barrel during a heavy rainstorm. He asked a domestic servant Blanche Cox, also twenty years old, to get him the extractor and as she approached him with it the gun went off and she was shot in the head, dying almost instantly. After hearing all the evidence the inquest jury decided that it was a case of misadventure and that Squibb should not face a charge of manslaughter as a result of negligence.

Another dreadful accident occurred in November 1876 at a time when the community was coming together for entertainment purposes. Two men, Armstrong and Turner, were using a three-inch gas pipe as a cannon to celebrate Guy Fawkes Night on Coombe Farm Hill. Three times the cannon fired correctly but on the fourth it exploded, wounding two children in the head and face and killing Thomas Sly aged eleven on the spot when a piece of iron, seven inches long and up to one and half inches wide, nearly split his head in two.

Perhaps the silliest accident which would have been comic had it not been so tragic happened to John Curtis of Pitcombe in January 1866. He went up a tree to lop off a limb but appears to have been either resting or sitting on the same branch. When it gave way he fell head first on to the road below and died the following day. (48)

While deaths did occur as the result of accidents, some people had lucky escapes, including John, 1st Lord Berkeley of Stratton and his family in June 1671. One of the appointments that he enjoyed after the Restoration of Charles II was as Lord Lieutenant of Ireland, based in Dublin. "My Lord Lieutenant, his lady, children, and many other persons of quality, as well as others, being met at the theatre there, the upper galleries thereof suddenly fell down, with the fall of which his Excellency, his lady and children were all hurt, though not much, but with it six persons were killed, and above thrice that number dangerously wounded." Berkeley was in the theatre to watch a performance of Ben Jonson's play 'Bartholomew Fair' and many Puritans took the opportunity to portray the event as a judgement from God on the frivolity of the Restoration period. (49)

It is also important to stress that while the local newspapers, especially in the nineteenth century, contained hundreds of accounts of accidents involving inhabitants from Bruton and the neighbourhood, the overwhelming majority of victims did survive. Some were unharmed while others suffered broken limbs and a range of injuries that may well have impaired their future lives.

Similarly, although local people were surrounded by many causes of death, life carried on and while there was the acceptance that some day death would come, it was not an issue which overshadowed their everyday existence. The economic circumstances of the overwhelming majority of the inhabitants of the town and neighbourhood meant that their concerns had to be elsewhere: they had to work in order to earn money to provide for themselves and their families. Health and safety issues lay far in the future and so in their time they had to do exactly what their employer required or they ceased to work and then faced the inevitable consequences.

3

DEATH FOR YOUNG AND OLD

a) The Young

With so many causes of death ever present it seems appropriate to consider life expectancy as a whole in Bruton. As Christians through the ages knew only too well, the Bible made reference to the allotted span of life being three score years and ten, but in reality people also knew that this was clearly not the case. The death rate amongst infants and children remained stubbornly high until at least the second half of the nineteenth century when medical improvements, developments in diet, housing, public health and later higher wages all played their part to reduce it. Table 6 gives some indication of child deaths as a % of total deaths in Bruton in a sample of some nine twenty-year periods.

TABLE 6 Child Deaths in relation to the total number of deaths in Bruton, 1590-1919.

Years	Number of Child deaths	Total number of deaths	Child deaths as % of total deaths
1590-1609	217	455	47.7
1630-1649	258	687	37.6
1670-1689	392	1054	37.2

Years	Number of Child deaths	Total number of deaths	Child deaths as % of total deaths
1710-1729	502	1087	46.2
1750-1769	337	824	40.9
1790-1809	314	840	37.4
1830-1849	328	936	35.0
1870-1889	147	635	23.1
1900-1919	59	447	13.2

A major problem in compiling these statistics is that prior to 1784 the age at death was not recorded. From that point a child was taken to be ten years old or under. Before 1784 the usual practice was to refer to a child as the son or daughter of a particular person, generally the father. For the purposes of Table 6 all such entries are assumed to relate to children under ten.

Parents expected infant and child deaths and so some historians have speculated that as a result they invested less affection in their children. There does not however seem to be any concrete evidence for this speculation. For the over-whelming majority of parents the death of a child was the most distressing of all deaths as for many people in previous generations, as in more recent times, it was far harder to lose a child than an elderly parent. Some parents also faced the dreadful grief of the death of children who had survived all the perils of early childhood only to die before them: John Cann, for example, had buried one son Henry Newman aged 7 in February 1843; he was followed by another son Thomas William aged 15 in January 1850 and then daughter Mary Anne aged 28 in April 1851.

For many parents the death of a child was the supreme test of their Christian faith and many, especially in the Victorian period took great comfort from the support of the Church and the idea that their child had been removed from a world of pain and suffering to be safe in the arms of Jesus. This was a concept that found expression on the gravestones of some children's graves. (See Appendix 6)

The oldest memorial stone which was erected to the memory of a child in the Bruton area and which survived into the twentieth century appears to have been originally on the outside of the east wall of the south chapel of Milton Clevedon Church.

> Under that Stone's a chi
> ld wrapt in Earth's mold,
> For whom canot his par
> ents griefe be told.
> In wit most rare noe
> lesse in grace was he;
> The sooner fit with
> Christ in blis to be.
> John Thacher Borne iv.12.1615.

The Burial Register shows that John, the son of the Revd. Peter Thacher, the Vicar of Milton Clevedon, was buried on 13th June 1622, when he would have been six and a half years old. (1)

The number of deaths of children under ten years of age in Bruton must have been devastating for parents. Between 1784 and 1814 some 524 children in this age group died and of these 479, or a massive 91.4%, were under five years of age, and 253 or 48.3% one year old or under. While the number of those aged ten and under who died fell dramatically between 1815 and 1900, the percentages remained virtually unchanged and infant deaths as a percentage actually increased. In a sample of eighteen years taken every five years starting in 1815, the number of deaths of children under ten decreased to 208 but of these 190 or 91.3% were five or under, and 107 or 51.4% one or under. If a child could reach the age of five then he or she had a reasonable chance of survival into adulthood.

Death it seems did not distinguish between the classes as children from all social groups were taken, for example, over a sixteen year period Sir Charles Berkeley of Bruton Abbey buried four daughters: Elizabeth in March 1636, Penelope in May 1639, another Penelope in March 1645, both being named after his wife, and Mary in April 1652. All these girls were between two months and five years old. Just over a century later on 9th May 1757 the Hon. Charles Berkeley buried a daughter, referred to as "Miss Berkeley" and on 19th August in the same year his son Maurice. These deaths may have prompted him to make his Will in November of the same year to include detailed provision for his two remaining daughters. When Charles himself died eight years later he had no direct male heir so the estate which included Bruton Abbey reverted to his elder brother John, the last Lord Berkeley of Stratton.

As may be seen above, Sir Charles Berkeley named two daughters Penelope and this in fact was a not uncommon practice with Christian names as so many children died. After the Berkeleys' daughter Elizabeth died in March 1636 they also named their next daughter Elizabeth when she was christened on 28th September in the same year. On 6th July 1703 Benjamin Sexey buried his son Benjamin and then on 26th May 1718 buried another son with the same name.

In some parts of the country families adopted the practice of giving the same Christian name to more than one child at the same time because of the expectation that at least one of them would die. An example of this practice may have survived from Bruton as in his Will of 15th April 1546 John Langyer bequeathed, "To my son John Langyer the younger a yearling. To my son John Langyer the elder ij oxen." (2)

Table 7 gives an indication of the months in which child deaths occurred in Bruton in two thirty-year periods.

TABLE 7 Months of most child deaths as a %.

Thirty year period	Months (inclusive)	Infants and under one	1 to 5 years old	6 to 10 years old
January 1784 to December 1813	January to April	43.2	36.7	43.5
	September to November	25.7	31.7	19.6
January 1870 to December 1899	January to April	49.5	45.0	38.1
	September to November	18.9	15.0	33.3

Table 7 shows that in the seven months covered for both periods nearly 70% of all child deaths occurred, although there was some slight change in the pattern. Deaths from respiratory disease normally associated with the winter months increased in % terms over the century, probably as a result of improvements in vaccination and public health that removed some the dangers of water borne and insect borne diseases. In the period 1784-1899 each of the above age categories displayed a marked decrease in deaths, in percentage terms to 54%, 64% and 55% respectively.

As so many different Parish Clerks completed the Registers through the centuries, various formats were used for entries for the burial of children. Prior to 1586 there is no indication at all as there is only a list of names and from then until the early 1650s the child's name is given along with "s of, d of". From the early 1650s until the late 1660s the Register reverts to the earlier form of just names, possibly reflecting more Puritan attitudes in relation to death. This system is then modified for some twenty years to include a name and alongside the words "a child". From 1686 until the formal printed Registers were adopted late in 1783 the name of the father is once again specified, except for a short period from the late 1740s to the late 1750s when the child's name was omitted and the entry simply reads "a child of", for example, there are twenty-five such entries in 1752 and twenty-seven in 1753. It was as if at times the whole affair was depersonalised and remembrance was not encouraged.

Finally, even in death the stigma of illegitimacy appeared in the records for infants. It was a mark of disapproval by the ratepayers who would in many cases have had to pay for the funeral out of the poor rates. Had the child lived and the father remained undiscovered, then the cost of raising the child would most likely have fallen on them as well: a pauper burial was the cheaper option. From 1589 to 1620 and from 1700-1782 the word "base" was added in the Burial Register alongside the name of an illegitimate child. At other earlier periods illegitimacy was indicated by the inclusion of just the mother's name, for example,

"1629 June 9   Aggnes, d. of Katherine Hickes
1652 September 1   Ralph, s. of Annice Gapper
1689 April 1   Sarah, ye daughter of Ann West."

There is no such indication after 1783.

b) The Elderly

Even though child mortality rates were high throughout the period under consideration that did not mean that some local inhabitants did not live to a ripe old age. On 7th March 1667 Barbara Hannam was buried aged 100; on 2nd October 1670 George Griffen, senior, aged 106; on 4th March 1777 John Barnes aged 96 and on 11th May Sarah Maggs aged 107.

John Pounsett of Cole died when he was 103 in April 1795. When John Curtis of Pitcombe died in July 1784 it was noted that his baptism was recorded as being on 25th January 1676, but it was added, "The day of his birth is uncertain; but he was told he was a large lad, and could walk when he was baptised." He too must have been at least 108 years old. That some of these ages were specifically identified in the Burial Registers and local newspapers may of course indicate that they were particularly unusual.

Through the nineteenth century similar examples were to be found such as Hannah Taylor aged 93 on 4th February 1818, John Bull for many years the postmaster aged 91 on 20th April 1820, Mary Croom aged 91 on 1st February 1831, Mary Biss aged 107 on 21st January 1846 and George Longman aged 91 on 7th March 1890. When Joseph Melhuish from Pitcombe died aged 109 on 23rd February 1838 it was reported, "he enjoyed excellent health to the last, and all his faculties were unimpaired; his hearing and memory were good, and he daily read his bible without the aid of glasses." When the death of Isaac Hill of Brewham in March 1860 aged 100 years and 6 months was reported, the local newspaper gave a fascinating insight into the insular life of one countryman: "He spent nearly the whole of his life in the above place, never having resided a month in any other." (3)

Until October 1783 the age at death was not recorded in Bruton's Burial Registers but one historian has estimated that nationally until at least the end of the seventeenth century only 5% of the population reached the age of 60. Once ages were included in the Burial Registers the true level of Bruton inhabitants living into old age became clear; between January 1784 and December 1813 some 410 men and women were over sixty years of age when they were buried and of these 119 were over eighty. One hundred years later in the corresponding thirty-year period there were 560 over sixty with 134 over eighty. This represented an increase of 37% and 13% respectively. What is even more noticeable is that in the earlier period fifteen lived to be over ninety compared with twenty-five in the later period, a 67% increase.

As Table 8 indicates there was also as significant difference in the % of men and women who died aged sixty and over.

TABLE 8 Percentages of men and
women aged sixty and over.

	January 1784 to December 1813			January 1884 to December 1913		
	60 and over	80 and over	90 and over	60 and over	80 and over	90 and over
Males	41.7	39.5	40.0	44.3	32.8	44.0
Females	58.7	60.5	60.0	55.7	67.2	56.0

It is possible that a man's working life in an agricultural area was not conducive to a long life or that women were much more capable of maintaining their existence in old age, possibly with the aid of family in which they could still play an active part.

While the young tended to die at two main periods of the year, for the elderly it was principally in the winter months between January and April with respiratory diseases. Of the 410 Bruton inhabitants aged sixty and over who were buried between January 1784 and December 1813 some 175 or 42.7% died in those four months. Of the 440 in the same age range who died one hundred years later, some 210 or 47.7% were in those hard, bitter months.

One localized factor which may help to explain why there was a tendency for some of the elderly to achieve a significant age was the presence of cottages used as almshouses for the aged from the early seventeenth century and then the newly constructed Sexey's Hospital from the late 1620s. The Visitors of the Hospital also continued charitable payments to some elderly people in the town who remained in their own homes. The actual number in the Hospital appears small, for example, at the time of the 1861 Census there were twenty-five elderly residents, with an average age of eighty. This total however represented some 16% of all inhabitants in Bruton who were over sixty at the time of the Census. Those who were fortunate enough to be elected to become residents were there for the rest of their lives, provided with a room, basic furniture, Hospital uniform, coal and a small payment each week. They thus enjoyed a far superior situation to many of their elderly friends who were outside this institution. (4)

Although this chapter has concentrated on the deaths of children and the elderly, the following two Tables give some indication of the number and % of those who died in each decade of life and the average age of death in twenty-year intervals from 1794.

Table 9 clearly shows both in terms of numbers and % a fall in deaths amongst the young and in % terms an increase in deaths amongst the elderly. It was only in the Victorian era and especially the latter part of it that the close association of death with old age became much more prominent. It was estimated that for England and Wales as a whole in 1826 one person in fifteen was over sixty years of age but by 1911 this had risen to one in thirteen. Table 10 illustrates this dramatic increase in life expectancy in Bruton at twenty-year intervals.

TABLE 9 Number and % of deaths in Bruton 1784-1900.

		10 and under	11-19	20-29	30-39	40-49	50-59	60 and over	Total
1784 to 1814	Number %	524 38.3	98 7.2	88 6.4	76 5.6	69 5.0	97 7.1	415 30.4	1376
1815 to 1900*	Number %	208 28.6	29 4.0	42 5.8	41 5.6	48 6.6	67 9.2	292 40.2	727

* Sample of 18 years taken at 5-year intervals from 1815.

TABLE 10 Average age of death in Bruton 1794-1914.

Year	Number of deaths	Total age in years	Average age of death
1794	51	1246	24.4
1814	39	1364	35.0
1834	33	960	29.1*
1854	56	1926	34.4
1874	30	1247	41.6
1894	39	2079	53.3
1914	27	1598	59.2

* There were eight infant deaths out of the thirty-three that significantly lowered the average.

By the late nineteenth century improved living conditions, along with better diet, the impact of public health reforms as well as medical improvements, all played their part in prolonging life. For some people this was a positive development but for others increased age created additional problems associated with lack of employment and declining health. In a period long before the Welfare State was created more and more of the elderly were forced to seek assistance from the Poor Law System and for some their days were to end in the bleak surroundings of the Wincanton Union Workhouse. (5)

4

ATTITUDES TO DEATH

Through the centuries attitudes to death have changed significantly. By the end of the nineteenth century the expectation was that death would come much more with old age and not with youth. In general deaths were at home, often in the presence of family, friends and neighbours, as well as in pre-Reformation days, a priest. (1) Unlike more recent times it was a topic that was always present and found expression visually in many churches and certainly in sermons. Gradually the idea decreased that the most auspicious place to be buried was within a church or monastery and so graveyards assumed much greater significance as a place of burial. As fears increased about the dangers to health, there was a move towards placing a body within a coffin and not just a shroud and then to mark the location of the interment with a monument of some kind.

Nevertheless the fear of death remained as within western culture it was felt to destroy everything that was unique and individual about the person who died. In their attitude to death therefore the Victorians moved more towards denial with the use of words such as "sleeping", "resting" and "gone before". They also developed an interest in spiritualism to allow them to contact "the other side." The fear of death found expression in the preamble to some Wills, such as that of Richard Holmede, a Tucker, in 1520, "fearing the owr of deathe make my testament and last will." When Margery Moleyns made her Will in September 1493 she spoke of "dreding the parting from this world." (2)

As life was probably going to be short, preparation for death was judged by some preachers and writers from the medieval period until the eighteenth century to be the most important function of earthly existence. People were exhorted to be firm in the Christian faith, repent, have a clear conscience and meditate upon death.

There was constant concern about the dangers of a bad death, which included the failure to make the necessary preparations, suicide and even sudden death. Occasionally within the Bruton Burial Registers such a death was clearly indicated, for example, when William Hoskins was buried on 6th August 1643 the word "suddenly" was added and for Thomas Wilton, a carpenter, on 9th August 1677, "suddainly". Both a former minister of Brewham, Rev. Edward Bennett, and his wife Mary, "by a suddain surprize fell asleep in Christ" some twenty-one years apart. (See Appendix 4b) Time being available before death has led one historian to point out that there was great emphasis placed upon the vernacular rhymes used by the laity throughout the medieval period at the elevation of the Host at Mass, often concerned with securing this grace in the hour of death.

> Ihesu, lord, welcome thow be
> In forme of bred, as I the se;
> Ihesu! For they holy name
> Schelde me today from synne & schame;
> Schryfte & hawsele, lord, thou graunte me bo,
> Er that I schale hennes go,
> And verre contryce one of my synne,
> That I lord never dye ther-Inne.

(See modernised version in Note 3)

The concept of a good death derived from that of Jesus Christ as recorded in the Gospels when he commended his mother to the care of one of his disciples and asked God to forgive those who were instrumental in the Crucifixion. For most people a good death would follow if all the necessary preparations had been made. During her last illness in 1596 Lady Magdalen Hastings of North Cadbury had three preachers with her who took it in turns on a weekly basis to give her instruction and support. When his mother died after a long illness and the day after taking leave of her family and with them at her bedside, Revd Woodforde noted in his Diary, "It has pleased Almighty God of his great good to take unto himself my dear good Mother...out of this sinful word, and to deliver her out of her miseries. She went out of this world as easy as it was possible for anyone. I hope she is now eternally happy in everlasting glory." (3)

The overwhelming majority of the dying faced death with humility, concerned principally for the future of their soul. Wealth, status, privilege and power in this world no longer meant anything. Just on a very rare occasion a glimpse is provided of the concerns which a particular individual had that there would be an appropriate funeral ceremony. While many of the very wealthy lavished large sums of money on their funeral arrangements, especially in the medieval period, it was perceived as being for the benefit of their soul. One instance of an element of pride at a particular status may be perceived. When Ursula, the widow of Hugh Sexey, made her Will in 1635 she included the instruction that she required "my bodie to bee buried in decent manner according to my birth and degree."

a) Medieval attitudes

In medieval society there was perceived to be a much closer link between the living and the dead as after death the Soul was waiting for the Second Coming of Christ when the general resurrection of the dead would occur. The Apostles and early Christians assumed that it would be in their lifetime but as it became clear that this was not the case, ideas developed and in particular the concept of the Last Judgement. It was at this moment that each soul would be examined and if found wanting despatched to Hell. From this point developed the idea of purgatory as most souls, while not being immediately damned, were not good enough to gain admission to heaven.

It was a very positive doctrine as the souls in purgatory knew that once their sins were exculpated they were saved. This belief was the one which linked the living and the dead closely together as it was considered that the prayers and intercessions of the living would aid the passage of the soul through purgatory. Obits, that is memorial services, could be held for ten or twenty years and Chantries could exist forever. For many of the dying, as well as for the bereaved, the knowledge that memory of them would be kept alive was a great comfort. One historian has commented, "The cult of intercession for the dead can be seen as...a means of prolonging the presence of the dead within the community of the living, and therefore as the most eloquent of testimonies to the permanent value of life in the world of time and change." (4)

The methods employed, along with the number and range of benefactions and meritorious deeds, which could be undertaken to assist souls in purgatory was extensive and many may be found in the few surviving late medieval Wills from Bruton.

i) Gifts to the Church

One of the grandest gestures was to establish or endow a monastery and most of the grants of land and other property to Bruton Priory suggest that the donors had an eye on the next world. Many of the documents contain phrases such as, "for the redemption of his sins", "for the souls of his ancestors and heirs", "for the good of the souls of his father and mother" and "for the good of his own soul and the souls of Aubrey his wife, John his son, and his ancestors." (5)

It was not unusual for a person making a Will at this period to divide it into two parts: the first part was a list of legacies, grants, gifts and donations to named institutions or people and the second part contained the instruction that the residue of the estate was to be allocated for the benefit of his or her soul. Unfortunately it is not possible to specify the relative weight given to each part for while the cash sums in the first part may be added up, the second part was usually covered by the word "residue". In 1509 for example John Harman directed that the residue of his estate should go to his daughter Agnes, "that she with her husband may dispose of part of it for the welfare of my soul and part of it for their own use." As the clergy and religious institutions were such beneficiaries in the medieval period it may be possible to speculate that some heirs did not in fact inherit nearly as much as they had hoped. Whether or not that created some tensions in the community is lost in time.

As the future of the soul was such an important consider-ation, to specify that the residue of an estate was to be used for the benefit of a soul was of course a subtle way of pressurizing the executor of the Will to implement carefully the last wishes of the deceased. When Richard Philippys made his Will in October 1509 he appointed his wife executrix and required her to deal with his goods, "that she disposes of them for the good of my Soul". In 1540 George Wylton left to his wife Jane "all my goodis movable and unmovable" with the instruction that she was to dispose of them "to the pleasure of God and for the wealth of my sowle." Margery Moleyns in September 1493 and Alianora Ede in February 1496 gave similar instructions but added that it was to be done as their executors thought fit. Symon Grene in March 1506 added other souls, "for the good

of my Soul and the Souls of my parents and benefactors."
In September 1471 Richard Dekyn had increased the pressure
even more, "to dispose for my soule in werkes of mercy and
charite, as she would I did for her in caas like."

John FitzJames, senior, was very specific with his gift and
dedicated it in such a way that he believed he would gain the
maximum benefit for his soul: "I will that my new missal
and my paxbrede of silver be used in the chapel of Redlynche
aforesaid in honour of Allmighty God and Mary his mother
and of St Anne and St Leonard and St Peter and all the saints
in heaven."

ii) Call upon Saints.

In the hour of their death and in their Wills medieval men and
women could invoke the name of the Virgin Mary and a host
of saints, especially John the Baptist, John the Evangelist and
St. Peter to be intercessors for them at the Judgement. Amongst
some of the educated laity who understood the current
theological priorities in the early decades of the sixteenth
century, there was the inclusion of the name of Christ but none
of the Wills that have survived from Bruton contained this
reference, probably because of their virtual absence in the years
immediately preceding the Reformation in the 1530s.

John Gregory was very brief in 1429, "I bequeath my Soul
to god" but the usual pattern in the early Bruton Wills was to
call upon God, the Virgin Mary and all the Saints: "my sowle
to almighty god to oure blessed Lady and to all the saints of
hevyn", as it was expressed by Margery Moleyns, and also
Richard Dekyn, Alianora Ede, Richard Philippys and in
February 1517 by Alice Brymmore. In August 1520 Richard
Holmede gave a slightly longer preamble, "my Soule to
almyghtye god maker and Redemr of almenkynde, to our
blessed lady queen of hyeve and Erthe and Moder of mcy and

to all the company of heven." It was only Sir John Fitzjames of Redlynch in 1538 who named specific saints, "I desire the good Lord, my Redeemer and Maker, that by the mediacion of the most blessed Mother, the Virgin Marie, of St Anthony, St Christopher, with all the Hollye Companye of Hevyn, that in manus tuas Domine commendo spiritum meum."[*into your hands Lord I commend my spirit*].

iii) Masses, prayers and remembrance.

A soul would receive considerable benefit from the Mass and so great emphasis was placed upon staging one or more Masses at the time of the burial and in the months and years thereafter. As early as 1417 Richard Bruton had left an instruction that 4d should be paid to each Canon or Chaplain present at his exequies, that is funeral rites. The same amount of money was bequeathed by Amice Gregory in April 1457 "to each priest serving in the said parish Church present at my obsequies" and in November 1498 Richard Vowell of Wells left 20s to the Canons of Bruton Priory "to say for my soul exequies and mass of requieum on the day of may burial." In March 1506 Symon Grene left the same instruction.

The very wealthy could afford many more masses and so Sir John Fitzjames requested "as sone after my decease as yt may be convenently 15 masses of the Fyve Wondes of Our Lorde by fyftyn most honest prestes, to each of whom saying one of the sayd masses I bequeath 2s." His request, however, fell far short of the 20,000 masses Henry V wanted for his soul.

There was clearly a hierarchy in the value of masses and prayers depending upon who delivered them and this was reflected in the money that was allocated. When the Countess of Salisbury died in 1415 she requested that the Canons of Bruton Priory should sing the requiem mass for which the Prior was to receive 13s 8d, each canon or priest 6s 8d an others 3s 4d. Symon Grene made a similar distinction in 1506, "I bequeath to each priest who makes intercessions for the dead on the day of my burial vjd. And to each scholer 1d." John Fitzjames senior in his Will in 1510 even made a distinction between the various levels of those in Holy Orders, so that on the day of his burial if they took part in his exequies, mass and prayed for his soul, "To each canon there being a priest 12d and to each canon not a prest 8d."

Masses and prayers could then be repeated for thirty days, called the Trental, although this could also entail thirty masses on the same day. A month after death, often referred to as a month's mind or remembrance, there would be another funeral mass, usually accompanied with bell ringing and the distribution of money to the poor. In 1471 Richard Dekyn gave priest John Cerne 2s 6d "to say a trentall mass for me" and in 1496 Alianora Ede gave three named priests 2s 6d each "to celebrate a Trentale for my soul." Symon Grene was more generous in 1506 and also in his requests reflected the different values placed upon those who performed the rites. "I bequeath to each priest offering exequies and mass on the thirtieth day after my death vjd And each Scholar and pauper who are there 1d." In 1545 John Turges of Redlynch appointed John Butley as his overseer and requried him to sell enough of his goods to see his "funeral with the months mind performed."

Once again it was the wealth of Sir John Fitzjames that allowed him to make detailed provision for the Trental on each of the days between his burial and the thirtieth day. "I will there be songe and sayd in the church where my body shalbe buryed every daye for one month 'placebo' and 'dirge' and 8 severall masses of Requiem in the morning by 8 honest prestes and 6 Clerkes yf they shall be gotten; one of the sayd masses to be songe by note, each prest having 12d at each 'dirige' and masses and each clerke 6d."

It is fascinating to speculate that towards the end of his life Fitzjames was becoming increasingly concerned about the fate of his soul. A number of his letters in the 1530s indicate that he tried to avoid returning to London and so decrease the risk of finding himself even more embroiled in the religious and political turmoil of that decade. As early as 1533 he explained to Thomas Cromwell that he was suffering from ill-health but in June of that year he was well enough to be present at the Coronation of Anne Boleyn, leading judges in procession to Westminster on horseback. Two years later while he was in residence at Redlynch he entertained men such as Cromwell and Sir Nicholas Wadham to dinner.

There may however have been some element of truth in his claims as he made his Will in 1538 and later that year or early in 1539 he resigned from his judicial role. Although he had the reputation as a lawyer of being honest and not corrupt, as the Lord Chief Justice of the King's Bench for some thirteen years, he had been involved in a number of the high-profile trials of the period such as those of John Fisher, the Bishop of Rochester, Sir Thomas More and Queen Anne Boleyn. Allegations persisted that he was therefore involved in judicial murders on behalf of Henry VIII. Interestingly and perhaps rather strangely, however, he does not appear to have made any attempt to save the Free School in Bruton, which he had helped to establish in 1519, when it was closed at the time of the Dissolution of the Abbey in April 1539.

There were so many of the practical arrangements specified in Fitzjames's Will that it does provide a good example of the care with which the living took their leave of this world. In addition his Will, like many others of the period, required the presence of an "honest" priest to perform the various rites. Alice Brymmore wanted her executor to select a priest who would meet with the approval of the Supervisors of her Will, one of whom was the Abbot of Bruton Abbey: "An honest prest by the sight of my Supvisors." Such stipulations were an indication that there were those within the Catholic Church who did not take their functions as seriously as they might have done. Allegations surfaced from time to time that some priests were prepared to take the payment and not say the mass correctly or the designated number of times. For the donor there was the great fear that this could put his or her soul in jeopardy.

While there were no such specific allegations made against the canons of Bruton Priory, there is no doubt that between about 1420 and 1448 it was at a very low ebb. The problems stemmed from two Priors, John Schoyle who was removed from office in 1430 and his successor Richard of Glastonbury who eventually died still in office in 1448. Bishops of Bath and Wells held various inquiries and imposed new regulations on several occasions but the abuses continued in this period. There was no specific reference to the failure to attend to these masses but it was clear that many of the canonical functions were either not being performed at all or in a very lax fashion.

The language of memory did not stop after a month as those who were wealthier in the community could afford to make provision not only for many months but also for years. Richard Dekyn in 1471 required his executors to find an honest priest "to sing divine service in the Chirch of Brewton aforesaid by a hole yere next suying my decesse." Alianora Ede bequeathed the large sum of nine marks or £6 for a priest to celebrate mass for a year for the souls of Thomas her husband, Thomas and William her sons and herself. Symon Grene in 1506 left the same sum for a priest to "celebrate for my soul and for the souls of my parents and benefactors in the parish church of Bruton for an entire year after my death."

For a few the period of time was even longer as in October 1429 John Gregory requested his executors to provide a priest "for three years at the altar of the Holy Cross in the parish Church of Bruton." In August 1526 William Burgess of Batcombe wished that the prayers for his soul should be offered not within the parish church of Bruton but in the Abbey, "I geve to the Abbey of Bruton to be praid for there by the space of five yeres, every yere 52s." A few months later Isabel Fitzjames did not specify a period of time but rather left a sum of money which was to be paid to the canons each week to say mass on a daily basis. She required her "executors fynd oone of the chanons of the monastery of Bruton to singe at my later hubonds aulter daily within the sd monastery praying for his Soule, my Soule and for all my good frendes Soules from the day of my obite till the summe of £20 in money be com up, giving away the said chanon every weke 12d." This requirement would suggest a period of between seven and eight years.

Potentially one of the most extensive series of arrangements was made by Alice Brymmore in 1517. She instructed her executors to find a priest "to sing before the Auter of or blissid ladye in the under pishe churche of Brewton" for three years for the souls of John Brymmore, herself, "And for all owr good ffreyndes sowles" for which he was to receive £5 13s 4d. In addition she left money to four grandchildren but being aware of the presence of death amongst the young, made the provision that if they all died before the age of twenty-one then the money was to be used to provide a priest to sing before the Altar of Our Blessed Lady in the south aisle of the church for the souls of John her late husband, herself, all the grandchildren, "And also for the Sowles of all or ffryndes or benefactours" until the sum of £4 6s 8d had been exhausted. Finally she required a mass to be held for fourteen years on the Anniversary of her death for the souls of her husband, herself and "owr frends."

As Alice Brymmore's Will indicates the concept of a mass being celebrated to remember a dead person on the anniversary of their death was also evident. The anniversaries of some of the patrons of the Priory seem to have been celebrated in some style. On the first anniversary of the death of Sir John Luttrell, the Dunster Accounts for 1431 record that some 33s 3d was spent in Bruton Priory and included payments of 12d each to fifteen canons, 6d each to 2 priests and 4d each to two clerks. Some fifteen pounds of wax was bought to make candles, as well as bread for the Priory along with fourteen gallons of ale for the canons and a separate gallon for the prior. To ensure that the anniversary was as widely known as possible the bedesman was given 1d for proclaiming it in the town. (6) Much more straightforward was the request of William Samford in December 1503 "that my said wife yerely during her life kepe my twelfmonethes mynde with two prests at dirige and masses."

Even more beneficial for the soul was to perpetuate remembrance forever and there were a number of ways in which this could be achieved. One method was the establishment of a Chantry at which a priest would celebrate mass on a regular and long-term basis. The most significant Chantry created in Bruton in the fifteenth century was that of Prior John Henton in 1458. He arranged that on every day of the year, except Easter Day, one of the canons would celebrate mass at the altar of St Aldhelm in the nave of the priory church "for the good estate of himself, his parents and the benefactors of the priory during their lifetime, and for their souls when they are dead, and also cause the exequies of the dead to be said with nine lessons.......The celebrant shall say aloud every day before the beginning of the mass the Lord's Prayer with the Angelic Salutation for the souls of the said prior and his parents, and of all the faithful departed." In addition the exequies of the dead with mass were to be celebrated "every year at the said altar on the day after the date of his death if possible, and in any case within five days for his soul and the souls of his said parents." Each year the sacristan was to receive 12d for candles and the clerks 20d for ringing the bells. (7)

Although there were chantries, at least within the Abbey at the time of its Dissolution, for some unaccountable reason Bruton escaped a visitation from Edward VI's Chantry Commission in 1547. By this time the site of the Abbey had passed to Sir Maurice Berkeley and it is possible that he was able to assure the King that such chantries had already been removed or it may be that the monastic buildings which had housed them had been demolished or converted to some other purpose. Any money or land that had been used to support the chantries had presumably already been seized.

A second, and probably the most straightforward and also cheaper method of ensuring that a name was remembered and that prayers were offered for a soul, was to make a gift of either money or goods to a gild based in the parish church. As a result a person's name was entered on the bede-roll and the whole of this list was read out at the annual requiem of the gild, which in the case of Bruton was at the time of the festival of the Virgin Mary in September. A person could thus be prayed for by name and perpetually. It also of course indicated that the donor had an identifiable place within the community in his or her lifetime and then ensured that it would be for all time. In addition the donor could be sure that the brotherhood would observe his or her funeral rites and undertake prayers and masses for their soul on other occasions during the year.

Exactly when such a gild was founded in Bruton Church is now impossible to determine but one was certainly in existence in the second half of the fifteenth century. Other evidence suggests that this was a period when the community seemed to have developed a more pronounced role within the parish church, perhaps reflecting the prosperity of the woollen trade within the town. At some stage in the mid to second half of the century the parish, possibly aided by the Priory, undertook the construction of the West Tower and all the expense that that enterprise entailed. (8)

The amount of money bequeathed by individuals to the fraternity varied and usually no purpose was specified. A common figure was 6s 8d, such as by Alice Brymmore in 1517, "Item to the ffraternyte of owr blissid lady in the said churche vjs viijd." The same amount had been given by Richard Dekyn in 1471 and Richard Philippys in 1509. John Harman in the same year gave 12s and Alianora Ede 20s in 1496. Symon Grene in 1506 was more specific, "Itm I bequeath to the fraternity of the aforesaid parish church of Bruton to the maintenance of one chaplain celebrating mass there 10s." The largest single bequest was £2 from Sir John Fitzjames in 1538, "To the Fraternitie of Or Lady in the Paryshe Churche of Brewton 40s"

While money seems to have been the commonest form of bequest to the fraternity in Bruton Church, there were occasional examples of specific items: items which must have been of particular importance to the donor. In 1493 widow Margery Moleyns bequeathed "to the brethered of oure Lady in the said Churche a maser" and in 1520 Richard Holmede, a tucker, left them "a grinding stone." There was also another fraternity in the parish church of Brewham for when James Wicks of Brewham made his Will in December 1539 he gave to the church there "to helpe to maynteyn the brothred priest a kowe." A similar bequest was made in the Will of John Exhall three years later "To the brotherhd of Bruham, a kowe and a paire of vestments."

A third way of ensuring that a name was remembered and that masses were said was to give to the parish church or the Priory a vessel, ornament or vestment, preferably with a suitable inscription. It was not unusual for a wealthy woman to leave a ring to a statue of the Virgin Mary, thus ensuring not only the remembrance of her name but also the possibility of Our Lady's intercession on her behalf. In 1493 Margery Moleyns did just that: "Item I Bequieyth to oure Lady in the

Priory church my wedding Ring." In addition she bequeathed "to the werkis of the parishe church of Bruton aforesaid a cuppe of silver."

The most ostentatious series of bequests was made in the Will of Richard Bruton in 1417. After allocating various gifts to the prior and canons of Bruton Priory, he specifically requested that he should be enrolled in their book of obits and his name added to the calendar of saints and benefactors. It would therefore be read out regularly and included in their prayers forever. This reference is the one and only piece of evidence which has so far come to light which indicates that such a book definitely existed in the Priory. Other conspicuous bequests from him included an altar frontal and two covers for the lectern, both of which were situated in the Chancel. He also gave a banner with the image of the Trinity "well and suitably adorned with gold and silk cloth well gilt." Finally he ordered that an image should be carved in wood of the Blessed Mary Magdalen the same height and width as one that already existed of the Blessed Katherine and placed next to it in the Chancel of Bruton Church. It was in that location that he wished his body to be buried so when all these items were taken together it would have made it very hard to forget him. (9)

Two years earlier the Countess of Salisbury had given to the prior and convent of Bruton a large silver or gold cup worth ten marks and to the prior a pair of blue vestments and other items of his apparel to the value of £10. When Prior Henton's parents financed a large bell for the conventual church and donated £400 in 1458 for the fabric of the same church and the cloister of the priory, it was arranged that both of them and their children should be taken "into the fraternity of the said church and priory and....they shall forever hereafter be participators in all masses and divine offices celebrated in the priory and all prayers, fastings, alms and other works of piety performed there." The same arrangement had been made for Mathew Carevill just over one hundred years earlier when he had agreed that the Prior was entitled to a messuage, rents and over seventy-five acres of land in Bruton, "the Prior received Mathew and his heirs into all the benefits and prayers of his church for ever." (10)

Widow Isabel Fitzjames ensured that her name would be remembered when she made gifts specifically to the Abbott, William Gilbert, "To my lorde of Bruton a Cruett of silver and gilt to serve him at his masse....I will that my lord Abbott shal have a vestment of white damaske braunched with golde and crosse of red satyn in the name of my mortuary."

The fourth, and undoubtedly the cheapest, method of remembrance could be the provision of some sort of light, such as candles, tapers or torches, although many of the surviving examples from Bruton seem to be on a larger scale. Light was an important symbol associated with death in the medieval period as it was seen as a way of dissipating the darkness. Above all, however, light represented Christ's salvation. Candles were placed in front of the images of specific saints or on the altars dedicated to them in the hope that a particular saint would keep them in mind and hence aid their souls as they moved on their journey from darkness to everlasting light. This may well have been the intention of John Harman in 1509 when he left 12d to the image of St Mary in the nave of the priory church of Bruton, although he did not specifically mention candles.

On at least two occasions during the Christian calendar candles and tapers assumed an even greater importance. One was Candlemas, the popular name given to the Feast of the Purification of the Virgin Mary on 2nd February. Candles were carried in procession to and in the church and offered to the priest who sprinkled them with holy water and perfumed them with incense before the altar. They then remained in the church as offerings, usually in the name of the donor. The second occasion was the Feast of All Saints on 1st November which was originally dedicated to the commemoration of all martyrs and saints not otherwise remembered and the Feast of All Souls on 2nd November which was dedicated to the souls of all the departed. Candles and the ringing of bells figured prominently on these days as it was felt that it brought comfort to the souls enduring the torments of purgatory.

Candles could, of course, be offered at any time. In 1362 John de Merston received a licence from the king to grant to the prior and convent of Bruton a messuage, two and a half virgates of land, 40 acres of pasture, 10 acres of meadow and 9s in rent in Charlton Adam, Bruton and Wyke Champflower "to find two wax lights burning daily at the high altar of the priory in the celebration of mass." Twenty-two years later in 1384 William Barwe and William Brewere received a similar licence to grant to the priory four messuages, one toft, one carucate of land, 12 acres of meadow, 10 of pasture and 4 of wood with 12s rent in Bruton and Brewham, "for finding a light to burn continually before the high altar in the Church of St Mary, Bruton."

Richard Bruton instructed that two candles were to burn at both the head and foot of his tomb in the chancel of Bruton church until the first anniversary of his death. When Prior Henton established his Chantry at the altar of St Aldhelm in the nave of the conventual church, he arranged for money to be paid on the anniversary of his death for "the maintenance of the lights when masses are celebrated thereat and for five candles to be provided at the said altar throughout the year, and double the number at every great feast..... and for five candles to be lit in the chapel of St Laurence the Martyr in the said church as often as mass is celebrated there."

Isabel Fitzjames also made arrangements for lights in 1526, "I will that my executors fynde and mayteyn a taper of a lb to brenne at all tymes convenient before the ymage of our blissid lady within the monastery of Bruton and specially at pardon masse tyme so long as the sum of 20s in money will endure." The bequest of Alice Marshall was much more modest in November 1540 when she left 12d to "the rode light and the torchys."

With huge numbers of candles being needed it was common for monasteries and even parish churches to keep their own bees in order to have a ready supply of wax. While this was probably almost certainly the case in Bruton, where the canons would also have required quantities of honey, no documentary evidence has as yet emerged.

One study for the county of Somerset has found that in the period 1480 to 1540 over £10,000 was given to monasteries for chantries, prayers and for the benefit of souls. The very size of this figure suggests that there was considerable confidence in the county with the state of the monasteries: that they were not populated by corrupt monks or in terminal decline as their opponents often alleged but that they were well-administered and would perform all the required functions. Bruton Priory, for example, seems to have flourished after the mid-fifteenth century reforms of Prior Henton and later under the direction of Prior Gilbert. The figure also indicates, of course, the generally conservative outlook of the wealthy donors as they were not, as yet, being influenced by the new ideas that were sweeping parts of Europe. (11)

iv) Free from debt.

As far as the medieval world was concerned it was absolutely essential for the benefit of a person's soul that he or she died free from all debt. It remained a common feature of Wills for centuries that a general statement would be included for all temporal debts to be paid. In addition there was often the recognition of spiritual indebtedness that led to a bequest to the high altar of a church or Priory for tithes forgotten. In 1415 John Venables included such a provision, "Item to the Prior and Convent of Bruton 20s for tithes forgotten." Nearly one hundred years later Symon Grene made a similar provision, "I bequeath to the high altar in the parish church of Bruton aforesaid for tithes forgotten vs."

v) Prayers of the poor.

There was a widespread belief in the medieval period that the prayers of the poor were especially potent in aiding a soul in purgatory. Many of the wealthy therefore instructed in their Wills that a number of poor men should play a part in funeral and subsequent activities, often carrying some kind of light. If such lights were held in the hands of the poor it was believed that they were a prayer in themselves and also a way of ensuring the powerful intercession of these men. At the deepest level the poor were symbolic for the image of Christ.

The Accounts for the arrangements for the first Anniversary of the death of Sir John Luttrell in 1431 indicate that four pounds of wax were to be bought from the Sacristan of Bruton Church and placed in four 'torchis' hired from him. Four poor men were to hold these 'torchis' during the obsequies and at the mass for which they were to receive 4d each. In 1417 Richard Bruton requested thirteen poor men hold thirteen tapers around his body. This number itself was also significant as it represented Christ and the twelve Apostles.

Some wealthy men provided the poor with gowns, usually black, to wear during these activities. In 1471 Richard Dekyn instructed that, "I will that myne executours yeve to 5 poore men 5 gownes, and also every Friday by an hoole yere next ensuing my decease 5d, to pray for my soule." Five was the number usually associated with the Wounds of Christ and was especially important if it involved a Friday, the day of the Crucifixion. In 1506 Symon Grene also included the poor: "Further I wish and ordain for six poor men of the town of Bruton to have six gowns of the 'freers' cloth to pray for my soul and the souls of my parents and benefactors."

As always it was Sir John Fitzjames who left the most detailed instructions in 1538: "I will that 12 por men shall kneyll about my herrse every daye at the time of the said 'dirige' and masse, every of theym having a Torche in their hands and there to pray for my Soule and all Christian Sowles; every of the same por men to have a blake gown and every day 4d until the sayde moneth be passyd." Twelve also symbolised Christ and the Apostles, although this time without Judas Iscariot and this Will highlighted that black was the expected colour.

Some stipulations were simpler, such as that of John Gregory in 1429 when he ordered, "And I wish that there be distributed to the poor on the day of my burial to pray for me 100s." This was a very generous sum at that period. (See comparison figures in Appendix 1.) In 1506 Symon Grene left 20s to be distributed at the rate of 5s a year for four years "to the poor living within Bruton.....to pray for my soul and the souls of my parents." The geographical specification was an indication of the concern that was occasionally expressed that the distribution of large sums of money attracted the poor from many other places in the neighbourhood which may not have been the intention of the donor.

vi) Acts of Charity.

There was a fundamental belief that acts of Charity would greatly assist a soul in purgatory. It was after all stated unequivocally in St Matthew's Gospel, "Insomuch as ye have done it unto one of the least of these my brethren, ye have done it unto me." (Matthew, 25,v.40) As always self-interest could be present, as expressed in two lines from a medieval poem:

"For man with-owt marcy, of marcy shall misse;
And he shall have marcy, that marcyfull is." (12)

It was not uncommon therefore for money to be distributed at a funeral, especially if the bellman had gone around the parish announcing a death, asking for prayers for the deceased and specifying the time of the burial. It was a signal for the poor to gather. On the other hand a Will could arrange for money to be distributed at a later time. Examples of both of these provisions exist for medieval Bruton.

In 1417 Richard Bruton's Will arranged for various doles to the poor, for example, in some thirteen named towns including Bruton and Brewham he gave "to each person lying in bed in their own or other houses not being able to go out by reasons of sickness.....6d." He also gave 1d, a fairly standard rate in that century, to each poor person who attended his burial. In a Codicil to his Will made on the same day as his main one, he wished "to be distributed amongst the poor for the soul of Custance Lyndraper of Bruton 13s." Finally he donated 6s 8d, "To the poor lying in 'le Spytelhous' in Bruton, to pray for me." At least three other men left money to the poor and sick in the Hospital or Almshouse at Lusty, for example Richard Dekyn left 20d "to the Almeshouse of Lusty" in 1471; Richard Grene 6s 8d in 1496; and John Brent 3s 4d in 1524.

In 1506 Symon Grene wanted £5 6s 8d "distributed amongst the poor and indigent" of Bruton on the day of his burial. As he had connections with Abingdon, he left a similar amount to the same categories there and a further 6s 8d to the poor in their almshouses. Twenty years later Isabel Fitzjames required £40 to be distributed to "prests and clerks and poor folks on the day of my burying" and again on the first anniversary of her death. Twelve years after that Sir John Fitzjames, her step-son, ordered his executors to distribute £5 "in almes yerely for five yeres" on four specified days each year to "the most poryst and nedy in Brewton, Weke, Pitcum, Shepton, Knoll, Stowke, Redliche and Cherlton Musgrove." All these places were within a short distance of his immediate estate at Redlynch and indicate an area of influence.

As several of these Wills specified the parishes or places that were to benefit, in addition to keeping out strangers, especially beggars and vagrants, they also demonstrated the importance of the parish community. For some people this was their world and for them it represented the limits of their everyday activities. This discriminatory aspect also perhaps foreshadowed the way in which the relief of the poor was to develop and be restricted in centuries to come.

While these Wills specified the poor as a group, others contained a more general reference to charity, for example, Richard Dekyn in 1471 required his wife as executrix to dispose of the residue of his estate "for my soule in werkes of mercy and charite." Acts of charity were not of course resticted to the poor but could appear in other forms. Not only did Sir John Fitzjames in 1538 make provision for each "por howseholder dwelling within onye parte of my inheritance" to receive 6s 8d, but also, more unusually "To every mayden of good conversacon, fatherless and motherless, unmarryed and dwelling within onye part of my inheritaunce 40s to her marriage." Householders had also benefited from the Will of John Hadley who lived near Dunster when in 1534 he left 4d to each of them in eight named places including Bruton .

Money was also left for apparently secular purposes, particularly the repair of roads and bridges. In reality many of the roads either linked Church and monastic estates or were the routes that directly connected the church with various parts of the parish: in some respects they were roads shared by both the living and the dead on their way to the parish church by the shortest route. In addition it has also been argued that if roads and bridges were well maintained then they contributed to the ease of travel and comfort of all inhabitants and so could be classed as an act of charity in that way. As there were a number of bridges in the Bruton area they may well have been included within any maintenance but there is no specific reference to them in the few surviving medieval Wills. (13)

In 1417 Richard Bruton bequeathed money to repair roads in at least five separate towns, including Bruton: "For repairing the way from the house of the sheepfold of the Prior of Bruton to Estrope and beyond 30s." Some ninety years later Symon Grene also left money for this purpose but he was less specific as to the exact location, "Item I bequeath for repairing and improving the ways around Bruton wherever the work is most needed xls." In 1550 widow Elizabeth FitzJames bequeathed "To the mending of the highways in the parish of Brewham 100s." In the period from 1480 to 1660 for Somerset as a whole some £905 was left in Wills for such improvements.

At the other extreme another charitable act was to donate money to a building, usually the parish church. Once again, although generally not stated, the hope was that through remembrance and prayers, the soul of the departed would gain spiritual benefits, especially in relation to purgatory. It was customary in the opening formula of many Wills to leave a small sum to the Mother or Cathedral Church of St. Andrew in Wells. There was not a set amount, for example, Margery Moleyns left 12d, Richard Philippys 14d, Alianora Ede 20d and Symon Grene and Alice Brymmore 3s 4d each.

Much more common was a gift to the parish church that took various forms: general or specific, cash or goods. In 1509

John Harman simply left 12d "to the parish church of Brewton", as did John Chaper als Nicolls in 1526. Generally it was a contribution towards the fabric or repair of the church: Amice Gregory left 3s 4d to the fabric of Bruton church in 1457 as did Symon Grene in 1506 with 20s but he added a further 20s specifically for the fabric of the nave. In 1509 Richard Philippys contributed 40d "for the repair of the parish church of Brewton."

When money was left for specific purposes it does provide some indication of the activities that were occurring in the church and the Priory in the late medieval period. Some of these may well reflect the growing prosperity of Bruton as a market centre and some the long-term, and ultimately successful, campaign of Prior William Gilbert to have his Priory raised to the status of an Abbey.

As early as 1417 amongst his many gifts to the parish church, including a statue, altar and lectern cloths and a banner depicting the Trinity, Richard Bruton instructed his executors to "cause all the glass windows to be mended and repaired and keep them so mended as long as they conveniently can." In 1500 John Vynyng alias Dyer of Wincanton left ten marks "to the edifying of our lady chapel of Bruton" and three years later William Samford left 20s "to the new Chapell of oure blissid lady in the Priory." In 1509 John Harman bequeathed 3s 4d "To the fabric of the said new chapel of St Mary of Brewton." These gifts suggest that building work was taking place within the Priory in the first decade of the sixteenth century. Within the parish church itself there was also work underway as in 1517 Alice Brymmore left £4 "for the newe bylding of pcell of the southe yle there" and three years later 20s was given by Richard Holmede "to the making of the bellis in the saide parishe Church." In 1544 Thomas Toar was prepared to leave 12d "To the maintenance of the bells of Bruton." The construction of the West Tower may well have necessitated such actions.

There were occasional gifts of goods to the parish church that were not specifically linked to a request for prayers for a person's soul, although the very presence of a tangible item, suitably inscribed, would ensure perpetual remembrance. In 1429, as well as donating 20s to the fabric fund of the parish church, John Gregory also gave "1 chalice of silver gilt." A similar gift was given by Margery Moleyns over sixty years later, "I bequeeth to the werkis of the parishe church of Bruton aforesaid a cuppe of silver."

Acts of charity were also extended to other churches and chapels which would increase the chances of remembrance with masses and prayers in those places as well: some were local but others were much further a-field indicating an area with which a particular person had a connection, possibly through family or business. While Alianora Ede left 20d to the chapels of St. John the Baptist at Brewham and St. Leonard at Pitcombe, Alice Brymmore did the same but added churches at Batcombe, Lamyatt, Castle Cary, Bratton and Milton, with each church receiving 3s 4d.

Unsurprisingly Isabel Fitzjames of Redlynch left 3s 4d to the chapel of St. Peter there, but Richard Philippys may have had a connection with Lyme Regis as he left 6s 8d to the fraternity of the Blessed Mary there. Richard Holmede gave 10s to "ye parish of Turbrigge" as well as sums of money to the Augustinian and White Friars of Bristol, the friars of Ilchester and of Bridgewater. Symon Grene was even more extensive as he left bequests to the parish church, fraternity and almshouses in Yeovil. He also gave money to two churches in Abingdon with one of them receiving two altar cloths "of white damask embroidered with golden flowers and images of the Holy Cross, Blessed Mary and St John the Evangelist." The almshouse and the poor of that town were likewise remembered in his Will.

It must be a reasonable assumption that acts of charity in the form of money and goods directed at a named priest or canon required masses, prayers and remembrance on their part even when no stipulation to that effect was included. In 1545 Jone Hardwell of Wyke Champflower was quite specific, "To Roger Neechollys to pray for my soul iijs iiijd." On the other hand in 1417 Richard Bruton simply left 6s 8d "to the chaplain of the parish of Bruton." A century later Alice Brymmore donated a similar sum to each of John Loty, the prior of Bruton, Robert Rotherham "prieste my Gostly fadder" and William Brymmore, a canon in the Abbey and presumably a son or relative by marriage. John Tyler, a cloth maker from Wells, also gave a bequest to a relative in the Abbey, this time his stepson, "To my wife sonne Sir Richard Bogy chanon of Brewton, 20s, a flatte pece of silver pond 8 uncs, [*weighing one pound and 8 ounces*] and 6 silver spones."

Priests often acted as the executors or overseers of Wills and as such received a gift. In 1509 John Harman gave Richard Bogy and Richard Vowells, two canons in the Priory "to each of them one sheep, or 20d that they may bear witness to the said bequests." Isabel Fitzjames also made gifts nearly twenty years later, "I will that Sir William Clement, priest, shal have a counterpoynt of verdor whiche nowe lyeth upon my bedde in the chamber. I will that Sir Robert Rotheram, parishe prest shal have a counterpoynt of imagery which nowe lyes upon me." Perhaps a little comfort in the unheated cells or dormitory in the Abbey.

For so long the concept of purgatory dominated medieval attitudes to death and great amounts of time and trouble were taken to make the necessary preparations and, particularly by the wealthy, to ensure that masses, prayers and remembrance were in place. Yet within just a few years the whole concept was swept away with the Reformation.

b) The Reformation and after

The Reformation period was to be one of both change and continuity as the ordinary people the length and breadth of the country came to terms with the momentous decisions that had been made by their monarch and his advisors.

One great change that came with the Reformation was the abolition within a relatively short time of the doctrine of purgatory. The last of the Ten Articles of 1536 still commended prayers for departed souls but by 1543 the term 'purgatory' was banned so death became the point at which a soul's fate was sealed. It meant therefore that there was no longer any need for elaborate rituals during the funeral or masses in the days following or on any anniversary. In 1547 all endowments designed to fund lights, prayers, masses in front of altars, images or in chantries were confiscated.

These changes also meant that in 1549 the burial service was significantly shortened, although for another three years it still included psalms and Holy Communion but these were omitted in 1552, along with many of the prayers for the dead. Some of these prayers were re-introduced in the Elizabethan Prayer Book of 1559 which was designed to be a compromise to re-unite the various beliefs.

In some respects the theological ideas prevalent at the time of the Reformation and immediately afterwards were to many of the laity much more severe than earlier. Luther expounded the doctrine of salvation by faith alone and Calvin the doctrine of predestination, that God alone would decide who would be saved, no matter how virtuous a life had been led or how many good deeds had been performed. Leading Protestant theologians argued that the soul's journey to heaven or hell occurred immediately after death. The saved would experience complete happiness after the final resurrection when they would be reunited with family and friends in the presence of God. The damned, for whom the sentence was irreversible, faced eternal damnation in the fires of hell, deprived of God's presence.

How far and how quickly these ideas were adopted in Bruton is impossible to determine with any degree of accuracy as only a small amount of evidence has survived and that exclusively from the wealthier in the community. It may be however that within the population as a whole there were a large number who subscribed to the view that God was too loving to send many of them to hell.

Bruton certainly suffered the same traumatic events as the rest of the country in the late 1530s as on 1st April 1539 the Abbey was dissolved with all the implications both spiritual and temporal which that entailed: from prayers and masses, to acts of charity, to employment and business. Swept away in the 1540s were many of the images and altars that had existed both in Bruton Abbey and the parish church, sometimes for centuries. Much more besides was removed as two former churchwardens, Christopher Chyck the younger and Robert Hilyar, were severely criticized in 1554 as they had sold off church items to the value of £28 without the consent of the parish, and had probably overseen the removal of the images of Mary and John. As this criticism was made when Queen Mary was on the throne it may indicate that there was still strong support for the old religious ways within the town. Certainly the wholesale removal of property from the interior of churches was occurring on a national scale so that in February 1549 a Commission banned the removal and sale of any more vestments, ornaments, plate, jewels and bells. (14)

One other change which potentially affected the dying and the dead in Bruton was the attempt by Edward VI in 1547 to restrict severely the ringing of bells: "do abstein from such unmeasurable ringing for ded persones at their burialls, and at the feast of All Sowles." The king ordered that only one bell should be rung "at soch tyme as sicke persones lyeth in extreme daunger of death..... and when the corps of any such dead persons shalbe brought to the churche to be buried then to ring also moderatelie in the time of the obsequies thereof, and no longer." Bells however do appear to have been rung extensively in Bruton for centuries thereafter. (15)

The radical change in theological belief may be found in some of the Wills of Bruton men and women from the 1540s and throughout the remainder of the Tudor period. Whereas before the Reformation there had been numerous requests for the intercession of the Blessed Virgin and various saints, this was transformed into commending a soul to God and increasingly expressing the hope of salvation through the suffering of Jesus Christ. Some men such as Nicholas Gilbert in 1566, George Stephen in 1573 and Francis Poole in 1597 made the simple commitment, "I bequethe my soull unto Allmightie god." Agnes Plumley was a little more explicit in 1560, "ffirst I bequeath my Sowle to god the father god the Sonne the holly goste three psons and one god."

In July 1542 Robert Chyk was already by implication hoping for salvation, "I Bequeth my soule to Almightye god beseching his goodness hit may be receavyed to his godly rest and to be accompanyed wt his blessid chosen." Later Tudor Wills from Bruton and its immediate neighbourhood developed the concept of salvation much more fully, such as that of Walter Tynbury of South Brewham in 1567, "ffirste and pryncipallie I bequethe my soul to the pleasure of Almyghtie God and to Jesus Christe his onlie sonne my saveior and redemer by whose deathe and passion I trust to have remyssion and for geanes (*forgiveness*) of all my synnes."

There was a similar sentiment in the Will of John ffrye in 1588, "ffirst and principally I comend my sowle into the handes of almightie god my creator and of Jhesus Christ my only saviour and redeemer by whose bitter passion and death I doe beleeve most stedfastly to be saved." Almost identical wording may be found in the Wills of Sir Maurice Berkeley in 1580 and Petronell als Purnell Spicer in 1589. There was clearly a set formula at this period so its inclusion in a Will did not necessarily reflect the exact beliefs of each individual testator, but that it was often included was an indication that it had achieved general acceptance.

Unsurprisingly however in rural areas traditional Roman Catholic beliefs remained important in some families. Elements of continuity were evident as a generation which had been born, had grown up, lived and worked for decades under such practices might well on the surface appear to embrace changes but secretly adhere to their old religion. There was after all a great deal of comfort to be found for the dying and the bereaved in some of the Catholic doctrines. The wording of a small number of Bruton Wills, especially in the 1540s and 1550s, suggest that some Roman Catholic beliefs remained deeply ingrained.

In 1544 Stevyn Broke left goods to the value of £3 6s 8d to his son Steven who was away fighting in the war against France, but added that if he did not return the bequest was to pass to Stevyn's wife Christian on condition, "that she find a priest to pray for me and all Christian souls." For several generations the Fitzjames family was to remain staunchly Catholic, for example, in her Will in November 1545 Dame Elizabeth Fitzjames, the widow of the former Chief Justice Sir John and the mother of Sir Maurice Berkeley who purchased Bruton Abbey in that year, instructed, "To be said for my soul the day of my burial fyve masses of the name of Jhu, fyve of the v woundes, thre of the Blessed Trinity and fyve of the fyve principall feasts of Our Lady, each priest having 8d." She gave black gowns to each of her children and servants who attended her burial or "month mynde" and required that "a priest be founde to say masse in the parish church of Brewton at Our Lady Aulter where my husband lieth buried."

A number of the older traditions may be found in a Will made in 1550 by Elizabeth Fitzjames, the widow of John Fitzjames who had died in 1534, several years before his father Sir John of Redlynch, leaving no direct heirs. Elizabeth left 8d to every householder in Combe and Horsington, "so that they take paynes to goo with my corpus to see yt buried." Status within the community mattered so she wanted her debts paid: "Proclamation to be made in the towns of Bruton and Sherbourn that persons are to come forward and prove their debts." Finally she ordered that half of the residue of her estate "be bestowed in mending highways, and on prisoners, and to the marriage of the poor." The latter was an idea that her father-in-law had championed in his Will some twelve years before.

In neighbouring Brewham parish church lights were kept burning in the early 1540s as they had been throughout the medieval period. In 1542, for example, John Exhall left 3s 4d "To the high roode light there" and two years later John Toogood gave "To the high Cross light xijd" and "To the maintenance of two torches iiijd."

Another element of continuity was that just as in earlier decades in the years before 1547 virtually every surviving Will from Bruton left a small sum of between 4d and 20d to the Fraternity of Our Lady in the parish church. These Wills included those of John Hoper als Smyth, George Wylton, William Gane, William Borne, Stevyn Broke, Thomas Toar, William Cleves, William Walter and Robert Bartlett. The expectation must have been the same as before, namely remembrance and prayers but only the will of John Stevyns in 1544 expressly stated it, "To the fraternity of our Lady of

Bruton to be prayed for xijd." Robert Chyke was much more generous when he donated 3s 4d to this body in 1542. With the Dissolution of the Abbey in 1539 it may well be that the Fraternity was thrust into a much more prominent role in relation to provision for the soul for a short period of time

When Edward VI abolished chantries, gilds and endowments in 1547 it is a reasonable assumption that the Fraternity of Our Lady in Bruton parish church ceased to exist. It is interesting to note, however, that during the reign of Queen Mary, when many Roman Catholics hoped that the old faith would be restored, staunch Catholic Henry Ottis alias Calowe, a successful chandler, maltster and rope-maker, bequeathed "To the fraternity of our lady at Bruton ij bushels of malt." It would seem that the former gild was revived but it must have been short-lived as no other references to it seem to have survived.

Virtually all of those testators who made a bequest to the Fraternity continued the practice of making one to the parish church of Bruton. Stevyn Broke and William Cleves did not wish to have a spiritual debt as each made a small gift of 12d and 20d respectively to the high altar for tithes forgotten. Cleves and William Gane made their contributions to the chapel of St. Leonard at Pitcombe rather than to the parish church. In other Wills men such as Roger Ames and John Langyer also left 4d each to Bruton church. Elizabeth Fitzjames was more generous with a gift of 10s.

In the reign of Queen Mary gifts continued, but interestingly while two were in cash, three were in goods, for example, Henry Ottis alias Calowe left another two bushels of malt and John Yonge a bushel of wheat. In 1554 widow Johan Peter donated a ring of silver and gilt, a clear return to pre-Reformation days. In most of these examples in the 1540s and 1550s the Cathedral Church of Wells continued to receive a small sum of money.

The majority of the Elizabethan Wills from Bruton maintained the practice of giving money to both the town's parish church and Wells Cathedral, except for John ffrye who only left money to the former. Although two of the contributions were just for 12d each, most were much larger ranging from 2s to 6s 8d, possibly reflecting an increase in prosperity in this later period, although inflation would also have to be taken into account. As there was no perceived benefit for the soul by this time, the donations had become an act of charity, usually for the "reparation" of the parish church. It is possible that it had become part of the expected pattern of a Will and that the scribe or clerk would remind the testator to make a donation, one which, of course, would be generally known about in the community and could be perceived as an indication of status.

In rare instances money was still left to a named priest, two in the early 1540s and one in the reign of Queen Mary, but included no specific request to pray for souls. In January 1544 William Gane left 3s 4d to "Sir Richard Busshop, priest of Pitcombe", he was a former canon of Bruton Abbey who had become the curate of the neighbouring village. In the same year Stevyn Broke left 12d "to Sir John Eryngton my curate." A decade later the same priest, referred to as "curate of Bruton" received 20d from Henry Ottis alias Calowe.

As in earlier decades there was great concern amongst the dying that their debts should be paid. Both Robert Chyke in 1542 and Henry Ottis in 1554 charged their sons "as sone as they can conveniently they se my detts paid" as Chyke expressed it and Ottis made the necessary arrangements, "they paying therefore my debts as they and I be agreed upon." By the latter part of the Elizabethan period it was customary to include a statement near the end of a Will that the residue of the estate was to be given to a named person or persons, once debts had been paid, "Item the rest of my goods and cattells moveable and unmoveable and unbequeathed my debts paide and my funeral discharged I give and bequeathe to…"

The final significant area that survived the Reformation and continued to operate for centuries was the charitable act to the poor. It would no longer be linked to prayers for the dead person's soul but was increasingly regarded as part of a person's Christian duty to help those who were less fortunate. For some people however there must have remained the older idea that such gifts might help to mitigate any sins committed during their lifetime. In addition large gifts were often publicly recorded on boards in the parish church so it was in fact still a way of ensuring that a name was remembered. Finally of course it indicated the social status of the donor or his or her family.

The abolition of the concept of purgatory which meant that there was no longer any need for the prayers of the poor, must have very adversely affected the well-being of this group within a community such as Bruton, especially as the traditional alms from the Abbey had also ceased. There was virtually no mention of money for the poor from 1539 to 1560 in the surviving Wills from the town. One exception was Henry Ottis who in 1554 directed that his wife, son and son-in-law "shall each yearly after my decease give to the poor for the term of their lives for my soul and all Christian souls xijd at the time and day of my decease, viz iijs iiijd amongst them."

From 1560 charitable gifts became more common again, possibly an indication that as the community was beginning to settle down after the upheavals of the previous three decades their true impact upon groups such as the poor was being more fully understood and appreciated. The amounts given varied significantly, such as 20s from Agnes Plumley in 1560, 40s from Nicholas Gilbert in 1566, 10s to the poor householders of South Brewham from Walter Tynbury in 1567, 12d from

John ffrye in 1588, 10s from Petronell Spicer in 1589 and 20s from Francis Poole in 1597. An interesting observation, very reflective of the Protestant viewpoint, was made by Sir Maurice Berkeley in a Codicil to his Will in 1580. "Item I will that my executor shall geve twentie poundes to the poore at the daie of my burial, by shillings, half shillings or groates at his discrecion, and though I know it wyll doe me no good, yet I am persuaded it will doe theme no harme."

While many beliefs had changed and the old certainties had been swept away by the Reformation, the importance of the parish church within the community remained and it was here that the dying wished to find their final resting place. Some, such as Stevyn Broke and John Plimpton, still specified that they wished to be buried within the church itself but the majority increasingly saw their resting place as being in the churchyard. They all remained content, as Robert Chyk expressed it, that, "my body to be buryed in hallowed grounde."

c) Seventeenth century attitudes to death

Although many theological developments had occurred at the period of the Reformation and immediately after, there were those, particularly the Puritans, who felt that the changes had not gone far enough. At the moment of death they viewed the soul and the body as being completely separated and as it was the former that was important, the disposal of the body was of less significance. They therefore felt no need for ceremony, prayers or even a Minister to be present, but unfortunately there is no surviving evidence concerning these arrangements in Bruton.

Wills from the town, however, clearly indicate that the emphasis was upon the salvation of the soul through God alone or through the merits, passion and death of Jesus. In that way there was the hope of everlasting life, eternal happiness and access to the kingdom of heaven. The Book of Common Prayer made reference to resurrection and about a quarter of the Wills from Bruton in this period expressed their belief in it, with a standard formula becoming prevalent after 1660.

Of thirty-eight seventeenth century Wills examined in detail some twenty-nine, or 76%, gave their soul to God alone or to God and Jesus specifically for salvation. Fourteen commended their souls to God, sometimes with additional comments, such as Hugh Sexey in 1619, "my mercyfull Redeemer, who hath redeemed me and all mankind" and Thomas Albin in 1603, "my maker and redeemer." In 1633 Agnes Morris referred to "Allmightie God my heavenly ffather" and in 1630 Thomas Wilton commended his soul into the hands of "Almighty God, my Creator in whom I beleeve most stedfastlie to be saved." With the exception of spinster Catherine Drew who made her Will in September 1695 and commended her soul into the hands of Almighty God, all of these references occurred before 1658. It was an indication perhaps that although Puritanism was not very strong in the area, it did lead to some simplification of the formulae used.

The other fifteen Wills added the name of Jesus Christ to their hopes for salvation and of these eight come from the post-Restoration period. Several such as that of James Plympton in 1613 expressed the hope of being saved through the passion of Christ, "I comitt my soule into the hands of Almightie god, my Creator, and of Jesus Christe my onlie Savior and Redeemer, by whose bitter passion and death, I doe believe moste stedfastlie to be saved." This sentiment was repeated by William Hellier in 1624, Alice Hill in 1640 and Edward Norton in 1660 and was usually referred to as the doctrine of the atonement

At least eight of these Wills placed an emphasis upon the role of Christ in aiding the remission and forgiveness of sins.

In 1629 John Mogg bequeathed "my selfe unto allmightie god and unto his dearely beloved Jesus Christ, by whose most pretious blood shedding I surely and fully hope to have forgiveness of all my sinnes and trespasses." After the Restoration of Charles II in 1660 the sentence became much more standardized, for example, in 1673 Robert Ludwell committed "my Soule into the hands of Almighty God as into the hands of a faithfull Creator trusting assuredly that through the Lord Jesus Christ all my Sinns are done away and I am freely iustified in the sight of my God."

The various hopes expressed throughout the seventeenth century gave some indication of attitudes to death at that period. In 1643 Robert Albin, and seven years later his widow Christian, both spoke of their souls being placed "in the Company of his heavenly Angells and blessed Saints." In 1647 Peter Tinnie hoped that his soul would "enjoy eternall happiness after this life endes." After the Restoration there were more references to everlasting life: William Day in 1678 hoped "to inherit Everlastinge life", as did John Yeadle, the former Minister of Bruton, in 1688 and Thomas Warner, mariner, in 1696.

A very elaborate and long formula, that covered most of the areas already considered, was to be found in the Wills of Sir Maurice Berkeley in 1617 and William Swanton in 1637. Berkeley stated,

"And ffirst I bequeath my soule into the hands of Almightie god the ffather the sonne and the holy ghost Three personnes but one Eternall incomprehensible and most mercifull god my Creator Redeemer and Sanctifier confidentlie beleevinge and affirming my selfe that by the death and passion of my lorde and saviour Jesus Christ and by faith in his bloud I shall be freed from all my sinnes and by his ressurection Justified and shall enioye and be made partaker of eternal glorie In the kingdome of heaven."

After requesting "decent Christian burial" for his body, he continued, "there to remayne untill the same shalbe raised upp againe and both soule and body reunited and shall meete my Saviour in the Clouds to the generall Judgement and togeather with him and the rest of the faithfull to enter into his glorie."

In their Wills both Berkeley and Swanton not only hoped to enter into eternal glory with their sins forgiven but also referred to the re-uniting of body and soul at the resurrection. A belief in the resurrection was one which seems to have gained increasing attention during the course of the seventeenth century, for example, Berkeley's widow, Dame Elizabeth, in her Will in 1626 hoped "at the general Resurrection to receive the same agayne not a vile mortall and corruptible Body as it is nowe, but a glorious ymmortall and incorruptible body lyke unto the body of my Savioure Jesus Christe."

In 1643 Robert Albin commended his body to earth, "nothing doubting but according to the Articles of my Creed I shall at the last day of the genneral Resurection receive it againe without spott or blemish." John Hodges in 1652 simply wished his body to be buried in Bruton's churchyard "in hope of a Joyfull resurrection." After the Restoration the Wills of William Morris in 1667, Robert Ludwell in 1673, Richard Dimond in 1676, Peter Walter of Wyke Champflower in 1686 and William Tice in 1687 all suggested that a standard formula was being employed. In each case the body was committed to earth, "beleeving stedfastly that at the generall Resurrection both Soule and Body shall be reunited and received into Glory."

In just one instance in the Wills examined there was no religious preamble at all but simply the distribution of an estate. This Will was made by Thomas Cornish als Allen in December 1696 and was indicative of the format that was to be increasingly used in the decades which followed.

Older ideas still lingered, most notably in relation to acts of charity towards the poor, gifts to the Church and the necessity of ensuring that debts were paid. If the hope did remain that there would be some benefits for the soul in these acts of kindness it was not overtly stated in any of the Wills of this period. What was interesting was that as more and more money was raised in the seventeenth century and beyond for the relief of the poor through the Poor Rates and to maintain the parish church with the Church Rates, that such charitable acts should continue at all.

d) Eighteenth century attitudes to death

Many of the Bruton Wills suggest that in the first half of the eighteenth century there was a general continuation of attitudes to death that had existed in the seventeenth century. Testators continued to commend their souls to God and hope that through the merits, mediation, death and passion of Christ there would be the same forgiveness of sins, salvation, eternal life and a place in the kingdom of heaven.

There was, however, an increasingly marked distinction emerging between the religious and the secular in the formulae of eighteenth century Wills. More and more testators entrusted their soul to God but made no other religious statement. Historians have suggested that this did not necessarily mean a change in attitudes to religion or death but an acceptance that the chief functions of Wills were to settle worldly affairs and to ensure a smooth transition to heirs. One reference to God that continued to appear in most Wills thanked Him that while the testator might be sick or weak in body he or she still possessed a sound mind. The Will of Richard Creed in 1744 was typical: "being weak and sick in Body but of Sound Mind and Memory for which I praise my God."

Throughout the century a number of Wills from Bruton commented upon the uncertainty of the time of death, an idea that had been much more prevalent in Medieval and Tudor Wills. Mary Griffen in 1722, Nicholas Goldesbrough in 1738, John Thomas in 1758 and Robert Pavy in 1796 each made their Will as they were "calling to remembrance the uncertainty of this transitory life", compared with "the certainty of Death." George King in 1719 felt that he had to make his Will "daily considering with my selfe the uncertainty of this transitory life and it is a race only unto death." Comments such as these tend to suggest that death continued to be an ever-present concept in the daily life of many people. There was a certain degree of resignation in the comment in 1733 by Lucy Temple, sister of Lady Berkeley, "My Soul I resigne to Almighty God whenever it shall please him to take me out of this World of Misery and Uncertainty."

In 1748 Peter Ames gave "my Soul unto God who gave it to me hoping to be saved through the Merits and Mediation of Jesus Christ my Saviour and Redeemer." Thomas Morren in 1701, George King in 1719 and Lucy Temple in 1733 expressed similar sentiments. Explicit references to resurrection were very rare although Mary Griffen was "hoping for a Glorious and comfortable resurrection" and George King also believed, "that at the General resurrection both Soul and body shall be reunited and received into Glory." For others there was the simple acceptance that, as Ann Creed stated, "Gods will be done."

Unusually there was one Will late in the century which contained a religious opening and that was the Will of Nicholas Everatt, a tanner, in 1797. "ffirst and principally I resign my Soul with the utmost Humility into the hands of Almighty God my Creator humbly hoping for a Blessed Immortality though the merits and mediation of a Blessed Redeemer Jesus Christ."

Much more common throughout the century, however, and particularly from the mid-1730s, was the practice of the majority of Wills not to make a religious statement at all but simply to contain a list of bequests, establish Trusts and dispose of property. Included within this category were the Wills of Henry Sampson in 1718, Richard Creed in 1744, William Pavy in 1763 and several members of the Goldesbrough family such as Nicholas in 1738, Austin in 1757 and John in 1767, the latter possibly being the most surprising as he was the Minister of Bruton and the Master of the Free Grammar School.

The parish church continued to be important in the consciousness of many members of the community as evidence from the Accounts of the Churchwardens indicates that on average two bodies a year were buried within the parish church of Bruton: it was after all quite a lucrative source of income for the Church. It was however indicative of the changed nature of Wills that none of those who sought interment within the church mentioned this fact in their Wills, such as for example, Nicholas Goldesbrough in 1738. The implication must be that either the necessary arrangements had been made by the individual before death or that the family made the request after death. (16)

e) Nineteenth century attitudes to death

Nineteenth century, and particularly Victorian attitudes to death were varied, complex and changed through time. For some writers such as novelist Charlotte Bronte, death was the grim reaper, "That dread visitant before whose coming every household trembles." For others such as the poet Alfred, Lord Tennyson, it was much more benign:

"like a friend's voice from a distant field
Approaching though the Darkness."

The magazine 'Punch' even published a cartoon in 1845 that showed death hovering at the end of the bed of a poor sick man who was living in a miserable hovel, under the title, "The Poor Man's Friend." For most Victorians, however, there was always hope and phrases such as, "Not lost but gone before" were frequently employed.

Religion continued to figure prominently in Victorian life with Church attendance playing a major part not only in the parish church but also in the two Non-Conformist chapels in Bruton. Newspaper accounts indicated that at times of special services such as Harvest Festival, the parish church was full to overflowing. On the other hand the religious statements that had previously started Wills were completely lacking in the nineteenth century, from William Saunders in 1804 to Stephen Penny in 1851 to Alfred Whalley in 1885. They tended to be concerned exclusively with money, land, and property in general.

The importance of Evangelicalism and Non-Conformity in the Victorian period, however, did a great deal to revive the medieval concept of a good death, which in their eyes required piety and fortitude in the face of suffering. When grocer Thomas Deacon died aged eighty in February 1838 it was reported to be "after a painful and lingering illness, which he bore with Christian fortitude. He is much regretted by his friends and large acquaintance." Nineteen years later when the Minister of the Independent Chapel, the Rev. William Skinner died in February 1859, it was "after a long and painful illness, borne with patience and Christian resignation." As one historian has commented, "In the Victorian Evangelical version, this good Christian death took place in the home surrounded by a loving and supportive family, whose affection expressed itself afterwards in sorrow for the dead." (17)

The Evangelicals and Non-Conformists stressed the older doctrine of atonement, where Christ had died as a substitute for sinful human beings and hence faith in his sacrifice on the Cross was required to ensure salvation. There was the assurance that their sins were forgiven, "Death had no terrors for the Evangelical…The Evangelical's confidence in the face of death was unusually comforting and homely; it lay at the heart of Evangelical religion." (18)

Most Victorians believed that individual judgement would occur at the time of death and the Evangelicals in particular stressed the role of punishment that for some was the 'poena sensus', that is the pain of the senses, represented by the fires of hell. Thomas Hardy conveyed these images in 'Tess of the D'Urbervilles':

> "She thought of the child consigned to the nethermost corner of hell, as its double doom for lack of baptism and the lack of legitimacy; saw the arch-fiend toss it with his three-pronged fork, like the one they used for heating the oven on baking days."

For other Victorians, however, the 'poena damni', the pain of loss, was much more important as they regarded this as the loss of heaven or the absence of God.

Some writers even began to see hell as being on earth, just as William Blake had already drawn attention to the "dark satanic mills". In 1845 Frederick Engels referred to the Old Town area of Manchester as "this Hell upon Earth." (19) Fortunately such squalor did not exist in Bruton, despite its manifold public health problems.

As death was common in Victorian society all ages, from children to the elderly, were familiar with so many aspects of it as it appeared widely in literature, as well as in the Bible and hymns. Sometimes death was used to encourage good behaviour and occasionally to frighten but more often than not it was used to prepare people for what was all around them.

Much of what was written and used as texts for sermons was also designed to provide hope, including the expectation of the resurrection: "Blessed be the God and Father of our Lord Jesus Christ, which according to his abundant mercy hath begotten us again unto a lively hope by the resurrection of Jesus Christ from the dead. To an inheritance incorruptible, and undefiled, and that fadeth not away, reserved in heaven for you." (1 Peter 1 vv.3-4) When Jesus was speaking to Martha he said, "I am the resurrection, and the life: he that believeth in me, though he were dead, yet shall he live: And whosoever liveth and believeth in me, though he were dead, yet shall he live." (John 11 vv.25-6) Needless to say these two extracts from the Bible were particularly popular at funerals.

In the second half of the nineteenth century many Victorians found great comfort in their religion. They continued to draw heavily on the appropriate verses of the Bible such as verse 4 of Psalm 23: "Yea, though I walk through the valley of death, I will fear no evil: for thou art with me: thy rod and thy staff they comfort me." One historian had commented, "The strategy now was not to frighten sinners into Heaven but to beckon them there by promising more of the good things they had enjoyed in life. So as Hell ceased to be a fiery furnace, Heaven became a cosy fireside where the long-lost loved ones congregated." (20)

Hymns of the period likewise carried the appropriate messages of exhortation, hope and comfort especially for the dying and the bereaved. Charles Wesley's hymns from the previous century were particularly popular with Non-Conformists and Evangelicals:

"Rejoice in glorious hope;
Jesus the Judge shall come,
And take his servants up
To their eternal home."

Some hymn writers stressed the rest that would come at the end of a journey:

"Rest comes at length; though life be long and dreary,
The day must dawn and darksome night be past;
Faith's journey ends in welcome to the weary,
And heaven, the heart's true home, will come at last."

(F.W. Faber)

So many of the hymns that were written specifically for children encouraged the belief in a delightful place in heaven:

"And our eyes at last shall see Him,
Through His own redeeming love;
For that child so dear and gentle
Is our Lord in heaven above;
And he leads his Children on
To the place where he is gone."

(Mrs C.F. Alexander)

"Looking upward every day,
Sunshine in our faces;
Pressing onward every day
Toward the heavenly places.

Lord, so pray we every day,
Hear us in thy pity,
That we enter in at last
To the Holy City."

(Mary Butler)

As so many Victorians became convinced that there would be a reunion in some heavenly home, the great danger developed of sentimentality creeping into writing about death in the period and also a denial that death had in fact occurred. Words such as 'sleeping', 'resting', and 'gone before' were frequently found on many gravestones, including in Bruton churchyard. Popular songs of the period also conveyed the same messages as the following examples show:

"Hark! A solemn bell is ringing,
Clear thro' the night;
Thou, my love, art heav'nward winging
Home tho' the night
Earthly dust from off thee shaken,
Soul immortal, thou shalt waken
With thy last dim journey taken
Home thro' the night."
                    (*All Thro' the Night*, Walter Maynard)

"Stretch out your hand to me, Douglas, Douglas,
Drop forgiveness from heaven like dew:
As I lay my heart on your dead heart, Douglas
Douglas, Douglas, tender and true."
                              (*Too Late*, D.M.M. Craik)

"We shall meet, but we shall miss him
There will be one vacant chair
We will linger to caress him
While we breathe our evening prayer."
                        (*The Vacant Chair*, Henry Washburn.)

(For a selection of other verses from popular Victorian hymns and songs, see Appendix 7.)

One other way in which the Victorians seemed to deny death was in their increased interest in spiritualism: the belief in the immortality of the soul and the possibility that contact could be made with 'the other side' through mediums. Spiritualism started in the United States of America in the 1840s and spread into the United Kingdom over the next two decades. Exactly when the interest in séances first reached

Bruton is impossible to determine but they were certainly being held in the late Victorian period. In July 1881 at the end of his "Magic and Mesmerism" entertainment Dr Smeaton staged, "A dark séance afterwards (*which*) was well patronized." In April 1889 Professor Dupres held a private séance for members of the Mutual Improvement Society and one report stated that, "The 'Dark Half Hour' was much enjoyed." No records have survived to indicate exactly what happened at any of these sessions. (21)

While wealthier Victorians believed that it was necessary to make preparations for their death by ensuring that their wishes were recorded, they also considered that work should continue until death or ill-health forced them to stop. At national level Lord Palmerston died in office as Prime Minister aged eighty-one in 1865, Benjamin Disraeli died aged seventy-seven, two years after he lost the General Election and was elevated to the House of Lords, and William Gladstone was finally persuaded to retire from the office of Prime Minister in 1894 aged eighty-five.

When Stephen Penny died aged sixty-six in October 1851 he was still acting as the Secretary of the Governors of King's School and only the year before had resigned as the Postmaster of Bruton, having "so long held the office." Former soldier Coles became a cutler when he left the army and died suddenly in July 1853 when he was sharpening a customer's razor at the age of eighty-four. On the death of John Jelley in February 1888, some two months short of his eightieth birthday, it was reported that it was only a few years before that he had been forced to give up the school which he run for nearly 50 years as a result of ill-health. (22) When Edward Thomas died in January 1909 aged 77, it was stated that he was still working at his trade of shoemaker. There was of course nothing new in this practice as the available evidence suggests that nearly three hundred years before Hugh Sexey was still pursuing his profession of auditor when he was well into his seventies.

There were some other changes in attitude towards death in the nineteenth century. First the Victorians developed the rituals of mourning that had really started in the eighteenth century. There were strict periods of time and a dress code for those in mourning, particularly widows, along with extensive condolence letters. Second and far more important there was the change in attitude towards the expected time of death, from infancy to old age as discussed in chapter 3. Along with this came the expectation that if Victorian medical men could not prevent death, at least they could alleviate pain, with opium widely used until the emergence of aspirin in 1899. How successful this pain relief was is difficult to assess for certainly there were a number of death notices in local newspapers which would seem to cast doubt. In 1849 spinster Mary Bennett died aged forty-eight "after a protracted and painful illness"; the Master of Sexey's Hospital, George Parfitt, died aged sixty in 1851 "after a long and painful illness"; and in 1899 Philip Hill, a painter and plumber "had been a great sufferer, and was confined to his house for a considerable period."

Traditionally the women of the family were expected to undertake the majority of the nursing care of the sick and dying, possibly aided in wealthier families by servants or nurses from outside. It must be hoped that Florence Nightingale's assessment of these nurses pre-1870 was exaggerated as she described them as "too old, too weak, too drunken, too dirty, too stolid, or too bad to do anything else." (23)

Finally, as scientific and technological developments occurred, the literal interpretation of some aspects of the Bible began to be questioned. For centuries burial in the ground had been the accepted method of disposing of a corpse but in the nineteenth century advocates of cremation were increasing heard. A debate raged over whether cremation was a suitable method to dispose of the body of a Christian in the light of references in the Bible to the resurrection of the body. The first crematoria were established in the mid-1880s and in 1902 the Cremation Act was passed which legalized and regulated the practice. Acceptance was slow, probably as a result of the continued strength of Christianity so that by 1908 there were only about 800 cremations a year nationally. The first recorded burial of ashes in Bruton churchyard was for Jane Ann Scott aged sixty-two on 8th April 1914, having been cremated in Manchester on 1st December 1913.

5

THE ROLE OF THE PARISH
CHURCH AND
THE CHURCHYARD

a) The Parish Church

Burial within the church was reserved for the wealthy or those of high standing in the community, often founders, patrons and benefactors of the building. Bruton church or the Priory became the resting place in the medieval period for various members of the De Mohuns and Luttrells, along with others who had made gifts, such as Sir William de Montacute in 1319 who had conferred on the Priory the rectory of Shepton Montague. As so many churchyards were small they became increasingly crowded which meant that existing burials were often disturbed. It was therefore regarded as much more peaceful to be buried within a church. The poor of course were excluded, although as one epitaph expressed it, this may not have mattered:

> "Here I lie at the chancel door,
> Here I lie because I'm poor;
> The further in, the more you pay;
> Here I lie as warm as they." (1)

In the medieval period to be interred in the Chancel, and particularly before the High Altar, meant that a body was in the most sacred part of the church, the place where the Mass would be celebrated each day. It was also believed to be a prime position when Christ came from the east to judge both the quick and the dead. It was no coincidence that clerics such as Richard Bruton in 1417 instructed that, "My body to be buried in the parish church of Bruton, in the chancel."

Those buried in the nave were slightly further away but were still much better placed than those outside. In addition interment near an altar or image of a saint was also much sought after. Wills made between 1417 and 1517 mentioned at least four altars placed in the area of the nave in the parish and conventual churches in Bruton, dedicated to Our Blessed Lady, All Saints, Holy Cross and St Aldhelm, as well as various statues and images: Blessed Katherine, Blessed Mary Magdalene, St Mary and the Crucifix. It was believed that a location near one of these would provide added protection for the soul. In 1496 Alianora Ede, for example, wished to be buried "by the image of the Crucifix near the tomb of the said Thomas Ede my husband." In 1517 Alice Brymmore wished to be interred "before the Awter of or blissid ladie." Both widows, of course, left large sums of money to the church.

There had in fact been a ban from the early medieval period on burying anyone in a church unless they were clergy or a founder or a benefactor but gradually, in order to raise money, this ban had been ignored. Exactly how soon burial within Bruton church became more accepted is not clear but was certainly in operation in the fifteenth century with the burials of Richard Bruton, John Gregory and Amice Gregory. The former was a cleric and it is possible that John and Amice Gregory were benefactors but no direct evidence of this has survived, although in his Will John Gregory made reference to a gown with the livery of the prior of Bruton on it. It was a practice which continued in the sixteenth century with at least three members of the Fitzjames family, John senior, Sir John and Dame Isabel between 1510 and 1543. It was also a wish expressed by William Samford, Richard Philippys and Richard Holmede. In each of these cases a donation was made to the church in the form of cash or goods.

The Tudor period produced many more Wills indicating that burial within the churchyard was required but some still requested in the church itself, such as Stevyn Broke and John Plimpton. In 1567 Walter Tynbury of South Brewham left instructions that his body was to be "buryed wthin the pishe churche of bruhm." There was a significant change in the seventeenth century as less than a quarter of surviving Wills from Bruton specified the church directly but over half of the testators required either a decent Christian burial or simply to be returned to the earth, it being left to the executors to determine exactly where, possibly taking into account any instruction that was given before death. "And my body I commit to the Earth from whence it was taken." Such a situation was not surprising as nationally in the first half of the seventeenth century at least, there was increasing opposition to intramural burials as some felt that the church was hallowed ground and it should not be dug into. In addition many writers complained that such burials could lead to unpleasant smells and possibly the spread of disease.

The Churchwardens' Accounts for Bruton which have survived from the middle of the seventeenth century, indicate that the practice of burial within the parish church continued throughout the eighteenth century and into the nineteenth century. The Churchwardens charged far more for such interments compared with those in the churchyard. Nationally there was in fact some criticism of the amounts demanded: "No ground in the kingdom is now sold so dear as a grave.....

the churchwardens of parishes sell graves in the church and churchyard like wares in their shops." (2)

For most of this period the Bruton Churchwardens seem to have charged 6s 8d for a single burial and 13s 4d for a double burial within the church, for example, in 1735 it cost 6s 8d each to bury William Pavy and John Cheeke's wife. In 1760 they received 6s 8d "For breaking the Ground in the Church for the Burial of Mrs Mary Pavy senr.", with the same for Mrs Elizabeth Sampson in 1788 and 13s 4d for the joint burial of Mr and Mrs Whitehead in 1799. For some unspecified reason the sum paid for the burial of Mr and Mrs Pritchard in the church was cheaper, being 10s 4d in 1801. It is possible to speculate that in some cases the amounts paid were advance payments as Elizabeth Sampson did not die until April 1790 and the Whiteheads died just over a month apart from each other in 1801.

The evidence suggests that on average two bodies a year were interred within the parish church throughout the eighteenth century which may have created problems. One structural issue that emerged was that some of the graves were not adequately reinforced at the sides and ends so that the floor of the church began to sink in places. In 1744 the Churchwardens and Vestry were forced to issue an Order, "that every body that shall hereafter bury in the Church, shall first wall up the Grave, or use some other means to prevent the gravestone from sinking beyond the true level of the Pavement of the said Church." The Order was clearly taken very seriously as in one instance in 1766 John Cox was paid 14s 4d "for a bar of iron wt 43lbs" to support the tombstone over a vault and £4 10s 0d was paid for the flat tombstone itself. The labour of three men involved in laying the iron bar and tombstone cost another 7s.

Another problem was overcrowding and so the Churchwardens were quite prepared to inter the bodies of different families in the same grave. This practice did not meet with universal approval amongst all parishioners. In the case of the Smart family, when Robert died in 1763 he directed in his Will that he was to be buried in the church in the same grave as his parents, Thomas and Mary, and he left money to the Churchwardens for its maintenance. He did however add the proviso that they would only continue to receive the money for as long as no other body was interred in their grave. To ensure that this requirement was kept he instructed that the information should be carved into the grave slab:

"By whose Will an Annuity is given to the
Churchwardens for keeping in Repair
The Vault underneath on condition they do not
Permit any other Corps to be interred in it." (3)

Finally, the church could provide a space for a suitable, lasting memorial to a person or family, a tendency that particularly developed in the eighteenth century. As the Berkeleys were the Rectors of the parish church, responsible, amongst other things, for the maintenance of the Chancel, it was natural that their memorials should be there along with families connected by marriage. When Phelps published his book on Somerset in 1836 he referred to various local families interred within the church and whose graves were marked, usually with flat stones: Goldesbrough, Wood, Cheeke, Albyn, Russ, Pavy, Mason, Brown, Saxton, Venn, Smart and Bruce. Nearly all were eighteenth century burials with the exceptions being John Russ in 1685 and former minister Emanuel Mason in 1653. (4)

b) The Churchyard

In many respects the history of churchyards is as dramatic as that of the church buildings themselves. One historian has assessed their role in the community: "For hundreds of years, the churchyard was used for various secular purposes, most importantly for commerce and leisure. Throughout the Middle Ages, it was indeed the principal place for open-air meetings of almost any kind." (5) Such occurrences were relatively easy as before the seventeenth century churchyards were generally open spaces with very few monuments of any kind. As hardly any graves were marked, except possibly with a small earth mound, the hope was always that the sexton would remember where burials had taken place and avoid digging up a site too soon.

Churchyards were often referred to as "God's acre", that is 'acre' in the sense of a piece of enclosed land, or "God's seed-field". Based upon various verses in the Bible, it was believed that bodies were sown there like seeds to await the resurrection. The body "is sown in corruption; it is raised in incorruption; It is sown in dishonour; it is raised in glory; it is sown in weakness; it is raised in power; It is sown a natural body; it is raised a spiritual body." (1 Corinthians 15, vv.42-22) It was a phrase still in use in the late nineteenth century when, for example, it was recorded on John Jelley's brass plaque in St Mary's Church in 1888 that, "His Body rests in God's Acre around these walls." (The phrase also appeared in early twentieth century dialect poetry, see Appendix 8)

Under Canon Law churchyards were ecclesiastical possessions but the laity usually had a customary right or privilege to be buried there and from the fifteenth century the area of a churchyard was frequently defined as the land some fifty to seventy yards wide around a church. In that sense Bruton churchyard was probably an exception as there was originally no such space for burials beyond the eastern end of the chancel and a much larger area at the western end of the church. Other local churches such as those in Pitcombe, Shepton Montague, Milton Clevedon and Lamyatt conform more accurately, although the distances are generally less

In some places markets, fairs, courts, church ales and a whole variety of games and sports, such as wrestling and cudgelling, took place in churchyards, although evidence for any of these occurring in Bruton churchyard has yet to emerge. Until at least the eighteenth century, however, Fives was commonly played in many Somersetshire parishes against the Church Tower and this may well have occurred in Bruton. (6) Animals often grazed in the churchyard and that was a useful method of keeping the vegetation under control. It did not always meet with parishioners' approval, such as in January 1799 when the Vestry complained that the Minister, Revd. Charles Roberts, grazed his horse there, "And whereas the Churchyard has for time Immemorial been Inclosed and kept in decent Order at the expence of the Parish... And that no Cattle of any Kind was ever permitted to Graze therein till Mr Roberts feed it with his Horse without the consent of the Inhabitants of the Parish." The Vestry added that they believed that the sole right to do so rested with Sir Richard Colt Hoare as Rector at that time.

With so many activities occurring in churchyards there was always the possibility of violence breaking out and as early as October 1311 Bishop Drokensford of Bath and Wells commissioned the Bishop of Cork "to reconcile the cemetery of the parish church within the enclosure of the Priory of Bruton after bloodshed." No details have survived to indicate what events necessitated this action. In October 1605 Robert Darby was charged in front of the Church Court with "Strickinge Mr Evans the cureat in the churchyard because hee reproved him for his drunkenness And for a common drunkard." Darby was excommunicated but absolved the following year when he claimed, "that he did not strike the said Evans willinglye but throwing a stone att another bodye, it lightend on Evans." In July 1588 an example of violence occurred in Pitcombe churchyard when Robert Lane was presented in front of the Church Court as "he stroaketh Thomas Mogge in the churchyard wheareby blud was shed." Unfortunately no details were given concerning the circumstances or the outcome.

A different type of violence may have been carried on in Lamyatt churchyard as in the 1780s it was recorded that, "Here is also a pair of stocks under a very venerable yew 13ft round in the body." Given the way in which local people tended to react to the unfortunate victims held in the stocks, there may well have been a great deal of raucus behaviour there. In the middle of the nineteenth century Bruton Churchyard was still a gathering place, not always for peaceful purposes. In August 1851 a fight broke out between two groups of men during which Joseph Bacon was stabbed with a knife by Alfred Durston and Robert Sheppard was wounded in the back by Abel Parker. Both of the accused were found guilty with Durston being sentenced to eighteen months imprisonment and Parker to twelve months. As in so many of the nineteenth century cases of assault "Both parties appeared to have been the worse for liquor." (7)

Needless to say such activities caused considerable concern amongst bishops and so very gradually from the thirteenth century secular activities were removed from churchyards. This process was particularly aided in the sixteenth and seventeenth centuries by a growing concern to separate the living from the dead. As burials within churches decreased and those in churchyards increased more and more the latter became reserved for interments: the wealthy joined the poor who had always been buried there. A few of the wealthier members of the community in Bruton had already expressed a wish to be buried outside the church, for example, in his Will in 1509 John Harman stated he wished, "My body to be buried in the burying place of the parishioners of Brewton wherever it shall please God." Margery Moleyns had been even more specific in her Will in 1493: "my body to be buried in the Churchyard of Bruton by gibbis mary." (8)

The location of a grave within the churchyard was of considerable importance, just as it had been within the church itself. The prime position was as near as possible to the eastern end in order to be first to meet the Risen Christ, who was expected to come from the east with the rising sun at the time of the general Resurrection. It was no coincidence that when Charles Berkeley was undertaking his reconstruction of the Chancel in 1743 and removed the bones and remains of the bodies that had previously been placed in the crypt beneath it, he re-interred them under an earthen mound at the then most easterly point of the churchyard, before the Victorian extension, and to the south of the Chancel. On the mound he constructed a square stone monument, topped with an urn and originally surrounded with an iron railing. A translation of his Latin text on this memorial reads:

"We are the dust and bones of the bodies previously lying in the charnel-house under the Sanctuary of this Church. Preserved under this monument by order of the Honorable C. Berkeley. Anno 1743" (9)

For most burials the south or west sides of the churchyard could be expected: here the sun's rays would have fallen upon the graves as the concept of light remained important. The one area to be avoided was the northern side, the dark side, generally in the shade, and sometimes referred to as the 'Devil's side.' It was here that the stillborn, the un-baptised, suicides, executed criminals and the excommunicated could be buried. When the Burial Register recorded that on 14th January 1604 four named condemned prisoners were interred, it was presumably on the north side without a Christian burial. As an act of mercy a bishop could permit the burial of a person in one of these categories to take place, often at night. Some were not so fortunate as alongside the name of John Wookke on 24th December 1624 was added, "excommunicate Buried out." The same had happened to

Edmond Klethero on 6th October 1597, "buried outt of the churchyard", but no reason was given.

Not everyone of course wished to be buried in a churchyard, as one epitaph apparently indicated:

"Rather be buried among thistles and briars
Then over there with thieves and liars."

In March 1772 when a labourer was digging for stone to repair the roads he unearthed a human skeleton "which mouldered to ashes as soon as exposed to air." Unfortunately no location was specifed and at the time it was thought to be a murder victim. Late in 1794 Rev. Richard Paget, who was collecting information to make additions to Collinson's 'History of Somerset' that had been published in 1791, noted that, "In Oct. 1794 the remains of a leaden coffin containing the bones of a female & two children, together with a comb made of bone & ornamented with rude carving, were discovered by some workmen quarrying stones in a field called Atkin's hill adjoining to Brewton." He was forced to add, "The coffin was so much mutilated & bruised in removal, and had suffered so much from the injuries of time, that it was impossible to ascertain its original form. No trinket or other implement was found in it beside the comb." The use of lead does suggest a person of wealth or status but the reason for burial in that location remains unclear.

The area around Creech Hill attracted burials through the centuries. The excavation of the site of the Romano-Celtic Temple on Lamyatt Beacon revealed a later Angle Saxon Cemetary with at least twelve bodies. In December 1849 some workmen digging for stone at an unspecified location on the hill found three human skeletons "which immediately crumbled on being touched." At that time it was felt that this may have been the site of a battle and the remains were of those who fell in that conflict. In the late nineteenth century when more stone was being quarried near Creech Hill Farm two bodies were unearthed although no details seem to have survived and it is therefore impossible to determine their age. As this area includes a Roman Temple and an Iron Age site, these last two groups of skeletons could have dated from any period because of the importance of the location to people in the past. In addition a medieval chapel dedicated to St. Lawrence was recorded on Creech Hill and so some of the burials may be related to that building. (10)

Churchyards themselves were not always well maintained, much to the concern and distress of the parishioners. In 1623 it was reported to a Church Court that at Shepton Montague, "Henry Bonly....doth rent the churchyard and keepeth horses therein in soe much that the said churchyard is much fowled thereby and the graves trodden." The same problem had existed earlier in Bruton Churchyard as in 1554 another Church Court held there complained, "Itm the Churchyard is fylthelye kept yt by the default of John Michell Smythe."

By the eighteenth century much more care was being taken with comments and payments appearing regularly in the Churchwardens' Accounts, for example, in 1738-1739, "The North Alley Pitched this Year of the Church Yard", and on 19th October 1782, "Paid John Duffett for trimming the Walks in the Churchyard 1s 6d." Together such entries suggest that formal paths had been created to give more access to graves. On 24th June 1810 the Churchwardens paid 4s 6d "for cutting the Grass in the Churchyard." Even so the state of this area did not always meet with approval as in May 1827 on a Visitation the Archdeacon of Wells commented, "The Church yard is full of weeds & long grass, it must be kept more neat." He added, "The Church-yard Gates to be locked", which may suggest that some unauthorized activities were still taking place there. (11)

At the same time there was a marked increase in the number of monuments to the dead placed in the churchyard, most of which were worked upon by local stonemasons and craftsmen and as a result tended to be rather plain, with the usual reminders of death, such as a skull and crossbones or a scythe. Other tombstones contained images of hope such as angels, cherubs and doves to symbolize divine messages, immortality and the Holy Spirit respectively.

In addition a small number of wealthier families began to select a chest-tomb, sometimes referred to as altar tombs. Some people felt that as space was becoming more limited within the church, it was better to have a site that was prominent outside, rather than hidden away inside. It did, of course, establish their family's burial territory as well. Early twentieth century postcards picturing the church and churchyard show that there were very few graves to the west and south of the church except for these chest-tombs. They were therefore somewhat isolated and as a result very, very prominent. Some of these weathered chest-tombs may still be seen in these positions just to the west of Bruton church, while most of the ordinary eighteenth century gravestones have been destroyed through age, weathering, safety concerns or the needs of modern maintenance methods.

Nineteenth century Churchwardens' Accounts suggest that the Victorians in Bruton were very punctilious in maintaining the churchyard and its associated graves: on 13th December 1852 James Upham received 18s 6d for "37 weeks cleaning Churchyd Paths"; on 18th April 1863 John Shears was paid 2s 6d for "weeding Hedge round new Chy." The most serious problem which the Victorians faced in Bruton churchyard was that, as burials had taken place in the same small location for a thousand years, and with the population having risen significantly in the eighteenth century, there was severe overcrowding developing. This problem was not unique to Bruton as in 1843

Edwin Chadwick's 'Report on the Practice of Interment in Towns' found that in large towns and cities many churchyards were overcrowded and unsanitary.

After the outbreak of cholera in 1848 one West Country writer condemned in no uncertain terms the state of many churchyards. "In a churchyard which is of ancient origin and overcrowded, a vast amount of animal decomposition is constantly going on, and the disturbance of the soil, by opening new graves and exposing fresh surfaces, has a most pernicious effect upon the health of the inhabitants. It is well known that under such circumstances, considerable exhalations are continually arising, impregnating the surrounding air with gaseous contaminations..... from the churchyard emanates a deadly human poison... a silent though certain destroyer of health." (12) In many towns and cities it led to the closure of churchyards to new burials and cemeteries being opened instead.

The solution in Bruton was different as the town was fortunate that it was able to expand its churchyard to the east of the Chancel, on to land that had belonged to the monastery, had passed to the Berkeley family who transformed it into parkland with Walks, and finally became glebe land. In 1844-1845 the parish raised £146 15s 2d by public subscription to purchase the land, judged to be about one acre, between the eastern end of the chancel and the turnpike road to Wincanton. The Turnpike Trustees took the opportunity "to widen the road at the Corner below the Arch" and paid the Churchwardens £9 7s 6d for a strip of land and spent a further £20 9s 8d building a retaining wall against the new Churchyard. Between 1845 and 1847 the Churchwarden's Accounts contained numerous entries relating to the extension in addition to the cost of the land purchased: there was stone from Marydown Quarry, haulage of the stone, building a new wall, laying paths, digging drains, planting twelve Yew trees and consecration expenses, in all over £100.

For some Victorians establishing and maintaining a family grave was an important activity, almost a social status symbol. Yet the wording on the gravestones could be quite simple as the older term "Here lieth the body of" was replaced more and more by "In memory of". Many of the larger family plots were marked with kerbstones or railings, the latter were then regularly cleaned and painted. In many instances there was a stone slab, covered with grass turfs or marble chippings, which could be lifted when required to give access to an underground vault in which coffins were placed on shelves.

The vast majority of these Victorian family graves, which tended to be to the east of the church or around the southern and western boundary wall in Bruton churchyard, were still in place in the mid-twentieth century, although by that stage as families moved away or died out, they were no longer maintained to the same high standards. Rusting railings with weeds and tall grass inside the kerbstones was a common sight. Most of these kerbstones or railings were removed in the second half of the twentieth century as they interrupted quick and efficient grass cutting by machine and some had become unstable. A few, however, were still being used for the burials of later generations of the family. (13)

It was felt by some Victorian families that they must be together in death and it was not unusual for a body to be brought some distance, aided by the development of the railway network. In January 1867 Walter Stockwell's funeral was held, "The remains of the deceased gentleman were brought by train to Bruton, and interred in the family vault." In December 1869 the remains of Mrs Tatham, a sister of J.G. Bord, were brought from London and placed in their family vault, as were those of Mrs Rich the following June.

Other bodies left Bruton for the same reason. In January 1884 Emily Dickens of Gower Street, London, petitioned the

Episcopal Court of Wells for permission to remove the remains of her father Major George Dickens, who had died in Bruton in March 1859 and was buried in the churchyard. His wife died in November 1883 and was interred "in the consecrated part of the Cemetery of Paddington" and Emily wished her father's remains to be placed there with those of her mother. (14)

Considerable care clearly went into the provision of gravestones in the churchyard. After three of his children had died, Josiah Jackson of Durslade Farm discussed the issue of appropriate memorials with a local stonemason in December 1895. "We agreed that he should put up 3 marble Head Stones, one each at Stuarts grave 4 feet high, one 3ft 6in high at Franklyn's & one 3 feet high at Dorothy's in Bruton Churchyard." They were ready to be put up on 18th January 1896. (15) (For the details of the inscriptions on these gravestones and that of Jackson and his wife see Appendix 6a)

Perhaps the most intriguing request for burial appeared in the Will of Anne Pitney of Lamyatt in 1764: "First I Will and desire my Body may be decently interred in Lamyat Churchyard as near my late Husband as may be but not under the same Tombe." The reason why she wished to be near but not with her husband has been lost through time.

6

BURIAL OF THE DEAD: GENERAL

After a death had occurred the rituals in the period that followed were of supreme importance: it was the time when the various religious and social duties towards the deceased were performed, including the funeral itself. It marked the point at which all the transference of property rights, obligations and status within the community were made to the rightful heir. Above all, it provided the opportunity for group support of the bereaved. In return the latter would discharge all the expected duties of hospitality and, in the earlier part of the period, of charity to the poor.

As religious and cultural ideas changed and developed through the centuries, the emphasis placed upon these post-death rituals varied. The importance of the immediate family became much more dominant, which has led some historians to suggest that the reaction to death has been transformed from a community or group one to an individualistic one.

Wills from before the Reformation indicated that the deceased often left detailed instructions for the arrangements to be undertaken after their death, including for their own funerals. They would specify the requirement for prayers, masses, attendance of priests, scholars, and tapers or torches;

examples of which may be found in the Wills of men such as Richard Bruton and Sir John Fitzjames. Some men even ensured that their tombs were actually ready before their death. Such was the case of Richard Fitzjames, born at Redlynch and brother of John senior, and who died of the plague in January 1522. He was in turn Warden of Merton College, Oxford, Bishop of Chichester, then Rochester and finally London. He was also one of the founders of the Free School in Bruton, to which he left an endowment of at least £10. In his Will dated 11th April 1518 he was very precise: he desired his body to be buried "in the nave of my Cathedral Church of St Paule, London, under the altar of St Paul of my own foundation, under the tomb of marble lately erected and prepared by me."

Increasingly however the actual arrangements were entrusted to an executor or executrix, in the case of a surviving widow or daughter. In 1617 Sir Maurice Berkeley, for example, wished his body "to be layd upp in decent Christian burial accordinge to the discretion of my Executors." In 1660 Edward Norton hoped "to be decentlie Interred by my Executrix", as did William Day in 1678. In 1710 Robert ffry displayed the same confidence in his daughter Joan, "And I committ the care and management of my ffuneral to the prudence of mine Executrix." Thomas Tice alias Rogers was slightly more general in 1683, "And my bodie I desire may bee decentlie buried according to the discretion of those to whom the care of my funneral shall bee committed."

Although Samuel Brodripp was content in 1707 to leave decisions to his Executors, he was careful to add the proviso, "My funerall charges not to exceed ten pounds." Eleven years later William Mogg of Shepton Montague was even more precise in his directions to his executors in relation to his funeral expences: "that a Sume not exceeding fffifty pounds nor lesse than forty pounds be expended thereon."

Executors, as well as taking into account any directions for burial left by the deceased such as within the church or in the churchyard, also had to be aware of prevailing ecclesiastical requirements on interment and any local customs. As most rural areas did not have a specialist undertaker, often until well into the nineteenth century, (1) executors had to rely upon a range of local people, from the women who laid out the body to the carpenter or joiner who made coffins as one part of his trade. Once coffins had become more standard at funerals the Accounts of the Overseers of the Poor for Bruton show regular payments, such as in April 1764 carpenter John Clarke was paid 15s 0d for supplying coffins.

All the evidence indicates that for the overwhelming majority of the population there was considerable concern for the body after death and that it should have an appropriate burial. First, in the medieval period and well beyond, it was customary for a person to sit with the body overnight. As medical expertise was so limited there was always the fear that the person was not actually dead and so might revive. In addition if foul play was suspected the body was watched so that it could not be tampered with before the Coroner held an Inquest. In general, however, it was perceived as a mark of respect often undertaken by a member of the family. After the death of a pauper in June 1740 the Bruton Overseers paid, amongst other amounts, a halfpenny for "A Watch Candle to burn with Wm Walter." Revd. James Woodforde recorded in his Diary that on the death of his father in May 1771, "old Alice Stacy....begged most heartily to sit up with my Poor Father, all night, which she did with Christian speed." In fact in total some six women, whom he referred to as "wakers", sat with his father's corpse all night and to each he gave "Black Lamb gloves."

Secondly, to ensure that the deceased's wishes for burial were implemented fully, bodies were sometimes carried considerable distances, which in the days before transport improvements could be a difficult and arduous task. It was, however, one which was deemed important enough to be undertaken. For this to happen of course the person concerned had to possess some wealth and it is perhaps ironic that it was the poor who were more often buried in the consecrated ground which they knew well as they travelled far less than the wealthy.

Sometimes the distances involved were not considerable, for example, the Burial Register recorded that on 22nd August 1764 Miss Mary Cheek (sometimes written as 'Chicke') was brought from Castle Cary. Before the body was moved Revd. Woodforde and his father went to the Chicke's house "to attend poor Molly Chicke's corpse to her Grave at Bruton Church to be interred there..... We had Wine and Cake at Mrs Chicke's before we set forth for Bruton. The Lord grant that she may be eternally happy; she died like a faithful Christian." Once again for him a good death was an important factor and it is interesting to note that in this case the hospitality took place before the party set off for the interment in Bruton churchyard.

Other bodies were transported greater distances, for example, on 3rd February 1767 Mary Penny was brought from North Cadbury and on 31st March 1679 Jone Pavy had been "brought dead from Glasto." (*Glastonbury*) A glimpse of how such a journey could be undertaken may be found in the details which Revd. Woodforde recorded on the movement of the body of the five-year old son of Giles Francis to Castle Cary on 7th June 1772. "The child died at Bath owing to a kick in the groin by another lad. Giles works at Bath, and he and his son brought the child in a coffin upon their heads from Bath, they set out from Bath last night at 12." (2)

Instructions were sometimes written into Wills concerning the return of a body to a particular church. When Richard

Bruton knew that he was dying in London in 1417 he added a Codicil to his Will: "I will that my body be brought or carried as soon as possible after my decease from London to the said parish church of Bruton." Such a request may imply that in his case some embalming must have taken place as the journey may well have taken a week or more. Sir John Fitzjames also expected to be buried in the parish church of Bruton but recognised that he might not be in residence at Redlynch at the time of his death. He therefore made his arrangements accordingly, "To every parish churche through which my body shalbe caryed towards my burying 6s 8d and yf my body rest in any churche one night then to that church 20s."

In 1600 Sir Henry Berkeley hoped to be buried in Bruton parish church with the proviso, "if it shall plese God that I depart this life ther, or wthin an hundred myles therof, so as conveniently it may be conveyd thither." The death of Admiral William Berkeley in 1666 cost the family a great deal of money as after he was killed at sea his body was captured by the Dutch and taken to Holland. The family paid for it to be returned to England where it was buried in Westminster Abbey. After Sir Charles Berkeley, 2nd Lord Fitzharding, died in Whitehall in London on 12th June 1668 his body was brought back to Bruton and interred in the family vault on the 26th of that month.

In a Codicil to his Will in November 1757 the Hon. Charles Berkeley expressed his wish to "be buried in the Chancel of the Church of Brewton near my ffather and my Children who lie buried there." If he died "at any Great distance from Brewton" his exccecutors were given the discretion to select a different location but he added, "remembering however the preference which I desire to be given to the Chancel of Brewton Church." After his tragic death in his own ornamental pond at Bruton Abbey in 1765 his wish was fulfilled.

A small number of other men and women who died in Bruton wished to be buried elsewhere, for example, when George Bathin, gent., died on 9th December 1588 at the Hart Inn in the town his body was "carried to Loockam (*Luccombe near Minehead*) to be buried." Lucy Temple, the sister of Lady Berkeley and who resided for much of the time at Bruton Abbey, requested in 1733 that her body be placed in the vault with her mother and father in Mortlake Churchyard in London. Such a distance was short when compared with the journey undertaken by the body of John Evelyn's friend Mrs Godolphin, a family linked to the Berkeleys through marriage. Evelyn attended her funeral in London and recorded that the body was then to be taken "all the way to the foote of Cornwall, neere 300 miles, & then as honourably interred in the Parish Church of Godolphin."

On the other hand there were those who required just a decent Christian burial and so the place was unimportant. The Churchwardens of St. Martins-in-the Fields, London, recorded that they received 2d in 1591 when on September "ye xiij was buried John Celey of Bruton in ye Countie of Som'set cloth." (3) In 1506 Symon Grene directed "my body to holy grave wherever it pleases God to separate my soul from my body." Sir Maurice Berkeley took the same view in 1580, "And my bodye to be buried in the Churche where I shall happen to depart this transitorie life." In 1758 John Thomas expressed the wish to be buried in or near the parish church of Bruton but added, "if it should so happen I Should Die in or near The said parish or near it but if I Should Die any Distance from The said parish I Desire That I maie be Buried where it should so happen."

Third, if a person went missing then efforts were made to retrieve the body for burial. A deliberate search could be undertaken such as in the case of Susannah Johnson in November 1738 when the Overseers of the Poor paid 2s "for beer for the men that serched for Sn Jonson in ye River." When her body was recovered they paid 1s 10ds for "Washing the Corps & bringing her home", along with 6d for "Horsehire." The rest of her funeral arrangements with shroud, coffin and grave cost 5s 3d with 3s 6d for beer.

Fourth, a decent burial was considered so important that the local community was prepared to spend money on any strangers who died in their midst, albeit usually cheaply from the Poor Rates. Both the Overseers' Accounts and the Burial Registers for Bruton indicated that strangers were present in the town and buried if required, some nameless, others not. In October 1739 the Overseers paid 6s for "A coffin for a Man that died at T Robins", and in January 1741 for "A Coffin Shroud and buring a Man that died at Carys 16s 8d." In March 1780 John Duffet was paid 2s 6d "for Burying a Stranger." While in the eighteenth century the word 'stranger' was often used by the Overseers, in earlier periods the Burial Registers tended to use other phrases, such as, "3 May 1571 A poore walking boy." On 19th December 1588 "A walking woman's child" was interred. If possible a name was recorded, "29 July 1635 Evans Davie, a stranger" and "9 June 1637 Dennes Briant, an irish child." It was not always the case, "25 July 1672 A poore man, a traveller, buried", depending on the circumstances. On 12th January 1768 Revd. Woodforde recorded that he buried a man found dead in the snow. There was no identification and no one knew him. It was a very sad end for a minority of the population.

Finally, there was the expectation that after a death and before burial a corpse would be correctly and decently laid out or stretched. This procedure would ensure that as far as possible the body was in an appropriate state to be viewed by relatives, friends and neighbours who came to offer their sympathy and support to the bereaved. This task was usually undertaken in wealthier families by a paid nurse or a trusted family servant.

By the late eighteenth century there was a very detailed general procedure to be followed. The mouth was to be kept closed with a handkerchief or piece of clean cloth tied around the head, eyelids closed and limbs straightened. Next the body was washed all over with soap and water, usually under a sheet or blanket for decency and for the same reason a strip of cloth was bound around the body from waist to thigh. At the same time the orifices were blocked with cotton wool or clean rags. The body was then redressed, often in a white nightgown, smock or shirt, hair brushed and arms folded over the chest. At that point it was ready to be viewed and remained in that position until the time came for it to be enclosed in a shroud or placed in a coffin.

How far this exact procedure was followed by the relatives of poorer people cannot be determined with any degree of certainty. Clearly some action was evident, for example in November 1735 the Overseers paid 1d for "A Dram at stretching out Eliz Walter", and in January 1742 six and a half pence was paid for "A Candle & laying out Wm Truman." The usual rate for much of the eighteenth century was 2s 6d, such as on 15th March 1746, "Pd Mrs Thridgould for laying Mary Hill." This system was also extended to strangers as in October 1705 the Overseers paid 6d "to ye Women stretching out a dead Child a Stranger at Jane Phelps's."

Such preparations and the funeral itself were very important for the bereaved and the community as a whole as not only did it confirm that the person concerned really was dead and so all could share the loss, but also, as one historian has written, it provided "an opportunity for re-establishment of the social group, for a reinforcement of its life and unity." Daily life had to continue. (4) From the religious perspective a Christian funeral was believed to aid the soul's passage to eternal life and, particularly amongst the uneducated, the resurrection of the body was taken literally so it had to be well-prepared and intact. In some parts of the country the concept was taken so seriously that even any teeth which fell out during a lifetime, including milk teeth, were collected, preserved and eventually placed in the coffin with a person when he or she died.

As the time of the funeral approached the body was enclosed in a shroud. Wealthier families provided a sheet from their own supply of linen but the Overseers of the Poor would purchase one for paupers if necessary, for example in July 1681 the Bruton Overseers paid John Albyn 4d "for a Shroud for John Smith." Each shroud was tied at the top and the bottom and sweet smelling flowers or herbs, such as rosemary or bay, were often enclosed, no doubt helping to disguise unwelcome odours. As a number of these flowers and herbs were also present at weddings it has been suggested that they were used to symbolize the continuation of life in future generations.

As a move to protect the woollen industry an Act of 1678 stipulated that all burials were to be in woollen shrouds. "No corpse of any person was to be buried in any stuffe or thing other than what is made of sheep's wool only.......the Act shall be publiquely read upon the first Sunday after the Feast of St Bartholomew every year for seaven years next following after Divine Services." Needless to say such a measure was not universally popular:

"Odious! In woollen! 'twould a Saint provoke,
(were the last words that poor Narcissa spoke)
No, let a charming Chintz, and Brussels lace
Wrap my cold limbs, and shade my lifeless face." (5)

In their Accounts the Bruton Overseers kept a record of the number of burials in woollen and in 1679 paid 1s "ffor Entering the Affidavits for Burying in Woollens in this Book." In the first six years of the Act's operation there were 180 burials in woollen recorded out of a total of 292 actual burials.

In crisis years such as between 1728 and 1730 when there were 187 burials some 161 were in woollen. Such statistics did not necessarily indicate widespread disregard for the Act as in some cases the burial may have been in coffins without a shroud and others without any covering whatsoever.

There were however some members of wealthier families who deliberately chose to ignore the Act and so faced a financial penalty. A Justice of the Peace had to be informed and he sent an Order to the Churchwardens and Overseers or the Constable to collect a fine or distrain goods to the appropriate value, usually £5. The first person to defy the Act in Bruton seems to have been Robert Ludwell, a prominent local merchant and Governor of the Free School, who was buried on 20th November 1679. "Mr Ludwells mony beeing 50 shillings was given away to 50 poore people for beeing buried in lyning and the other 50 shilling was given to Mr Tho Ludwell who informed of the same."

When Henry the son of Mr Thomas Sampson was "buryed in Lining contrary to the Act of Parliament" in September 1692, a J.P. was informed by Ann Gane and Margaret Chinick, possibly women responsible for laying out the body, who jointly received the 50s. The information on Mrs Ann Drew in May 1695 was provided by Ezeckial More, who duly received his reward. (6) The receipt of half the fine provided a good incentive to impart the necesssary information but there is little surviving evidence of how extensive the practice was or whether it was possible for wealthy families to use any inducements to prevent such actions.

While burial in a shroud had been the most common practice in the medieval period and beyond, partly on the grounds of cost and partly to aid decomposition, from the mid-sixteenth century coffins were increasingly used and this trend was to gain momentum, especially amongst the wealthier members of the community, in the seventeenth century. Some churches even possessed a communal coffin to carry the corpse to the grave, but evidence for one in Bruton has not emerged.

Many people felt that burying a body in a coffin hid it from view and gave added protection if the grave was disturbed. For some in the community the provision of a coffin by the family was an indication of social status. In addition as not all bodies were buried at a suitable depth, there was a genuine concern about unpleasant smells and health matters as the body decomposed, especially if it was interred within the parish church.

It has proved impossible to determine how early and to what extent coffins were used in Bruton. Although many of the surviving Wills contained detailed arrangements for the testator's burial and specified where, none of them referred to the provision of a coffin. As the Berkeleys were being interred in the crypt under the chancel from at least 1581 it would seem reasonable to assume that their bodies were enclosed in a coffin of some kind. The first reference in the Overseers' Accounts was much later as it appears to be on 1st September 1694 when 7s 6d was "Payd to Joseph Smith for a coffin for Dorothy George." Underneath this entry was added in darker ink but by the same hand, "This is to be no precedent, the woman dying in Travel, & not to be buried without it."

During the next twenty years there were many references in the Accounts to the provision of shrouds but it was only from the 1720s that coffins were mentioned more frequently, for example, in December 1727 some 8s 6d was paid for a "Cofin and burying Chapman's wife." In December 1731 a slightly smaller sum of 7s 6d was paid for "a Cofin for Anne Seymore & Burying her." By the early nineteenth century the Overseers were paying a standard charge of 8s for an adult's coffin and 4s for that of a child.

Once in a shroud or coffin the body was carried to the church, in the former case presumably resting upon a solid object such as a plank of wood, usually by relatives, friends and neighbours. In the nineteenth century once the Wincanton Poor Law Union, which covered the Bruton area, was established, any pauper who died within the Union Workhouse in Wincanton was usually carried by other inmates to the town's parish churchyard and then, once that was judged to be full, to the new cemetery nearby. Towards the end of the century bodies could be returned to their own parish. The poor physical condition of the inmates involved in carrying the corpse did create problems and led to a contractor being employed. (7)

In the Victorian era it was not uncommon for the corpse of a wealthier and well-respected inhabitant to be followed to the church by a large procession of the townsfolk, many of whom would be wearing the appropriate black mourning clothes or some other black item. When Daniel Ward, the former owner of the Silk Mill died in February 1859, "All the shops were closed, and the funeral procession comprised all the leading tradesmen and others of the town, and the employees of the Silk Factory, at the head of whom walked the children of the National Schools, who have lost one of their truest and warmest friends." When the Vicar, the Revd. James White died in July 1868, there was a large procession of parishioners with at least seven other local clergymen in attendance "and immediately preceding the corpse, were the organist and members of the Church choir." The church itself "was filled in every part, even the children's galleries being crammed long before the commencement of the service." Some 200 people were said to have lined both sides of the road when Dr. Heginbothom was carried from Patwell House to the Church in June 1879. This crowd included Freemasons with black armbands and white gloves and the Foresters in mourning regalia.

A freemasons's funeral could entail a procession such as that of J.H.M. Balch, a solicitor, in March 1878. Although he lived in Bruton he was to be buried in the family vault at Brewham. Freemasons left their lodge-room and went to his house from where they escorted the body to Brewham Church where the service was conducted by one freemason, the Revd. M. Shackleton, and another Brother Hayter played the organ. As the body was lowered into the grave the brethren threw in sprigs of acacia, an evergreen considered sacred by the Hebrews, many of whose rites and ceremonies were revived by the freemasons. For them the acacia was a symbol of immortality and during the funeral service it was said, "This evergreen is an emblem of our faith in the immortality of the soul. By this we are reminded that we have an immortal part in us, which shall survive the grave, and which shall never, never, never die."

By the end of the century flowers in general had become an important part of the burial process. In June 1892, for example, when the body of Charles Welch was conveyed from Lamyatt to Milton Clevedon Churchyard it was reported that there were many wreaths so that "The funeral car was covered with rich floral tributes of love and respect to the deceased" and that the grave "was beautifully lined with moss and flowers." (8)

Bells remained important in spite of the attempts at the period of the Reformation to impose restrictions. Originally as a person neared death the passing bell would be tolled – usually nine strokes for a man, six for a woman and three for a child, followed by one stroke for each year of age. This happened at all hours of the day and night as the occasion demanded. "Ringing his knell" was a phrase frequently found in funeral expences in the Tudor and early Stuart periods although at exactly what stage was not specified. Certainly by the seventeenth century the older system seems to have faded away as the bell was generally rung just at the time of the actual funeral. "18th October 1673 ffor making Wm Allens grave and ringing the Bell 2s 0d", was a common type of entry in the Overseers' Accounts at that period and beyond.

This method still existed in the nineteenth century although by that time it did not seem to have met with universal approval. On one occasion the Rev. Stephen Hyde Cassan complained to a Churchwarden that the ringers insisted on ringing the bells after funerals and that many "respectable parishioners" disapproved of this practice. That his vicarage was so close to the west tower may have had some bearing on his complaints. Nothing appears to have been achieved by his efforts as at the time of the Revd. White's funeral it was reported, "The muffled peals from the tower spoke the worth of the departed." The same bell tolled not only for local inhabitants but also for the deaths of royalty and national figures. On 5th January 1853, for example, the Sexton, Joseph Gurney, was paid 2s 6d "for Toling the Bell on the day of the funeral of the Duke of Wellington."

In some parts of Somerset through the centuries it was not unusual for tenor bells to have appropriate inscriptions on them:

"I to the Church the living call,
And to the grave I summon all."
or
"I sound to bid the sick repent,
In hope of life when breath is spent."

It would appear that most coffins continued to be physically carried into Bruton Church until January 1889. In the previous year members of the Mutual Improvement Society had resolved to give some kind of testimonial to Dr. Stockwell as a result of all the instruction and training he had given to them. "The doctor, however, said he should take it as a personal favour if the parishioners would subscribe towards a wheel bier for the town, and he would accept that as a testimonial." This request was duly acted upon and it was reported that the new bier was first used in January 1889 at the funeral of a son of William Clarke junior of West End. (9)

While the corpse was in the church and carried to its grave it was usual for it to be covered with a pall or a burial cloth. In some areas the pall was placed over the corpse as it was taken from the house of the deceased to the church but there is no evidence for this practice in Bruton. St. Mary's possessed several burial cloths but it is not clear at what period each one was purchased. One was definitely in use long before 1764 as on 7th March of that year Thomas Bond was paid 1s 6d "for mending the old Black Burial Cloth." This attempt may not have been completely successful as two months later on 7th May the Churchwardens paid Mr Whitehead £2 2s 0d "for a new Black Burial Cloth." When the Churchwardens listed the "Implements of the Church" in 1785 they included, "Two Old Burial Cloths and one New One." All may not have been well by 1827 as in that year the Archdeacon of Wells ordered the Churchwardens to purchase a new Pall. Later in the nineteenth century there appeared to have been some refinements in the system as a distinction was made between the Pall and other Cloths used at the time of burial.

A funeral sermon was standard practice for the wealthiest or those of high rank in a community. Before the Reformation it was usually delivered during the mass, at a month's mind or even at an anniversary. Post Reformation it became part of the burial service itself, just prior to interment and remained as such until the eighteenth century. From that period there was some variation as the Church of England favoured delivery on the first Sunday after the funeral service whereas Protestant Dissenters preferred a few days after the burial, which might also be a Sunday. Revd. James While was buried on a Thursday and his funeral sermon was preached by Revd. John Creeser the following Sunday evening. After the minister of Bruton's Independent Chapel was buried in the grounds of the chapel in Wincanton on a Friday his funeral sermon was also on the following Sunday evening.

William Clarke, senior, aged eighty-eight died on a Thursday in late August 1899 and was buried the following Sunday "in a polished oak coffin with brass fittings." As a result in the evening service it was recorded that "appropriate hymns were sung, and the Vicar suitably alluded to the death of the deceased." As well as attending church regularly, Clarke was in fact that man who had supervised the restoration of St.Mary's Church in the early 1870s and this was felt to "be a lasting testimony to his skill and ability."

Funeral sermons followed a typical pattern: the first half, based upon a suitable text, reminded the congregation that life was short, death came to all, and that the future life would be eternal bliss for the good but eternal damnation for the wicked. The second half of the sermon was usually an account of the deceased, stressing his or her merits and virtues. One popular text, which was the one chosen for the Revd. White's funeral sermon was from Revelation 14 v.13, "Blessed are the dead which die in the Lord.....that they may rest from their labours." A second popular text was, "I have fought a good fight, I have finished my course, I have kept the faith. Henceforth there is laid up for me a crown of righteousness." (II Timothy 4 vv.7-8). Finally, "That ye sorrow not...for if we believe that Jesus died and rose again, even so them also which sleep in Jesus will God bring with him." (I Thessalonians 3 vv.13-14).

Just as in the pre-Reformation period money was given to priests to say mass and offer prayers for the souls of the departed, so in later times some clergy could significantly augment their income by preaching funeral sermons. While it may have generally been left to relatives or executors of Wills to make the actual arrangements, there appears to be only one surviving Will from Bruton which specifically requested a sermon and that was the Will of John Mogg which was made in February 1629, "Item I give to a preacher to preach my funeral sermon vjs viijd." Six years later Ursula, the widow of Hugh Sexey, who by this time was residing in Shaftesbury, also left money, "Item I give to the Preacher that shall preach at my ffunerall twentie shillings." She also gave 5s to each of "the men which shall carry mee to the Church to bee buried." On 12th August 1765 Revd. Woodforde noted that, "Mr Upcott desired me himself to preach a Funeral Sermon if he died." Two days later after his death Woodforde did so in Castle Cary Church and received 10s 6d. (10)

Finally the corpse in its shroud or coffin was lowered into its grave which was usually dug on an east-west alignment with the head placed at the west end, facing the rising sun and the direction from which the Resurrection was expected. In many places the traditional depth of a grave was six feet but it may well have been less than that in Bruton churchyard. The reason may relate to a fairly solid layer of stone or drainage problems, the latter being an issue which the Churchwardens had to address on several occasions. Alternatively the damp conditions here may have facilitated rapid decomposition at whatever depth.

In August 1840 a Vestry Meeting ordered "that the depth of a grave for an Adult be four feet and a half, and for a child two feet, but should the Sexton be required to dig a grave to a greater depth than four feet and a half that then he is to be paid one shilling per foot for such extra depth." This latter provision may have been made to allow two adults, such as a husband and wife, to be interred on top of each other rather than side-by-side. There were occasional double interments, such as on 21st August 1668 when it was recorded in the Burial Register that, "William Sweet & Joane his wife were both buried in one grave." There were many other occasions when a married couple followed each other rapidly to the grave, such as Thomas Ames on 18th December 1716 and his wife Edith on the 29th of the same month. On 28th May 1799 Mary Michell was buried and on 3rd June her husband, Revd. Edward Michell. On February 2nd 1895 Hannah White followed her husband Daniel to the grave as he had been buried on 10th January.

A popular verse which was once to be found in the churchyards of South Brewham, Pitcombe and Shepton Montague, carved on several of the gravestones of those who died in the period 1750 and 1805, recorded the double burials:

> Behold the Husband and the Wife,
> Now join'd in death as once in life,
> Whose Souls are now at rest we trust
> In the blest mansions of the just.

(For other examples see Appendix 6)

In the overwhelming majority of cases the grave was correctly dug and well-prepared but there could be occasional problems. On 7th March 1765 Revd. Woodforde recorded that he buried Master Shorte who had died the day before but "In the middle of the Burial Service I was obliged to wait while the Grave was made longer." Over two centuries later after pauper Edwin Lanning died in the Wincanton Union Workhouse in September 1896 his body was returned to his native parish of Charlton Horethorne for interment. His burial was delayed however when it was found that the grave was six inches too short as the Porter at the Workhouse had given the wrong measurements to the Master. (11)

After the burial it was customary for the mourners and other guests to receive some hospitality provided by the deceased's family. It was perceived not only as an act of remembrance towards the departed but also of support for the bereaved and a recognition that life had to continue. In some cases there was the necessity to demonstrate the on-going social status of the deceased and his or her heirs. In 1417 Richard Bruton directed that after his funeral the canons of Bruton Priory were to receive "drink and other necessities......as the custom there is." William Walter's funeral expenses in 1584 included provision "for the meat and drinke for the neighbourrers after they came home from the buryall." Fourteen years later Edward Collins' wife made a claim for "drinking for the neighbours after the burial." In 1625 Ann Marsh, widow of John Marsh, expended money "for meate and drinke spent at his said funerall." Thomas Albin's widow Tabitha regaled mourners with "Dakes Beere" after his funeral in 1641. (12)

When one of the Governors of the Free School was buried in 1626 some 3s 4d was paid "to Mr Cheeke for Bread & beere for the company." The provision of some refreshment also accompanied the burials of the inmates of Sexey's Hospital. In 1652, for example, the cost of the burial of William Smith was 10s, which included "Ringing, Shroude and making ye people to drinke." After the funeral of "Old Higham" 2s 6d was spent on "bread beere and Cheese."

The custom continued both in the Hospital and in Bruton in general but it was so commonplace that it was often not recorded or became covered within the general term, "funeral expenses." There were however occasional exceptions such as in November 1832 when after the death of James Clarke his widow Mary paid 19s 5d to John Clarke "for meat at the Funeral" and a further 8s 6d to "H. Ball for Bread." (13)

All that remained was for the funeral expenses to be paid and one study for Somerset as a whole has found that the median funeral costs were 10s in 1581, doubled by 1616 and rose to 40s in 1641. As only a few individual examples have survived from Bruton no such definitive statement may be made. The total cost of William Walter's funeral, which included shroud, bell, interment and refreshments was 22s, whereas that of John Dicer just four years later in 1588 was only 8s. In 1625 widow Ann Marsh faced funeral expenses of £2 10s 0d for her husband John. Tabitha Albin "laid out in and about the funeral of the said deceased to witt a coffin a Shroud making the grave, ringing the knell for Dakes beere and other necessary expenses in and about the funeral 1 10 0". These costs were very small when compared with the funeral expenses of Mrs Godolphin, which Evelyn estimated cost "her deare husbande not much lesse than 1000 pounds." (14)

By the nineteenth century the cost of funerals had risen sharply so that the funeral expences of James Garland, a Cordwainer, in August 1825 were assessed at £10 1s 0d, for spinster Susannah Cox the following year £19 17s 51/8d, for Thomas Raishley, also a Cordwainer, in April 1827 £6 10s 0d and for James Clarke in 1832 just over £24. (15)

Accounts such as those of the Bruton Overseers indicated that each aspect of a burial, laying out, shroud, coffin, grave digging and bell, had a set charge and that these varied through the centuries. In August 1840 the Vestry produced a comprehensive list of fees that included the charges for the depth of the grave.

"The following is a List of the said Fees

	Clerk			Sexton		
	£	s	d	£	s	d
For a Burial when the Pall is used		5	0		5	0
For a Burial when the Best Cloth is used		4	0		4	0

For a Burial when the Common	3	4	3	4
Cloth is used				
For a Pauper Burial when paid	1	6	1	6."
by Overseers				

In addition 6s 8d was to be paid to the Clerk and Sexton for tolling the Bell if a corpse was taken out of the parish for burial. Before this date the Clerk had received two-thirds of the fees and the Sexton one-third. The Vestry amended this list on 31st March 1864 to give the Sexton two-thirds and the Clerk one-third of the fees, presumably reflecting much more accurately the involvement of each person. (16)

7

BURIAL OF THE WEALTHY

a) Medieval

All the evidence for burials in Bruton in the later medieval period comes from Wills which were made by people who actually had something to bequeath. It follows therefore that these testators were amongst the wealthier members of the community. It is extremely unlikely that the mass of the inhabitants of the town received the same treatment in death. These wealthy men and women were in a position to ensure that at the time of their burial everything possible was undertaken for the benefit of their souls.

For the wealthy it was anticipated that there would be a series of services in Latin that commenced the evening before interment with 'the placebo' – the Vespers of the Office of the Dead, which in fact Sir John Fitzjames requested in 1538 should be said or sung everyday for a month after his burial. He left similar instructions for 'the dirige' – the Mattins of the Office of the Dead, which was normally said at any time after midnight. This could include Psalm 23, "The Lord is my Shepherd" in which many of the bereaved found comfort and near the end of this mass was reference to the living Redeemer and the bodily resurrection.

Before the interment there was the Mass for the Dead or Requiem Mass which included the plea, "requieum aeternam dona eis domine et lux perpetua luceat eis." ("O Lord, grant them eternal peace and let the everlasting light shine upon them.") The body was then interred, often after many mourners had departed as it was the health of the soul that mattered and not the decay of the body. The priest at the graveside pronounced the words of absolution, often written on a parchment scroll as well and this was placed on the corpse's breast. Holy water was sprinkled on the body twice and incense passed over it the same number of times. There was a prayer for a quiet sleep in the grave and then resurrection with all the saints. Finally the priest threw earth to form the shape of a cross on the body in the grave, committed earth to earth, ashes to ashes, dust to dust and commended the soul to God.

For those who could afford to pay priests, the funeral services were repeated seven days later and on the thirtieth day, 'the month's mind.' In 1506 Symon Grene left 6d to each chaplain and 1d to each scholar and poor person "being present at exequies and mass on the 30th day after my death." A variation was a 'trental', that is thirty masses to be celebrated either on one day or on thirty consecutive days. In 1471 Richard Dekyn left 2s 6d "to Sir John Cerne to say a trentall mass for me" and in 1496 Alianora Ede also left 2s 6d to each of three named priests "to celebrate Trentale for my soul." Finally the mass could be repeated on the anniversary of a death, known as the twelve-month mind or year obit. In 1517 Alice Brymmore directed that mass be celebrated for the souls of her husband, herself and those of the friends on the anniversary of her death for a period of fourteen years.

In the medieval period it was common for the Will of a wealthy person to go into some detail about the arrangements for his or her funeral. Of prime importance was ensuring the attendance of as many clergy as possible to say mass and pray for the soul. In 1417 Richard Bruton arranged for each canon present at his burial to receive 4d. Given the nature of his at times rather disreputable career with allegations of corruption, burglary and even murder, his soul needed all the help which he could generate. (1)

By 1510 the cost had risen as John Fitzjames senior granted "To each canon there being a priest 12d and to each canon not a priest 8d if they are willing to be present at my exequies and mass and to pray for my soul." His son, Sir John, specified the presence of fifteen priests to say masses. In 1457 Amice Gregory bequeathed 4d to each priest "serving in the said parish Church at my obsequies", and in 1526 Isabel Fitzjames ordered that £40 should be distributed "to prests and clerks and poorfolks the day of my burying."

Some of the wealthy were very insistent that there should be torches or candles, usually held by the poor, at their burial. Richard Bruton specified thirteen poor men "vestiti cum xiij Tapres in minibus portantibus." ("provided with clothes with 13 Tapers carried in their hands.") Sir John Fitzjames wanted twelve poor men, "every of theym having a Torche in their hands." In each case the symbolism of light and of the Apostles was present.

Many of the Wills of the wealthy inhabitants left detailed instructions about the exact location of their grave, usually within the church itself. For them it was consecrated ground with which they were familiar but as some of them tended to travel much more than the poor, they sometimes had to leave directions for their bodies to be transported long distances, such as Richard Bruton. Some like Richard Philippys in 1509 made a general request to be buried in the parish church while others such as John Gregory in 1429 were more specific as he wanted to be interred in the church next to Eleanor his deceased wife.

Some very precise locations were given, such as Richard Bruton in the Chancel, Alianora Ede in the middle of the church in front of the image of the Crucifix and Alice Brymmore before the Altar of our Lady. John Fitzjames decided upon "a certain arch on the south side of the holy water stoop there", and Richard Holmede in the south aisle by the font. As has already been discussed, location near altars and images of saints was considered very advantageous for the soul. There was, of course, nothing new in selecting a precise or prestigious location. The discovery of at least twelve Anglo-Saxon burials on the site of the Roman Temple on Lamyatt Beacon indicated that the cemetery was placed on or near a site that was known to have once been a sacred place. (2)

For those who were founders, patrons or benefactors of a parish church or a priory, there was the expectation that they would be favoured in death with a prime location within that priory or church. For them it meant that they were close to the canons and would receive the benefits of their prayers. After Bruton Priory was founded by the de Mohuns a number of members of the family were buried there, such as John who died between 1252 and 1254 in Gascony and whose body was brought back to England and interred in the Priory, while his heart was buried at Newenham Abbey before the High Altar. Nearly one hundred years later in 1342 another Sir John de Mohun left his body to the canons. When the Luttrells succeeded the de Mohuns as patrons they followed the tradition with John Luttrell buried in the Priory in 1430. (3) As the de Montacute family also endowed the Priory, at least two members of their number found a resting place there, Sir Simon in 1317 and Sir William, who made his Will in 1319 in Bordeaux.

The burial of patrons in or near a priory or church provided status and a sense of tradition for that institution, especially if the person concerned was of local, regional or possibly even of national importance. The desire to possess such a body could lead to unfortunate actions. It appeared that another member of the de Mohuns, also named John but this time of High Ham in Dorset, on his deathbed in 1221 gave instructions that he wished to be buried in Salisbury Cathedral. As his body was being transported there it rested overnight in Bruton Priory and the canons took it upon themselves to bury it there. The Bishop of Salisbury was furious and eventually the Prior and Convent made a public written apology and undertook to return the body or such part of it as remained. (4)

As John FitzJames, senior, was able to request burial within the priory church on his death in 1510, it implies that at that period he was a significant benefactor of the Priory. In his Will in 1429 John Gregory bequeathed a gown "with the livery of the Priory of Bruton " to his servant Thomas Welles which suggests that he had been admitted as a lay brother by the canons for his generosity and so there would haved been no problem honouring his desire to be buried alongside his first wife in the parish church. There were other benefactors who had been admitted as lay brothers such as William Baily als Rawlyns who died in Wareham, and left "To the house of Brueton whereof I am brother 40s." In September 1468 Prior John Henton agreed to perform various services of commemoration for Hugh Sugar, the Treasurer of Wells Cathedral, who was admitted "into their spiritual confraternity." Exactly how much Sugar gave to the Priory was not specified but probably amounted to a signifciant sum as at the same time he gave £40 to the abbot of St Augustine's Abbey in Bristol.

The wealthy were prepared to commit large sums of money to the day of their burial. Considerable amounts were expended to ensure a suitable attendance of priests, canons, scholars, local inhabitants, friends, neighbours and the poor, the latter in expectation of food and drink as well as alms. John Gregory, for example, requested that 100s be given to them and Isabel Fitzjames £40. For the fortunate few there was the possibility of black cloaks or other black clothes. Unfortunately no precise figures may be attributed to Bruton as men like Richard Bruton and Richard Holmede gave money to every canon or monk in a whole range of monastic institutions but did not specify the numbers that were actually involved in each. The Luttrell Accounts indicated that the family was prepared to spend 33s 3d in Bruton in 1431 to celebrate the first anniversary of the death of Sir John Luttrell. (5)

For those who had the money a permanent memorial could be arranged. Richard Bruton not only wanted to be buried in the Chancel but also ordered that a marble stone should be placed above his body carved with the effigy of a high-ranking priest, "cum ymagine sacerdotis superius sculpto." The word "superius" may also be translated as "abovementioned" so it was just possible that Bruton envisaged the carving as a representation of himself.

b) Post Reformation

The Reformation period and the century or so that followed witnessed a number of changes in burial rituals. Not only did the Edwardian Prayer Book abolish prayers for the soul and significantly limit what remained, such as removing the Holy Communion during the funeral service in 1552, but also it translated these services into English. For the first time many ordinary people would have had a much clearer idea of what was being said and actually happening. The priest met the corpse at the entrance to the churchyard and conducted a short service which included a reading from I Corinthians 15, centred on the resurrection of the body in a transformed state, "But we shall all be changed, In a moment, in the twinkling of an eye, at the last trump: for the trumpet shall sound, and the dead shall be raised incorruptible, and we shall be changed." (vv.51-2)

Such alterations meant that Protestant funerals were normally completed in one day.

Reflecting the Puritan ideas of the time, in 1645 the 'Directory' stipulated that while the corpse was to be "decently" attended to the grave, there was to be no praying, reading or singing going to or at the grave. While this format was often retained by later Non-Conformists at their burials, the 1662 Book of Common Prayer allowed the Church of England to revert to the pre-Civil War system.

It is very clear from the surviving Bruton Wills that there were a number of changes taking place in burials there. First, there was a pronounced tendency to specify burial in the churchyard or "cymitorie" as Thomas Walter called it in January 1544. This trend may be found in the majority of Wills prior to the Restoration in 1660. A smaller number, however, such as John Plimpton in 1554, Agnes Plumley in 1560 and Joane Sampson in 1648 wished to continue the practice of being interred within the parish church. So too did Elizabeth Fitzjames in 1545 but in her case it was to be buried by her late husband.

Second, from at least the 1620s more and more testators in their Wills left the matter of the funeral arrangements to their executors, "to be buried in the Church or Churchyard of Brewton aforesaid by the discreation of my Executor", as William Hellier expressed it in 1624. Third, and exactly at the same time, the use of the words, "And my Body I committ to the Earth from whence it was taken" became standard in virtually all Wills throughout the seventeenth century. A small number such as James Plympton in 1613 and Alice Hill in 1640 specified that they wished, "my body to be buried in Christian burial."

A fourth change that became evident in the mid-sixteenth century was for very wealthy families to create a family vault.

In addition to providing greater privacy and the avoidance of disturbance, there was a social status element as well. The surviving evidence would suggest that the system was initiated in Bruton by the Berkeley family, but when and how far it was copied by other local families is impossible to determine. In his Will made in 1600 Sir Henry Berkeley ordered "my body to be bureyd in my parishe Church at bruton in the vawlt wch I made for my father." As his father, Sir Maurice, died in 1581 this would seem to date alterations to the crypt under the chancel to that time. There is, however, no record of Sir Maurice's interment in the Burial Register, probably as this was one of the periods when it was not being kept accurately. In 1617 Sir Henry's widow, Dame Margaret, also expressed the wish, "to be buried in the vaulte within the parisshe Churche of Bruton."

Subsequent generations of the family were interred in the vault throughout the seventeenth century, such as Charles, second Lord Fitzharding on 26th June 1668 and his wife, Lady Penelope, less than a year later on 29th April 1669. Maurice, third Lord Fitzharding expressed the wish to be "decently interred with my Ancestors in the Church of Brewton" and this was accomplished on 10th June 1690. It was presumably some of these family members, along with other remains, which Charles Berkeley removed in 1743.

There was some variation in the speed of burial, for example, on 6th December 1612 the Burial Register recorded that, "John Chicke died upon Scte Andrewe's day in the morning & was buried the s.(*same*) day." On 6th May 1606 Johan the daughter of William Lane was interred, "being borne & bapt: the day before." In her Will in 1617 Dame Margaret Berkeley expressed the wish that she be buried "the next daye after my Deacease." On the other hand for others there could be a delay, especially if they died some distance from Bruton, for example, Sir Maurice Berkeley died on

1st May 1617 and was interred on the 8th of the same month, just over two months after his mother. Perhaps the most unusual was an entry in the Burial Register in 1663, "Mrs Sedbury was buried June 1, being kept a yeare & halfe unburied." No explanation was given.

Aristocratic families could expect Heraldic Funerals which were controlled by the College of Arms or in the days of Elizabeth I by the Queen herself or Lord Burghley. They were considered to be important as they symbolized the continued cohesion, continuity and strength of the aristocracy after the death of a prominent member. As the necessary detailed and complex preparations had to be made such funerals occurred a while after death, bodies therefore had to be embalmed and organs removed. It was customary for a Herald of the College of Arms to be in attendance and the overall result was that they could become very expensive.

With their aristocratic connections various members of the Berkeley family were likely to have been considered for such a funeral, although because of cost and the dislike of being cut open some, such as Dame Margaret, gave detailed instructions about where and when they wished to be buried in order to avoid this happening. One prominent member of the family did have an heraldic funeral in 1560, "The xij day of Marche was bered at Dytton my lade Barkeley, the wyff of Ser Mores Barkelay, knight, with a pennon of armes and a iiij dosen of skochyons, and a Harold of armes, master Rychemond." The deceased was Katherine, the first wife of Sir Maurice Berkeley of Bruton and daughter of Lord Mountjoy.

As such funerals became more and more extravagant and elaborate, there was something of an aristocratic reaction to them so that in the seventeenth and eighteenth centuries there were some significant changes. It was certainly the case that there were those within the aristocracy who did not like the concept of embalming and wanted a quicker and cheaper burial which placed the emphasis upon genuine mourners being present, rather than attendance for political consider-ations. Some of the aristocracy turned to nocturnal funerals, the darkness of which could symbolize death but with the flickering candles providing the concepts of light and hope.

As early as 1626 Dame Elizabeth Berkeley wished "to be buried in the Churche next adioyning the place of my decease And the solemnities thereof to be performed in all private mann." When Charles, Lord Fitzharding, was buried on 26th June 1668, the Clerk recorded in the Burial Register that he "was between 12 & one of the clock in the night after a sermon preached by Mr John Randall, then Minist: of Brewton, buried in the vault in the Chancell in a coffin of lead." In April of the following year there was an almost identical entry for his wife, Lady Penelope, except her service was an hour earlier. Nearly one hundred years later the Hon. Charles Berkeley directed "that my ffuneral shall be performed in the most private manner and with the least Expense that decently may be."

In 1668 John, 1st Lord Berkeley of Stratton purchased the estate of Twickenham Park from Henry Martin. It contained a large house which four years before the Hearth Tax Returns had rated for thirty-four hearths. It was an ideal location for a courtier's country estate: a few miles from the centre of London but linked to Westminster and other key locations by the River Thames which flowed past it. Lord John maintained a family pew in the parish church of Twickenham and it was in a vault there that he was interred in 1678. The year before his brother, Sir William from Virginia, had died in Berkeley's mansion in Berkeley Square and he too was brought to this church with his body apparently tightly encased in lead and buried first in the middle of the chancel and then the following year placed in the vault with his brother. In 1785 the antiquarian Edward Ironside recorded, "on opening this vault about a year ago... the body of Sir William Berkeley was found lying on the ground without a coffin cased in lead exactly fitted to the shape of the body, shewing the form of the features, hands, feet, and even nails; and appears to be beat firmly to it, and looks like a figure in armour." (6)

c) 1700 and beyond

Most of the Protestant funeral practices continued into the eighteenth century and beyond. For many of these believers it was their own way of confronting the fact of death and preparing for their own. In the sharing of grief they found considerable solace as they were discharging a duty. For the bereaved it acknowledged a continuing relationship with the living and confirmed acquaintances. In that context it remains surprising that it was rare for women from the wealthier classes to attend burials until well into the Victorian period. This was ostensibly on the grounds that for a decent burial mourners must be able to control their grief at funerals and behave with fortitude, and it was felt that most women could not do so. Funerals became therefore a time to demonstrate self-control and act bravely.

It is very noticeable that in eighteenth and nineteenth century Wills from Bruton no mention was made of funeral and burial arrangements, a marked contrast from pre-Reformation days. As members of some families, such as the Smarts, Goldesbroughs and Pavys were buried within the Church and others such as the George's in the churchyard, it is likely that the wishes of the departed were discussed with family or executors at some time prior to death. If a family vault had been created then it would be the natural assumption that all members of the family would find their last resting place within it.

In a small number of cases testators made a specific request, such as Lucy Temple in 1733, "My Body I desire may not be opened but put in lead and buryed privately and decently without Velvet or Linnen." Although she came from an aristocratic background, she clearly wished to avoid being embalmed and having an extravagant public funeral. Peter Ames the elder, a yeoman from Wyke Champflower, in 1748 simply wished, "my body to be decently Interred" and left the arrangements to his executors. A similar request was made by Nicholas Everatt in 1797, with responsibility also passed to his executors. In 1823 Richard Biggs specified that, "my body may be decently interred in the Church Yard of Bruton."

Various members of the Berkeley family continued to be interred in their vault in the eighteenth century: 23rd November 1704 Anne, Lady Fitzharding; 28th March 1741 William, 4th Lord Berkeley of Stratton, some four days after his death. On 12th April 1744 Lady Jane Berkeley's coffin was added and on 5th August 1765 that of the Hon. Charles Berkeley, the man who just over twenty years before had been responsible for its clearance. One female relative, Lady Elizabeth Egerton was also interred on 15th November 1765, seven days after her death at Bruton Abbey. She was a cousin of Lord John and the daughter of the 1st Earl of Portland.

Finally on 26th April 1773, nine days after his death, the lead coffin of John, 5th Lord Berkeley of Stratton, joined the rest. In his Will made the previous year he had expressed the wish that if he died in or near London he should be buried in Twickenham Parish Church close to his mother and two sisters but if he died in or near Bruton he should be interred there. As he died in the Abbey Mansion it was the latter. In addition he stated that, "It is my express will and desire that in which ever place I shall be buried my funeral shall be performed in the most private manner and that no Monument or Inscription whatsoever be placed over my poor Remains." He was clearly following the Berkeley tradition started in the previous century. He was the last of the direct male line of this branch of the family and with his death their various titles became extinct and the connection between the Berkeleys and Bruton was broken.

William, Lord Berkeley, appeared to have been enthusiastic about Latin phrases and so may well have been responsible for many of these which were recorded in and around Bruton Abbey in the eighteenth century. He directed that the Berkeley of Stratton family motto should be engraved on the plate on his coffin: "Pauca Suspexi Pauciora Dexpexi." (7)

For the wealthier members of the community who were not aristocratic but of the "middling sort", gifts of black items and wearing them became particularly fashionable at funerals in the eighteenth century. Revd. Woodforde included references to this custom in the area, for example, when his mother was buried in a vault in the chancel of Ansford Church in February 1766 he noted that, "We had all Crepe Hatbands and Cloaks." When his father was interred five years later in May 1771 he recorded that the Pall Bearers had "black silk Hatbands and shammy gloves", the under-bearers "black Lamb gloves", and the Clerk "a black silk Hatband." As was the custom, his father's servant, William Corpe received a gift of "a black crape Hatband and buckles and a black broad cloth coat and waistcoat given him by us."

Revd. Woodforde himself was often given black items when he officiated at funerals, such as the burial of Thomas Roach of Bruton who died of smallpox in September 1768, "I had a black silk Hat band & a pr of black Gloves sent me for burying him by his good Brother." Three years earlier in November 1765 he had received, when burying a Mr Roach in Castle Cary, "a silk Hatband and a Pair of gloves", although he did not specify the colour. More unusual was an entry in his Diary for 29th January 1765, "Mr John Penny sent me a small Plumb Cake and a pair of White Gloves this Morning - I buried his little Maid this Afternoon." (8)

The expectation throughout the eighteenth and nineteenth centuries was that the deceased should be buried well, that all the formalities and customs should be observed, including attendance, condolence letters, and sympathy expressed. On 18th June 1901 Josiah Jackson buried "our dear Annie", his second wife. He was clearly very pleased that, "Many friends came here and many met us in the Road. Beautiful wreaths of Flowers were sent....and a lot of respect and sympathy was shown & given to us." On the other hand Revd Woodforde was appalled at the way the funeral arrangements for his sister Jane of Cole were conducted by her son-in-law in December 1798, "None of her Relations invited to attend her to her last home. No Pall-Bearers & also even a Pall partly refused." (9)

8

BURIAL OF THE POOR

To discuss and analyse the burial of the overwhelming majority of the inhabitants of Bruton is extremely difficult as, being predominantly poor, they have left little written evidence. While their age at death and some of the likely causes may be available the actual methods by which they were committed to the earth through the centuries remain elusive. What is certain was that they did not find a place within the church itself: theirs was the ground outside, often in a shallow grave, unmarked except for a short time by a small green mound. As some labouring families did become more prosperous they could afford a permanent marker, at first a simple wooden cross, a handful of which were still to be seen in the churchyard in the mid-twentieth century, and later still by a very plain headstone with no elaborate carvings, just their name and dates, possibly a religious text and often the work of a local stonemason. Many of these headstones seem to have been made from inferior Keinton stone which weathered badly and flaked extensively.

It must be hoped that through the changing times the priests, ministers and curates who said the masses, prayers and read the burial service for the wealthier in the community, did the same for the poorer inhabitants of the town. The bereaved that the poor left behind needed the same support at the graveside as their wealthier counterparts, perhaps even more as they often faced a very uncertain future, especially with the death of the main breadwinner.

a) Help from the Parish

For certain groups, however, it is possible to piece together a more complete picture. The first of these were the paupers, the poorest of all, as they frequently received help from the Overseers of the Poor. In addition these parish officers in exceptional circumstances could give assistance to those who were poor but who normally managed to remain independent of the official Poor Law system (1)

As for the wealthy, the initial process for the poor was stretching or laying out the deceased and the Overseers could make a contribution towards this, although the amounts granted varied significantly. In the first twenty years of the eighteenth century 6d was the usual amount:

"1711 May   Paid for laying out John Orams   0   6
              widow
 1719 Dec.   Paid for laying out Joan George   0   6."

By the middle of the century women such as Mrs Thridgould and Mrs Butler were regularly receiving 2s 6d for this process:

"1746 March 15   Pd Mrs Thridgould for laying   2   6
                  Mary Hill
 1752 May 23   Pd Mrs Butler for laying   2   6."
                  Sarah Mundy as usual

In the nineteenth century the amount had risen to 3s 0d, for example, after his death in September 1819 William Meade's wife was paid that amount for laying him out.

The corpse of the poor person was also enclosed in a shroud and there were many examples of this in the Overseers' Accounts: in December 1719 "paid for a Shroud for Joan George 4 0." Frequently, however, the actual cost of the shroud was not identified as a separate item but linked with others, for example,

"1658	ffor a Shroud & burying of Edw Loveless	6	6
1726 Nov	John Highams shroud and burying	6	6
1730 Nov	Ryals shroud and for Burying him	7	0."

The number of purchases of shrouds indicated that not only was a decent burial provided for a pauper but also that the Overseers did not possess just one shroud in which the body of each dead pauper was enclosed while in the church and which was then removed at the graveside and reused.

With one exception which the Overseers themselves did not wish to set a precedent, references to the provision of coffins for paupers began in the eighteenth century. It was probably at that stage that there was increasing concern about the nature of the decomposition that occurred. The initial cost of an adult pauper's coffin was 6s which increased to 8s in the early nineteenth century, and that for a child was 4s.

| "1739 Nov. | A coffin for a Man that died at T. Robins | 6 | 0." |

This expenditure probably related to an entry in the Burial Register for 3rd November 1739 "A poor man, stranger." The custom of a decent burial even for a stranger still existed.

"1804 Feb 2	For Mary Creeds Coffin	8	0
1805 Dec 24	For Elizabeth Singars Coffin	8	0
1806 Feb 2	For John Hoars Child Coffin	4	0."

It would seem that in some instances when a family was probably not completely destitute the Overseers would make a contribution but not pay the whole amount, for example,

"1694 Ap. 14   Towards the ffunerall   4   0
               of Mary Ames
    1711 May   Paid towards a Coffin for   4   0."
               Orams widow

The funerals of children were clearly much cheaper, for example, in July 1742 when the Overseers paid 11s for a coffin, shroud and for burying adult pauper Anne Hill, it cost them 6s for the same items for Martha Ames, a child, and in her case with the provision of beer. When Martha Batt's infant child was buried in February 1740 it cost in total 4s. Much earlier in 1686 William Wornall had received a contribution of 1s "to help bury his Child." This was probably Grace Wornall, a child, who was interred on 21st March 1686.

As in the case of Anne Hill, many of the eighteenth century entries were for a composite amount, such as

"1749 Ap 29   A coffin Shroud Beer & Burying   10   6."
              Robt Pope

A few entries gave a greater breakdown;

"1719 Dec   Paid for layng out Joan George   6
            Paid for a Shroud for Joan George   4   0
            Paid for burying Joan George   2   6."

A more unusual entry occurred in April 1740,

"A Shroud 10d An Extraordinary Large Coffin   11   4."
for Jn Dibbings 8s & Burying Him 2   6

In this instance it does appear to have been a remarkably cheap shroud.

The Overseers also paid for the grave to be dug by the Sexton, the corpse inserted and the grave filled in again:

"1686 Aug   ffor burying Wid ffezzard   2   6

1711 May   Paid for burying John Orams widow 2   6."

This amount seems to have been a fairly standard charge in the late seventeenth and eighteenth centuries and which may also have included ringing the bell:

"1673 Dec 13	ffor making Wm Allens grave and ringing the bell	2	0
1684	For ringing and making Robt Parkers grave	2	6
1694	Payd Wm Ames for making a grave and ringing for Joane Pawley	2	6
1771 Sept	Didging the Grave and ringing the Bell for Cabel's wife	2	6."

As the 1840 list of charges already cited indicated, by that period the whole process had become much more expensive, although a pauper's funeral still remained cheaper.

Just as for the wealthy, a bell was rung for the poor and there were references to such ringing from the moment the Overseers' Accounts began in 1653. Unfortunately there was no indication at what stage this occurred, although in July 1804 there is just one reference to the Passing Bell. Before the Reformation this bell had been rung as a person lay dying. There was also the knell which was rung just after death and then a bell at the time of burial. As many of the references in the Accounts are linked with the digging of a grave, it would seem most likely that for the poor in Bruton a bell was rung just at the time of the actual interment.

The Overseers seemed to have been quite generous as most of the entries for burials indicate that beer was provided:

"1661   Item for beere when Peter Walters child   1   6."
         was buried

In 1686 for widow Elizabeth ffezzard's burial the Overseers also spent 1s 6d but on this occasion it was "ffor washing and beer for her ffunerall." This beer was not a celebration but for the bearers, for example, at the funeral of Elizabeth Walter in November 1735 some 3s 6d was allowed for "Beer for the Barrers" and the same sum in April 1737 for "Beer for the Barers" of Ann White. Throughout the eighteenth century one of the commonest entries relating to burials was, "A Coffin, Shroud, Beer & burying..." There is no evidence from Bruton that any money was provided for any food or drink for the bereaved or for those attending a funeral, as did occasionally occur elsewhere.

The Overseers of the Poor maintained their role until 1834 when the Relieving Officers of the new Poor Law Union super-seded them in granting relief. The position of the former within the community had been crucial in providing aid to the poorest in their time of bereavement and the numbers who benefited increased through the years, especially in the eighteenth century, although as this was a century when the population of Bruton rose significantly, in percentage terms there was probably much less of an increase. During the period for which Overseer's Accounts exist for the town, the cost of pauper funerals rose markedly, from as little as 4s to 6s in the 1660s to 10s 6d a century later for the whole process and to 8s for the coffin alone in the early 1800s. It is important to stress however, that while these costs fell upon the ratepayers, they represented a very small fraction of the Overseers' total disbursements.

A pauper's funeral was cheap and basic but it was decent, it showed respect for the dead and was in keeping with the Christian precepts operating at particular times. In at least the nineteenth century some of the poor considered such a funeral to be shameful and tried to save during their working life to avoid such a perceived fate. It is however sometimes difficult to discover how far this idea was one promulgated by the Victorian middle class which they reflected back to the poor to encourage habits of thrift, and how far it was a matter of genuine concern to the really destitute. The reality of course could be different as for example in a three year period between 1862 and 1864 out of a total of 104 funerals conducted in Bruton Church some sixty-eight were classed as pauper and paid their 3s each. It was nevertheless the case that towards the end of the century, more and more bodies of those who died in the Wincanton Union Workhouse were removed by relatives and friends for burial: five in the 1870s, fourteen un the 1880s and seventeen in the 1890s. This was however out of a total number of deaths there of nearly 600 in the last thirty years of the century so represented no more than 6%.

b) The poor of Sexey's Hospital

The second group of the poor for whom evidence survives were the fortunate ones who were housed in the Hospital of Hugh Sexey or who received a regular pension from the Visitors. From the early seventeenth century Sexey, a native of Bruton who pursued a successful career in London, including being appointed one of the Auditors of the Exchequer for James I, had housed some poor families, including elderly tenants, in cottages on the north side and at the western end of the High Street. In 1616 he had transferred most of his property to twelve Trustees and after his death three years later they resolved to build an almshouse or Hospital to house twelve elderly inmates, a number which rose to twenty-eight by 1815. Their intention to include twelve boys, increased to fifteen in 1822, to be educated and then apprenticed was delayed until the 1660s. By the 1870s the apprenticeship scheme was no longer considered appropriate and so it was amended to provide girls with domestic training in preparation for domestic service and surplus cash devoted to other educational projects. (2)

The benefits for the young people admitted to the Hospital, particularly for the boys, were enormous. They were clothed, fed, educated, trained and then apprenticed. The hardships of their lives were mitigated and many lived to be successful employees and also employers. Not all of them of course avoided the illnesses or death that afflicted so many of their age group, for example, in 1662 the Visitors "paid for burying one of the boyes 12s 6d." Twenty-two years later on 20th February 1684, "John Coles, a Lad of ye Almeshouse" was interred in the churchyard. In December 1825 they paid £1 3s 0d for a Coroner's Inquest on the body of John Brown and a further £2 3s 1d for "the Funeral Expences of John Brown one of the School Boys. " He was in fact buried on 30th November aged thirteen. (3)

For the elderly who were admitted to the Hospital there were similar benefits with clothes in the form of the Hospital's livery, warmth with a coal allowance and blankets, and a small sum of cash each week in a room of their own. Once they were admitted, provided that they did not break any of the rules and regulations, such as becoming intoxicated, they were guaranteed their room for the rest of their lives. If they became too ill or too feeble to look after themselves properly help was provided. In addition one of the elderly female inmates always served as a nurse. In 1652 the Visitors granted 5s 6d to William

Smith "in his sickness & pay for one to attend him" In 1892 the Master of the Hospital requested that as a result of the Medical Officer's Report, Ann Eaton should be moved to a larger room and have a nurse provided as she "was not in her right mind." She was eventually interred aged seventy-six on 28th December 1894. In February 1895 the Visitors agreed to "allow a sum of not more than 2/6 a week, for an assistant to help look after Martha Young", but she died that month aged 100 years and three months. A similar attendant was arranged for Miriam Williams aged eighty-one in 1899, as she "was very ill and physically incapable" and she lived until 26th January 1900.

The result of these beneficial conditions was that many of the elderly within the Hospital lived to a significant age. The 1841 Census, for example, indicated that the thirteen old men then resident had an average age of seventy-three, with Isaac Coles and Thomas Parker both aged ninety, and that the twelve old women had an average age of eighty-two. Included amongst the females was Mary Biss who when she eventually died on 15th January 1846, was just a few days short of her 108th birthday, "having been born 2nd Feb. 1738. Up to the period of her decease she retained her faculties, and until very recently attended the daily Chapel."

Only occasionally did the Burial Registers indicate that a person being buried was a resident from the Hospital, but in two periods between July 1869 and July 1879 and November 1892 to November 1902 such information, along with ages, was included. It showed that of thirty-seven inmates of the Hospital buried in the churchyard, twenty were on their seventies, fourteen in their eighties and one over one hundred. When Charlotte Amor died on 9th November 1909 she was eighty-seven years of age and had been a resident for twenty-eight years, and it was also noted that her brother, Edmund Williams, was still there aged ninety-one. (4)

Death of course did finally arrive and was a commonplace in such an institution, for example, of the twelve old people who received their allowance in the first week in September 1638, two were dead before the Deed of Incorporation bearing the inmates names was signed on 10th December of the same year.

Their burial arrangements followed the same procedures as those of other poor people but were rather more generous. A shroud was provided, such as in May 1662 "for a shroud for Old Higham 5 0", and then, "pd for making the grave & Ringing the Bell 4 0." One important difference was that the Visitors allowed a small amount of money for food and drink after the funeral, presumably for the other inmates in their somewhat enclosed community. When William Smith was buried in 1652 the payments included money for "making ye people to drinke." On the death of Old Higham arrangements were made "for bread beere and Cheese at ye ffunerall."

The cost of the funeral was borne by the Hospital and the surviving Accounts from the 1650s to 1680s indicate that it was generally 10s, for example, that of William Smith in 1652,

"And for his burial, in Ringing, Shroude and making ye people to drinke   10   0."
"1663 pd for Burying Old goody White   10   0."

The funerals of "Old Tabor" and "Old Buffin" cost the same in the mid 1670s. Just over a century later the funeral expenses of men such as William Sweetman and Henry Godfrey were 12s 6d. Between the years 1816 and 1822 it was reported that the funeral expenses averaged £4 3s 51/2d a year. (5)

As the Hospital had its own Chapel it is reasonable to assume that through the centuries all or part of the burial service was conducted there. In addition as the Chapel was surmounted by a bell some of the ringing may have been internally arranged but as payments were made regularly for ringing some of it may also have occurred at the parish church.

The Hospital possessed its own burial cloth or pall in the same distinct blue that the inmates wore. While the pall may have existed from the earliest days of the institution, the first definite reference to it occurred in an Inventory of 1704 when Robert Elliott was installed as the Master, "One Blue Burying Cloth, 2 Callico-sheets, 2 Linen Sheathes thereunto belonging." The distinct pall was still in use at the beginning of the twentieth century as it was reported in July 1907 when Elizabeth Farrant aged eighty-two was buried, "The quaint pall belonging to the institution was used at the funeral. It is of dark blue with the letters 'H.S.' in white." It must have been an impressive sight if it was used to cover the coffin on its journey from the Hospital to the churchyard." (6)

c) The role of Friendly Societies

The third source of evidence for the burial of the poor is derived from the Friendly Societies which existed from the eighteenth century. A number were formed in Bruton and in the surrounding villages from about 1760 and their rules and regulations contain many similar provisions. One Bruton Friendly Society, based in the Blue Ball Inn and which had been established in 1818, required all its members to pay 1s on the death of another member and the same was the case of the Shepton Montague Friendly Society founded in 1853, which also required the payment of 1s on the death of the wife of a member. In both instances the money went towards the funeral expenses. The North Brewham Society founded in 1828 was slightly different in that it paid two guineas towards the funeral expenses and required that each member contribute 1s which was paid to the widow and children. In every case the money was not paid in the event of suicide. (7)

When it came to the time of the burial of a member there was a large public demonstration of support in the form of a procession. Although the Independent Order of Odd Fellows in the Manchester Unity tended to attract wealthier labourers, artisans and craftsmen because of its level of fees, its funeral activities were typical. When a member, William Vickers aged thirty, was buried on 30th December 1843, the other members of the Order, "resolved to pay their last tribute of respect to his memory, and to accompany his remains to their last resting place in public procession." About fifty members from Bruton and the district met at their headquarters in the Old Bull Inn in Patwell Street, "attired in deep mourning, wearing black sashes and gloves, and aprons trimmed with black ...proceeded to the residence of the deceased, and formed in procession."

The procession was headed by the Lodge officials and then all the members in pairs, followed by the corpse and the friends of the deceased with two Lodge members at the rear. After the Revd. White had read the funeral service in the parish church, the members formed a circle around the grave and "Brother Parfitt, the Secretary of the Loyal Brue Lodge.....delivered with much effect the impressive and sublime funeral oration of the Order." They then accompanied the relatives back to the house and returned to the Old Bull Inn. In the afternoon all members attended the church again where the Revd. White preached a sermon based on 14 Revelation v.13, "Blessed are the dead which die in the Lord." The local newspaper added that, "everything connected with the arrangements of the funeral was conducted with great decency and propriety." (8)

Thirty years later the Ancient Order of Foresters experienced the first death since their formation of a branch in Bruton in 1863. About thirty of its members assembled to form a procession at their headquarters in the Blue Ball Inn "and after donning the funeral badges of the Order, proceeded to the house of the deceased, where the ceremonies prescribed by the ritual of the Order were performed." In this case the body was carried by the members of the Foresters and followed by family and then the rest of the brethren two by two. "The brethren wore black silk sashes with deep silk fringe tied with green riband, white gloves and neckties." The report added, "The ceremony was a most impressive one."

Reports in the early twentieth century indicated that the Foresters were still attending the funerals of their members, such as James Young aged fifty-one in November 1905: "his funeral was attended by brethren in regalia." There was also a Juvenile Foresters' Branch and when one of its members, Stanley Clark, aged eight, was accidentally drowned in the River Brue in April 1907, "members took part in the funeral procession." (9)

While the evidence contained in this chapter offers a glimpse into the burial of a small number of the poor, the practices used in Bruton for the vast majority of the poor before 1900 were never recorded and have faded from memory. The poor as a group was not usually regarded as equal to the wealthy in life: they were certainly not equal in the arrangements in death.

9

BURIAL OF CHILDREN

The death followed by the burial of children was deeply distressing for most parents. The same funeral rites were followed for children as for adults which once again was indicative of the importance placed upon a decent burial. The grief experienced by all parents must have been profound, even though before the end of the nineteenth century death was commonplace and even expected. For some parents it must have been devastating when they faced multiple deaths amongst their children, for example, in December 1828 the Overseers of the Poor paid for the funerals of three of Jacob Brown's children. In 1895 Josiah Jackson buried three of his children within a period of two months and a fourth less than a year later.

An important distinction was made between those who were baptised and those who were not. Such was the significance of baptism, especially in the earlier part of the period with the concept of purgatory and the fear of eternal damnation, that the Church permitted midwives to baptise a newly born child if it was felt to be in danger of imminent death. By the latter part of the nineteenth century such fears had declined and as a result the time span between birth and baptism seems to have extended, often into the third and fourth weeks of life.

The fear of death before baptism, however, remained deeply ingrained in dwellers in rural areas. On 26th May 1606 the Burial Register for Bruton included Johan Lane who had been "borne & bapt: the day before." In April 1768 Revd. Woodforde recorded one occasion when he was called out by parents at eleven o'clock at night to baptise privately a child who had been born that day and was suffering convulsions. He added a memo: "Never did I any ecclesiastical duty with more pleasure as it gave such satisfaction to its Parents, and that they were so good and charitably disposed to have it done." Unfortunately the baby boy did not survive as he died the next afternoon and two days later Woodforde buried him, grateful that he had baptised him, "a very happy turn for the dear Innocent." Just over two years earlier he had noted, "I privately baptised a Child this Afternoon at our house, it being ill and not come to its time, by the Name of Elizabeth". He did, nevertheless feel compelled to add that she was "base born."[1]

After death great care was exhibited towards the baptised child, especially by members of wealthy families, such as the Hon. Charles Berkeley who interred two of his children in lead coffins in the family vault under the chancel in Bruton church and then in his own Will expressed his wish to be interred near them. In 1895 Josiah Jackson demonstrated the same care for his three children. He obtained the death and burial certificates that had become necessary after the passage of the Registration Act in 1836 and then ordered a coffin for each child from Allen Green who went up to the farm and took the necessary measurements. He also saw the Sexton and selected the appropriate locations in the churchyard. This last action was perceived as an important duty for a member of the family, especially for children who would have expressed no preference while alive.

Jackson then visited Amor the stationer and printer to order Memorial Cards that were usually edged with black and gave brief details of the deceased. He arranged for photographs to be taken but it is not clear in these instances if they were to accompany the Memorial Cards or were just for close family members. For the photograph of Dorothy who died first, Jackson borrowed a camera from Mr Osborne, "he lent me his Camera & I brought it up & took as well as I could a Photo of Dorothy's face & took it back again." He may have judged his efforts to be less than successful for on Franklyn's death he contacted a professional photographer, Goodfellow of Wincanton, "& he agreed to come over & take poor Franklyn's likeness which he did." Rather significantly he added, "and some of the others." At least when Stuart died a couple of weeks later the photographs of him were already in place.

The funerals of these children were all conducted by the Vicar, Revd. Thomas Ridley, to whom Jackson, following the old custom, gave a pair of gloves. His comments in his Diary indicate that he was clearly pleased with the wreaths and flowers that were placed on the graves. The family also received many letters of sympathy: a practice that had become common by the end of Victoria's reign. On the Sunday following each burial, Jackson attended Morning Service in the parish church and then the evening one in his regular place of worship in the Wesleyan Chapel. In the latter on each occasion the lay preacher delivered a sermon based upon an appropriate text, all of which Jackson recorded. "Let us come boldly unto the throne of grace that we may obtain mercy and find grace to help in time of need", "It is expedient for you that I go away", and "If a man die shall he live again." (2)

For the burials of the children of the poor the Overseers paid or contributed, for example, in 1661 they paid 1s 6d "for bringing Peter Walters children to Earth." In September 1778 they spent 2s 4d "for burying Mary Trask's Child" and two years later in July 1780 some 3s 6d "for Burying & a Shroud &c for Fishes Child." One of their smallest sums was just 1s in

April 1807, "Burying Severa Quances ch", presumably only a contribution rather that the full cost.

The Overseers would also provide a child with a coffin and spent 2s 6d on one for Mary Trask's child. By the early years of the nineteenth century the standard cost of a child's coffin was 4s. For children too a bell was rung, for example, in June 1779 1s 6d was paid to "Jn Duffet for ringing ye Bell for Jas Smith's Child." After birth the standard practice was for the mother to be churched, that is, to attend a church, usually within forty days, to be purified and to give thanks for a safe delivery. If however the baby, who had been baptised, died before the mother was churched it would be wrapped for burial in the same white cloth in which it had been baptised, called the chrisom.

Even in death the immoral activities of its parents were recorded alongside the name of the child, at least from 4th March 1588 with "William Roe, base s. of Barnabe Roe." 'Base' was the word used to indicate illegitimate and on page after page it or "BB" (*Base Born*) continued to be used for over one hundred and ninety years. The last such entry in the Burial Register occurred on 31st March 1782, "John, son of Martha Young, base." Such children, however, continued to be identified in the Christening Registers usually, and especially after October 1788, by recording just the mother's name.

For the un-baptised child the procedure was very different. As late as the sixteenth century midwives were required to swear an oath, "If any child be deadborn, you yourself shall see it buried in such secret place as neither hog, dog nor any other beasts may come unto it.......you shall not suffer any such child to be cast into the lane or any other inconvenient place." (3) That such detail was included is a clear indication that these practices had been, and possibly were, still occurring. The implication was that as baptism had not taken place these infants were not fully regarded as human beings.

There is no surviving evidence as to how extensive this practice was in the Bruton area but there is no reason to suppose that it was in any way different from other parts of the country. One complicating factor was that in various Burial Registers there was a tendency at particular times not to name a child being buried but to include a phrase such as, "A man child of" or "A woman child of." In some instances it is possible to trace a baptism at an earlier date that may refer to the same child, such as on 15th August 1596 there was the burial of "a girl child of Stevin Bugley." The Christening Register recorded that on 2nd December 1592 "Agnes Bugley, d. of Stevine B." was baptised. For many more, however, no baptism was recorded. This may suggest that as an act of mercy for some of the grieving parents, the Clerk and the Sexton were prepared to undertake and record a burial, presumably without a minister being present and without the burial service being read. The north side of a churchyard was sometimes used for this sort of interment.

Two nineteenth century examples demonstrated that the practice of such interment for the un-baptised without any ceremony was still occurring in Bruton. In December 1872 Dr. Wybrants held an Inquest on the body of a child, the daughter of a labourer James Fry, "which had been previously interred without a certificate." The child had become ill and Dr. Cox expressed the opinion that death was near. "It shortly after died, and was buried by the Sexton." The jury returned a verdict of "Died from natural causes", but the Coroner warned the Sexton "not to bury a body again without a certificate." The second case came in 1896 when on 18th March Josiah Jackson's wife Annie gave birth to a baby boy but he died four days later. The following day Allen Green "made a little coffin for Baby" and Jackson obtained the necessary death and burial certificates, "I saw W. Lucas (*the Sexton*) about burying it this evening at 8 o'clock." His last entry in relation to this unnamed baby was, "Mrs Popes (Nurse) &

Mrs Hisgrove took Baby to Churchyard to be buried." None of the family attended: so different from the arrangements he made for his other dead baptised children. (4)

In neither of these examples is the death recorded in the Burial Register. In practical terms therefore this must mean that the number of interments in the churchyard was far greater than the official records in the Burial Registers would suggest. Such interments continued into the twentieth century but some seem to have been recorded, such as on 12th March 1904, "An unnamed infant, the son of Patrick Francis Murphy", who was "A few hours" old and was buried, "Without the service prescribed by the Book of Common Prayer."

In a few instances death may have come so unexpectedly that one child was baptised and the other not or one was stillborn. On at least two occasions the dead children were interred together:

"1629 Dec 9. 2 sons of Robert Ames the one Steven & the other not Baptised."
"1662 Sept. 8, Mary Iles, with a brother unchristened."

In both of these examples the children would appear to have been twins.

Very few children's epitaphs have survived on gravestones in Bruton churchyard. One was added for Susanna Jeffery who died in February 1890 aged two years and four months,

"Their not gone from memory, not from love,
But gone to their father's home above."

For Josiah Jackson's son Stuart there was a question and answer: "Is it well with the child? It is well." (See Appendix 6)

10

BURIAL OF NON-CONFORMISTS

Through the centuries Bruton has been home to various religious groups that did not conform to the official beliefs of their day. This was particularly a problem in the post Reformation period for those men and women who continued to adhere to their traditional Catholic faith and then the development of a number of groups which did not conform to the requirements of the Established Church, generally referred to as Non-Conformists. As parishioners it was customary for them to find a resting place in the local churchyard but there was no obligation for the Minister of the Parish Church to read the Burial Service or say any words at the graveside.

Needless to say some families whose members had been brought up in the Catholic faith before the Reformation continued, openly or in secret, to adhere to their older beliefs in the immediate post-Reformation period and beyond. In so doing they were prepared to pay the heavy financial burden which was imposed upon them as recusants. They did, however, accept the church building and the churchyard as their final resting place. In reality of course they had little choice as no Catholic churches survived in the immediate area and most of these believers did not have access to a private family chapel. In some parishes up until the early eighteenth century Catholics were allotted their own small area in a churchyard and sometimes buried at night but there is no evidence for this practice in Bruton.

Quakers were residing in the town from at least 1661 and some such as William Willis, Florence Beasley and William Ellett faced persecution for their beliefs. Until the Toleration Act 1689 Non-Conformists were not permitted their own burial grounds but that did not stop Quakers from interring their dead in their own way, even though they were heavily fined as an example from Alford indicates:

"Att the Buryall of Samuel Clothier on 29th of the 6 mo. 1670 ffines sett & Leavyed by Robert Hunt's warrt ffor Burying the dead.
    Who exprist bad words also Saying they buried him like a dogge there being noe prist noe supstitious Ceremony But the Corps decently interred."

In all fifteen mourners, including Clothier's wife and children, were fined 5s each. (1)

In general Quakers tended to have plain coffins, no pall, no special mourning clothes and the actual burial was in silence. Their graves were in rows with bodies interred in the order of death rather than in family graves or vaults and usually without gravestones or monuments. In this way they felt that they were better able "to assist than to oppose the laws of Nature." After the funeral there would be a meeting for worship which constituted a particularly important aspect for them as it allowed relatives and friends to talk about the dead person and share memories. For them there was no other external form of grief, "If you wish to honour a good man who has departed this life, let all his good actions live in your memory." (2)

After the Toleration Act 1689 Quakers were fairly rapid in establishing their own burial grounds but one does not appear to have existed in Bruton, even though they had various meeting places in the town. As a number of the local Quakers were fined for the non-payment of tithes to the Church of England, their names have been recorded. None of these seem to have been officially buried in Bruton churchyard and so may have been carried elsewhere.

Perhaps the general beliefs and wishes of Quakers at death may be best expressed in the opening of the Will of Thomas Whitehead of Bruton in April 1691: "first and principally I commend my soul into the hands of Almighty God my Creator having an assurance of eternal life through Jesus Christ my lord and Saviour My body I commit to the earth to be decently buried at the discretion of my Executors hereinafter named in some burying place of my friends the people called Quakers when it shall please God to take me out of this transitory world." (3)

Thomas Whitehead moved to Bruton from North Cadbury and became a major clothier in the town, employing a large number of local inhabitants. He was very active within Quaker ranks and was fined and imprisoned on numerous occasions for his activities. When he died one tribute stated, "Thomas Whithead aforesaid in ye Ministery dept this life ye 13th of ye 2nd mo 1691 he had a public testimony for trueth more than thirty yeares and was serviceable in ye Church of God, and is entred into rest." (4)

The Independents, later called the Congregationalists, were present in Bruton in the eighteenth century and had various meeting houses until they opened their first chapel in 1803. They were joined by the Wesleyan Methodists for a short while in the late 1770s and early 1780s and then from the mid-1830s with their chapel being built in 1842. Although both Chapels attracted large congregations in the nineteenth century, neither applied for nor opened their own burial sites. The actual location of each chapel was not appropriate for that purpose. The Independent Chapel was on the south side of the High Street with a very steep slope behind it down to Lower Backway. Although the Methodist Chapel at West End was on a flat piece of land, the area available for burials was very small.

Most members of these congregations accepted, albeit sometimes reluctantly, that their final resting place was to be the parish churchyard. There were exceptions such as Revd. William Skinner, who died in February 1859 aged fifty-five, and who had been the Minister of the Independent Chapel for over thirty years. He was interred in the Independents' Burial Ground in front of their Chapel in Wincanton where several other members of his family were already interred, including possibly four of his five children who pre-deceased him. His wife was to join him in 1870. One tribute ran, "His unaffected piety and amiable, gentle, manners, combined with highly intellectual attainments, had greatly endeared him to all classes." (5)

For Non-Conformists the most significant development came in 1880 with the passage through Parliament of the Burial Law Reform Act, although it was strongly opposed by the clergy of the Church of England with some 15,000 or 75% of them signing a petition against it. The Act allowed Non-Conformists to select a minister of their choice to conduct their burial service.

11

BURIAL OF THE DEAD: MISCELLANEOUS

For many of the bereaved the funeral service ending with burial gave closure to a very difficult period in their lives. It marked the point at which they had to accept that the person concerned was really dead and that they had to go forward with their lives. How they did that depended on so many factors, from the support that they received from relatives, friends and neighbours, to their own state of mind. Some made the transition to a different existence relatively quickly and easily, at least to outward appearances, especially if there were children who needed to be cared for and brought up; others found it much harder and for them there could be repeated visits to the churchyard and the grave. Their comfort was in keeping the grave and any monument in good condition as a tribute to the deceased. (1)

As the Burial Registers for Bruton cover such a long period of time from 1554, one feature that does become noticeable was how frequently a married couple followed each other to the grave within about a year. In June 1768, for example, John Ashford "sexton of Bruton Church" was buried and his widow Margaret in February 1769. In August 1886 Jane Sugg aged seventy was buried and her husband John, also aged seventy, the following April. The Rawlings were quicker, with John aged sixty-one in August 1883 and Hannah aged sixty-four in October of the same year. John Cox aged seventy-six and Betsy Cox aged seventy-nine were reunited in less than three months late in 1888. Age clearly played an important part in many of these cases, with one partner feeling unable to continue without the other.

There were instances when deaths were much closer together, which may suggest that death was the result of illness. On 28th May 1799 Mrs Mary Michell was interred and the following entry for 3rd June was "The Rev. Mr Edward Michell, husband to the above lady." In 1668 the Burial Register recorded for 21st August, "William Sweet & Joane his wife were both buried in one grave." As plague was in the town at this time that may account for the two deaths.

Before the introduction of printed Registers in October 1783, there was a greater opportunity for the Clerk, or possibly a minister, to insert a comment or other piece of information. A few unusual entries may be found in Bruton's Burial Registers: on 2nd February 1587 "Ould mother Colins" was buried, to be followed on 4th May 1592 by "Ould Mother Coward". Alongside the name of William Walter on 15th January 1642 were written the unusual words "flesh and bloud," with no indication of their meaning. On 15th January 1687 Henry Bizby was "First buried after ye porch was done." No other evidence has survived to indicate the nature of what was undertaken or even where. It may have been some repairs or alterations to the area under the North Tower, the place used to transact parish business, or just possibly it was the time when the wooden Screen was placed inside the west door to create a new porch.

One of the most intriguing entries was made on 28th February 1731 and recorded the burial of "Pedro Chocolet, servt. to ye

Rht. Honble. Ld. Berkeley." As it was very fashionable at this period to employ a black servant, this may well have been the case here.

Just occasionally a remarkable and unsubstantiated claim was made in the report on a deceased person in a local newspaper. In March 1842, for example, it was claimed that Mrs Mary Norris, who was the only daughter of John Griffen of Bruton, "was a lineal descendant in the male line from Cadwallander, the last king of the Britons, and was the last of her race."

12

PROSPERITY IN DEATH

The surviving documentary evidence for Bruton indicates that as the centuries advanced an increasing number of inhabitants of the town became more and more prosperous. Wills and inventories revealed men and women with money, property and other items to bequeath to surviving members of their immediate families, other relatives, friends and servants, as well as to a range of other beneficiaries, most notably the Church and the poor.

A range of factors contributed to this development, some national and some local. The Black Death in the fourteenth century had decimated the population and there was an acute labour shortage for decades. It meant therefore that there was the possibility of labourers achieving higher wages if they were prepared to be mobile. In addition it allowed many of the 'middling sort' to make substantial progress because of their specialized skills that were much in demand: lawyers, clothiers, weavers, merchants, butchers and yeomen farmers – all of whom were to be found in the Bruton area. It was no coincidence that a number of the surviving medieval Wills were from men in these categories.

Secondly, the Dissolution of the Monasteries in the 1530s led to the emergence of a new generation of landowners, often with Court connections. Such was the background of Sir Maurice Berkeley when he bought Bruton Abbey and its local estates in the 1540s. He had been in the household of Thomas Cromwell and was clearly an able enough politician to survive his fall from grace and subsequent execution, to become a Standard Bearer of Henry VIII. Connections with a powerful family that had both national and local importance may have aided his ambitions for land – he was after all the stepson of Sir John Fitzjames of Redlynch, the Chief Justice of England.

The sale of former monastic lands continued throughout the reign of Queen Elizabeth I, changing hands on two or more occasions through purchase or long leases. Many enterprising men of the 'middling sort' seized the opportunity to participate in this rapid expansion of land ownership and it was at this time that Hugh Sexey made much of his fortune, as well as reaping the rewards of being a London-based financier and prominent Auditor.

Third, during the medieval period and beyond, Bruton was a successful market town and from the early 1530s had its two annual Fairs as well. Together these markets and fairs attracted a wide range of tradesmen, merchants, artisans and craftsmen, some of whom settled permanently in the town, such as Gabriel Felling the goldsmith. Their activities brought them and the town increased prosperity. New houses were built and more and more of the existing ones given a fashionable facade, especially in the eighteenth century.

Finally, after the death of the last Lord Berkeley of Stratton in 1773, most of his Bruton estate was purchased by the Hoares of Stourhead. As the family had their Georgian mansion located there they had no wish to live in what must have consisted in parts of very old and inconvenient former Abbey buildings. The whole enterprise may well have been under-taken as a longer-term investment in relation to the acquisition of land. Within some twenty years the Abbey Mansion had been dismantled and every conceivable stone, door, tile and window frame sold. More significantly, however, in 1799 Sir Richard Colt Hoare disposed of much of the actual land. In all some fifty-seven local inhabitants, fifty-one men and six women, paid over £12,126 for this property. In a further sale of land in 1812 ten men spent over £1,523 on their acquisitions. (1)

These two sales transformed the property-owning situation in Bruton for while there were still large landowners, such as the Hoares who retained some property, the Earl of Ilchester at Redlynch and Sexey's Hospital, much of the land in and around the town was in the hands of a wide range of local inhabitants, such as farmers, solicitors, clergymen, shopkeepers and innkeepers. During the rest of the nineteenth century they and their heirs became the prosperous middle class leadership of the town.

Inventories gave an indication of the wealth of a few of the inhabitants of Bruton but for many more the level was in general very imprecise. Once a Will had specified various legacies and a range of items which were to be bequeathed to other beneficiaries, the tendency was to leave the residue of an estate to a named person or persons, usually a spouse or son. What actually constituted this residue was never stated.

a) Medieval

In the medieval period the overwhelming majority of testators in Wills gave considerable thought and attention to their souls and, as has been discussed, there were frequent legacies to the Church and religious gilds for the establishment of Chantries, along with masses and prayers for their soul, often in perpetuity. Some Wills such as that of Symon Grene in 1506 referred to virtually nothing else.

There were a very small number of wealthy men in Bruton in the medieval period and as was to be expected they tended to devote considerable time and effort to disposing of an extensive range of personal items, as well as land. In 1510, for example, John Fitzjames, senior, of Redlynch, left a silver spice plate to "my most dear brother, Richard bishop of London", and a silver bowl to each of his daughters. Isabel, referred to as "my most dear wife", was bequeathed a range of silver cups and goblets as well as "my best bed at Redlynche with all its belongings and her own bed with sheets, table cloths and garments." She also received a feather bed that was formerly at Bristol, where he had been an M.P., and two more from Redlynch. His son and heir, John, likewise received various other beds, silver dishes, goblets and cups.

In his turn by his Will in 1538 Sir John Fitzjames, as he was by then, passed on these items and many others to his heir at Redlynch, although his wife was to receive five beds with their various covers and blankets. There was also a reference to "my gilte pottes of sylver.....two saltes of sylver and gilte...my standing cupp of sylver called 'the bryde cupp'". In spite of the turbulent times in which they lived the Fitzjames family managed to remain a very prosperous family.

Beds appear in many of the early Wills for a number of reasons: in the first place they represented a very large financial investment as they were often huge, highly decorated, carved wooden constructions, generally of oak and with pillars and canopies. They frequently had elaborately woven or embroidered curtains and covers as well as multiple mattresses. But more important, they had a symbolic association as they represented the process of life and death: in the same bed a person could be conceived, be born, conceive his or her own children and die, a cycle that was repeated generation after generation.

There were at least two other very wealthy men in the medieval period associated with Bruton and a small number of others who had enough wealth or sufficient possessions to justify making a Will. Undoubtedly the wealthiest was Richard Bruton who had made a fortune by ruthlessly exploiting his large number of ecclesiastical preferments. During his lifetime various allegations of corruption were made against him, as well as ones of burglary and attempted murder. He was rash enough on one occasion to be overheard declaring that he was prepared to spend £6,000 deposing Henry V in 1415. This potentially treasonable utterance did not appear to have been followed up. The sum of money mentioned was enormous for the period and, if correct, gives an indication of his wealth. Certainly his Will, made some two years later, bore this out as he distributed huge sums of money for the benefit of his soul, which judging by some of his actions during his lifetime, was more than necessary. (2)

The other particularly wealthy man was John Gregory, a lawyer and one of the escheators of the Crown in Somerset, that is he received, managed and disposed of estates which had no heirs or where the owner died intestate. In his Will he left sums of money to family, friends and servants, as well as the Church, but in addition this was the first surviving Will from Bruton that specifically bequeathed personal items. As well as basins, pots and ewers there were several fur-lined gowns, rosaries, one with gold beads, weapons, including a bow and twenty-four arrows and a horse.

By the early sixteenth century household items appear more regularly, for example, in 1510 John Jeffreys als Cockes, who was an Alderman of Bath, bequeathed a range of items "Unto the churche house of Brewton." These included, "a doseyn silver sponeys of the which knappys be gilt the syne of strawberys and also a doseyn of garnyshe vessell that is to sey a charger, xii platters, xii potyngers and xii sawcerys also two brygandysse two brochys a mete clothe and a towell." One Bruton tucker, Richard Holmede, was concerned that the tools of his trade should be passed on and so he made particular reference to them in 1520, "Item to Xpian (*Christian*) my daughter iiij peyre of Tuckers sheris." He was also in a position to leave her some household items, "Item vj platters six podingers and six saucers too Crocks a basyn a Laver of brasse a Chafing disshe iiij Candelstycks Item a new flockbed." Holmede was clearly successful in his chosen trade and just five years before his death was leasing a tucking mill from John Fitzjames of Redlynch at an annual rent of 6s 8d. (3)

In 1503 William Samford made various bequests in cash amounting to over £16 and he was so confident of the value of the contents of his house and the goods which he owned that he instructed his wife Margery, who was his executrix, to "selle such goods as will make the hole seid summe of £16 13s 4d." Although these were clearly men of some substance, they appeared to be very few in number. It was only in the post-Reformation period that wealth increased and may be traced to a greater range of Bruton's inhabitants.

b) Post-Reformation and seventeenth century

Unfortunately many Wills at this time did not contain a reference to occupation but in the period 1550 to 1700 as well as three Gentlemen and ten Yeomen making Wills in Bruton, there were also two clothiers, shoemakers and mercers, with a weaver, cutler, husbandman, cloth worker, maltster, woollen draper and a Clerk in Holy Orders. Even this small sample indicates that Wills were being made by a far wider section of the community than previously. Greater wealth was spreading.

Between 1543 and 1555 the Inventories for nine surviving Wills reveal an average value of £18 8s 3d, ranging from £3 6s 8d for Thomas Walter in 1544 to £51 6s 8d for John

Plimton a decade later. At other times in the sixteenth and seventeenth centuries the value of personal and household goods varied significantly as may be seen in Table 11.

TABLE 11 Value of personal and household goods 1584-1736.

Year	Deceased	Value £	s	d
1584	William Walter	34	0	0
1588	John Dicer	4	14	0
1598	Edward Collins	35	5	6
1621	Edward Knewstubbe	43	10	5
1641	Thomas Albin	106	7	7
1683	Thomas Tice als Rogers	1158	13	0
1691	Thomas Whitehead	6806	16	6
1736	William Wilton	302	7	0

The list of Thomas Whitehead's personal and domestic possessions was formidable and revealed a high standard of living with considerable comfort. (4) (See Appendix 5)

For wealthy landed families it was of crucial importance that their affairs should be settled before death to ensure that their intentions were clear to all concerned. It was not unusual therefore in this period for members of such families to make a Will while they were still fit and healthy. Both the first Sir Maurice Berkeley in February 1580 and his son Sir Henry in May 1600 made their Wills, "cawlinge to memory the sertenty of death, & the unsertenty of the time therof" while "beinge in heathe of bodye and of whole and perfecte memorie, thankes be geven to god." Probate for Sir Maurice was granted on 16th November 1581 and Sir Henry was buried in Bruton on 1st October 1601, some seventeen months after he made his Will. Sir Henry's son, the second Sir Maurice, was not so fortunate as he was already "sicke in bodie" when he made his Will on 26th April 1617. He died a few days later on 1st May and was buried on the 8th. His eldest son, Sir Charles was clearly taking no chances as when he made his Will in December 1666 he described himself as "being in Indifferent health of body." He did however survive for some eighteen months, being buried on 26th June 1668.

Each of these men, except Sir Charles, produced very long detailed Wills which dealt with all aspects of their landed estates, money, household contents, animals and, in the case of Sir Henry all his armour, "all my armor & furnyture of warrs, also my tents & such other thinges as are in my armory at bruton." Each one of them arranged that their respective wife would retain Bruton Abbey and its contents during her life before it passed to the eldest male heir. Once again items such as beds and their attachments, silver and furniture figure prominently.

One very interesting feature in these Tudor and Stuart period Wills was the detailed arrangements made in death for younger sons, for example, amongst other bequests the first Sir Maurice gave land in Buckinghamshire and Coombe Farm to his second son Edward, Horsley Farm to his third son Francis, land in Kent to fourth son Robert, and the youngest John received the lease of lands in Wanstrow and Batts Farm in North Brewham. Sir Henry gave his second son Henry the manor of Yarlington and third son Edward the Manor of Pyll. If the family remained a close unit and favourable marriages were entered into, then there was the possibility of an enhanced position within an even larger geographical area. On the other hand the major weakness of this sort of arrangement was that it did divide landed estates into smaller portions and had the potential to decrease power and influence. It may well have been this sort of concern which led the second Sir Maurice to make provision for his younger sons, Henry, Maurice, William and John, but in the form of the rents from large parts of his estate to be jointly divided between them rather than a gift of actual land. (5) He also made provision for his daughters: Margaret was to receive £2,000 "for her marriage portion or advancement in marriage", and Jane £1,500, provided that they married with the consent of his widow or eldest son Charles.

While the Berkeleys were the wealthiest family in Bruton for several generations, it was very noticeable that other men started to leave much larger sums of money on death in the sixteenth and seventeenth centuries. In 1637 along with a number of bequests of land, William Swanton could easily leave £150 to each of his three unmarried daughters. In 1687 William Tice left £5 a piece to six sons and grandsons and another £20 to his eldest son and in 1679 Robert Ludwell bequeathed £250 to a younger son and £200 each to his two daughters, Christian and Mary, when they attained twenty-one years of age.

In some instances of course a Will belied the wealth of a man at the time of his death. A good example of this was Hugh Sexey who made his Will on 19th August 1619 and was buried the next day. In his very brief Will he allocated in total £1,140 to various relatives and servants, with the resi- due, including an unspecified amount of cash, to his second wife Ursula. One litigant in the 1620s was subsequently to claim that his personal estate was worth some £10,000. He had, however, amassed a very large estate of land and property but had conveyed most of it to twelve Trustees in 1616, undoubtedly to ensure that his charitable activities would be continued. When transferred this estate was estimated to have had a capital value of over £4,400 and two years later had a clear income of well over £200 a year.

As with the Berkeleys, these men were increasingly making provision for younger sons, for example, in 1542 Robert

Chyke gave his second son £26 13s 4d and another son £20 and each also received a horse. He also left £6 13s 4d for his married daughter Alice to be paid to her husband, William Cottisholde, but with an interesting proviso that it "be payde by the descrecion of my wife at such tyme as she hath dew prof that he dothe well use and prosper wt that whiche he hath Recevyed at my hande allredy." If there was any doubt in her mind then the sum was to be given directly to Alice, "for the comfort of my daughter."

Near the end of the seventeenth century very large bequests were made by Thomas Whitehead to his younger children, for example, son John received £400, and Thomas and George £500 each, daughters Hannah and Jane £400 a piece and Mary £500. On the other hand eldest son Manasseth received just 10s as he "has had a considerable portion already."

Throughout the sixteenth and seventeenth centuries various indicators of prosperity at the time of death were common and seemingly more extensive. Firstly, a number of men left clearly defined land to their heirs, for example, in 1542 Robert Chyke referred to his occupancy of "my grounde callyd Collyns Heyse" and "the Capeland." Within a century some of this property may have passed to the Albin family as in 1643 Robert Albin left land "knowne by the name of Collens Hayes being now divided into six severall Closes conteyning in the whole threescore and six Acres", along with fifty acres "called by the name of Great Chawley" and a smaller piece of ground called "little Chawley."

A mercer, Robert Ludwell senior, in 1673 bequeathed various pieces of land to his son Robert including "my Close called Scholehouse Close and my close called Rye Ash", a house in Discove, "Loridge" and "Dallens Close" with four acres and "all my Grounds called Cogley Grounds." In his turn Robert junior was to pass on this property in his Will in 1678 to his sons but interestingly his was one of the very few Wills which identified the location of a house by name or in a particular street. The usual practice in a small community where everyone knew everyone else was just to refer to the house as "my dwelling house." Robert Ludwell junior left his tenement called Roper's Tenement to his wife. (6) The only other seventeenth century reference to a dwelling house in a specific location seems to be one in 1623 when Benjamin Ellis left to his son William "All that Messuage or Dwellinghouse in which I now reside situate lying and being in Quaperlake Street in Bruton."

Secondly, items of silver appeared more frequently, for example, in 1544 William Gane left three silver spoons to his wife and two silver spoons each to his two daughters. In the same year Stevyn Broke bequeathed to his son Steven, "four spoons of silver, that have my name inscribed or graven upon them......and a silver salt, double gilt." Twenty-three years later Walter Tynbury of South Brewham left "a dossen of sylver spones a sylver salte and a sylver goblett equallie to be devided" between his two sons John and William. In 1676 Richard Dimond gave his son Richard "my Silver Tankard and my silver Bowle." William Day may have possessed more silver items as he gave his son John, "One Hundred pownds and one of my Silver Tankards." He also left his daughter "one silver Candle Cupp and Cover and the wrought Bedd", but in both instances his wife was to have use of them during her lifetime.

Third, household goods continued to proliferate, for example, in 1544 Thomas Walter left his son Richard two platters and his daughter Agnes "the greatest pan" along with a cow. In 1546 William Cleves gave Isabel his daughter "j crock and iij pewter vessels." A decade later John Yonge left a variety of goods to four different recipients: a crock, a pan, two saucers and a pottinger. John Plimpton in 1554 was very specific and indicated the value which could be placed on what in more recent times might be judged to be an immoveable object, as not only did he leave to his son John "the table board, the cupboard and the chair that remaineth in the parlour" but also "the cilinge in the hall."

Thomas Cornish als Allen was particularly concerned to ensure that all his beds were distributed as he wished in 1696. There were two feather beds in his Great Chamber, one of these with "Bedsteeds, Curtaines, Rallins, Bolsters, Pillows, Ruggs and blanckets" he gave to his son William and the other to daughter Ellinor. Another son Thomas received, "my best fflock Bed and Bedstead and all things thereunto belonging." William was also given "two other fflock Beds and three Bedsteeds", along with "the Cupboard in the great Chamber." Earlier in the century in 1652, having left his three grandchildren three of his best silver spoons each, John Hodges gave one of them "my side table", another "Dew Bartas" (*pots*), and the other, "my Press and Cubbert." In 1681 William Kenniston left to his three grandchildren "my great brass pot.....my great bell metal pot.....a feather bed." One of his sons also received a coffer. In 1639, amongst many bequests, Thomas Wilton left one of his granddaughters "the great brazen pann" and to another "my wives golde Ringe." The following year James Hodges of Milton Clevedon left to his grandson Bartholomew Greene "one great Silver boll." As wealth increased a significant development occurred as more references appeared not just to sons and daughters but also to the next generation.

Fourth, items relating to a particular trade made many appearances, for example, in 1554 Henry Ottis alias Calowe left to his son John "all my brewing vessels, trindles, vats, trows, a malting pan, and all other vessels and instruments or necessaries belonging to my craftes of Chandling or roping." Two years later in 1556 John Yonge bequeathed to his son Richard "all things in the shop and in the lime pits." Shoemaker Thomas Wilton in his Will made in 1639 was certain that

Nicholas Wilton and his wife would follow in the trade as to them "I doe bestowe all my shoes and leather." Finally in 1696 clothier Thomas Cornish alias Allen left to his two sons Thomas and William, "my Shop of Tools Instruments and Materialls of Trade and my three ffurnaces."

Fifth, another sign of prosperity which emerged in the sixteenth century was the increasing number of references to horses being bequeathed in Wills. In 1542 Robert Chyke disposed of various animals: he gave his son John "my white mare with her foal and thencresse of her tyll he come oute of his yeres of prentyshod" (*apprenticeship*); to William Chyke the younger he gave "my Baye horsse callyd my stalyn"; and Nicholas Chyke received "my Sorel mare wt her colt." John Langyer had just one yearling which he left to his son John in 1546. In 1678 Robert Ludwell the younger bequeathed to his brother Thomas "my black gelding."

Sixth, while some wealthy inhabitants had owned or leased various pieces of land in Bruton or its immediate neighbourhood for generations, in the seventeenth century there was a tendency for some men to possess land further a-field. In 1638 Lawrence Goolde left his house in West Pennard to his wife during her natural life; in 1650 as well as land and other property in Bruton and Brewham, John Albin bequeathed land in Street called Stockwood to his son John. In 1673 Robert Ludwell the elder left property in Brewham and Charlton Musgrove and in 1696 Thomas Cornish alias Allen held the leasehold of the White Hart Inn in Wells which he passed to his son William and daughter Ellinor.

Finally as some men's prosperity increased they were in a position to lend money to others. Two examples appeared at the time of the English Civil War in the 1640s and may therefore be related to it and to the uncertain times faced by some families or used to help finance the support that they gave to one side or the other. In his Will in 1647 Peter Tinnie made a reference to a debt of £60, money which he had lent to Philip and John Cruse of Corten Denham. Much more substantial was the sum of £500 that Robert Albin had lent to Sir Charles Berkeley and which was mortgaged against land in Norwood Park. In 1643 Albin instructed that this money could either be repaid in full or as an annuity of £40 a year to his widow.

c) Eighteenth and nineteenth centuries

Wills and inventories indicate that the level of prosperity of some men in Bruton continued to rise throughout the next two centuries, for example, in 1808 the effects of William Meachem of the Old Bull Inn were assessed at around £1,000 and those of boot and shoemaker John Mills at £800 in 1838. Once again large sums of money were bequeathed, for example, in 1714 John Whitehead gave £1,500 to each of his sons Thomas and Joseph and £1,000 to daughter Mary. Four years later Henry Sampson bequeathed £100 to a younger son John and £200 each to three daughters, Jane, Elizabeth and Grace on their marriage, provided it was with the "advice good liking and consent" of his wife. In 1738 Nicholas Goldesbrough, the late Master of the Free Grammar School, gave £300 to son Austin and £600 to daughter Anne to be paid within one month after his death without any conditions.

One of the wealthiest men and the most generous in his range of bequests as he had no children or direct heirs, was Robert Pavy in 1796. He donated £100 to Bristol Infirmary and £200 to Bath Hospital. He also allocated £200 a piece to however many of his father's and mother's cousins were still alive and a further £2,000 to be divided between their children. In fact an advertisement had to be placed in local newspapers requesting claimants to come forward with the necessary proof. In addition he left a total of some £1,135 to his servants and other local people, including £40 to Daniel Vigar one of his gardeners, £300 to Joseph Ive "my late apprentice", £50 to his solicitor Edward Michell, £10 to "My servant Thomas Baily" and even £5 to "Mary Jeffery my washerwoman". There were also a number of grants to various people in areas outside of Bruton.

Great concern continued to be exhibited in the transference of what became increasingly valuable land and property. The evidence suggests that more and more men were taking the opportunity to lease or purchase additional property, especially with the sale of a large part of the Hoare family estates in Bruton. The very fact of purchase was in itself an indication of an enhanced level of prosperity within some families. In 1718 Henry Sampson left a house called "Waddon" with adjoining land to his wife Christian, along with other meadow and pastureland at Henley and Sledges Close. He also owned a house and lands at South Brewham. William Russ possessed two dwelling houses in Bruton, "Near the High Cross" along with at least thirty-six acres of land, mainly Capon Lands. In 1757 Austin Goldesbrough senior was able to pass on to his wife not only his own house with a garden and orchard in Bruton but also to his two daughters Ann and Sarah land in Black Pitt and two acres upon Charldon, along with four dwelling houses on the south side of the High Street.

Multiple house ownership or leasing seemed to have become much more common as wealth increased, for example, in 1805 William Meachem, in addition to the Old Bull Inn which he left to his son John, gave "3 tenements facing the Cross" to his daughter Betty Stone. The reference to the Cross was indicative of how names remained in use as the Cross itself had been dismantled some fifteen years earlier. In 1830 John Mills the shoemaker detailed a house and land in Wyke Champflower, several pieces of land in Huish Field, two fields called Lady Wells, a Close in Black Pit, a house at Hardway and one in the

High Street opposite the entrance to Cats Lane. As well as his own dwelling house in the High Street, Edward Dyne owned in 1849 two other houses in the town, Gants Mill with lands attached as well as Cock's Plot, Park Wall Close, Lusty Close and arable land in Charldon Field.

Household goods continued to proliferate with, for example, Robert Fry in 1711 bequeathing "my Chest of walnut drawers....my Little Clock.....my white bedd in the garrett and the bedstead bolster pillows two blankets and rug belonging to the same." He also included amongst his gifts a large number of silver items: son Robert received "my Large Silver tankard and my Silver hilted Sword." His daughter Joan was given "my silver cup sixteen silver spoones ffour small Silver salts and one Silver porringer and my great Clock." His wife Susannah retained "my two Silver candlecupps with their Covers and my Six Silver fforks during her natural life." In 1831 spinster Lucy Lloyd bequeathed to William Lloyd "my silver pint cup and two table spoons with the initials LL engraved on them."

John Whitehead also referred to silver items in the form of a Tankard, two Cans, CandleCupps, Salver, Snuffers and box. He directed that five named recipients should be given "one piece of broad gold" and Elizabeth Lloyd two pieces. As a clothier, following in the business of his father Thomas, John arranged for the stock in trade to be passed on to his eldest son Thomas or to the next son Joseph if the former declined to enter his trade: "my dyeing furnace press and all and singular my tools and implements of my trade." He was, however, very realistic because as both boys were still minors he recognised that neither might wish to enter the business and so he directed that then the property was to be sold and the money divided between them.

In 1757 another clothier, Austin Goldesbrough, also bequeathed the goods of his trade to his son Austin and this time it included not only "the Workhouse necessary and by me used for carrying on the Clothing Trade" but also "all my broad and other Woollen Cloth.....and all my Wool Yarn List Oil Soap Dye Stuff and other Materials for making Cloth and all my sheering Tools Leads Scales Weights Scribling Horses Wood Baskets Dying ffurnaces Handles Racks and all other utensils for dying Dressing or otherwise making or manufacturing of Cloth."

In 1797 tanner Nicholas Everatt left to one son, Robert, "my Estate called the Tann House and two ffields belonging to the same", and to his other son, Joseph, a house in the High Street "together with all the Chandling utensils thereon the premises." He also possessed a number of other properties in Bruton and Wyke Champflower which were divided equally between his two sons and his wife Mary.

An inventory of the goods and chattles of William Wilton, referred to as a "Stocken Maker", who died in 1734, reached a total of £302 7s 0d, including 29 pictures, 178 pounds of wool and a further 95 pounds of wool ready for the pinions or spindles. There was another "Thirty two pounds of Worsted in Knitters hands", an indication that the Domestic System was still very prevalent in this part of Somerset. An inventory of the effects of shopkeeper Thomas Hannam on his death nearly one hundred years later in 1832 valued the contents of his shop and associated areas at £50 10s 0d. His overall assets were assessed at some £974 11s 2d. His stock included over 4 cwt of clover seed, 45 sacks of oats, 5 sacks of peas and 20 sacks of beans as well as two dozen rakes and 8 picks. (7)

The spread of insurance meant that householders were able to obtain greater protection for their belongings. In 1847 builder William Clarke, who lived at West End, insured his household goods and furniture for £80 with the Phoenix Fire

Office of London. While he was residing in Tolbury House in 1868 retired Army Officer Lieutenant Colonel Edward Hall insured his household goods for £800 with a further £50 for China and Glass and £30 for Pictures and Prints. A decade later in the same house T.O. Bennett judged his household goods and furniture to be worth insuring for £1000, with £250 for China and Glass and £65 for Pictures and Prints, although six named pictures were additionally insured for between £25 and £100 each

As the level of prosperity of some men increased so did the complexity of their Wills, especially if property or money was put into a Trust for either a widow or children or both. John Ludwell was clearly childless when he died in 1726 and so he arranged for all his property to be put into a Trust designed to exist for a thousand years. The revenue derived from this Trust was to be available to his widow during her lifetime and then to his niece Elizabeth Dampier and her heirs. Daniel Morgan of the Blue Ball Inn had the foresight to take out an insurance policy for £1,000 and in his Will in 1853 he established a Trust under the control of his wife and two other trustees to invest the money and use it for the education of his two children who were both minors and then "for the purpose of settling my said son in some respectable trade profession or calling" and also paying his daughter up to £500 on her marriage, provided that his widow approved. There were additional clauses affecting any money which his widow received in the event of her remarriage.

William Saunders had arranged a slightly different Trust in 1812 when he granted all his lands and property to his widow for her natural life or until such time as she remarried, referred to as "intermarriage with any other Husband." In such a case his Trustees were to ensure that all the property was used for the benefit of his two sons and to ensure their "custody tuition and Guardianship" until they were twenty-one years of age and then to set them up "in any profession trade business or employment" for their advancement. At least one of them, Thomas Viney Saunders was to follow his father in the medical profession in Bruton.

A Trust established in 1764 by the Will of Anne Pitney, a widow of Lamyatt, was borne of necessity. After a few small bequests, mainly to her two servants, she left all her property in Lamyatt, Ditcheat and Ansford to her son Matthew. The problem was that, as she acknowledged, he "has for sometime past been disordered in his senses." Two local men, Gerard Martin and William Melliar, were to adminster all this estate and any which her son had received as a result of his deceased father's Will. As Matthew was to die without issue the estate was later divided between various other relatives.

The Trust established in 1767 by John Goldesbrough, another Master of the Free School, was extensive and detailed. He placed his estate in a Trust to be administered by two men, Walter Burton and John Dampier, and the rents and profits from it were to go to his eldest son John and then to his male heirs in turn, "for the first second third fourth fifth and all and every other the Son and Sons of the body of my said Son John lawfully to be begotten." If son John had no male heirs the money was to pass to his second son, Richard Nicholas and then his heirs in the same order as for those of John, but if he had no male heirs then it gradually passed down through his remaining four other sons and their heirs. In the meantime as several of the boys were minors the Trustees, along with his widow, were to oversee "the Custody Tuition Guardianship and Education of all my said Sons" and to arrange for their "Maintenance Learning and Education at the Universities Trades Professions or otherwise as they shall think fit."

One very interesting and unusual arrangement was made in the eighteenth century and concerned the Berkeley family and

Bruton Abbey. When William, 4th Lord Berkeley of Stratton, who had purchased the estate back from Sir John Brownlowe in 1719, died there in March 1741, the family title passed to his eldest son John but the Abbey Mansion and its associated property did not. All this Lord William bequeathed to his third and youngest son, Charles, as his second son William was already dead. The reason for this action was not explained at the time: it may relate to the fact that Lord William considered that the title and a vast amount of other property, especially in London, was sufficient for John and therefore he wished to make provision for his youngest son. There is just the suggestion, however, that there may have been division within the family as it is possible that John married without his father's consent a bride who was considered unsuitable. Certainly for most of John's remaining life she almost disappeared from sight. In the end as Charles died with no surviving children the Bruton estate eventually passed back to Lord John in 1765 and he lived there until his own death eight years later.

d) Wealthy females

All the cases examined so far in this chapter have been male but there were a number of females in Bruton who were very wealthy at the time of their death and who also benefited from the increase in prosperity which was apparent. In general until the 1882 Married Women's Property Act when a female married all her property passed to her husband and so she became very dependent upon him, owning little in her own right. There were, however, three main categories of females who did possess property: the first was a woman who remained a spinster and so could retain, purchase, own and administer her own money and property; the second was a widow who did not remarry. As in reality few women from the wealthier classes who were above thirty years of age seem to have remarried, there could be a number of them living in a particular locality. Third, there was a much smaller category of those females who were married but were left money or property in Wills for their own absolute use.

In very exceptional cases there were wealthy widows who challenged the provisions of a Will, such as Ursula, the widow of Hugh Sexey. She in fact remarried very quickly after his death, this time to Sir Gerrard Sammes. One or both of them considered that she had not received from Sexey's very brief Will all that she should have done and so within five years of his death, Sammes initiated legal proceedings on behalf of his wife against Sexey's Trustees, obtaining for her the Manor of Wanstrow. (8)

In most cases a widow did not have land or houses to bequeath at the time of her death as it was customary for her late husband to have left her a life interest in a property and then the remaining instructions in his Will came into force, usually ensuring that the property passed to the next male heir. A widow might possess landed property in her own right if she had purchased it after the death of her husband. In his Will in 1744 Richard Creed had left his wife Ann "all and singular my real Estates of what Nature or kind soever and wheresoever for and during the term of her natural life." As he had no male heir it was then to be passed on to his daughter Judith. By the time that Ann Creed died in 1760 she had purchased additional property, "All that my Messuage or Dwelling House situate at a place called Toppeny corner or Tolbury Corner in Brewton.....with the Stable Curtillage and Garden there unto adjoining and belonging." Ann Creed willed the property to the same daughter Judith, who was by that stage married, but with an interesting stipulation, "to her own Sole and separate use Barring all other Persons from Intermeddling or having any thing to do therewith notwithstanding her being Married." She may have wished to give Judith more independence or it was possible that she considered that her husband, yeoman Thomas Butt, would gain enough of her property as a result of the Will of her husband.

Although widows did not generally possess their own property at death, they did have money so the distribution of some of it figured prominently in their Wills. For Somerset as a whole between 1480 and 1660 women represented just under 15% of all donors who gave money for charitable purposes, with religion and the poor being the most prominent. In total they gave about 6% of all the money that was donated. (9)

As with their male counterparts, widows' Wills from the later medieval period, such as those of Margery Moleyns in 1493, Alianora Ede in 1496 and Alice Brymmore in 1517, devoted various sums of money for masses, prayers and other beneficial measures for their souls and the souls of family and friends. Isabel Fitzjames left £20 to be used for the provision of a canon of the Abbey to pray at her husband's altar daily "for his Soule, my Soule and for all my good frendes Soules." In the decade after the Dissolution of the Monasteries Elizabeth Fitzjames also left money for priests to say masses on the day of her burial.

Widows also gave money in the form of bequests, for example, in 1457 Amice, the widow of John Gregory, gave her granddaughter Eleanor Weston "10 markes of silver" and in 1589 Petronell als Purnell Spicer left 20s to each of two sons and 12d to each of her grandchildren. Half a century later in 1640 Alice Hill was in the position to leave £20 to one grandchild, £50 to another and £100 to a third. In 1648 Joanne Sampson was even more generous as she left each of her grandchildren £100, to two boys when they reached the age of twenty-one and to her granddaughter on the day of her marriage. These widows were clearly prosperous in their different periods. From her wealthy privileged position Dame Elizabeth Berkeley was able to be more lavish with money as she gave sums which ranged from £2 to £10 to a number of servants, as well as £50 each to her two youngest sons and added £70 a piece to the £100 that her two daughters had been left by one of their grandmothers.

The increased prosperity of some widows may be seen in the way in which a number of them acquired in their own right a range of silver items; this was particularly the case within the Fitzjames and Berkeley families, for example, in 1526 Isabel Fitzjames gave to the Abbot of Bruton "a Cruett of silver and gilt to serve him at his masse." Nearly twenty years later in 1545 Elizabeth Fitzjames was very precise in her descriptions, " To my son Sir Morice Barckley, knight, two salts with the dolphyn upon them, my two wine pottes of silver with the Dolphyn and the Conysse upon the covers, five spones with blue animell upon the knappes." Dame Margaret Berkeley in 1617 left to her servant Dorothy Cole, "my Little Silver Sault and fower Silver Spoones." As a wealthy spinster Lucy Temple left a large collection of silver items including candlesticks, spoons, cups, medals, even a warming pan. She also had a number of items made in gold such as a jewel box and toothpick case.

As early as 1457 Amice Gregory possessed a range of silver items which she bequeathed: she gave her granddaughter Agnes Weston a silver pot and her grandson John Weston a silver cup, one piece of silver plate and a silver belt. She also gave to Thomas Palinton six silver spoons.

The vast range of household items that made an appearance in female Wills was indicative of the comfortable lifestyle of some of these wealthier women. Once again beds and all their belongings figured prominently in the Wills of various Berkeley widows and also in those of others such as Agnes Morris in 1633. She also added tablecloths and table napkins. In 1545 Jone Hardwell left her sister Agnes Gowldow "a pair of sheets, a pair of blanketts and a 'keverynge'." In some instances the list was more varied, such as that of Johan Peter in 1554 when she left to her son James, "iij sheets, a pair of blankets, my best coverlet, a crock, a cauldron, ij platters, a great candlestick." By 1902 Ann Bowring was able to detail a long list of items, mainly despatched to nephews and nieces, including silver cream jugs, a cake basket, bedstead, wardrobe, dressing table, looking glass, pictures, washstand and a clock.

From occasional references it is possible to deduce not only the degree of comfort in wealthy families but also how female members of these families were expected to spend some of their leisure time. In 1626 Dame Elizabeth Berkeley bequeathed to her daughter Margaret, "a Neddlework Carpett of my owne making and all the Neddleworke stooles in my Clossett not yet finished. Item I give unto my daughter Jane a Needleworke Carpett wch my Mother gave me haveinge the Killigrewes Armes thereuppon." Such rich items, which may well have hung as tapestries on the walls, must have made the required impression upon visitors and servants.

Within male Wills the distribution of wearing apparel received scant mention and then it was often in the most general of terms. Females tended to be much more specific as it was an area over which they seem to have had complete control and the items bequeathed gave some indication of their wealth. In her lengthy Will in 1527 Isaballa Fitzjames instructed that, "My cosin Alice Storke shall have my best bonet and a frontlet of tawny velvet; Joan Compton, daughter of the said Alice, my best worsted Kirtle." In 1545 Jone Hardwell left her sister a kirtle and a 'kercher' and to Jone Nye "a blue frock and a kercher." Nine years later Johan Peter left among other items, "a black kirtle and a woman's hood." Just four years after that Agnes Plumley had a much more extensive wardrobe as she referred to four gowns as well as "my Scarlat kyrter....a blacke worsted kirtle.........my best hoode......my best redd petticott." There were also two smocks, three neckerchiefs and three kerchiefs, "a cassocke...my russet ffrocke.....a gowne of clothe...my violet cappe......my hatte."

In 1633 Agnes Morris also possessed at least one whittle and three petticoats along with a "best Holland apron" and two other aprons. She also had different clothes for different days as to Melior Hogges, her daughter-in-law, she left "my hatt and my gowne wch I doe weare sondaies." To another female, Kathleen Perry, she gave "my gowne wch I doe weare satterdaies." Perhaps the two days of the week when a woman could be most prominent: attendance at the weekly market on Saturdays and Church on Sundays.

It was possible that widow Joane Sampson who died in 1648 had sufficient cash to be in a position to lend money. In her Will she made a reference to two bonds due to her: one for over £80 from two men in Langport and one for £60 from three members of the Mogg family of Shepton Montague. She also left to her married granddaughter money due from several other bonds that had been arranged by her late husband, but in these instances the sums involved were not specified.

Finally there was a third category of females who could own property in their own right, even if they were married. These were women who had been specifically bequeathed property or money in a Will and the necessary declaration of intent made. In 1690 Maurice, Lord Fitzharding, bequeathed to each of his two daughters £500 and directed that their respective husbands "shall not have to doe with or be concerned in and have any benefitt" from the money or its interest. In addition his daughters could dispose of the money as they saw fit "without or against the consent of their respective husbands." Twenty-two years later his brother John, the next Lord Fitzharding, established a Trust for his two daughters, "Exclusive of their said husbands and wherewith their said husbands shall not intermeddle."

In 1823 Richard Biggs made a similar arrangement for his god-daughter, Elizabeth Mead, the wife of farmer William Mead of South Brewham when he left her a legacy of £100 in cash and an annuity of £30 a year for life: "that the said annuity and legacy to the said Elizabeth Mead shall be for her own separate use independent of her present or any future husband and not subject to his debts engagements or control and that her receipts alone shall be sufficient discharges for the same." In 1855 Richard Sly of Shepton Montague bequeathed to his granddaughter Martha Sims a house and garden in Charlton Musgrove "independent of the Debts control and engagements of her husband."

No matter how wealthy these men and women had been in life or how much their prosperity had increased as a result of their labours, good fortune or bequests from relatives or friends, the fact remained that in the end they in their turn had to make the necessary preparations to distribute it to others as they could not take it with them.

13

THE WORLDLY
CONSEQUENCES
OF DEATH: WILLS

a) Alternatives to Wills

As men and women, especially from the wealthier ranks of society, faced the inevitability of death, their concerns mounted about a number of issues. In the medieval period it was essential to ensure that all the necessary arrangements were in place for their funeral and that adequate provision was made for the health of their soul. In the centuries that followed as prosperity increased and it found expression in more tangible objects such as houses, land, personal items and money, they wished to ensure that all their worldly goods should be transmitted to subsequent generations as they intended. The consequence was that over time the production of a last Will and Testament became much more commonplace: its detail and careful construction would ensure that final instructions could not be ignored by the trusted men and women who were charged with its implementation.

The overwhelming majority of the population, of course, did not need to make a Will as they had nothing of any value to leave and in some instances nothing at all. It was taken for granted that any material goods such as a chair or earthenware pot would pass to the next in line, usually the eldest son. As the leases of their dwellings were generally for a number of years and for up to three lives, that is designated persons, they just descended to the next named person, on payment of a small fine. In the medieval period and beyond even many of the wealthier in the community did not make a Will and so other systems were in operation.

A traditional method of deciding property rights was to hold an Inquisition Post Mortem with a jury of local men and amongst its functions was to establish who was the rightful heir and if he (or possibly she) had achieved the age of majority. Documentary evidence indicates that such Inquisitions Post Mortem were held in Bruton throughout the medieval period, for example, on 10th July 15 Edward I (1287) a jury heard testimony from William de Godmanston, William de Gratelegh and William Chamflour that John was the son and heir of the late Ralph Huscarl, that they had attended his baptism in the Church of St Mary in Bruton and that he was over twenty-one years of age. On 27th October 7 Henry VII (1492) another Inquisition Post Mortem established that William Basyng was the son and heir of Edward Basyng and that he was aged twenty-five.

Early deaths meant that the heir to property could be a minor and that raised issues of wardship. On the death of Robert de Draycote in 1293 his son John, who inherited his estates including Redlynch was just eleven years old. When William de Monte Acuto died in 1320 he had extensive estates in several counties including the manors of Shepton Montague, Yarlington and Knolle, all of which passed to his son William who was aged eighteen. When he died some twenty-five years later he was to leave an heir who was just fifteen years old. Thomas Lovell held the manor of Milton Clevedon which his wife Joan had inherited and when he died in 1401 it passed to their son Thomas who was thirteen years old. Another Joan, this time the daughter of Thomas Beauchamp, inherited the manor of South Brewham when she was fifteen years old on the death of her father in 1488.

In most of these cases the wardship passed to the monarch and provided a fruitful source of income. On the death of Richard, the lord of the manor of Brewham, in the reign of either King Richard I or King John (the jury were not sure which) his son and heir John was a minor and the wardship passed to the monarch until King John sold it to William de Monte Acuto. In 1363 it was reported that the heir to the Redlynch estate was once again a minor and as such was a ward of Edward III.

Such Inquisitions Post Mortem were still being held in the sixteenth and seventeenth centuries. On the death of Nicholas Fitzjames of Redlynch in 1550 one established that his property included the Manor of Redlynch, Knoll and Wyke Champflower, where as well as cottages, he possessed a water mill. There was also property in at least six other local parishes. The jury declared that James Fitzjames was his son and heir and that he had reached thirty years of age. A similar Inquisition Post Mortem was taken on 19th May 1620 at the Guildhall in London, to examine some of the affairs of Hugh Sexey. The jury established that he possessed various properties in London, such as in Aldersgate Street and elsewhere in the parish of St Giles without Cripplegate. They also concluded that his nearest heir was Anne Paynes, then the wife of Thomas Banckes, an issue that the latter was to pursue with Sexey's Trustees throughout the 1620s without much success.

This last case demonstrated the fact that such an Inquisition could not necessarily resolve all the issues. As early as 1341 the Bishop of Bath and Wells, Ralph of Shrewbury, had received an order from Edward III to enquire into the case of John Baskyn and Joan his wife. They alleged that Henry Selyman had seized a house in Bruton that John Cribbe had given to Stephen de Bydiston and Gunnora his wife and their heirs. As Joan was the heir of these two, John made the claim that she should have inherited the house. Henry on the other hand alleged that Joan was a bastard. No outcome is recorded. (1)

An Inquisition Post Mortem also pronounced on what property the deceased owned or leased, a not unimportant issue in troubled times when access to original documentation was far from easy. On 10th April 5 Edward III (1332) a jury decided that John de Perham leased 160 acres of arable and twenty-four acres of meadow in Charlton Adam from the Prior of Bruton. A second Inquisition on his death the following year found that the holding had decreased to 107 acres of arable and sixteen acres of meadow. In 1409 on the death of Ela the widow of Richard de Sancto Mauro, knight, it was found that she possessed three messuages and six virgates of land in Shepton Montague with an annual value of £2 10s; seven messuages and six carucates of land in Pitcombe with an annual value of £7 and five more messuages and four carucates of land in Cole with an annual value of 100s.

The estate which William Basyng inherited from his father Edward in 1492 was assessed to be a messuage, twenty acres of arable land, twelve acres of meadow and one hundred acres of pasture in Bruton which he leased from the Prior of Bruton and was worth 30s 8d. When Sir William Weston died in 1594 the jury recorded that he owned land in various parts of Somerset, including "Gauntesmills in Bruton" but at that time they found that his son and heir Thomas was just 15 years 1 month and 24 days old and so a minor. The Inquisition Post Mortem on the death of Henry Southworth established that he owned, amongst other property, the Manor of Wyke Champflower with some twenty houses and gardens, six cottages, a water mill and several hundred acres of land. (2)

Occasionally in the case of a few very unfortunate people the jury at the Inquisition Post Mortem decided that they owned nothing. Such was the case of Joan Cole at Bruton on 27th November 23 Henry VII (1508), "She has been an idiot since birth. She has never alienated any lands; nor have any lands ever descended to her, nor has she ever possessed any lands or goods which she could alienate or dissipate."

It is clear from the large number of Inquisitions Post Mortem which have survived that in some instances considerable amounts of land and other property could be involved. This did open up the possibility of illegal activities being undertaken by a corrupt or disreputable official employed by the Crown. In 1419 an Inquisition was held into the conduct of John Lannoy, the former escheator for Somerset and Dorset. By virtue of his office he had presided over an Inquisition Post Mortem at Shaftesbury where a bronze boiler belonging to the Abbess of Shaftesbury valued at 100 marks passed into the king's hands after William Ferebeter drowned in it. Lannoy seems to have concealed what happened, retained the bronze boiler for himself and subsequently sold it back to the Abbess for ten marks when she was at Bruton. Exactly how his actions came to light were not stated nor was the outcome. (3)

A second method that was often used to record decisions and the course of action taken was to register a death in the Church Court which was held during an annual Visitation. Although most of the business of this Court concerned immoral behaviour within the community, oversight of the clergy and churchwardens in the performance of their functions and a range of other local concerns, increasingly the Court dealt with administrative matters such as the registering of deaths, whether or not there was a Will. (4) In the medieval period it was the Testament that was used to dispose of personal property in which the Church Courts had particular jurisdiction. In practical terms they could not interfere in the disposal of real property such as houses and land. It was no surprise therefore that it was the Church that encouraged various items to be included in the Testament: the soul given back to Almighty God, the body to be buried in consecrated ground and a bequest to the Church.

In many cases the Church Court in Bruton recorded what had happened and the situation as it was perceived on the day the Court sat. In 1617, for example, the Court noted that the wife of Walter Ponter died "and whether she mad a will ore noe wee knowe not And that the said Walter possesses her goods." In the same year in Shepton Montague, "That Richard Crosse aforesaid died and his goods remayne ther in his wives hands." Six years later it was noted, "that Joanne Hodges is likewise deceased and William Coles of Bruton her sonne in law possesses her goods." Such a record was particularly important if a person with something to leave died without making a Will, "that the said John Atkins is lately deceased intestate Agnis his wife possesses his goods." Sometimes when a Will did exist it was not proved by the time that the Church Court occurred, "Richard Coles is deceased and his will as yet not proved Christian Coles his relicte being executrix." (5)

A number of Wills were in fact proved in the Church Court when it assembled in Bruton, for example, on 3rd March 1544 those of Thomas Walter, William Gane, Roger Ames and John Togood. A decade later on 24th September 1554 that of widow Johan Peter and John Ottlye were proved "in the church of Brewton." Others were proved further away such as those of Isabel Blackmore on 25th January 1556 and Roger Hurman on 22nd February 1556, both in Wells Cathedral.

A third method was to record a death and present any subsequent actions or information at the Manorial Court. These Courts had administered the affairs of manors through-out the medieval period but unfortunately documentary evidence from Bruton only survives for a much later period. The normal procedure was to record the death of a tenant in the manor as this could have financial and tenancy implications. When the person who died was the last of the named lives originally listed on the lease then the property passed back into the hands of the Lord of the Manor. On the death of John Robins in 1813 "a tenement on the North side of the High Street is fallen into Hand." The same was also reported for "a Tenement called Dropping Land Grounds" on the death of John Middleton.

Under the terms of most leases on the death of a tenant a heriot, usually best goods, best animal or a sum of money became due to the Lord of the Manor. A Survey of Bruton in 1669 included eighty-six unspecified heriots, sixty in money ranging from 1s to £6, with 6s 8d, 10s and 13s 4d being the most common, two of the best beast, three of the best goods and five of best beast or best goods. Some twenty-one premises paid no heriots but at least half of these were Shambles. A further survey in 1713 provided a little more detail for while the number and range of the money heriots was similar to the earlier Survey, it also showed that in eighty-five instances the heriot was the best goods. It listed just nine premises where no heriot was payable which may suggest that a new Lord of the Manor was exploiting his estate more rigorously.

When the Court Baron was convened in Shepton Montague in December 1760 it recorded,

"Thomas Sutton to be Dead Since the Last   1   10   6
Court and a Heariote
Peter Stone Dead Since the Lords Corte and no
Herriot Done."

When John Young died in Bruton in 1815 a heriot of £2 13s 4d became due on the tenement he had leased and the death of

Mrs Joanna Mellior four years later led to a number of heriots on several properties including, "£1 3s for Capon Lands payable to the Lord and £1 9s 7d for Long Close to the Lord." (6)

As prosperity increased it was in the interests of more and more people to ensure that deaths were registered and all the necessary administrative matters undertaken as quickly and accurately as possible. As the decades progressed the majority of the dying chose to settle their affairs through a Will and Testament.

b) Wills: General Considerations

i) Executors and Overseers.

The role of the executor was to ensure that the provisions in a dead person's Will were implemented. In the overwhelming majority of cases when a man was married, he nominated his wife for that role, usually leaving her the residue of his estate as well. Examples may be found in many of the Bruton Wills, such as Simon Grene in 1509, Henry Ottis als Callowe in 1554 and Edward Norton in 1660. Before the Reformation it was not unusual for an additional male executor to be added as well but so much depended on factors such as whether a wife was already deeply involved in helping to run a business or farm. Older women were often given sole responsibility but in cases where the wife was young and there were dependent children additional support was brought in from a person in whom the testator placed great trust.

In cases where a husband or wife was already deceased the role passed to the next generation, for example, in 1589 Petronell als Purnell Spicer made her son John Eliott her sole executor and in 1652 John Hodges gave the role to his daughter Jone, "my rightfull Executresse." In 1493 widow Margery

Moleyns made her son-in-law John Brokway and his wife Alice her executors and in 1554 widow Johan Peter likewise made her son-in-law Robert Rodway her executor. In a very small number of instances a generation was by-passed and the role was allocated to a grandson, such as by Christian Albin to her grandson James in 1650. For those who were unmarried there was more variation, for example, in 1695 spinster Catherine Drew placed power in the hands of her "kinsman" Thomas Ludwell, Lucy Temple in 1733 to her niece Ann Berkeley and in 1763 William Pavy designated his brother Robert.

On those occasions when the testator considered that the instructions in his or her Will would be implemented over a long period of time and given the prevalence of death, it was not unusual for the task of implementation to be extended to the "Executors, Administrators and Assigns" of the initial executor.

When an executor was not necessarily a direct beneficiary of the Will, it was customary, especially in the earlier part of the period, for that person to be given a small sum of money or an item for their trouble. In 1690, for example, Thomas Whitehead wished his executors to each be given "a good pair of Gloves." A particularly generous example may be found in the Will of Sir John Fitzjames in 1538 when he appointed four executors: "my very good master Sjr Geyles Strangwiche, knight, to whom I bequeth my flagon of sylver, my trustie and lovyng cosyn Sir John Horsay, knight, to whom I bequeth my two dosen Trangers of Sylver – they coste me beyond £20 – and my shaving bason of sylver and my trustie friends, William Portman and Geyles Penye. To William Portman my standing cup of sylver that I had of Sir Phillippe Fulforde and to Geyles Peny my standing cup gilt that ys comenly used to drynke claret wyne in."

When he originally drew up his Will in 1757 the Hon. Charles Berkeley directed that his three executors should receive £100 each "as a small acknowledgement for the trouble they may have in proving my Will and the Execution of the Trusts hereby in them reposed." In 1813 John Dalton of Pitcombe was also generous towards his two executors, Henry Hobhouse of Hadspen and Rev. Samuel Serrell of Wells, as he gave them one hundred guineas each. A decade later in 1823 Richard Biggs gave two of his executors, John Birt and Thomas Bennett, fifty pounds each.

One problem which the Executors faced occasionally was actually finding the nominated heir. In the vaste majority of instances the issue was clearcut as those named in the Wills were still in the locality or in contact with the testator in the period before his or her death. When this was not the case an advertisement in a newspaper was sometimes used, as may be seen from the following example which appeared in 'The London Gazette' on 22nd December 1681:

"These are to give Notice That John Cary, Senior, and his wife, of the parish of Bruton, in the County of Somerset, are both lately Deceased, and the Estate which they left, is fallen to Joseph Cary their eldest Son, (if Living) The said Joseph Cary upon this Information (wherever it comes to him) is desired to shew himself at Bruton, or otherwise to certifie the Lord of the Mannor under his own Hand, that he is alive."

While a Mrs ffrances Cary was buried in Bruton on 15th December 1681, there is no record of a burial there for John Cary at this time.

In the earlier part of the period under consideration once an executor or executrix had been named, it was also customary to appoint Overseers, sometimes referred to as Supervisors of the Will. It was their function to act as advisors and give help and support to the executor who, as well as often suffering grief from the recent bereavement, might have little or no experience in dealing with some of the necessary administrative matters. In 1660, having appointed his wife Elizabeth as executrix, Edward Norton then named two Overseers, "desireinge my very good frends Mr Thomas Jarvis of Brewton and Mr Edward Morrice of Stoake Lane to bee overseers hereof and to bee Aydeinge and Assisinge to my Poore wife, and my said child by their best Advice and Councell." In 1678 William Day appointed his son-in-law John Russe, his son John Day and Thomas Allen, gentleman of Bruton, to be "my Supervisors of this my Will and Testament not doubting but they will bee ready att all tymes to direct and Assist my said Wife in the due execucon thereof."

The inclusion of a few appropriate and well-chosen words within a Will might help to ensure that the Overseers took great pains to perform their functions as desired. In November 1653 William Ewens of Hadspen did just that, having made his wife Margaret his executrix. "And I earnestly desire my loveing kinsman Baptist Austen and loveing friend Richard Gane to bee overseers of this my Testment last will assuring my selfe that they will see it truly pformed in all points according to the true meaning thereof."

Appointing locally influential people as overseers could be viewed as a way not only of ensuring the implementation of a Will but also as a means of providing some protection for the bereaved. In 1509 Simon Grene nominated amongst his overseers John Fitzjames, senior, of Redlynch and in 1542 Robert Chyke included "my good lady Fitz-james, to whom 40s, desiring her ladyship to be friendly to my wife and children." It was customary to give either cash or goods to overseers for their trouble. Simon Grene gave John Fitzjames 26s 8d and his two other overseers 20s each. In 1544 Stevyn Broke made John Plymley and Hewe Sherwode his overseers and left two shillings between them. A decade later Henry Ottis als Callowe gave his two overseers Robert Plynton and William

Nervall "to each of them a pair of hose." In 1580 when Sir Maurice Berkeley appointed three of his nephews his overseers he "doe geve to everie of theyme a ringe of goulde, weyghinge one ounce with a deademannes head graven in it." Payment and a mourning ring at the same time.

With the production of many more Wills in the seventeenth century and with the wider experience gained of the necessary procedures, far fewer testators appointed overseers, leaving the task to the executor alone. Overseers as such were extremely rare in Bruton Wills in both the eighteenth and nineteenth centuries. There were occasional exceptions such as Austin Goldesbrough who, in his very lengthy Will in 1757, appointed his wife and son joint executors and then his three brothers-in-law Abraham, Charles and Joseph Clavey "to assist my said Executors in the performance thereof." In reality these men were acting as Trustees for part of his Will and so on other occasions Trustees may be seen as fulfilling part of the function of overseers in previous generations.

ii) Witnessed.

The overwhelming majority of Wills were signed by one or more witnesses, although in fact as long as the testator had signed the Will there was no need for such witnessing. When Lucy Temple made her Will in 1733 and then added a Codicil on the same day, neither had any witnesses and there was just her own signature. In this case before her Will was proved John Timberline, described as a servant, and Rachael Rudd, a spinster, had to swear that as they were "well acquainted with her Manner Character and Way of handwriting" that the Will and Codicil were "totally wrote and subscribed by and with the proper handwriting of the said Lucy Temple deceased."

In reality the presence of witnesses when a Will was drawn up and written down by a scribe would prevent any potential controversy at a later date. For some testators such as Thomas Walter in 1544 there was just one priest, John Eryngton, as a witness but others clearly took witnessing very seriously, especially in the earlier part of the period when multiple signatures of witness were common, for example, there were eight signatures "wt many others" on the Will of Margery Moleyns in 1493.

In the pre- and immediate post-Reformation period it was the standard practice for one of the witnesses to be a priest. In the 1490s Edward Huchins signed Wills as the parochial chaplain, followed by Robert Rotheram until 1526 when he was replaced by John Eryngton. The latter does not seem to have been a canon of the Abbey or, if he had been, to have retained a position there as his name does not appear at the time of the Visitation of 1526, on the document of Surrender in 1539 or the subsequent Pension List. He was however remarkably successful in retaining his position during the turbulent times of the Reformation as he continued to witness Wills as curate of Bruton until 1554, although Robert Antell also signed as curate in 1542-1543. Eryngton may have died in 1554 but he certainly did not survive the accession of Queen Mary as in 1554 and after John Whitwyll signed Wills as curate.

In the decades that followed there was a marked decrease in priests signing Wills, although they continued to appear from time to time, such as Meredith Evans as Minister in 1589 and John Randall in 1667. How far local inhabitants had utilized the skills of the canons in the monastery in relation to the preparation of their Wills can only be a matter for conjecture as the names of so few of the religious have emerged. Amongst those who witnessed the Will of Margery Moleyns in 1493 were Willm Clerk and John Monk, but there was no indication if it was their surname or profession that was given. The Will of Richard Philippys in 1509 was more specific as in addition to the curate it was signed by "John Blake chaplain John Bisshoppe chaplain Roger Stere sacritore."

From the late sixteenth century it was more common for the testator to give his or her own manual authentication using a phrase such as "in wytnes wheareof I have hereunto set my hand and seal." This in theory removed the need for the oral testimony of other witnesses but even so in the seventeenth and eighteenth century Wills from Bruton generally had either two or more usually three witnesses who of course could be used to authenticate the signature. By the nineteenth century the majority of Wills were drawn up by solicitors and their signatures along with others of a suitable status appeared, for example, in 1813 the Will of Elizabeth Meachem was signed by George Parfitt, clerk to Mr Dyne, solicitor and W. Saunders, surgeon. Saunders own Will, which he had made in 1804, had been witnessed by attorney Edward Mitchell. Edward Dyne, attorney, along with his clerk Thomas Jelley, signed that of John Mills in 1830 and Henry Dyne, solicitor, and John Crouch, surgeon, added their signatures to the Will of Daniel Morgan in 1853.

One interesting fact to emerge from an examination of the witnesses to Bruton Wills is that, with two main exceptions, for a period of less than one hundred years females signed as witnesses. The earliest authentication that has emerged so far was the mark of Agnes Bennett on the Will of John French in 1630 and the latest that of Alice Gray on the Will of Robert Fry in 1713. Why this should be the case in this period is not clear although unlike in pre-Reformation days it was a time when a number of people could be in the room as a person lay dying and so made a Will. The seventeenth century also saw a decline in the influence of the Church which may have previously acted as a barrier to female participation.

There were two exceptions outside of this timespan. In 1510 the Will of John FitzJames, senior, was witnessed by

Elizabeth Vowell and Mary Fitz-James and in 1804 the Will of William Saunders was not only signed by attorney Edward Mitchell but also by Harriett and Louisa Sweeting. Such a situation must indicate that while there was no legal impediment for females to act as witnesses it was for some reason not the accepted practice. The small number of females involved may be misleading as on the copies of Wills made for probate purposes the names of some signatories were included but then the phrase "and many others" was used.

On at least two occasions the female witnesses, Agnes Bennett and Alice Burge, were unable to write their own names but made their mark instead, which may suggest that they were trusted servants in the household. In only one instance was an occupation specified as in 1688 Jane Graves who signed John Yeadle's Will was referred to as his nurse. Robert Fry in 1711 ensured that his Will was only known to one other family as it was witnessed by Michael Atkins, senior, Margery Atkins and Michael Atkins, junior, none of whom benefited from its terms. Just one Will, that of Susanna Gatehouse in 1652, was signed by two female witnesses, who were her kinswomen and no one else.

The question of authenticity was of crucial importance and so witnesses were a major element in this. After the names of the three witnesses to John Ottlye's Will of 1554 was added the phrase, "who recordeth this to be trew." In reality, however, any Will that was written in the testator's hand was regarded as valid even if there were no witnesses at all or had not been signed by the deceased. In at least two instances just initials were included, probably as the person concerned was so sick and near to death that a full signature was no longer possible. One such may have been Dame Margaret Berkeley in 1617 who described herself as "beinge weak of bodie" and she was in fact buried some eighteen days later.

The second instance related to the Will of Hugh Sexey in 1619 and demonstrated that using just initials could lead to disputes. An allegation was made by Thomas Banckes on behalf of his wife Anne, who claimed to be Sexey's direct heir, that Ursula Sexey "wished to acquire not only his personal estate worth £10,000 but also the property, and tried to get him to alter his Will on his death bed. Half an hour before his death she caused a supposed Will (including a gift to herself of the manor of Blackford for life) to be read to him, put a pen in his hand, and caused him to subscribe 2 imperfect letters as his hand writing on the Will. She put wax on the Will, made an impression with the seal and guided his hand to take it up." Banckes amongst other claimants also alleged that Ursula Sexey and some of the Trustees of Sexey's property destroyed a former Will that was in his house in Bruton. The Trustees denied all the allegations but the main weakness with Banckes' case was that while these actions were taking place he was actually present at the death bed, although he claimed "he was overcome with sorrow" and did not know at that stage that his wife was Sexey's heir. (7)

It is interesting to note that in the seventeenth century many testators did not sign their Wills but made their mark instead. Out of thirty Wills examined drawn up in the period from 1620 to 1687 some thirteen or 43% contained the mark of the person. Of these thirty Wills six were made by females of whom four made their mark. It did not necessarily mean that these people were illiterate as amongst them there were two yeomen, a cloth-ier and a prosperous cloth worker. Nine of the thirteen acknowl-edged that they were "sick of bodie" and so may have been too feeble to inscribe their full name. In fact a number of them such as Alice Hill, William Wilton and Richard Dimond were all buried within nine days of making their Wills.

A few testators were still making their mark in the nine-teenth century, such as Mary Talbot in 1806 and Daniel Morgan in 1853.

If a Will was not appropriately signed or witnessed it could create problems for the executor and then the potential beneficiaries. The usual procedure was for a reliable person to make a declaration on its validity. On 25th February 1629 John Mogg made his Will while "being sick in bodie but of good and perfect memorie" and then placed it in his chest. When he was on his deathbed just over a month later three men recovered it and added a memorandum, "that the said testator did acknowledge this to be his last will and testament the xxx daie of Aprill last past beinge found in his chest in the psence of us." Thomas Tice did not sign his Will in November 1683 but the following month one of the two witnesses was able to offer a reason, "that for about three quarters of a yeare before the death of the said deceased hee the said deceased was not able by reason of a Lamenesse in his right hand and arme to write his name."

Even when a testator could sign his own name an addition to a Will was sometimes judged to be so trivial that no signature or initials were added, but the authorities took a different view. Nicholas Goldesbrough duly signed his Will in 11th April 1738, as did three witnesses including Robert Yeatman who had drawn it up. Before the Will was sealed a memorandum was added on the back giving eight named people £1 each to buy a mourning ring. When this unsigned memorandum was queried Yeatman replied that he read it to Goldesbrough and he approved of it but Yeatman "apprehending the same not to be Material did not desire the testator to subscribe his name thereto." The Will was proved on 1st July in the same year, nearly two months after Goldesbrough was buried.

Another problem was that occasionally an error was made when a Will was drawn up. When the Hon. Charles Berkeley arranged his Will in 1757 he apparently bequeathed to his wife "my Silver Basin and Silver Candle Stick with Snuffers." The following year however he signed a Codicil to point out that there had been an error in transcribing his instructions and it should read "my Silver Basin CandleStick with Snuffers." Lucy Lloyd signed her Will in April 1831 but then added a Codicil on which she just made her mark apparently in September 1830 – some six months before the Will itself. Solicitor Christopher Moresby of Frome who had drawn up the Will was required to appear before the Commissioner in London in June 1835, four months after her burial, to explain the difference. He was able to report that when the Codicil had been added the word 'one' had been omitted in error and that he had the correct date of September 1831 recorded in his own Books and Accounts. The explanation was accepted and the Will proved in August 1835

In exceptional circumstances a Will could be oral, such as that of John Swanton, gentleman, in February 1640. Three witnesses, Thomas Holte, Thomas Ludwell and Richard Hackman, swore on oath that Swanton "beinge sicke in body butt of good remembrance" told them "that his brother ffrancis Swanton Esquier should bee his whole and Sole Executor, or hee used wordes to this effecte.....and shortlie after dyed." Probate was granted in April.

iii) Timing.

In the medieval period and far beyond there was the knowledge that all life must end in death and that preparations must be made. Yet it was not until the Tudor period that the formulae at the beginning of Bruton Wills acknowledged the certainty of death and the uncertainty of the time of it. The first surviving Will which made such a reference was that of Sir Maurice Berkeley in February 1580, "And callinge to remembrance the certentie of deathe and the incertentie of the tyme of the same." It was a sentiment that was to find expression in Wills in the seventeenth century such as in that of Sir Henry Berkeley in 1600, or expressed slightly differently by James Plymton in

1613, "calling to mynde the instability of this mortall lyfe and nowinge that nothinge is more certaine then death."

While some Wills, such as that of John Thomas in 1758, continued to use the same phrase, many others in the eighteenth century, such as John Whitehead in 1714, Mary Griffen in 1722 and Robert Pavy in 1796, used a shorter phrase such as "calling to mind the uncertainties of this life." Death appeared to be a word which they did not wish to mention, placing the emphasis instead either upon resurrection or simply starting with the distribution of their worldly possessions without any other preamble.

There is evidence to suggest that many people were not inclined to make a Will well in advance of their deaths as there was the fear that in some way the action would bring death closer or would weaken that person's authority within the family once it was known what he or she intended to do with their possessions. The tendency in Bruton therefore was to make a Will shortly before death. Table 12 indicates that of forty Wills made between 1554 and 1754 for which the date of the Will and the date of burial may be traced with certainty twenty-six or 65% were drawn up within fourteen days of death.

TABLE 12 Short time between a Will made
and burial in Bruton 1554-1754.

7 days and under	8 to 14 days	15 to 21 days	22 to 28 days	Over 28 days and under 2 months	2 months and over	Total
17	9	5	3	2	4	40

In addition a further eleven out of thirteen Wills were made and proved within two months which means that in total some forty-six out of fifty-two Wills or 88.5% were made within two months of death.

On the other hand as Table 13 indicates a much smaller number of Wills were made considerably further in advance, sometimes years, which may suggest that some people were able to contemplate the possibility of their own death, including in particular circumstances.

TABLE 13 Longer time between a Will made
and burial in Bruton 1554-1754.

3 to under 6 months	6 to under 12 months	12 to under 24 months	24 to under 36 months	Over 36 months
2	1	3	2	0

A further five Wills were made and proved within a period of two to five years. One of the longest periods was that of the Will of William Swanton which was drawn up on 27th May 1637 and proved on 17th May 1642, some ten days short of five years. It may have been that in a few instances there was the belief that a person was dying, made a Will but then recovered. Others may have felt that as they had significant estates to distribute, they wished all their affairs settled long before death, such as Sir Maurice Berkeley who made his Will in February 1580 but it was not proved until nearly two years later.

By the very end of the eighteenth century and throughout the nineteenth century it was not uncommon for the period between a Will being made and death occurring to be over a year, such as in the cases of Nicholas Everatt and William James. Lucy Lloyd made her Will over four years before her death but the longest period would seem to be that of William Saunders whose Will was originally made over fourteen years before his death. Some of course remained very short such as

Richard Biggs aged eighty-four who was buried just twelve days after he made his Will.

Those intrepid few undertaking long or hazardous journeys also tended to make Wills in advance. In 1624 Humphrey Wootton of Brewham, gent., made his Will when he was "About to take my journey into the Newfoundland." When Sir William Berkeley, the Governor of Virginia, was recalled by Charles II, he took the precaution of making his Will on 2nd May 1676, "being in perfect health of body and mind." He was after all judged by contemporaries to be the wealthiest man in the Colony, owning some 17,000 acres. He survived the journey back across the Atlantic but died in England in July 1677. In the same year as Berkeley was recalled his Secretary, Thomas Ludwell of Bruton, was in England preparing to travel back to America and so he too made his Will, "being bound on a voyage to Virginia." It was to be his last journey as well as he died in the Colony the following year, and found prominent resting places, first under a large inscribed gravestone on his estate 'Rich Neck' and then from the mid-nineteenth century in the graveyard of Bruton Parish Church in Williamsburg, Virginia.

Before he set out on his ambassadorial mission to Paris in 1675 John 1st Lord Berkeley of Stratton did not make his Will but took the precaution of transferring the management of his affairs into the hands of his friend, the diarist John Evelyn, who commented that it was "upon the great importunity of my Lady and Mrs Godolphin to whom I could refuse nothing."

In the seventeenth century it became increasingly common for sailors to make a Will before embarking on a ship and in November 1696 Thomas Warner of Bruton did just that. He referred to himself as a "Marr. now belonging to his Maties Ship Grayhound Capt James Atkins Comander." His Will indicated that he was resigned to the fact that his death would quite likely occur at sea, "And my body to be disposed of at the will of the Almighty being bound to the Seas and in consideration of the incertainty of this transitory life and that it is appointed for all men once to dye." He left everything he possessed to "my loving ffriend Humphry Emptage of Deal in the county of Kent Yeoman to be disposed of by him at his own will and pleasure." In January 1713 Robert Fry also described himself as a Mariner but did not specify a ship, although in his Will he gave £10 to Capt. Henry Lawrence. Fry was probably already in Bruton when he made his Will as he was buried there on 23rd January 1713, eighteen days after signing it.

The expectation that death would strike at any time meant that many testators included alternatives in their Wills in case they outlived a particular beneficiary. As early as 1429 John Gregory left 100s to John Barbow "if he shall be living, and if he shall not live to the age of 12 years, I will that they be distributed by my executors amongst the poor for my soul." In 1544 Stevyn Broke also arranged that if his son did not come home from the war then his wife Christian was to use the money to provide a priest "to pray for me and all Christian souls."

In 1542 Robert Chyke decided that a legacy should pass to a younger son: "And farther that that I have geyved to Robert Chyke the son of William Chyke shall remayn to the next eldyst brother of the sayd Robert yf god thak hym from the Worlde before the age of Twenty yeres." Agnes Plumley arranged in 1560 that goods that she gave to her son William should pass to the children of Richard Tabor and John Plumley "yf yt happeneth the Saide Willm to die before he hath wyef and children."

Such arrangements continued through the next two centuries with increasingly legacies being divided between survivors, for example, in 1656 Thomas Mogg left £20 each to his six children but instructed that if one or more of them died the sum was to be divided equally between the rest. The development of Trusts, especially in the later eighteenth and nineteenth centuries, meant that very detailed directions could be included to take into account premature deaths. Sometimes as in the case of the Goldesbrough family these instructions could cover many pages.

iv) Administrative matters.

One task that developed in importance through the centuries was to revoke any previous Wills and Testaments, although as many Wills were made near to death, especially in the earlier part of the period, few people in fact needed to do so. The first occasion when this revocation appeared in a Bruton Will was during the reign of Elizabeth in the Will of John ffrye in 1588, "Item I utterly revoke and adnull all and every other former wills Legacies testaments and bequests by me in any wise before this time made, willed or bequeathed." This sentence or very similar ones remained in use for the rest of the period under consideration.

In practical terms the inclusion of such a statement was designed to help prevent any disputes or challenges to a Will, as in fact was the case with Hugh Sexey's Will in 1619. For the Wills that did include this stipulation it is impossible to determine how far it was successful. In reality between 1588 and 1688 out of over forty Wills only thirteen contained such a statement, itself an indication that most people had not made an earlier Will. From the beginning of the eighteenth century, however, its inclusion became much more standard and appeared in the overwhelming majority of Wills for the next two centuries.

A second administrative task was to ensure that directions given in a previous Will by another deceased person that related to the present testator should be repeated, honoured and carried out. In 1588 John ffrye recorded in his Will that at an earlier date Lady Berkeley (probably Elizabeth, the second wife of Sir Maurice Berkeley, who made her Will in 1584) had left £20 "to be imployed to the use and releife of fower poor folks of the towne of Bruton" and that he and Richard Blackwell had "oversighte and disposeinge of the same." He designated "in my place my welbeloved in Christ Richard Hyll" continue the process. In her Will in 1626 Dame Elizabeth Berkeley ordered that one hundred pounds that was in her possession and had been left to her daughters Margaret and Jane "by theire Grandmother Killygrewe" should be handed over.

Nearly one and a half centuries later the practice still continued as in her Will of January 1775 Susannah Hunt of Pitcombe left all her household goods, furniture and plate to her daughter Elizabeth, "except such part of the plate as belongeth to my late husband's ffamily and which by his Will is directed to be divided between my two Sons."

A third administrative task was for the testator to remind his survivors of any arrangements which had been made for property before death. These men were not only wealthy but also very prudent. In 1566 Nicholas Gilbert included in his Will, "Item as concerninge my Lande I will that it gooe and remeyne hereafter accordinge as my Evidec. And Writings doo shewe." Thomas Whitehead had clearly made some earlier provision for his eldest son Manasseth as in his Will in 1690 he left him just 10s as he "has had a considerable portion already." Exactly what form this had taken was not specified but he clearly did not inherit the main business as this, along with Thomas's house, passed to his second son John. Manasseth, however, was later described as a clothier of Bruton so Thomas may have established him in a separate business.

The most successful and in the long term beneficial action for the town was the transference by Hugh Sexey in 1616, some three years before his death, of most of his lands and property to twelve Trustees. The proceeds from his estate were to be devoted "to such Charitable and good uses as they or the greater number of them shall sett downe, lymitte, nominate and appoynte." (8) As his subsequent deathbed Will was so brief no mention was made of this transference although its existence was never challenged.

That other men and women had made some provision for various members of their family may be inferred from the way in which a nominal sum of 1s was bequeathed to some children, often married ones. In 1656, for example, Thomas Mogg bequeathed £20 each to six of his children but only 1s each to the two eldest sons, Richard and Felix who were both over twenty-one, and to his married daughter Hannah Barnard. In 1722 Mary Griffen left the whole of her estate to her son George except 1s that was to be given to daughter Anne. A family problem may be implied by the Will of William Morris in 1667 as he left 1s to his son William but added later in the document, "Item I doe release unto my sonne William Morris the Judgement of Two hundred pounds which I have against him."

Finally there was clear evidence in a number of Wills of the concern by the dying person that the terms of the Will should not be breached and so appropriate provisos were included. The simplest method was to insert a clause placing a restriction upon a bequest. This procedure was adopted by Ann Creed in 1757 when she gave property to her daughter for her sole use and barred "all other Persons from Intermeddling", even though she was married. One of the most strident provisos was written by Sir Henry Berkeley in 1600 and may well indicate pronounced tensions within the family. "Itm my wyll ys that yf my eldest sonne or any wth his pryvetey or consent, shall goe about to frusterate or make voyd this my wyll or any pt therof, or shall impeache his mother of her Joynter, or any pt therof, that then yt shalbe in the powre of my sayd wyfe to dispose of my leas of norwood to my two younger sonnes duringe the lyfe of my eldest sonn so as yet after his time the sayd leass may then to his heyrs male." This clause was significant in financial terms for when Sir Maurice Berkeley, the eldest son, made his Will in 1617 he referred to some £4,500 being derived from Norwood Park in "Rentes, Issues and profitts." He had clearly undertaken no action that would have threatened his inheritance.

Robert Ludwell used a similar ploy in 1673 when he granted his son Thomas "All my Grounds called Cogly Grounds and all my Estate therein" on condition that within two years after Robert's decease Thomas paid his mother £400, an indication of the value placed upon some land in the vicinity of Bruton. If he failed to do so "then it shall be lawfull to and for myne Executrix and her assignes To enter into the said Grounds and to dispose of them at her and theire Will and pleasure."

Placing a restriction upon the receipt of money in relation to marriage was used in a number of Wills, for example, in 1567 Walter Tynbury of South Brewham bequeathed to "Edythe Nyxon my daughters daughter to her maryage twentie nobles so that she be ruled and maryed by the consent of her gramother and her uncles John Tynbury and Willm Tynbury." The second Sir Maurice Berkeley gave £2,000 to his daughter Margaret and £1,500 to his other daughter Jane, both with the proviso that they would receive nothing if either of them "shall marrie without the consent or good likinge of my said wife and sonne Charles Berkeley or one of them." Just over a hundred years later in 1718 Henry Sampson used exactly the same proviso when he bequeathed £200 each to his daughters, Jane, Elizabeth and Grace.

In 1560 Agnes Plumley gave a similar direction but on this occasion it was designed for her son, "I will also that my Sonne

Willm shall not marry without the concentt of my overseers." She did, however, proceed to add an incentive for his future conduct, "yf my saide overseers doe expectant that he doe give hym selfe to thrift and honestie and soe doe continewe I will that they then do deliver parte of the goodds or the hole at their discression to the said Willm."

c) Wills: Bequests of the deceased to family

Throughout the centuries one of the principal objectives of the dying person was to ensure that their possessions should be bequeathed to the appropriate members of their family. In the medieval period the Wills from Bruton followed the pattern that once arrangements had been made for the dead person's soul and for their body to be buried, then the Will simply moved on to include a list of items to be bequeathed elsewhere. In the Elizabethan period the formula at the beginning of a Will had been developed to make reference to the distribution of worldly goods, as for example, in 1588 John ffrye stated, "And for the disposinge and bestowinge of my goods I give them in manner and form followinge."

In the seventeenth century a few Wills reverted to the medieval idea of just disposing of goods without a comment, such as John Mogg in 1629, John Hodges in 1652 and Thomas Cornish als Allen in 1696. The vast majority however referred to their belief that God had bestowed their goods upon them, for example, in 1630 John French declared, "And as concerninge those transitorie goodes wherewith it has pleased god to blesse me withal I doe dispose and give in manner and forme as followeth." Most Wills used the word 'bless' but a number such as Thomas Mogg in 1656 favoured 'bestowe' and Edward Norton in 1660 'lent me'.

At the beginning of the eighteenth century there was a very abrupt change in format as all references to God bestowing worldly goods ceased immediately. It was never used again in any Bruton Will throughout the next two centuries. Wills remained a way of transmitting property to family and friends but they ceased to have a spiritual dimension, except for committing a soul to God and often giving thanks for a sound mind.

i) Bequests to a wife.

As a married man approached death there was inevitably concern on his part to ensure that sufficient provision was made for his widow. In the overwhelming majority of cases therefore a widow received a life interest in property or other goods before they were passed on to the next heir. An all-embracing clause was often used such as that in 1743 by Richard Creed, "that my beloved wife Ann Creed shall have Hold and Enjoy all and singular my real Estates of what Nature or kind soever and wheresoever for and during the term of her natural life." John Goldesbrough was even more specific in 1767 when he bequeathed to his wife Anne for her natural life "all my ffreehold Messuages Lands Tenements and Hereditaments Situate lying and being in the County of Somerset or elsewhere."

Provision for a widow could take various forms. First it was not unusual to permit a woman to retain any goods that she had brought with her on marriage. In 1600 Sir Henry Berkeley declared, "I doe geve to my sayd wyfe, all such plate as she brought wth her, & if any of that be sold then my wyll ys that she be recompensed wth as much money or plate, at her choyse." In 1624 William Hellier decreed that his wife Agnes was to retain "all such howsehold stuffe as she brought with her at the time of our marriage." Later in the century in 1690 Thomas Whitehead required his widow to divide all his household goods and plate between his children, "but all such maiden goods as she brought with her I wholly give her to dispose as she shall think fit." In the same year in a Codicil to his Will Maurice, Lord Fitzharding, left to his wife his coach and coach horses and in addition she was to retain "all the jewells and Plate her Mother gave her and the flowerpott Hangings all wch were hers before."

As part of her marriage settlement Richard Amor's mother had retained Yard Barton and Hooper's Close in Pitcombe. On her death these passed to Richard and in his Will in 1822 he bequeathed them to his younger brother John as he appeared to have no direct heirs.

In the eighteenth and nineteenth centuries some Wills made reference to recompense for a wife's dower but it was often linked to other customary rights such as a third and so was impossible to distinguish on it own.

Second a widow could receive a cash payment. In 1542, for example, Robert Chyke gave his wife £66 13s 4d and in 1600 Sir Henry Berkeley arranged for his wife Margaret to receive £100 a year "out of my parke of Norwood." By 1643 part of these lands were mortgaged and from the repayments Robert Albin specified that his widow could be paid an annuity of £40 a year by Sir Charles Berkeley. In 1738 Nicholas Goldesbrough simply gave his wife Judith "the Summe of Seven hundred pounds to be payd her within one Month after my decease."

Third, and much more common, was for a widow to receive a quantity of household goods. Some men used a general clause such as John Kenniston of Redlynch in 1678, "My wife shall have use of all my goods for life." In 1738 as well as the sum of money Nicholas Goldesbrough added, "I likewise give to my Wife any part of my Plate or Goods as she shall think proper to take." Occasionally a single item was identified, such as in 1718 George King wished that his widow "shall have the use of my Silver Tankard during the term of her natural life."

A small number of extremely wealthy families identified a whole range of goods so the list became very long. In 1538, for example, Sir John Fitzjames left to his wife £100 worth of plate, "two of the best beddes of downe at Redlinch....with fustians and coverledds, three feather beds and thre mattras with coverledds and blankets, two payre of best sheetes, all such chaynes, flowers, ringes and other jewels as she hath used to were." There were also tablecloths, napkins and a range of animals. There were many similarities with the bequest of Sir Maurice Berkeley in 1580 to his widow, "to may saide wieff all the furniture in the chamber in the toppe of the howse, commonlie called the gallorie chamber, as well hangings, beddes, bedsteedes, testers, with the pallet & canapye there, and also three palletts in the gallorie and the bedde in litleease with all their furniture." She was also to receive half of all the linen, brass and pewter in Bruton Abbey.

As houses became more and more comfortable other items began to be mentioned, such as in 1711 Robert Fry included not only "pewter brass bedding Linen Hangings" but also "Chaires Cushions Looking glasses Tableboards and Other my household goods." Some items were much more personal, for example, the Hon. Charles Berkeley gave to his wife "all the Jewells Watches and other things usually worn by her as the Ornaments of her Person" and she was also to receive "for her Life the use of all my Plate that was her late ffather's."

Fourth, some testators specified a particular property or lands that they wished to be passed to their widow for the period of her life. In 1678 for example William Day left to his wife Alice, "All those my Lease hold Tenements with thappurtenances wherein I now live Scituate lyinge and beinge in Discove." In 1718 Henry Sampson granted to his wife Christian not only "my Messuage or dwelling house lands tenements and hereditaments....situate lying and being in South Brewham" and which were leased to William Tice, but also "All that my Messuage and Tenement called Waddon and the several Closes thereunto belonging, and also one other Close of Pasture called Veincoats Close."

Finally, over and above all these specific bequests, in a very large number of instances the wife also received the residue of the estate, after other legacies and items had been arranged. What actually constituted the residue was never stated but in some cases it left the widow in a very favourable position for the rest of her life.

Not all of the gifts to wives were unrestricted and various conditions could be imposed, as in the Will of John Ottlye in 1554, "And for my goodess without anye other legacyes other to churche or children, to Johan my wife whom I make executrix, on condition she leave all goods remaining at her decease to James my son." A note was added, "where unto Johan beynge called dyd fullye agree and concente." Much more common, however, was a restriction that centred on re-marriage. For some men there was clearly a deep concern that money, property and goods which they had either received from their ancestors or had amassed during their lifetime and so wished to pass on to their children, could be diverted to the children of a second or subsequent marriage. In addition they did not believe that they should continue to provide financial support to a former wife as that burden should be transferred to her new husband. In 1643, for example, Robert Albin decreed that the annuity of £40 a year to his wife should cease if she re-married. In 1718 Henry Sampson arranged that all his bequests to his wife would pass to his children on "her day of marriage with any other after taken husband." Daniel Morgan specified in 1853 that his wife Susan should only retain the Blue Ball and Wellington Inns "so long as she shall continue my widow and unmarried."

Austin Goldesbrough's Will in 1757 was possibly more severe from the point of view of his widow as he gave her his dwelling house along with its contents and land adjoining during her natural life, "or the end of three Months next after the Marriage of my said son Austin." At that time it appeared that his widow Katharine was required to vacate the property. In this instance however the clause was not activated as Austin junior was to follow his father to the grave in February 1763 aged thirty-nine and unmarried, whereas his mother finally died in July 1791 aged eighty-nine.

From the evidence of Bruton Wills it would seem that when a man was in a position to make a Will, adequate provision was included for his widow. While it has been possible to examine some of the areas where she was granted a legacy or bequest, it has not been feasible to place an overall value on what was actually received. In addition to 'the residue' not being defined, there were other imponderables: these Wills rarely mentioned a wife's customary right to one third of an estate and what that was worth. In 1711 Robert Fry, for example, gave his wife "two closes lying at Brewton aforesaid called dropping Lane Closes....in compensation of her third or dower." Sometimes a wife received goods that were described under the general terms of 'moveable and unmoveable' but were never defined.

On occasions when all the property and lands were placed in a Trust which was to benefit a widow during her lifetime, the amounts involved were not specified. In this connection the Will of Samuel Mead of South Brewham in 1827 was particularly interesting as he ordered his three Trustees to sell all his property after the decease of his wife Mary but he gave her power to dispose of one half of it as she saw fit. Marriage settlements and the implications from them were rarely discussed in Wills, although in his Will in 1757 the Hon. Charles Berkeley honoured his Marriage Covenant which was made with his wife, Mrs Frances Killigrew, on 24th May 1745. By the terms of this arrangement he was to give her £1,000 for her own use if she survived him and the sum was to be paid within three months after his death.

Mention of a wife in a Will brought forth a range of terms of endearment from the dying husband, at least from the seventeenth century. In reality there do not seem to be any such words or phrases of affection in surviving Wills from Bruton itself before 1600. In 1568 in South Brewham, however, Walter Tynbury referred to "my welbe loved wyffe Edythe." While such terms may well have become part of the general formula in a Will, that they were not included in all Wills may indicate a genuine level of feeling in some instances.

The first occasion when such a phrase appeared in a Bruton Will was in that of Sir Henry Berkeley in 1600 when he referred to Dame Margaret Berkeley as "my welbeloved wyfe." It was a term also used by John Thomas in 1758 and shortened to 'beloved' by Richard Creed in 1743. In the late seventeenth and throughout the eighteenth centuries the word 'loving' was applied to a wife by men such as William Tice, Henry Sampson and Nicholas Goldesbrough. The commonest term used, however, was 'dear' which was included in the seventeenth century by men such as William Morris and Richard Dimond. It seemed to have been in standard usage by the nineteenth century being included by Thomas White, John Mills and Daniel Morgan.

A variation which appeared on a number of occasions in the seventeenth century was 'deere loving' or 'dear and loving', as witness the Wills of Sir Maurice Berkeley in 1617, William Swanton, Robert Ludwell senior and William Day. One Will that was rather more flamboyant was that of Sir William Berkeley in 1676 when he left all his goods and property to "my dear and virtuous wife, the Lady Francis Berkeley." This endearment appeared despite the fact that the influence and actions of his second wife were felt by many contemporaries to be the main reason for his fall from grace with Charles II.

Berkeley made reference in his Will to "my dear sister, Mrs Jane Davies." A small number of other Wills also included a term of endearment for another member of the family. Thomas Ludwell bequeathed money to "my dear Mother" and land to "my dear brother." Anne Creed made "my Beloved Daughter Judith Butt" her sole executrix and Thomas White hoped that his widow would take care of "My Dear Children." When it came to overseers Thomas Albin appointed "my loving brothers" and William Morris "my loveinge ffreinds Robert Ludwell Richard Beaseley and John Ames."

The decision that a testator made could have huge implications for his estate once it was in the hands of his wife, especially if there was no male heir. Although John de Mohun was a successful and distinguished knight he was heavily in debt, possibly as he spent huge sums trying to marry his daughters into various other aristrocratic families. He arranged therefore that the management of his vast estates, including Dunster and Minehead, should be placed in the hands of his wife Joan. After his death in 1376, as there were no sons from the marriage, she agreed to sell the reversion of the estate to Lady Elizabeth Luttrell, who was the great granddaughter of Edward I, for 5000 marks. This meant that on Joan's death the estates would be transferred to Elizabeth and, although such a sale was not a common practice, it provided a good example of the economic power of wealthy widows and the part that they could play in society. In fact Lady Elizabeth died before Joan and so in 1404 it was her son, Sir Henry Luttrell who succeeded to the lands and lordship of Dunster which included the patronage of Bruton Priory and therefore after more than two hundred and fifty years the de Mohun connection with the Priory ended and the Luttrell family became the patrons

ii) Bequests to children.

Throughout the centuries under consideration children were undoubtedly the largest single category of legatees as a very significant proportion of Wills included them. The eldest son as the male heir was usually the principal beneficiary but, as has already been discussed, there was a tendency through time to include younger sons as well. In many cases of course the full inheritance of the eldest son did not materialize until after the death of his mother. In instances where the father was probably already a widower or sufficient provision had been made for the widow, the residue of the estate passed to the eldest son immediately, as happened in the Will of William Swanton in 1637 and Robert Albin in 1643. Occasionally it was divided between mother and son as occurred in the case of the Will of Thomas Albin in 1603.

Not unsurprisingly the tools of a trade were passed on to a son, such as those of the chandlery and roping business given by Henry Ottis als Calowe to his son John in 1554. In 1691 Thomas Whitehead bequeathed to his son John "my Cloth press and shop of tools with my furnace standing in the Dye house", along with £400 worth of "cloth wool and yarn." In 1696 Thomas Cornish als Allen, another clothier, left to be divided equally between his two sons, Thomas and William, "my Shop of Tools Instruments and Materialls of Trade and my three ffurnaces." In 1757 Austin Goldesbrough passed on to his son not only the tools of his cloth business but also the necessary premises as well.

In some instances a deceased father was in the favourable position of being able to leave a legacy in money: so for example, in 1577 Matthew Grene left his son John 100 marks and his youngest daughter Mary 200 marks; in 1647 Peter Tinnie was able to give two of his sons 10s each, another £32 and the fourth £40, which reflected the fact that the first two were already adults and probably married with children of their own, as witness the number of grandchildren bearing the same surname. In 1738 Nicholas Goldesbrough left his son Austin not only property in Gillingham in Dorset but also £300 in cash. A few years earlier in 1704 John Baynard of Wanstrow had arranged for £2,700 to be divided between his children and this was to include Ralph the youngest with the proviso "if he be bred a scholar."

Household and other items appeared in abundance, for example, in 1543 Thomas Walter left his son Walter, "a Crock, a pair of hose and my plough harness.....to Richard Walter my son two platters." In the same year William Gane left to his son John "xli, a great crock and iiij silver spoons. To William my son xli, a great crock, a cow and a bed." Thomas Cornish als Allen left to his sons and daughters "two feather beds in the great Chamber and the Bedsteeds, Curtaines Rallins, Bolsters, Pillows, Ruggs and blanckets to the same belonging." There were also three other fflock beds and son William received "the Cupboard in the great Chamber" and Thomas "the Presse in the Hall Chamber."

The household items which Robert son of Thomas Albin was bequeathed in 1603 were varied and provide an interesting example of what was judged to be moveable at that period, "the standing bedstead and truckle bedstead in the parlour, the benches seelinges, tackes and glasse there, the boordes and benches in the hall with the glass of the windows and seelings in and about the house." In fact in the medieval period and beyond windows, doors and even chimneys were regarded as personal property and so were often bequeathed separately. So valuable were windows that many were constructed in such a way that they could be taken down and stored in a place of safety when the householder was away from home. In the reign of Henry VIII judges ruled that windows were part of a house and should not be removed separately but the practice was still common in the reign of Charles I a century later.

It was no surprise that in such a rural area, and especially in the earlier part of the period, animals and agricultural implements were bequeathed as well. In 1544 Thomas Walter gave sons Thomas and John a colt each and Hugh a yearling; Roger Ames in the same year bequeathed his son Steven a cow and a heifer; and in 1546 William Walter gave his sons Christian and Philippe a yearling each. Two centuries later Peter Ames of Wyke Champflower left to one of his sons, also named Peter, amongst other items, "Six of my Cows, One yoke of Oxen, one Mare, my old Waggon.....one Tull or Plow." Earlier in the century in 1713 James Bisse of Batcombe had left his son Thomas "a white cow and all my sheep."

Provision was made for daughters and they too received the practical bequest of animals, especially at the period of the Reformation. In 1543, for example, John Hoper alias Smyth gave his daughter Isabel "three cows, also a sheep, a lamb and a gray gelding." The following year Thomas Walter left his daughter Agnes a cow, along with "the greatest pan." In 1546 John Langer also left his daughter Mary a cow.

When a man was a widower and had no surviving male heirs the expectation would be that his estate would pass to any daughters. In 1851, for example, Stephen Penny was in that position and so he bequeathed to his two daughters, Elizabeth and Mary, "All and singular my real estate whatsoever and wheresoever And also all my personal estate of what nature or kind soever."

The commonest bequest made to daughters throughout the period under consideration was money. On occasions this was linked to marriage and was clearly designed to enhance their marriage prospects, especially within the wealthiest families. In other cases it may have been designed to give a small degree of independence, although with married daughters such gifts usually passed to the husband.

The sums of money given outright without being specifically linked to marriage varied significantly. In 1509, for example, Richard Philippys left his two daughters Alice and Anne £10 each. His Will was in fact the only surviving pre-Reformation one from Bruton that named daughters. By 1673 Robert Ludwell was in a position to leave his daughter Mary £500 and in 1738 Nicholas Goldesbrough bequeathed his daughter Anne £600.

A distinction was often made between those females who were still single and those who were married and had therefore already received a cash settlement. In 1647 Peter Tinnie gave his married daughter Joane Beaslie 10s but his unmarried daughters Mary and Elizabeth £60 each. In 1676 Alice Wood, one of the married daughters of Richard Dimond received just £2 and the other Margarett Berriman "the Table board in the Parlour Chamber which is next to the doore." Some fathers were more generous as in 1597 Francis Poole gave one married daughter Annas ffry £20 and the other Agnes Coward £10. Robert Albin was in a similar position in 1643 as to two married daughters Edith Hole and Christian Howe he gave £10 a piece and to a third Mary Jeffery £100 along with "one of my best featherbeds and all things thereunto belonging."

When Thomas Wilton drew up his Will in 1639 he appeared to have had no male heirs and therefore much of his estate was given to his five daughters with the eldest Agnes Neale receiving his house and the other daughters from £5 to £20 each.

In a number of instances the money bequeathed to daughters was directly linked to their marriage day, as for example Sir Maurice Berkeley in 1580 arranged for £600 to be paid to each of his daughters Anne and Margarett "to the furtherance of theire marriage." His grandson, the second Sir Maurice, was more generous, bequeathing his two daughters Margarett and Jane £2,000 and £1,500 respectively, "for her marriage portion or advancement in marriage." A suitable marriage for a daughter could have immense social or political implications for landowning families in the Tudor and Stuart periods when so much land was changing hands.

Amongst other families the amount of money available to be paid to daughters towards their marriage days varied considerably, so that, for example, in 1588 John ffrye was in a position to give each of his two daughters, Margarett and Agnes £1, "to be payde her att the daye of her marriage." In 1655 William Ewens of Hadspen gave each of his three daughters £40, to be paid within one year of the marriage day and in 1691 Thomas Whitehead bequeathed his daughter Hannah £400 for the day of her marriage but if she did not marry this sum was to become an annuity of £20 a year.

Thomas Albin, a yeoman, was fortunate that although he had a large family of surviving children, he had sufficient wealth to provide for each of them. As well as four sons he had five daughters, one of whom, Joane Walter was already married and who received £1. His four single daughters, Dorothie, Edith, ffraunces and Margaret, were each promised £26 13s 4d "to be delivered unto her at her daie of marriage." Each one of them also was given two silver spoons.

Silver items were also bequeathed to their daughters by other men, for example, in 1544 William Gane gave two silver spoons each to his two married daughters, Agnes Foyle and Isabell Sledge. Silver spoons were clearly an important item at this early period as in the same year Stevyn Broke gave four silver spoons to each of his daughters Christian and Agnes, the latter also received "a pan of a bushel." Silver remained an easily transmittable bequest so in 1710 Robert ffry gave to his daughter Joan, "my silver cup sixteen silver Spoones ffour small Silver salts and One silver porringer", along with "my great Clock." Over one hundred years later in June 1823 Harry

Sims of Shepton Montague gave one of his daughters his silver tankard and the other his silver pint cup.

Household items could be of practical value to daughters so in 1546 Isabell, daughter of William Cleves of Cole received "j crock and iij pewter vessels." Roger Hurman's daughter Mary was bequeathed "ij crocks, ij pans, ij caldrons, a hat, two cappes and a kirtle." Richard Creed, on the other hand, in 1743 simply arranged for his married daughter Judith to receive all his household goods after the death of his wife.

Daughters were occasionally left the wearing apparel of their mother on her death, a type of bequest that did not appear very often from father to son. It would be presumed in the latter case that a wife receiving the residue of her husband's estate would take the necessary action in disposing of his attire. In 1626 Dame Elizabeth Berkeley willed to her two daughters, Margaret and Jane "my wearinge Clothes." In 1648 Joanne Sampson gave to her two married daughters, Alice fflower and Anne Baylie, "all my wearing apparel and to gold rings equally to be divided betweene them." In 1833 Mary Clarke left all her wearing apparel to her married daughter Ann Allen except "my Silk Shawl which I give to my Granddaughter."

More unusual, but apparently prevalent in the sixteenth century, was for tools of a trade to be bequeathed to a daughter, generally in families where there was no direct male heir. It may also be the case that the particular daughter was already involved in that trade. In 1520, for example, Richard Holmede, a tucker who leased a mill on Combe Brook from John Fitzjames, left his daughter Christian, amongst other house-hold items, "iiij peyres of Tuckers Sheris." Just over twenty years later in 1543 John Hoper alias Smyth arranged that, "After the decease of my wife I give all my implements belong-ing to a smith's trade to my said daughter Isabel." Over three centuries later in 1857 a slightly different arrangement was made by Clock and Watch Maker Charles Oram as he bequeathed to his daughter Maria Evans his "stock in trade."

As families purchased more property, especially in the nineteenth century, it became much more common to bequeath houses to daughters, so for example, in 1805 William Meachem gave "3 tenements facing the Cross" to his daughter Betty Stone, along with £340, with the proviso that she support her aunt Betty Small during her life. If these two females were unable "to agree to dwell together" the latter was to receive 4s 6d a week from Betty Stone. Perhaps there were tensions within the family. Another interesting arrangement was in the Will of William James in 1817 as he gave to his daughter Sarah, "all such parts of the House in which I now reside with the Buildings and Appurtenances thereunto belonging as are not leased by me to my Son Henry James." As William James was a Whitesmith he may well have carried on his trade in one or more of the buildings attached or close to his house. Sarah also received £400 in cash, to be paid within twelve months from William's death.

The property arrangements made by Charles Oram for his daughter Maria Evans in 1857 were more complex. She was to receive immediately not only the cottages that he had erected on a garden in Silk House Barton but also two of the four cottages he leased in South Brewham. The other two cottages there were given to his granddaughter Mary Ann Oram provided that she returned to Bruton within one year to claim them. If not, they too passed to Maria.

For some daughters and their children an inheritance was delayed and probably unexpected, such as in the case of the Sampson family. When Thomas Sampson made his Will on 26th August 1811, and which was proved on 21st June 1813 after his death in April aged eighty-five, he left his estates in places such as Bruton, Evercreech, North Brewham and East

Pennard to his wife for her natural life and then to his son Thomas and his heirs. No further provision was made and so after the deaths of both his wife and son with no heirs, his three daughters resorted to a private Act of Parliament, Sampson' Estate Act 1845 (8 Vict 1845), to ensure their inheritance, especially as two of them, Ann Ward and Elizabeth White had seventeen children between them who were still living.

As in the case of widows it was impossible to determine the extent and value of many of the bequests to children. In a few instances they were bequeathed the residue of an estate, such as John, son of William Gane in 1544 or Joan, daughter of Robert ffry in 1710 and what that entailed was not recorded. In addition although children were often named as 'lives' on a lease, reference to that lease, with the dwelling house and land passing to them, rarely appeared in Wills. In some cases where most of the estate was left to a wife and there were surviving young children, there was the implicit assumption that she would take care of and provide for them from the bequests she received from their father. In cases where children were already married no mention was ever made of what they had been given by way of a marriage settlement by their father.

Potentially one of the most generous of bequests was made by John Ludwell when he was dying childless in 1726. He placed all his property in a trust for his widow Agnes during her life but added a clause that, "in case my said wife shall happen to have any Issue by me or any other Husband that shall live to the age of one and Twenty years or be married that then (*the Trustees*) shall grant and convey the said premises to such Child or Children of my said Wife", and in such proportion as she deemed appropriate. In fact four years after John's death Mrs Agnis Ludwell married Mr Robert Cheeke by licence on 7th December 1730. The Parish Register does not record any christenings for them in the years that followed. The beneficiaries therefore became three nieces and nephews.

Perhaps one of the most poignant bequests appeared in the Will of Richard Dekyn in September 1471 for it demonstrated the ever-present reality of death which he himself was facing. Knowing that he would not live to see his offspring he nevertheless felt it incumbent upon him to include the following "Item, I bequethe to the child in my wife's wombe, if God fortune hit to have cristendome and live, 5 marc, when it commyth to full age."

iii) Bequests to other relatives.

An examination of surviving Wills from Bruton indicates that the dying were concerned to ensure that bequests were left to other relatives: sometimes as a gesture of generosity and sometimes as there was no wife or child. In a very small number of instances the actual relationship was not specified but a general word such as 'kinsman' was used. In 1429 John Gregory bequeathed to John Barbour "my kinsman one gown and xxs." In addition he gave 100s to John's son, also called John. In his Will in 1538 Sir John Fitzjames made a very large number of detailed bequests but added that the residue was "to be distributed among my por kynnesmen and women that have much nede and little helpe." In 1650 widow Christian Albin gave "my Kinsewoman Johane Hopkins.....a Cloath cotton gowne", and two years later Susanna Gatehouse made provision for "my two kinswomen Marie and ffrancis Clynton." Finally in 1676 Richard Dimond gave 10s to Elizabeth Hartry "my Kinswoman."

Usually, however, the relationship was specified and the commonest was to leave a legacy to grandchildren. While there were a very small number of early references, such as in the Will of Amice Gregory in 1457, these bequests definitely appeared in Bruton Wills with increasing frequency in the later Elizabethan period, such as the Will of Petronell als Purnell Spicer in 1589 when she gave "to every one of my children's children twelve pence a peece." Legacies to named grandchildren appeared regularly in seventeenth century Wills but more rarely in direct form thereafter as increasingly Trusts were established which left money and property to a son or daughter and then their heirs, without naming grandchildren. Examples of this sort of arrangement may be seen in the Wills of Austin Goldesbrough in 1757 and John Goldesbrough a decade later.

In six out of fourteen Wills that gave money to grandchildren between 1589 and 1676 the sums bequeathed were £1 or less: Thomas Albin in 1603 left 3s 4d each to four grandchildren and Richard Dimond in 1676 "to each and every of my Granchildren that shall be lyving at the time of my decease Twenty shillings a peece." At the other extreme three testators left £100 to grandchildren such as Alice Hill to her granddaughter Elizabeth Dawe in 1640 and William Morris to his granddaughter Elizabeth Sharpe in 1667. The third was Joane Sampson who left the money to three grandchildren in 1648: the female one on the day of her marriage and the two males when they attained the age of twenty-one. One of these grandsons, John, also received the residue of her estate. James Albin became the recipient of a similar bequest three years later. It is impossible to determine exactly what or how much these two grandsons received but judging by the other bequests which their respective grandmothers made, they were both wealthy widows.

In a few instances grandchildren received goods of different kinds. In one of the earlier references to a grandchild Elizabeth Fitzjames bequeathed to Richard Barckeley, whom she described as "my sonne's son" when he reached the age of twenty-one, "a bason and ewer with the dolphyn and the conysse in the mydes of the bason.... All my cattle and household goods in Gloucestershire." In 1652 John Hodges gave each of his three grandchildren one "of my best silver spoones", and in addition one of them received "my side table", the second "Dew Bartas", (*pots*) and the third "my Press and Cubbert." In 1710 Robert ffry bequeathed to his granddaughter Susanna Sharp "my white bedd in the garrett and the bedstead bolster pillows two blankets and rug belonging unto the same."

In at least two cases grandchildren received a combination of money and goods, for example, in 1639 Thomas Wilton left each of his grandchildren £1 and in addition one of them, Mary Wilton, was given "the great brazen pann", another, Agnes March, "my wives golde Ringe" and a third, Margarett Hardinge, "one of the lesser Crockes." Widow Amey Gibbs in 1740 left £5 to one of her grandsons, Mathew Gibbs, while the other, Henry Ricketson received £2 along with "three spoons and all my books except my largest bible." Granddaughter Mary Rutherford was also given £5 along with "all my wearing apparel one pair of sheets my mauning ring one large spoon." In a direct reference to one more generation, her great granddaughter Amy Ricketson was to receive £2 when she reached twenty-one years of age. In 1806 Mary Talbot left all her money, securities, goods and chattels to her granddaughter Mary Lacey, but no indication was given of the extent or range of any of them.

The Will of William Mogg of Shepton Montague in 1718 was more unusual as after he had bequeathed his grandson William Mogg Woolmington lands in the village he gave him up to £150 to be apprenticed: "to put him out apprentice to any trade and Master that the said William Mogg Woolmington shall choose by and with the good liking consent and approbacon of the said Thomas Woolmington his father Provided always that he be not bound unto his said father." Thomas was a taylor from London and this proviso prevented him from gaining the legacy.

Brothers and sisters appeared regularly as beneficiaries, particularly from the reign of Elizabeth I. It has been suggested that this occurred when a dying person was single or childless but the evidence from Bruton Wills does not appear to substantiate fully this view as there were more surviving Wills which clearly indicated the existence of other close family members such as a wife or children.

In most cases it was a sum of money which was bequeathed, for example, in 1589 Edward Spicer gave his sister Anne Wyne £20 and in 1690 Maurice, Lord Fitzharding left his sister Jane Berkeley £200. In 1696, after many other family bequests, Thomas Cornish als Allen gave his two sisters, Joane White and Patience Allen £3 and £2 respectively. The Whitehead family tended to remember brothers and sisters as in 1690 Thomas Whitehead gave to his three sisters, all of whom were married, £1 each and in 1714 his son John in his turn gave to his older brother Manasseth "one piece of broad gold" and £5 each to his other brothers Thomas and George. Finally in 1816 Thomas White gave his three brothers and one sister £20 each, after having made arrangements for his wife and children.

In a few instances it was goods of various kinds that were bequeathed, for example, in 1542 after a long list of bequests to his immediate family, Robert Chyke gave to his brother Stephyn "a gowne clothe of mouster coler and furr of blake lamb." While widow Agnes Plumley left most of her goods and money to her son William, she also distributed some items to two sisters: Alice Tabor received amongst other things a featherbed with attachments, "my second best beades......my second harness girdle a blacke worsted kirtle my third gowne wit my best hood"; Maude Sendall was give "a cassocke my fowrth harness girdle and a kerchief." Ninety years later widow Christian Albin gave "unto my sister Johane Jordan my bedd whereon I lie furnished." The bequest to the brother and two sisters of James Plympton was more substantial as in 1613 they were promised his dwelling house after the death of his wife, even though he also had a daughter Joane.

On just one occasion when the deceased was survived by a wife, was a brother given the residue of the estate. In his 1624 Will William Hellier was not over-generous towards his wife Agnes as he allowed her to retain what she had brought to the marriage, gave her his "wearinge lynnen togeather with my best Bedd and boulster" and an annuity of £8 a year, payable quarterly. As there were no children the residue passed to his brother Symon Hellyer.

Needless to say there were men and women who died while they were single or had no surviving dependents and so brothers and sisters were the obvious recipients. Just before he died in February 1640 John Swanton managed to tell witnesses that he wished all his estate to pass to his brother Francis. Mariner Robert Fry was clearly a bachelor when he died in 1713 as he gave £200 a piece to two sisters, £50 to a third and the residue of his estate to his brother John. A century later John Dalton of Pitcombe placed all his property in trust, first for his sister Elizabeth and then after her decease for his brother Nathaniel.

When he died in Ireland in 1708 Samuel Brodripp, formerly of Wyke Champflower left the vaste majority of his estate to his brother John who still lived there. As well as household goods this included "my watch, Sword, Gould ring & Silver Tabacco box." Included in his Will was the rquirement that John should pay "Twenty shillings to the poore bachelors of the town of Bruton" within one year of his death. This appears to be the only surviving Will from this area which gave money to this category. Edge tool maker George King had no family of his own in 1719 and so as a token he left 1s each to four brothers and sisters and one guinea to another sister. In the same year William Russ bequeathed the majority of his landed property to his brother John and "my Plate household Goods and utensils of Household unto my sd two Sisters Elizabeth Russ and Jane Russ."

As a wealthy woman when spinster Lucy Temple died in 1733 she distributed her money and personal possessions far and wide, including twenty guineas apiece to "my Sister Portland my Brother Palmerston and my Brother Temple." Susanna Gatehouse, who died a spinster in 1652, had a much smaller estate but was still able to give her sister Joane Daggett six pounds. Mary Mead of South Brewham was a childless widow in 1827 when she made her Will and so she left everything to her two brothers and one sister.

In two other instances dying bachelors gave a brother the residue of their estates. The first was Thomas Tice alias Rogers in 1683 when he named his brother William as the executor as well. The second was William Pavy, a mercer in 1763, who also required his brother Robert to administer a fairly extensive estate as executor. Robert himself was to die a very wealthy man in 1796 without a direct heir but William had assumed that he would have heirs and therefore made his Will with the proviso that everything he bequeathed to Robert should eventually pass to them as his nephews and nieces.

Nephews and nieces were another category of potential family recipients. In 1543 for example, John Hoper alias Smyth, amongst various gifts to family gave "To Alice Madocke my sister's child one sheep with a lamb. To Edith Butler the child of my other sister one sheep with a lamb." This particular gift to these family members was very early as all the other surviving references to nephews and nieces appeared to date from at least the late seventeenth and eighteenth centuries, such as when in 1683 Thomas Tice alias Rogers gave his four nephews £50 each.

Samuel Brodripp bequeathed to his niece Mary £5 "when she comes to Ealeven yeares old" and a similar sum to his nephew John "when he comes to thirteen yeares old." If one died the money was to go to the other. In 1726 John Ludwell arranged that if his wife did not have any children then on her death £400 would be given to his niece Elizabeth Dampier, and nephews Thomas and William Dampier would have his ffee Simple Lands, and Leasehold and Copyhold Estates respectively.

In 1733 Lucy Temple was in a position to be generous to her nieces as she gave £500 to Lady Barbara Bentinck, £200 to Mrs Trevanion, £100 to Miss Ederton and £50 to Miss Rebecca fflower. In 1773 John, 5th Lord Berkeley of Stratton, having no children of his own left just under £50,000 to a large number of nephews, nieces, great nephews and great nieces. Four years earlier in 1769 shopkeeper Ellis Paine was nowhere near as wealthy and so he was only able to give £20 each to several nephews and nieces. In 1817 widow Ann Hallett left bequests to three nephews in the Laurence family in Bruton and to three nieces, including Elizabeth Laurence "my two leasehold cottages situate in the parish of Milton Cleavedown with garden and orchard belonging."

The same practices were occurring in neighbouring villages, for exmple, in Ansford fifteen nephews and nieces shared a bequest of £650 from farmer Thomas Barnes, aged forty-eight, with his widow receiving £350. It was noted that he had "acquired a fortune of more than £1000, by industry and frugality, as he worked when a boy for a penny a day and his victuals." In 1733 William Dibben of Shepton Montague bequeathed sums of between £10 and £80 to various nephews and nieces and then the majority of his estate to his nephew James Chaffey Cowper. In Pitcombe in 1822 Richard Amor left his property to a nephew and two nieces and in 1878 in Shepton Montague spinster Elizabeth Pickford gave most of her estate to six nephews and nieces.

In 1823 two Bruton nephews of fishmonger Richard Biggs benefitted extensively under the terms of his Will as he had no surviving children. One nephew, Richard Griffin Hole, received a house and garden in Silver Street, along with three closes of pasture, Bittomswell, Henley Close and Knacknells Ball; the other, William Hole, was given three houses in Patwell Street, one only after the death of Richard's former servant who was given a life interest, and a close of meadow called Dicketts Moor. In addition the residue of his estate was to be divided equally between them. Richard Biggs seemed to have conducted his business operation in London and this he left to another nephew Henry Creed so he was able to state, "And whereas I have granted to my nephew Henry Creed a lease of my house and premises at Temple Bar and have also given him the goodwill of my business I consider that I have amply provided for him."

Finally in 1902 widow Ann Bowring gave money and items to at least eleven different nephews and nieces, mainly in the Longman family, which included £125 to each and a range of items such as "my Clock under dome....My Spirit Stand and bottles......my wearing apparel....Silver Cream Jug."

In a small minority of instances the dying person made a bequest to the former generation, once again possibly indicative of no marriage having taken place, no family produced, the death of a partner or the relative youth of the testator. In 1471 Richard Dekyn included his father in his Will even though he was married with a pregnant wife, "Item, I bequethe to my father John Dekyn my best gown and my best hate, and in money 40s." One bequest that was more unusual was that of Roger Ames in 1544 for although he had a wife and two children who benefited from his Will, he also gave "to my father John Ames two acres of corn in the field and a debt due to me of 1s." It may have been that he operated in some sort of partnership with his father to work the land. Similarly in 1613 James Plympton had a wife and daughter for whom he made provision but the residue of his estate as left to his father,

James the elder. The case of William Pavy was more straight-forward in 1763 as he had no wife or children and so gave £100 each to his father and mother. In addition if his brother Robert failed to produce an heir then all William's large estate was to pass back first to his father and then his mother.

A different example appeared in 1817 in the Will of William James and seemed to be expectation rather than anything definite. He noted that, "I lately had the Misfortune to lose my Eldest Son William James in the West Indies and it is probable that by his death I may be entitled to part of his property." If that in fact proved to be the situation he went on to make arrangements for it to be divided equally between his remaining sons and daughters.

In two instances it was a mother alone who benefitted which may suggest that the father was already deceased. In 1816 Thomas White left to "My Dear Mother" £30, but in 1676 Thomas Ludwell had been much more generous as before he set sail again for Virginia he arranged that all the money he possessed in London should be placed in trust and "the whole interest to be paid to my dear Mother during her natural life." On her death the principal was to be divided equally among his four sisters.

In just one case it was an aunt who was to benefit, as in 1690 Thomas Whitehead gave £1 to his aunt Alice Wayford. When spinster Catherine Drew died in 1695 aged thirty-three her two grandmothers were apparently still alive as she made bequests to both of them, "Item I give to my Grandmother Mary Berriman widow the Summe of ffive pounds.....Item I give to my grandmother Margaret Drew widow the Summe of five pounds."

Another family member to be of some concern to the dying, and for whom provision was sometimes made, was often referred to, especially in earlier Wills, as a 'cosyn'. It was, however, a word that was used to describe a number of relationships and not necessarily the first cousin. Some clearly were of course, such as in 1557 when Richard Bower left 12d each to three 'cosyns', Agnes, Elizabeth and William Whylton, while at the same time giving the residue of his goods to his two uncles Walter and Raff Whylton. Such a close relationship was also evident in 1695 when Catherine Drew left an annuity of £4 a year "to my Aunt Mary Berriman her daughter."

On other occasions the term 'cosyn' was less clear or possibly more distant, for example, in 1538 Sir John Fitzjames made reference in his Will to his 'cosyns' Aldred and Nicholas Fitzjames and also "To my cosyn Roger Blewet a standing cupp of sylver, on of the three which I had of my Lorde of London, which cupp my Lord bequeathed to myn Aunte, his Grammother." This would make Roger a second cousin at least. John's widow Elizabeth in 1545 made bequests "to my cosyn Joane Fostewe my gown of black chamblett lyned with frise, and my curtill of taffata." Another 'cosyn' Anthony Gilbert was one of her executors and received a third of the residue of her goods. In 1719 William Russ gave his "cousen Mary Hodges" one third of all his household goods.

There are occasional references to other family members but they are very infrequent. In 1512 John Tyler included in his Will his stepson as "my wife sonne Sir Richard Bogy chanon of Brewton", to whom he bequeathed 20s and "a flatte pece of silver pond 8 uncs, and 6 silver spones." In 1545 Elizabeth Fitzjames left her daughter-in-law Dame Katheryne Barckleye "my second best velvet gown" and in 1554 John Plimpton gave his three daughters-in-law £1 each.

Elizabeth Fitzjames also made bequests to her two sons-in-law: the first Gibbes received "a standing cup" but the second

William Fraunces, who was married to her daughter Mary, was given much more, " a great goblet pownced and my trussinge bed in the porche chamber, a pair of shetes of calacowe, and a pair of pillowe towes." Nearly a decade later in 1554 widow Johan Peter gave the residue of her goods to her son-in-law Robert Rodway. A similarly named brother-in-law John Drew received 5s from Catherine Drew and her two sisters-in-law Edith Drew and Anne Smith received £50 and 5s respectively. In 1878 Elizabeth Pickford of Shepton Montague bequeathed to her widowed sister-in-law "two large Table spoons nine Pewter Dishes Seventeen Pewter plates my bell metal pot two brass Kettles and the sum of Twenty Seven Pounds."

A number of those who were facing death clearly took their responsibilities towards god children seriously and left them a small legacy in their Wills. What was very noticeable in the surviving Bruton Wills was that the majority of such bequests predate 1633 and nationally it has been noted that there was a marked decline in these gifts after the Civil War. It may well have been part of the change in attitude towards religion that occurred during that century.

In three instances a godchild received goods: the first came in 1527 when Dame Elizabeth Fitzjames bequeathed "to my godson Thomas Malet, a goblett gilte with the arms of Portcullis and the Rose, and 6 sylver spoonys"; the second came in 1560 when Agnes Plumley gave her godson Richard Tabor a heifer and the third in 1633 when Agnes Morris left her goddaughter Margaret Eliot "my best taffetu apron." More usual was for a small sum of money to be given, for example, in 1517 Alice Brymmore bequeathed "to evy of my Godchyldren viijd"; in 1554 Henry Ottis als Calowe gave 4d to each of his godchildren and twelve years later Nicholas Gilbert did the same but increased the amount, "To everie of my god children twelve pence a peece." In 1624 William Hellier's godson, John Baker, received £2.

Only four legacies appeared at a later period: the first was in 1695 when Catherine Drew gave one goddaughter, Catherine Bird "all my Woollen Clothes" and to another, fflorence Randall, 30s "which I lent her mother on the Pledge of a Silver Cup." The second was in 1733 when Lucy Temple was more generous as she gave her goddaughter ffany Trevanion £100 and in the same year William Dibben of Shepton Montague left his godson Mathew Pitney of Lamyatt £10. The fourth was in 1823 when Richard Biggs left his goddaughter Elizabeth Mead £100 and an annuity of £30 a year. It is perhaps interesting to see that of the ten bequests noted, five were made by godmothers and five by godfathers.

iv) Bequests of animals.

As agriculture was such an important activity in the Bruton area, especially in the earlier part of the period, it was unsurprising that animals appeared amongst the bequests of the dying. It would be expected that they would be distributed by the Wills of those most closely associated with agriculture, such as yeomen, although very few called themselves by that name. In 1557 yeoman John fflenger gave to "Raff More my wyves sonne my littell wandell cow." (9) Ten years later 'yoman' Walter Tynbury of South Brewham was much more specific in his bequests: he gave to his grandson Osmonde Nyxon "to oxen that Willm Clement my neyboure of South bruham hath nowe at hyre of myne and also I geave to the said Osmonde a mare and a colte or els a cowe and a calfe." This bequest gives an interesting insight into rural life with the oxen being hired out to neighbours. Five other grandchildren received twenty sheep each with the residue of his flock going to his younger son William. William was also given a choice: his elder brother John inherited the farm at South Brewham and John could "uppon his ferme fynde and pasture yerelie for his brother Willm Tynbury duringe his lyffe three wenlinge calves and also shall grase hym to beaves", or William could "have the use and occupacion and enioye the grounde called the psonage close in South bruhm", paying his brother John an annual rent of 6s 8d.

In 1613, amongst other items, James Plympton gave to his wife one cow and in 1697 widow Joane Pride of Knowle bequeathed "all my living flock of Cattle for the use of my said Grandchildren." Half a century later in1748 Peter Ames of Wyke Champflower, yeoman, left a range of goods to his son Peter which included, "Six of my Cows, One yoke of Oxen, one Mare, my old Waggon."

What was perhaps more remarkable was the emphasis that members of the local wealthy families placed upon animals and which revealed their continuing close connection with the land. In 1510 John FitzJames, senior, left to his son John, "20 oxen and 20 cows and all my sheep being at Lyde.....to the said Isabel my wife 20 oxen and 10 cows and all my sheep at Milton Clevedon." Amongst a long list of items which Sir John Fitzjames bequeathed to his wife in 1538 were, "the best plough of oxen wt weane, sowle and other things belonging at Yearlynton or at Redliche, all my sheepe at Smalden.......12 mylche kyne at Redliche, six of the best horses or geldings in stable or at grasse." In her turn Dame Elizabeth gave to her grandson Richard Barkley all her cattle in Gloucestershire and ordered her executors "to sell all my sheep, cattle, and horses as well rother as every other kind." (10)

The Berkeley family also retained a detailed interest in some of their animals. When the first Sir Maurice Berkeley was distributing his estate among his various sons, he was careful to specify in each case that when he bequeathed them a farm, such as Coombe Farm or Horseley Farm, that it should include "the Stocke upon the same." For different purposes he bequeathed "to my saide wief her Coche with the twoe horsses and the furniture to the same belonginge, and also three good geldinges."

In 1600 his son Sir Henry Berkeley made a similar arrangement, "I doe geve to my sayd wyfe her choach & any fower of my best geldings at her choise." He also gave his eldest son "my best horss after his mother hath chosen" and to two of his younger sons a gelding or a nag. He recognised that there were debts to be paid and so ordered the sale of "all such stocke of cattell as I shall have at the time of my death."

The second Sir Maurice did not go into so much detail in his Will in 1617 but he did require his wife to give two of his executors, Henry Bainton and Toby Pearce, one gelding or nag each. His widow, Dame Elizabeth, in her Will in 1626 distributed a few animals: "Item I give unto my Cosyn Grace Dugdale three of my Weanelinge Calves shee making election out of them. Item I give unto my Cosyn fflorance Pearse one Cowe calfe....Item I give to my oulde servente Rose Evans a heifer calfe.....Item whereas oulde John Coles and his wief had twoe Cowes Grasse in liewe of theire wages I give unto them for the sayd twoe Cowes Pasture ffourtie shillings a peece." The latter bequest in particular provides a fascinating insight into the operation of a rural community and the interaction between the wealthy and some of the poorer members of it.

In 1757 the Hon. Charles Berkeley left a legacy of £20 to John Stabler, his aptly named groom, along with "any one of my Horses Mares or Geldings that he shall Choose not being above the value of Twenty Pounds." He did however permit his executors to pay him another £20 instead.

In a number of instances while it is not always possible to discern the social status of the deceased from their Wills, they did demonstrate the importance of animals at the time of their death. As early as 1429 John Gregory bequeathed "to John son of Gregory Millelband one cow." In 1573 George Stevens gave to his daughter Margaret "three kyene" and in 1678 Richard Dimond gave to his wife "all my Cowes and Heyfers." Sheep were also bequeathed, for example, in 1504 William Bysshop gave each of the canons in the Priory one ewe, presumably in the hope of their prayers for his soul. In 1517 Alice Brymmore gave to her granddaughter, Margaret "lx wethers of my flocke of Badcombe" and in 1544 Roger Ames of Wyke Champflower gave to his daughter "Johan Amys vj sheep" with a further six to son Steven who also received "a whole wain." (*wagon*)

Occasionally there was a combination of animals, for example, in 1545 Jone Hardwell gave to her sister Agnes Fowldow "a cow, a ewe and a lamb." Three years earlier John Exhall had bequeathed "To John James a yerling of twelmonth age. To Stephen Twyney, a bullock of twoo yeres ages."

Horses were clearly also bequeathed but as the type was not usually specified it is not always possible to determine which were for riding and which were for working purposes. Robert Chyke had a number of horses which he disposed of in 1542: to son John he gave "my white mare with her foal and thencresse of her tyll he come owt of hys yeres of prentyshod"; William Chyke the younger received "my Baye horsse callyd my stalyn Wylling suche as shalhave the rule of my wyll to se hym usyd to the best behofe for the pfytt of the por ladd." He also gave Nichas "my sorel mare wt her colt."

The following year John Hoper alias Smyth had several horses in his possession as he gave his daughter "a gray gelding" and "to William Bilstone my bay nag" and "to Robert Griffith my dun mare." In 1546 John Langyer had just a yearling to pass on to his son John. On the death of Sir Joseph Killigrew in 1617 he gave Sir Maurice Berkeley "my gray horse" and his brother Sir Henry of Yarlington "my bay mare

'Tarbuckle'." Finally in 1775 widow Susannah Hunt of Pitcombe left to her daughter "my chaise horses and Cows."

For some families their few animals represented their most valuable asset, not only in terms of providing for their daily needs with such foods as milk and cheese but also in the case of oxen and horses as an aid to their labour. As a longer term investment there was always the hope that the animals would breed and so increase the overall wealth of the family. There was obviously some sort of hierarchy in the value or status of animals as none of the Wills mentioned pigs or goats. Similarly chickens, ducks and geese did not appear.

d) Wills: Bequests to the Church

In the medieval period and up until the Reformation those preparing for death were deeply concerned to ensure that every possible benefit was arranged for their soul. The result, as was discussed in Chapter 4, was that in total large sums of money and sometimes goods were given to the Church for masses, prayers, chantries, to individual priests, the local monastery and its residents and to the Fraternity of the Blessed Virgin. To a lesser extent these practices continued in the 1540s and 1550s.

While nationally from the beginning of the reign of Queen Elizabeth in 1558 there were fewer gifts on death to the Church or donations made for church repairs, the surviving Wills from Bruton indicate that the practice was still widespread there. Out of some twenty-nine Wills made between 1558 and 1650 twenty-one or 72.4% left money to Bruton Parish Church. The Cathedral Church of St Andrew at Wells did not benefit nearly as much as it appeared in just 27.6% of Wills and usually for the standard figure of 12d.

It may well have been that in Bruton, as with a few other aspects of life, religious attitudes were fairly conservative amongst some of the leading families and so gifts to the parish church continued. It also reflected the high regard with which St Mary's Church was held by various sections of the community. The major break came in 1650 as after that date only one more gift of money appeared during the remainder of the seventeenth century: 2s 6d from Thomas Mogg, yeoman, in 1656. Puritan attitudes and the devastating impact and implications of the Civil War in both economic and religious terms had caused opinion to change irrevocably.

In the period up to 1650 the sums allocated by the dying to the parish church varied with 12d and 6s 8d being the most common, but went as high as £2 in a few instances with just one much larger gift from Sir Maurice Berkeley in 1617 when he gave the Churchwardens £8 "towardes the repayringe of the Church." A note was added in the margin, "My meaning is that this Eight pounds shalbe payd to Godfrey for making Battlements to Church which I bespoke." The only other person to specify repairs was William Swanton in 1637 when he left the Churchwardens 10s "towards the repayreing for the Church there."

Although a number of those who requested burial inside the Church bequeathed a larger sum such as 6s 8d from Agnes Plumley in 1560 and Thomas Coles in 1650, only John Mogg in 1629 made a direct linkage, "I give unto the use of the church to be buried therein vjs viijd."

One testator specifically ordered that goods be provided for the Church and that was Catherine Drew in 1695 when she gave "to the Parish Church of Brewton aforesaid one brasse Candle Socket of the value of about tenn pounds." When this was installed it was a brass chandelier with sixteen sockets for candles and hung in the nave. This gift may well have been reflecting the much older idea of having a name remembered. Three men gave money not to the Church, but directly to the

Minister. In 1688 John Yeadle, the former Minister of Bruton, ordered that his estate should be divided into five equal parts and that the interest on two of these parts should be given to the Minister and the Clerk, "who are and shall be from time to time appointed to read and attend at morning prayer in the parish church ...while they officiate in the protestant Religion as by Law now established." In 1738 Nicholas Goldesbrough simply left the Minister five guineas and in 1757 the Hon. Charles Berkeley gave the then Minister, the Revd. John Goldesbrough, £50. As a slight variation in 1733 William Dibben of Shepton Montague gave John Ball the parish clerk there 40s.

When cash gifts to the Church stopped after 1650 other trends developed such as the Churchwardens charging a specific amount for an interment within the parish church, as was discussed in Chapter 5. In addition the practice became increasingly common for a donor to make a gift during his or her lifetime and not at death. In 1706 Mrs Grace Wason donated a silver flagon and in 1726 Robert Ludwell gave two Bibles. Later in the century in 1744 Richard Wood donated a Silver Flagon and a Silver Alms Dish and John Wood a Silver Plate. Richard Wood also provided another brass chandelier which was identical to the one that Catherine Drew had financed half a century earlier. In the same year John Gilbert gave a pair of silver candlesticks

The church in Lamyatt also benefitted from such gifts, for example, in 1740 Mrs Ann Pitney gave a silver Patten for the Communion Table and six years later the Revd. Trethewy Tooker donated "one large silver Flaggon" to be used there.

Presenting constructive gifts to Bruton church continued into the nineteenth century as in 1844 Daniel Ward donated "two very handsome Altar Chairs" and in 1866 Thomas Stockwell provided a new clock for the West Tower. In 1888

St Leonard's Church in Pitcombe received a brass lectern in memory of Catherine and Elizabeth Hobhouse, the daughters of the Rt. Hon. Henry Hobhouse of Hadspen House, from their nephew Henry Hobhouse. A plaque on it gives basic information on them and refers to them as "Lifelong friends to the People and Church of Pitcombe Parish."

With all these specific practical gifts to the church there was not only a continuation of the medieval idea of a name being remembered but also an indication of the social status of a person or family within their community.

e) Wills: Bequests to the Poor

Up until the Reformation the prayers of the poor, and even their attendance at a funeral, were considered to be particularly beneficial for the soul of the departed. As has been discussed in Chapter 4 gifts to the poor for that purpose occurred in large numbers of surviving medieval Wills. At first sight it appeared that the abolition of the concept of purgatory in 1547 meant that their attendance and prayers were no longer of importance.

Charitable gifts to the poor however continued for some two hundred years. It may well have been that many testators still clung to the older beliefs or the hope that there would in fact be some spiritual benefit. In reality it is clear that by the mid-Tudor period the motivation for charitable giving had become much more complex. There was a greater awareness of social need, along with a move towards secularisation such as supporting almshouses, hospitals and schools but at the same time accepting the directions of the Protestant ethic which continued to place emphasis upon charitable activites. Increasingly there was the realization that dire poverty created discontent that could lead to instability in town and country, threaten the regime and ultimately the very state.

Bequests to the poor appeared in the majority of seventeenth century Wills but became much rarer from the middle of the eighteenth century. This did not necessarily mean that attitudes to charitable giving changed dramatically but rather that more was donated during a person's lifetime as opposed to after death.

There were of course a few who did both and in Bruton that was most notable in the case of Hugh Sexey. For many years before his death in 1619 he had been financing poor people in cottages that he had acquired and paying pensions to a number of other individuals in their own homes. His transference of the majority of his landed property to Trustees in 1616 ensured that after his death the poor continued to benefit with pensions and other payments but above all with the construction of a new Hospital. He had also been a strong supporter of, and further endowed, the charity which his first wife Dorothy wished to be established in Otley in Yorkshire after her death. This one provided a small sum to help young tradesmen to become established and "upon ten poore sinegle yong mades at their marriages." (11)

It is very clear that in virtually every Will in the period 1500 to 1700 when money was donated to Bruton Parish Church, and often to Wells Cathedral, a gift was also made to the poor in Bruton. The impression is created that the Church of that time favoured such bequests and when the scribe was writing the Will he had a list of items available that would jog the memory of the testator.

In the period 1560 to 1660 the poor were gifted money in some twenty-three Bruton Wills, with sums which ranged from 12d from John ffrye in 1588 to four gifts of £20 each by four members of the Berkeley family. The commonest amounts were 10s, of which there were six and £1, of which there were seven. The following one hundred years witnessed far fewer bequests with just ten but they tended to be more generous, ranging from two of £1 to one of £40 and one of £50, an indication not only of inflation but also of increased prosperity.

Most of those who left money to the poor did so as a straightforward grant and it was presumably the task of the executors to make the necessary arrangements: the will of Thomas Ludwell in 1676 was typical, "To the poor of Bruton in Somerset £10." Occasionally more specific detail was included such as in the Will of William Wilton in 1654, "I give unto the poore of Brewton the some of Tenn Shillings, to be distributed at the discretion of my Executors and Overseers." Dame Margaret Berkeley made a similar request for her £20 bequest in 1617, "to be distributed in such manner as my executors shall thinke most fittest."

In some instances the task of distribution of money was given to the Overseers of the Poor and the Churchwardens. In 1643, for example, Robert Albin stated, "Item I give to the poore of the towne of Bruton 4li to be distributed at the day of my burrial by the Churchwardens and Collectors of the said Towne of Bruton for the time being." This was one of a limited number of occasions in the seventeenth century when testators reflected the much older idea of money being distributed on the day of burial. It did of course ensure a good attendance with the poor present in the hope of reward. In 1640 Alice Hill gave "unto the poore of Brewton twentie shillings to be disbursed att my funerall" and in 1673 Robert Ludwell made a similar arrangement when he left "fforty shillings to be distributed at or presently after my funerall." On the other hand for a few there was not a sense of such urgency, for example, in his Will in 1637 William Swanton gave " to the overseers of the poore of Brewton" 10s for the relief of the poor "to be delivered wthin one yeare after my decease."

A more unusual arrangement was made by Nicholas Gilbert in 1566 when he bequeathed to Elizabeth, the wife of William

Packesford, who was referred to as a servant of Sir Maurice Berkeley, "my howse standinge in the Northeside of the westende of the Towne of Bruton." She was to receive the Indenture and enjoy all the rents and profits from the house, "so that he paye one noble yerelie oute of the saide howse to the poore people of Brewton aforsaide." In addition Gilbert's neighbour, John Dyser, owed him £16, which debt he forgave "savinge fortie shillings whiche I give and Bequeth to the saide poore people of Bruton."

Other testators included details and imposed a range of specific conditions upon their bequests, such as John Fraunces of Alford, yeoman, who in 1578 left 10s "to 30 poor people of the town of Bruton." Two years later the first Sir Maurice Berkeley directed that his £20 legacy should be distributed "at the daie of my buriall, by shillings, half-shillinges or groates at his (*the executor's*) discrecion." In true Protestant style he added "I know it wyll doe me no good, yet I am persuaded it will doe theme no harme."

His grandson, the second Sir Maurice arranged in 1617 that his £20 bequest "shall remayne as a stocke forever and then lente unto the poore Tradesmen and other poore to each of them a parte for one yere uppon good securitie." In 1757 the Hon. Charles Berkeley arranged for the Minister and Churchwardens to distribute £20 to the poor of Bruton "who do not receive Alms of the Parish." Finally with his very generous bequest in 1796 Robert Pavy instructed the Minister, Churchwardens and Overseers of the Poor that the sum of £100 should be "disposed of to and amongst such poor objects of charity of the Parish of Bruton as to them may seem most deserving and who shall not then be in the Parish Workhouse or receive relief of the Parish." In these last two instances the beneficiaries were perceived to be the deserving as opposed to the undeserving poor, a concept that became increasingly important in the late eighteenth and especially in the nineteenth centuries.

The poor in neighbouring villages also received money from Wills, for example, in November 1653 William Ewens of Hadspen left five shillings to the poor of the parish of Pitcombe. In 1718 William Mogg of Shepton Montague gave £7 to the poor there and then added a further £3 in a Codicil the following year. The poor of the same parish also benefitted from the Will of William Dibben in 1733 when he left to the poor there "as have no Relief" the sum of £5.

After the spectacular generosity of Hugh Sexey towards the poor, that of his widow, Ursula, was very limited. In her Will in 1635 she left the parishes of Cloford in Somerset and Little Totham in Essex £5 each for the poor to be administered by the Overseers and £10 for the poor in the parish in which she died. In each case it was with the strict instruction that it was "for the setting the poore of the respective parishes on work... for that onely purpose." She was perhaps foreshadowing future developments and attitudes towards the poor.

From the very end of the seventeenth century legacies of money that were to be used to purchase designated items became more prominent. In the eighteenth and nineteenth centuries this practice may be seen as a reaction to the growing belief that if the poor were given money directly they would squander it on their perceived vices, most notably drinking and gambling. As early as 1695 Catherine Drew left £50 for the poor of Brewton "to be disposed of to them in Cloathing and other charitable uses by the discrecion of my Executor and the Overseers of the poore."

Coal to heat the cottages of the poor in winter was mentioned in two Wills: in 1733 Lucy Temple gave, "To the Poor of the Parish of Bruton fforty pound to be layd out for poor ffamilys in Coals at ffive pound a year for eight years." As late as February 1878 it was reported that on her death

Mrs Peplar of Prospect Cottage left instructions for the periodic distribution of coal to fifty old and afflicted poor people

The most common commodity to be designated in Wills became bread. In 1718 Henry Sampson left forty shillings "to be laid out in bread", but in his case it was to be "distributed by three Penny Loaves on the day of my ffunerals." In 1763 William Pavy directed that his executor, who was his brother Robert, was "to distribute the value of ffifty Shillings in Bread amongst such poor of the parish of Brewton as are not in the Workhouse." This arrangement was to last "for the space of Seven years next after my decease" and specifically "on the day of my Birth in every year (which I think is on the twenty third day of November old Style)". The Christening Register shows that a William Pavy, son of Robert was christened on 28th November 1726, so his speculation is likely to have been correct. Considering that he was wealthy and probably educated and was still unsure of the date of his birth, it was no surprise that many of the poor had little idea of exactly when they were born.

The most significant and long-lasting bequest of money for bread, however, came in the Will of Robert Smart in 1763. He gave to the Churchwardens of Bruton an annuity of £2 2s 0d a year, derived from the rent of some of his land. This money was to be used to maintain his family vault in the parish church and the residue to be distributed amongst the poor "in Christmas in every year in bread meat & coals or either." Subsequent annual accounts by the Churchwardens showed that they decided on 6d and 3d loaves. Each year long lists of the names of recipients appeared in their Accounts, such as forty-nine of the poor receiving a 6d loaf and seventy-seven a 3d loaf in 1776 and fifty-three and sixty-nine respectively the following year. These two years were fairly typical as most years up to about 130 of the poor benefitted. The annuity ceased, no doubt much to the distress of the poor, in 1806 when the land was sold and in the conditions of purchase was an indemnification, under the terms of the Statute of Mortmain, against all previous gifts. It was a great loss to the poor of Bruton, especially as they continued to experience very hard times during the Napoleonic Wars. (12)

The charitable gifts to the poor of John, 5th Lord Berkeley of Stratton followed a slightly different pattern. He gave £100 to the Minister and Churchwardens of Bruton to distribute to the poor but in addition he concentrated on hospitals. He bequeathed £1000 to St George's Hospital near Hyde Park Corner in London, "to be appled towards carrying on the charitable designs of the said Hospital." A similar sum was given with the same instruction to each of the Middlesex Hospital for the reception of Sick and Lame and Lying-in Married Women, the City of Bath Hospital and the City of Bristol Infirmary.

f) Wills: Bequests to Servants

After relatives servants constituted the second largest category of named beneficiaries on the death of a wealthy person. This action was the case in Bruton particularly in the sixteenth and seventeenth centuries up until about 1650, after which their appearances became much rarer. This change could have meant that some provision was made for them during the lifetime of a specific man or woman but more likely it was a reflection of the way in which, especially in the eighteenth and nineteenth centuries, the wealthier in the community moved further and further away from such close contact with poorer people.

It was perfectly possible that some of the servants, especially in the earlier part of the period, were also relatives, placed within a family for training, apprenticeship or to improve their prospects. Although Hugh Sexey did not identify her in his

Will, he appeared to have employed within his household for a short period in the 1590s a young girl who was a relative of his first wife, Dorothy, probably her niece Ann from Yorkshire. In one letter in July 1594 William Flessher enquired of his "welbeloved Brother Saxey and to my Sister, youre bedfellowe.....how youe like of my little girle." A subsequent letter in March 1595 referred to her "as yor dutifull servant." Within a year however the arrangement had broken down, Ann had returned to her father and Sexey complained that he "hathe spoke most injuriouslie to my wife, and geven the farr greater credit to his daughters wordes then to myne or my wyves." (13)

How extensive gifts to servants were from their former masters in the medieval period is impossible to determine with any degree of certainty but some of the earliest Wills from Bruton did include bequests. In 1417 Richard Bruton gave 40s to his servant Robert along with a brass pot, a bowl and "half a doseyn of Pewtre vesselles." He also left 10s to each of his two cooks, Hugh Olun and Master John Olun. Ten years later John Gregory included a range of bequests to his male servants, Gregory, Nicholas, John Wattys and Thomas Welles and to his female servants, Edith and Isabell. In 1506 Symon Grene left 10s to "Robert Lassellys formerly my servant."

In the vast majority of instances servants received money on the death of their employer. This cash would have been a welcome gift as in some cases that death presumably meant the termination of their employment and the need to find another way of earning a living. In 1589 Edward Spicer bequeathed to "Elinor Rodwaye my servant fortie shillings" and in 1648 Joane Sampson gave "my now maide Servant Sibilla Roberts three pounds." Some testators did not name individual servants but made a general bequest, for example, in 1619 Hugh Sexey left a sum to be distributed among his servants, "I give to the rest of my Servants now dwellinge with me Forty pounds to be equally divided amongst them." In 1643 Robert Albin adopted a similar approach, "Item I give to my Covenant servants that shallbe dwelling with me at the time of my Decease 10s a piece."

Robert Chyke was careful to insist in 1542 that the money he gave to his servants on his death should be in addition to their usual wages, "Item I give to Olyver my sevnt in money above his wages vjs viijd Item I give to every of my mayde sevnts in money above their wages xxs."

In a small number of Wills the actual role of the servant within the family or employment of the deceased was specified and provides a glimpse of life in various periods. In 1538 Sir John Fitzjames gave "To Margery my woman in my Chamber 5 marks." In a list of at least twelve servants Sir Maurice Berkeley left in 1617 the sum of 10s each to Nurse Maunder and Nurse Lennys. The latter, who was referred to as "my Nurse Christian Lynnys", also received a further £2 in the Will of Dame Elizabeth Berkeley in 1626. Over a hundred years later in 1733 Lucy Temple bequeathed "To my Nurse Mrs Wilkinson Twenty pound a year during her life to be laid out on her with Care."

In 1639 Thomas Wilton, a shoemaker, remembered to give "unto Robert Gibson myne Apprentice the some of twentie shillings." In 1796 Robert Pavy was much more generous as he granted to his late apprentice Joseph Ivie £300. If the latter had not already established a business he would have had little difficulty in doing so after that legacy. Hugh Sexey gave to his two clerks, Martyn Prechard and Thomas Laude, whom he employed presumably in London, £20 each.

There would appear to have been a strong paternalistic attitude amongst the two wealthy landowning families in Bruton towards their servants. This found expression in the sixteenth century not only in granting money, occasionally in addition to wages, but also by sometimes ensuring that they would have time to find other employment. The first evidence of this sentiment came in the Will of Sir John Fitzjames in 1538, "To each of my houshold servants that take any wages, one yere's wages and meate and drynke in my howse yf they luste to take hit to my month mynde be passed, and four markes to every of those that take no wages, at my months mynde."

A similar sentiment was expressed by Sir Maurice Berkeley in 1580: "ffurder I will that all my howshould Svntes shall have theire whole yeres waiges, suche as theye weare wonte to receyve at my hande of my gifte, shortly after my departinge, and also one monnethes enterteynement that theye maye better provide for theme selves." His son, Sir Henry, in 1600 granted all his household servants one year's wages, which was the pattern followed by his daughter-in-law Dame Elizabeth in 1626. Her husband, the second Sir Maurice, had just resorted to listing at least twelve servants and giving them either 10s or 20s each.

In 1712 John, Lord Fitzharding gave various sums to named servants and then to each one of his servants who had been in his service for six months, a year's wages. The Hon. Charles Berkeley also gave his servants one year's wages but this time they had to have been in his employ for a year or more.

Loyalty was clearly a virtue that was much prized and the appropriate phrases appeared in Berkeley Wills, for example, in 1690 Maurice, Lord Fitzharding gave £100 "to my faithfull servant Edward Perro." In 1712 John, the next Lord Fitzharding gave £50, his year's wages and mourning to John Shaw "for his faithfull Service to me....And to his Eldest son Twenty pounds in consideration of his Wives faithfull service to my late dear Wife deceased."

Some of those classed as servants were far from being low level domestic help and may well have played a vital role in the management of the house and its finances and possibly the whole estate. In 1617 Sir Maurice Berkeley referred to one of his servants as "Arthure Upton, gent", leaving him 20s. Dame Elizabeth nine years later was to call him "Arthwer Upton my servaunte" and leave him £50. Both left money to Thomas Dale: the first 20s and the second £10. Dame Elizabeth continued her paternalism even when a servant had left her employ, "Item I give to my oulde servente Rose Evans a heifer calfe." A very useful and practical bequest.

The largest group of legacies to servants by a member of the Berkeley family came with the death of the last Lord Berkeley of Stratton at Bruton Abbey in 1773. Amongst a range of other sums given to his servants was £600 to his gentleman, £500 to his valet de chamber, £500 to his housekeeper, £100 each went to a group of named servants, including his butler, coachman, housemaid, laundry and chamber-maids and £50 to six more, including his gardener. These sums were to be in addition to any wages and other money thast was owed to them at the time of his death. The total of these bequests came to some £2,400. In addition the wife and two daughters of one servant received £100 each and the wife of another £50.

More unusual was leaving money to someone else's servants but there were two clear examples from Bruton. The first was John Yeadle who had no close family and was the former Minister of the parish church and chaplain to the Berkeley family. In his Will in 1688 he made such a bequest, "I give to each of my Ld ffitzhardings meniall Servants living in Bruton house five shillings and likewise all my wearing apparell and other Lumber I give to be Sold, and the money to be equally distributed among the other Servants whome his Lordpp employes elsewhere." Second in 1733 spinster Lucy Temple, who also spent a significant amount of the year at the Abbey, specified "to my Lord Berkeley Servantes if I dye in his ffamily Twenty pound." In death both wished to express gratitude for the care that had been taken of them in life.

There were bequests to servants other than in cash and one of these was wearing apparel. In 1429 John Gregory left to "John Wattys my servant one gown" and more specifically "to Thomas Welles my servant 1 gown with the livery of the Priory of Bruton fur lined with fox." Presumably as a result of his standing within the community John Gregory had been accepted as a lay brother of the Priory. In 1545 Dame Elizabeth Fitzjames gave "To my woman Elizabeth Marshall my frocke of Russett worsted and my kirtill of Saye." In the fifteenth century and before Bruton was well known for its Russett cloth, for example, one ship owner loaded at Bridgewater amongst other commodities bound for Ireland, "2 dozen of Briweton Russet." Perhaps therefore Dame Elizabeth had had this item made locally although, as it was a coarse cloth it was more often worn by poorer people, but it must have been very warm. The material that was used to make her other dress was, however, a fine serge-like cloth.

A small number of servants received specific household items, for example in 1429 John Gregory left to one female servant Edith "1 bason with ewer 1 brass pot" and to another Isabell "1 bason and 1 pot." His widow Amice left to her servant Amice in 1457, "one brass vessel holding 6 gallons and one linen sheet." William Gane was generous to his servant Isabell Mogg in 1544 when he gave her "a pair of sheets, a pair of blankets, a coverlet, a bolster and two pillows, half a dozen pewter vessels, a cow and a heifer." This gift would suggest that she would be in a position to set up a house of her own.

It was, however, more common for goods to be left with some cash, as the following examples illustrate. In 1429 John Gregory bequeathed "to Gregorie my servant one gown with fur lining and xxs......to Nicho my servant one gown and vjs viijd." In her turn in 1457 Amice Gregory bequeathed "To George Mulward, my servant, one brass pot, one cover one sheet and 3s 4d." In 1566 Nicholas Gilbert gave to "Edithe Bilstone widdowe that kepe my howse fortie shillings a flock Bedd a Bollster a pare of sheets and a redd Coverlett apperteyninge to the same." Dame Margaret Berkeley was particularly generous to her servant Dorothy Cole in 1617 because as well as £5 she gave her "my Little Silver Sault and fower Silver Spoones, and my new Pewter att Brewton." Lucy Temple was similarly generous as she gave her servant John Loyd £50 and a year's wages along with a bed and Elizabeth Higgen £10 a year during her lifetime, a bed and "all my wearing Cloaths of all kinds." Nearly a century later Lucy Lloyd left " my faithful Servant" Charlotte Coward £100, "my feather bed Mattrass Bedstead and furniture Pillows bolster two pairs of sheets and three blankets with other furniture standing in the Kitchen Chamber And also all my Wearing Apparel."

While the latter was a generous gift it had been surpassed by the bequest made in 1823 by Richard Biggs to his maidservant Susannah Cox. She received not only £100 in cash and an annuity of thirty pounds a year for life but also his house and garden in Patwell Street for her natural life as long as she remained single, and he added, "she paying the taxes and keeping the same in repair." With the house came "all the household goods and furniture of every description which shall be in my said dwellinghouse at the time of my decease for her own absolute use and benefit."

While servants worked in close proximity to a family or may even have been related, in two instances a much broader group of workers was included. Both Thomas Whitehead in 1690 and his son John in 1714 took the opportunity to reward the workers in their Mills and those who spun for them in their own homes. As both were staunch Quakers they were imbued not only with Christian beliefs but also with the concepts of hard work and industriousness. They were well aware that the wealth that they had acquired was in part due to the same attitudes in their workers. The sums involved were not very large but they were a gesture, one which does not seem to have been replicated by any other Clothiers in Bruton. Thomas Whitehead made two types of bequests: cash and clothes, "Item I give to all my spinners six pence apiece. Item I give to my weavers scribblers and shear men unto each of them a pair of gloves." John chose just cash: "And I give unto all and singular my shearmen and Scribblers who shall actually be in my Service at the time of my death five shillings apiece."

g) Wills: The issue of debts

There were many reasons for debts: the vast majority were acquired in normal day to day living such as ordering or purchasing a commodity or item from a tradesman or crafts-man and not paying at the precise moment of delivery; work could be undertaken on a cottage or house and a bill submitted but not paid immediately; employees were often paid weekly or monthly and sometimes even quarterly and if death intervened during this period money would be owed; some men found themselves in some financial difficulty and resorted to borrowing money for a short or long term period and so were in debt. Whatever the reason for the debt its repayment was a crucial issue near death

Before the Reformation it was the function of the priest attending the dying person to ensure that he or she died in faith, hope and charity. One of the key elements of dying in charity was to have dealt with all debts. Virtually none of the surviving Wills for this period from Bruton made any specific reference to the payment of debts, probably for two main reasons: the first was that the dying person may have had enough time to deal with them before death; the second was that it was implicit in the instructions to executors to undertake actions for the benefit of the soul. One exception was Richard Dekyn in 1471 as he left the residue of his goods to his wife "after the debtes which of right I owe paide."

In a few instances to ensure that there was no possible debt to the Church itself, the deceased would arrange for a small sum to be given to the High Altar of the parish church, adding the words "for tithes forgotten." This practice continued into the 1540s when on one occasion in 1544 Roger Ames left "To the high altar for forgotten tithes a sheep" and in the same year Stevyn Broke gave 12d. The bequest of John Turges in 1545 was a little different: "To the chapel of St Peter of Redlinche, in full recompense for such debts that I do owe the said Chapel when I was warden vs."

An indication of the processes which could be involved in the settlement of debt may be found in a Deed of Confirmation signed by James Fitzjames in August 1564. In 1518 the Prior of Stavordale had granted to goldsmith Walter Love of Bruton various lands in the area, including a house, garden, orchard and close on the north side of the High Street and an acre of land in the north field "nighe tolburie". In his Will Love bequeathed all this property to Nicholas Fitzjames "for the payemt of the saide Walter Loves debts" He leased the property to Walter Walter of Bruton "towardes thaccomplishment & satisfaction of the Detts of the saide Walter Love" On the death of Nicholas Fitzjames his son and heir James confirmed the grant to Walter Walter. So the payment of Love's debts seemed to have continued.

In the post-Reformation world it became the standard practice to mention the payment of debts, so in 1542 for example Robert Chyke requested his executors "as sone as they can conveniently they se my detts payd." Three years later Dame Elizabeth Fitzjames instructed her executors to retain control of her farm at Smaldon which returned a rent of £13 6s 8d "to pay my legacies and detts." Her daughter-in-law, also named Elizabeth, was so concerned that her debts should be paid that she directed in her Will in 1550 that, "Proclamation to be made in the Towns of Bruton and Sherbourne that persons are to come forward and prove their debts."

By the middle of the Elizabethan period a reference to debts was included in the formula near the end of Wills when the residue of the estate was being considered: "the rest of all my goodes and cattels moveable and unmoveable and unbequeathed my debtes payde and my funerall discharged I give....." The Bruton Wills of George Stevens, John ffrye, Petronell or Purnell and Edward Spicer and Francis Poole all included this direction. In 1567 Walter Tynbury of South Brewham adopted a more direct approach when he instruced his executors "to receive and tak my dettes and paye my dettes that shalbe proved to be my very true dettes."

In 1600 Sir Henry Berkeley was very precise as he ordered, "that all such stocks of cattell as I shall have at the time of my death eyther at norwood, bruton, yarlington, & Smalden, shalbe sold for the payment of my depts." His grandson, Sir Charles who was also the second Lord Fitzharding, instructed his executors to sell first his Manor of Yarnfield in Somerset and then sufficient property and land which he owned anywhere in England and Ireland to pay his debts and satisfy the legacies which he bequeathed.

By 1700, and for the rest of the period under consideration, the direction was simplified so that the executor was to see that debts and funeral expenses were paid. As Henry Sampson expressed it in 1718, "my just debts being paid and my funeral charges being defrayed." This did not mean that the payment of debt was viewed as being less important and in fact in many cases after the testament regarding soul and body, for some men it was the first item which appeared in their Wills when they came to dispose of their worldly estate.

In 1667 William Morris was particularly eloquent and reiterated the traditional Christian concept: "And First for that I ought to have a carefull regard in the duty of a Christian for the payment of such debts as I shall Justly owe att the tyme of my death I do hereby give devise and bequeath..." Others such as John Yeadle in 1688 were much more brief, "ffirst I will that my debts and ffuneral expenses be paid." In the middle of the following century Richard Creed in 1743 and John Thomas in 1758 both started their Wills with the wish that their debts should be paid, although in the case of the latter he added, "if aney should There be." In the nineteenth century many Wills, such as those of William Saunders, Richard Biggs and Lucy Lloyd, began with the same declaration that their debts and funeral expenses must be paid.

It was a function that the executors of the Wills took very seriously and a number of the surviving Accounts which they prepared made reference to such debts. Their first task was to ensure that all the creditors were aware of the death of a particular individual and so in 1598, for example, the widow of Edward Collins claimed expences of 5s for "her charges of diet for herself and of her neighbors wth her at Wells at the time of the pclamacon to call in the credditors of the deceased and for the publishing of the same in the market at Brewton." Market day was one of the main occasions in a week when a large number of lcoal people would be gathered together and so information could be rapidly transmitted. The Account of Tabitha Albin in November 1641 after the death of her husband Thomas showed that she paid out over £141 to some nine creditors, with William Gane of Cole receiving the largest sum of £31 18s 0d.

With the publication of more and more local newspapers in the eighteenth and nineteenth centuries it became increasingly common for executors or the family solicitor to place an advertisement there to announce a death and request creditors to come forward: in February 1795, for example, "All persons who have any claims or demands on the estate and effects of Mr John Blackmore, late of Bruton in the county of Somerset, are requested immediately to deliver in the same to Mrs Blackmore, his widow and administrix." When both William Jerrard and his wife Grace of North Brewham died in 1829, "All Persons having any Claims or Demands on these Estates, or either of them" were requested to contact two named executors.

It was also of course the time when debts could be repaid to the estate of the deceased and so Edward Collins's widow received £4 13s 4d from William Smythe of Weston Bampfield as "a pcell of debt dewe" When James Cock of Hadspen died in 1860 his Executrix placed an advertizement in *The Sherborne Mercury* on 30th October requesting not only that anyone to whom the deceased was indebted should immediately "furnish me with the particulars of their claims" but also that all outstanding debts should be repaid.

Just occasionally a debt that was owed to the dying person was passed on to the heirs, for example, in 1544 Roger Ames gave his father 1s that was "a debt due to me." In 1589 Edward Spicer recorded in his Will that he was owed £210 by Thomas Sherwood and Richard Hodges and this sum he required to be paid to his executrix so that it could be distributed to cover his various legacies to his children and others. Sir Maurice Berkeley adopted a similar approach in 1617 but without details, "and all the debts owinge to me shall goe and be disposed for and towards the payment of my said debts."

Surviving Bruton Wills also revealed the practice of the dying person forgiving existing debts. In 1554 Henry Ottis alias Calowe gave to two of his sons six "rother beasts......they paying therefore my debts as they and I agreed upon" but then he continued, "I forgive all my debts that I can challenge for my 'strettes' of old before the date of these presents." In 1589 Edward Spicer likewise forgave a debt, "Item I give and bequeathe to Mr John ffitzjames the elder suche some or somes of money as he doeth owe unto me by a bill of his hand." Well over a century later in 1713 Robert Fry stated, "And I doe forgive my said Brother Gauntlet what he owes me." He also took the opportunity to give him £50 and "my best Wigg", the only occasion when a reference to this type of item appeared in surviving Bruton Wills.

At Lamyatt in 1764 widow Anne Pitney made a simlar gesture: "Also I give and fforgive unto Mr Seth Burge of Castle Cary in the County afordsd Stocking-Maker the sum of One Hundred Pounds which the sd Seth Burge owes me on Bond."

Potentially one of the most generous acts of forgiveness of debt came on the death of John, 1st Lord Berkeley of Stratton. He and his older brother Sir William Berkeley, the Governor of Virginia, had agreed to divide the profits of the Office of the Clerk of the Treasury of the Common Pleas at Westminster between them. At some stage Sir William had borrowed £1,300 from his brother and Lord John forgave him this debt provided that he paid Lady Berkeley £500 out of the profits of the Office and he also gave William a legacy of £100. This clause however was never implemented as by the time of Lord John's death in August 1678 Sir William had already been dead for over a year.

It was similarly possible to forgive part of a debt with the implication being that the remainder would be repaid, although this was not explicitly stated. In 1539 George George of Wescombe in the parish of Batcombe recorded in his Will that Elizabeth Fitzjames owed him £4 which he had loaned to her late husband "Maister John FizthJames....in the Chambre of the Halle in William North's house in Bruton." He then added, "for the greate goodness that I found in his Maistershipp (Jesu pardone the soule) I forgyve the one half."

Finally only one person gave money in a Will to aid debtors and that was Lucy Temple in 1733, "ffor the Reliefe of poor debtors out of Prison that are there for Losses not owing to their own Extravagancies." It was customary to bury a debtor according to his or her status and ignore any debts but there are no identifiable surviving examples from Bruton.

h) Wills: Specific items

As death approached many people were confronted with making a decision about their worldly estate as they recognised that it was not going to accompany them on their journey. Their Wills of course clearly indicated that depending upon the period their primary concern centred on the future of their soul, salvation and resurrection. In life however there had been items that mattered to them and they wished to ensure that such goods were passed to the person or persons that they judged to be the most appropriate recipient. In some instances there was a material value but in others it was something which they treasured irrespective of its worth.

Areas discussed so far demonstrate that beds and their attachments were held in high regard and found frequent mention in Wills, especially those made before 1700, although as late as 1817 William James left his daughter Sarah "the Bedstead with all curtains in the Middle Bedroom and the Bed and Bed ffurniture thereunto belonging" She was also to receive the same from the room in which she normally slept. Silver items of all types were also identified and bequeathed usually to a named individual. A vast array of household items was specified and arrangements made for their disposal and for those in a particular occupation or trade it was often necessary to ensure that animals or tools of that trade were passed on to the appropriate recipient.

In an age when the defence of the realm and the maintenance of law and order in the countryside rested with the landed gentry and the wealthy inhabitants in general, it was not unusual for weapons of war to be prized possessions for a man. In 1429 John Gregory bequeathed to his son (most likely his stepson) Richard Weston, "all my weapons" and to Thomas Broun one bow and twenty arrows. He also gave to his kinsman John Barbor, "1 iak de defence de serico" which translates as "a short defensive tunic of silk."

The Berkeley family were well prepared to fulfil their military role as in his Will in 1600 Sir Henry stated, "I doo geve to my sayd sonn Morys, all my armor, & furniture for warrs, also my tents & such other thinges as are in my armory at bruton." In his turn Sir Maurice was to pass these items on to his son and heir Charles in 1617. Maurice had in fact been a notable soldier in his younger days as he was knighted at Cadiz by the Earl of Essex in 1596 for conspicuous gallantry. As late as 1710 Robert ffry bequeathed to his son, also named Robert, "my Silver hilted Sword", which was obviously an important item to him.

As horses constituted such a significant means of transport and for work, harnesses were prized items and so were passed on with care. In 1520 Richard Holmede bequeathed to his daughter, as there was apparently no male heir, "too harness gyrdells oon is a sangwyn corse wt gilt harness and the other is a blewe corse wt white harneyis ungilte." In 1543 Thomas Walter ensured that his son Walter should receive "my plough harness." In her Will in 1560 Agnes Plumley distributed four "harness girdles" to different recipients.

Wearing apparel in general or specific items were often distributed on death so the Wills of widows such as Dame Elizabeth Berkeley and Agnes Plumley contained numerous references to pieces of clothing, itself an indication of their wealth in the sixteenth and seventeenth centuries. Similarly in families where there was no direct male heir clothes could be distributed, such as by Richard Holmede in 1520 who gave to William Blakmore "the best apparell that longeth to my bodye as my best gowne my beste dublet my best shirte my best hosyn and my beste cape." As John Togood of Brewham only had a wife and daughter, in his Will in 1544 he gave "To Edward Morgane a frieze coat with a shirt. To William Collyns a jerkin with a doublet." Many decades later in 1713 Robert Fry gave "to my loving ffriend Robert Pattison my best suit of wearing apparel now in the Country and two of my best Holland Shirts laced to my Cousin Edward ffry." Even when there was a son and heir clothing could be bequeathed elsewhere, for example, in 1429 John Gregory referred to at least six gowns that were given to six named individuals and in 1714 John Whitehead "that all and Singular my woollen wearing apparel shall be distributed amongst my poor relations."

John Turges of Redlynch may well have suffered the loss of his wife shortly before he made his Will in 1545 as he left "To Isabel Wenefricke my wife's say kirtle….To Agnes Fellell my wife's apparel, except her gown….To Alice Albusell my wife's gown." He also bequeathed "my best doublet" to John Otley.

Treasured items of furniture could expect to be detailed in Wills, for example in 1710 Robert ffry gave his wife "my Chest of walnutt drawers" but it was only for her use during her natural life whereas John Whitehead gave his daughter Mary, "all and singular my Chinaware and my Cabinet marked M:D and all and everything that at the time of my death shall be found within the same Cabinet and my dressing box in the parlour chamber." In 1827 widow Patience Hicks bequeathed to her son Thomas "my Mahogany Bureau Silver Pint Cup Looking Glass and other furniture" which was in her former house in Brean. By the time of her death she had moved to Shepton Montague to be with her married daughter.

Nearly one hundred years earlier in 1733 Lucy Temple left to Lord Berkeley "my little Walnutt tree Cabinet" and to her niece Lady Barbara Bentinck an Indian Cabinet. She also bequeathed a number of paintings, such as one of King William to her brother, Palmerston, and "to Mr fflower his own Picture....To my Cozen Wooly her own picture."

In her estate in 1696 widow Mary Allen also included paintings such as those of her brother Sir Edmund King and his wife and one of the late Queen Mary that she left to Mrs Webbe. The largest bequest of paintings, however, came with the death of the last Lord Berkeley of Stratton in 1773 when all the extensive collections of paintings in Bruton Abbey, including those by Van Dyke, Rembrandt and Sir Peter Lely, were given to his nearest male relative, Earl Berkeley of Berkeley Castle in Gloucestershire.

In general, however, it was smaller items which seem to have occupied the attention of the dying much more. For some testators books were clearly important as in 1429 John Gregory gave a Psalter to the Prior of Stavordale and "one book called Sydirck de gallic" to the Prior of Witham. The former Chief Justice of England, Sir John Fitzjames gave "to my cosyn Aldred Fitzjames all my bokes of lawe in recompense of suche bokes as I had of his father, except my greate boke of Statutes in vellum or parchment, which I give to my cosyn Nicholas Fitzjames."

As a clergyman John Yeadle was educated and well read. He possessed a collection of books, five named volumes of which he gave to Wells Cathedral, along with two volumes of Dr. Tillotson's Sermons to Mary Ludwell, and two books and all his pamphlets to Thomas Ludwell. All the rest of his books and papers he left to his kinsman Mathias Earbery if he was still living, but if not they were all to be sold and "the money be given by equall porcons to poore Tradesmen of the parish of Bruton to encourage them in theire respective Trades", at the discretion of his executors and the Overseers of the Poor.

Books continued to be prominent in the eighteenth century, for example, in 1740 widow Amey Gibbs bequeathed "all my books except my largest bible" to her granddaughter Mary Rudderford otherwise Rutherford. The family Bible was given to Amey's son Matthew. John Goldesbrough must have possessed a substantial collection of books as in 1767 he bequeathed "all the books in my two Libraries and all other my Books and Manuscripts" to be divided between his two sons, John and Richard Nicholas. Some of these books may have formed the basis of more than six hundred volumes that were sold after the death of a later Mrs Goldesbrough in 1855.

For one man facing death, the knowledge that he had a book that did not belong to him seemed to have weighed heavily upon his conscience as in his Will in 1417 Richard Bruton specifically ordered that, "I will that there be restored to the priory of Bruton 'Paulus super Clementinis' which is amongst the books in my dwelling house at Wellys." This volume was one of several books which appeared in his Will that he wished returned to various monasteries or clergymen. Like all priories Bruton would have possessed a library but there are no known books or manuscripts that may be definitely attributed to it, although in the 1890s it was considered that a Courtenay Prayer Book that was illuminated with about 500 coats of arms may have been produced there.

A number of Wills made reference to watches and clocks, for example, in 1626 Dame Elizabeth Berkeley left her watch to her daughter Jane and in 1714 John Whitehead gave his daughter Mary, "one gold watch and one gold chain." In 1902 Ann Bowring left her nephew Henry Longman "my watch and chain and appendages." The last two testators also bequeathed clocks, John Whitehead to the same daughter, who was to receive "my Clock in the parlour" and Ann Bowring gave "my Clock under dome" to another nephew Frederick George Longman. Lucy Temple was also in a position to make several bequests as she gave her clock to Mr Berkeley, "my gold Striking Watch" to Charles Berkeley and another gold watch to Miss Rebecca fflower. In the nineteenth century clocks and watches were more common so in his Will in 1821 baker Seth Smith bequeathed to his wife Edith, "my thirty hour clock and case and two of my silver watches." His daughter Mary received "my eight day clock and case and my two other silver watches."

Above all it was small items of jewellery that appeared most often in the bequests of the dying, not only very personal but also potentially valuable. In 1584 Dame Elizabeth Berkeley, the second wife of the first Sir Maurice, left her daughter Margaret, "3 Coffers with the jewels in them." Once again it was Lucy Temple who made a number of gifts: diamond earrings to Lady Barbara Bentinck; "my Braslets and Diamond Cross and Common Prayer Book with gold Clasps" to Miss ffany Trevanion; and a pearl necklace, described as "the least" to Miss Rebecca fflower. In 1902 Ann Bowring left her sister-in-law Rachael Longman, a "Jewel Case and Contents."

Gold rings were the most common of the items of jewellery, particularly in the seventeenth century and often family ones, passed on through the generations especially if a wife was already deceased. These rings were distinct from the ones that were given for mourning purposes, although at an earlier stage in their existence they might have originally been designed for the purpose. In 1560 widow Agnes Plumley gave "my golde ringe" to Sir Maurice Berkeley who was one of her overseers. He also received the same gift from Nicholas Gilbert six years later for performing this service. Dame Margaret Berkeley passed on "my weddinge Ringe wch I had of his father" to the second Sir Maurice in 1617. Widower Thomas Wilton in 1639 gave his granddaughter Agnes March, "my wives golde Ringe." In 1695 spinster Catherine Drew bequeathed to her sister-in-law "my late dear mothers wedding Ringe" and the following year Thomas Cornish als Allen, a widower, passed on his wife's wedding ring to his daughter Eleanor.

Some of the dying made arrangements for their own rings, such as Robert Albin who in 1543 left to his son, also named Robert, "my gold ring wherein my name is engraven to be kept and worne by him in rememberance of me." In 1648 widow Joane Sampson gave two daughters one gold ring each, whereas in 1691 Christian Ludwell left her two daughters, Christian and Mary, "all my rings and wearing apparel." Occasionally a description suggested a more ornate ring, for example, in 1626 Dame Elizabeth Berkeley left "My Diamond Ringe" to her brother Sir Robert Killigrew and his wife. Over a hundred years later Lucy Temple gave her niece Jane Berkeley a ring set around with diamonds and to Lady Byron "my Ring with 3 Rubys."

Finally, times changed, as did the habits of the wealthier in society, so that in 1831 Lucy Lloyd gave to Mary the wife of Theophilus Perceval, "the Sopha standing in my parlour with the Covering and Window Curtains corresponding." Two years later Mary Clarke was able to bequeath to her granddaughter, Elizabeth Creighton, "my Tea Caddy and Spoon.

i) Wills: the unusual.

Until the format of Wills became increasingly standardized in the eighteenth and nineteenth centuries, occasional unusual bequests appeared or the dying person included a statement that threw an interesting light upon a family, family relationships, attitudes to certain items or provided a glimpse into what was happening in and around Bruton at a particular time.

By the late thirteenth century a Hospital existed near Bruton, known as St Catherine at Lusty. It served as an almshouse for the poor and may also have housed lepers at one stage. There are in fact very few surviving references to it in the medieval period but it was included in a number of Wills as the dying man bequeathed money to it for the benefit of his soul. In 1417, for example, Richard Bruton gave 6s 8d to the poor in "le Spytelhous" in Bruton specifically "to pray for me." There were several other later charitable bequests as in 1524 John Brent left 3s 4d "To the Spetill house of Brewton." In 1471 Richard Dekyn called it "the Almeshouse of Lusty" when he donated 20d and in 1496 Richard Grene of North Cadbury left 6s 8d "To the Hospital of Bruton." Although it existed into at least the seventeenth century, it did not appear in any other surviving Wills. (14)

Another building that was mentioned by a dying man was the Market Cross. Traditionally, based upon the description of John Leland, the construction of this commercial centre was attributed to Abbot John Ely of Bruton Abbey in 1533. In his Will in 1542, however, Robert Chyke made the following bequest, "Item to the pformanc and bylding of the newe Crosse xxs." If nothing else this donation may suggest greater involvement by leading inhabitants of the town who would of course have had a vested interest, as did the Abbey, in the success of the weekly market. (15)

When making gifts of various household items, especially beds, a number of Wills, such as those of Thomas Albin in 1603, William Wilton in 1654 and Thomas Cornish in 1696 referred to the layout of their houses. The design usually included a hall and parlour with chambers over them. The most detailed description was given by Richard Dimond in 1676 when he gave his wife for use during her natural life the Parlour with the inner chamber above it, along with the Buttery between the Hall and the Parlour and she was to have access to the Hall and the Kitchen. She was also permitted to enjoy "that part of the Garden next the joining end of my Parlour as farr as the Beehives." All the rest of the rooms, outhouses and gardens went to his son Richard. In the days before the introduction of sugar honey was an important ingredient in many foods as well as candles and keeping bees was presumably part of the domestic economy of many homes.

At Redlynch Sir John Fitzjames also referred to "the greate chamber over the parlor" and his wife, Dame Elizabeth, gave to her son, Sir Maurice Berkeley, a bed and other items "being in the chamber called the Lord Lyssle's chamber and the ynner chamber belonging to the same, wt all the stuff in the utter chamber and the chappell annexed." Prior to the Reformation both Lord and Lady Lisle had been patrons and benefactors of Bruton Abbey. By the time that Sir James Fitzjames made his Will in 1579 different names were in use, "the Stourton chamber, my Lady Barkeley's chamber and the chamber over the buttery, and of the three new Testers of imbroderings that were last made."

In the Abbey Mansion the first Sir Maurice Berkeley left to his wife, "all the furniture in the chamber in the toppe of the howse, commonly called the gallorie chamber." This was likely to have been a large room as it included tapestries, beds, bedsteads, testers and three pallets. This reference may suggest that by 1579 either some significant building work or alterations had occurred to an original Abbey building or that Berkeley had built a new Mansion incorporating design features favoured in the Tudor period.

As agriculture remained such an important part of the daily lives of so many people it was perhaps no surprise that in at least two Wills crops were bequeathed. In 1544 Roger Ames left to his father, "two acres of corn in the field", and ten years later Henry Ottis alias Calowe granted to his daughter Alyce after his wife's death, "all the crop growing upon the ground, corn and grass."

The Will of John fflenger in 1557, who described himself as a yeoman, indicated some of the range of activities that a farmer would undertake. Having bequeathed her a cow, he also gave Cicilia More "my furnes wh is in the Slateer howse"; his son Nicholas amongst other things received "ij payre of lomes at the age of xvj years"; and "ij paire of the best lomes wh he will chouse & my presse for to presse clothe" to his stepson Raff More. Raising animals, slaughtering them, presumably shearing his own sheep and then spinning their wool to weave on his own looms, was all very much indicative of the domestic system of cloth production.

The attempts that were made to extend the use or life of an item may be glimpsed in the Will of Agnes Morris in 1633 for, although she was a wealthy woman, she was still able to leave to her daughter-in-law Melior Hogges, "one paire of Canvas sheets beinge lengthened both at one end." In 1560 Agnes Plumley had also left bedding but for a rather different purpose, "Item I give to the use of the poore women lyinge yn with childe a paire of blankets a paire of sheets and a coverlet." There was no indication as to whether these items would be sent to the cottage of a woman about to give birth or whether the woman was moved into a parish house which was used for that purpose.

It was not always the case that the recipient of a bequest was in this country and knowing the uncertainty of life the testators usually made alternative arrangements. In 1633, for example, Agnes Morris left money and various household items to her son John but stipulated that they should be passed to his son "if John my sonne doe not come into England to clayme and to receive the same." Over thirty years later in his Will, William Morris possibly a younger son of Agnes, left £100 to his son John, "To be paid when he returnes into England But if he return not then to remaine to my sonne Edward." No reason was given for these two members of the Morris family being out of the country but service in some branch of the military could be possible. In 1710 Robert ffry left various items to his son Robert but also made other arrangements for them if he "shall happen to dye during his present voyage at sea." He did, in fact, survive this trip but was buried in Bruton just two years after his father.

Life style and family problems emerged from several Wills, for example, in 1743 Richard Creed, a baker, disposed of all of his goods but then added, "And my further will is that the persons who are my Baile to the Sheriff shall in the first place be Indemnified and Saved harmless before any devise or Legacy shall take place." Whether this was as a result of a security required because of the nature of his occupation or of a crime with which he was charged and was awaiting trial was not specified.

The Will of Edward Norton in 1660 is interesting for two main reasons: the first was that he dealt with the issue of illegitimacy. He bequeathed most of his estate to his wife but some property he gave "unto Elizabeth Grymes my wives daughter, and my reputed daughter, whom I looke upon as my owne child though in the eye of the Law (beinge borne out of wedlock) shee cannot bee soe Esteemed." The child was a minor and so his wife received all the appropriate rents that he wished to be devoted to the "Educacon of my said reputed daughter untill shee shall Attaine her full age on One and Twentie yeares or be married."

Secondly, Edward Norton then went on to deal with the case of his brother John who had been the Minister of St Leonard's

Church in Bristol and a canon of the Cathedral, "But by reson of some distemper of mynde which hath Continued upon him about sixe and Twentie yeares last past (and yett doth) hee became incapable of dischargeinge his ffunction and dutie in those places." The Bishop had agreed that he should be allowed £10 a year, "Butt hath since these unhappy Warrs been wholly deteyned." Edward and his late mother had therefore supported John during that time and so he went on to establish an annuity, "that thereby hee may bee the better Provided for." Such a long period of illness must have been devastating not only for the sufferer but also for his family at a time when any treatment would have required payment and the whole matter was complicated by the disruption caused by the Civil War and the Commonwealth period.

Illegitimacy was also dealt with in the Will of Maurice, Lord Fitzharding in 1690. He made generous provision for Francis and Maurice Rutley whom he referred to as "my naturall sonns." Each was to receive £500 on attaining the age of twenty-one and some property in Ireland was to be divided equally between them. In addition their mother, Mrs Mary Rutley, was to receive £500. Whatever the moral issues involved, Fitzharding was at least continuing to accept his responsibilities. From a different point of view it must have been a sad situation for him as he failed to father a legitimate male heir and so his estate passed to his younger brother John. Unfortunately as Maurice had led an extravagant lifestyle he had been forced to mortgage the Bruton lands to the Brownlowe family of Lincolnshire and after a suit in Chancery Sir William Brownlowe assumed control from 1697.

Much later the Will of William Greenstock of Pitcombe in 1856 touched upon the question of illegitmacy. He placed £80 in a Trust for the benefit of his daughter Sarah who was by that time the wife of Uriah Hawkins. After Sarah's death the Trust was to benefit her children "including her daughter Mary born out of wedlock."

When widower Thomas Wilton made his Will in 1639 he had no surviving sons and so he adopted the practice of granting one of his daughters, Agnes Neale, a life interest in his house and its contents. As there were four other surviving daughters he then added that on the death of Agnes, "my Will is that the howse and the howsehould goods that is left in the howse to remaine to the rest of my children that be alive and to my childrens children." This was to be achieved by a sale and to ensure that this process was fairly undertaken, "I would that it should be devided by the Constables and Churchwardens of the Towne, Alsoe I doe desire you to sell awaie theis things for the use of my children and my childrens children as well as you can." He then included a provision which seems to have been unique amongst Bruton Wills at that period, "And at your cominge together about this busines for the makinge sale of theis things (but when God knowes) notwithstandinge, my desire is when the time is that you spend five shillings in Honie and Cakes."

In the centuries that followed there were occasional sales of property after a death which were held in various inns. In those circumstances it was not unusual for some form of alcoholic refreshement to be made available, not only as a courtesy but also presumably in the hope of encouraging potentional bidders to be more generous. In 1833, for example, Mary Clarke paid "an Inn Bill for Punch at the sale of Houses" when she sold the remaining years in the leases of two properties in the High Street which had been held by her deceased husband James.

The wording of Sir William Berkeley's Will in 1676 suggested that there may have been tensions within the family, especially if some of its members had disapproved of his younger second wife. He left everything to her except for £100 to his sister Jane Davies, £10 to Mrs Sarah Kirkman to buy a ring "that I may be remembered of so virtuous a good woman", and another £10 to his cousin Francilia "to buy her cloths for wedding." He added "And I do further make this declaration that if God had blessed me with a far greater estate I would have given it all to my most dearly beloved wife; for my brother, the Lord Berkeley's children have no want of that little I can dispose of and to the rest of my kindred, all but my dear sister Davies, I am far from having any obligation to." Recalled from Virginia in some disgrace he may have considered that his very influential family had done nothing or too little to support him.

Just under a hundred years later the Will of the last Lord Berkeley of Stratton also indicated family problems. His estate was divided between various relatives, such as nephews, nieces, great nephews and great nieces and cousins, especially his second cousin Anne Egerton, and a distant relation, the Earl of Berkeley. In the case of the latter the reason was specified in his Will: "And all this I do being the Last Male of my ffamily and desirous of Nourishing the Root from which it Sprung and wishing the Stock may continue to fflourish and put forth new Branches as long as any kind of Civil Government shall Subsist in this Country." This was despite the fact that he was married to Elizabeth, the 5th Lady Berkeley who survived him by three years. There is no mention of her in his Will and she hardly appeared in his life at all, which may well be explained by his string of transient love affairs that placed an intolerable strain on their marriage. Their failure to produce an heir may have been a contributing factor to the breakdown of their marriage. It has also been suggested that she was not from the same social status as her husband.

The Will of John, 3rd Lord Berkeley of Stratton was interesting for a different reason and that was his bequest of 200 guineas in gold to a famous actress of his time, Anne

Bracegirdle. She was the heroine of all Congreve's plays and with her black sparkling eyes, white teeth and fresh rosy complexion, was said to have charmed all the men who came into contact with her. Berkeley's relationship with her however was probably purely platonic as one contemporary wrote, "Tho' she might be said to have been the universal passion, and under the highest temptations, her constancy in resisting them served but to increase the number of her admirers.....It was even a fashion among the gay and young to have a taste or *tendre* for Mrs Bracegirdle." (16)

The Will of bachelor clergyman John Yeadle was very precise in 1688 and demonstrated the charitable inclinations of a man who had no direct male heirs. After the bequests of a small amount of cash, his wearing apparel, books, a clock and some pieces of silver, he directed that the residue of his estate was to be divided into five equal parts: the first two parts of which were to go, as has already been discussed, to the Minister of Bruton Parish Church and the Clerk. Another fifth was to be divided between his Executor Thomas Ludwell and his sister Mary. The next fifth was to be allotted "To the binding of poore boyes of the aforesaid parish of Bruton to Apprentices." The final fifth was to go to the poor of the town, "to be laid out one third parte of it in Bibles, where they are wanted, and in paying the House rent another third parte in cloathing; another parte in fewell for the Winter."

In the second half of the seventeenth century, and well into the eighteenth, there was a Quaker presence in Bruton, including the influential Whitehead family who were significant employers as clothiers. When Thomas Whitehead made his Will in 1690, amongst many other bequests, he established a Trust for his son George who was still a minor. All nine of the trustees were fellow Quakers and included Philip Allen, a maltster of Bruton, but were drawn from as far away as Lancashire and Cumberland, the home area of his first wife

Jane. He also gave to George Fox and George Whitehead, leading Quaker speakers, "Broad Cloth to make each of them a Coat."

His son John likewise made bequests to fellow Quakers, for example, "I give unto my friends commonly called Quakers belonging to the meeting at Weston Bampfield in the said County of Somerset ten pounds.... And I give unto my poor friends commonly called Quakers living at or near the several parishes of North Cadbury and South Cadbury ...five pounds." Before establishing their business in Bruton the family had been living in North Cadbury.

As Thomas Whitehead had such a strong religious conviction, a faith which had led to imprisonment many times, he did impose very strict conditions on his children: "it is my will that All my Children that shall or may expect any benefit by this my last will do keep in the fear of God..... if any of my said Children depart from the fear of God and refuse to be subject (*to the advice of his trustees*) and be unruly and dispose themselves in marriage without the consent of my trustees or the major part of them and be of an Evil Conversation that then such of my said Children shall have no benefit of this my last will and testament."

While a large number of Bruton Wills expressed the testator's hopes for their soul and body beyond death and a small number bequeathed money to the local Minister, only one arranged an endowment to spread contemporary Christian beliefs. In a Codicil signed on 28th April 1617, two days after he made his Will, Sir Maurice Berkeley established such an endowment.

"Nowe for as much as I would willingelie have a Reverend and a learned Preacher provided for and brought to Bruton wth much desire for instructinge and Teachinge the people in the service and feare of god: And my will is that the said Preacher doe preache everie Saboth daye in the forenoone and Catechise in the afternoons throughout the yeare or as farr forth as god shall enable him. And for and towardes the mainetenannce of such a Reverend preacher I desire my lovinge wife and my sonne Charles Barkeley to procure a convenient howse and a garden thereunto for him and to give yearlie unto him for his zealous endeavour in his function the full some of ffortie poundes of lawfull money of England which maintenance I doe hereby appointe to remayne for ever."

The presence of more than one clergyman in Bruton in the years before the Civil War may indicate that this request was fulfilled. Extreme Protestantism or Puritanism was not strong in Somerset as a whole so only Bruton and Bridgewater were the two main recipients of these preacher endowments.

Included towards the end of the lengthy Will of Isabel Fitzjames in 1527 was the request that "William Clements, scholar of Oxford, shall have a peir of blankets, a bollster, and 26s 8d in money to his exhibicion." As he does not appear to be a member of the family or a canon at the Abbey, it is possible that he was formerly a pupil at the Free School which her stepson John had helped to found in 1519.

The Will of the Hon. Charles Berkeley was made in November 1757 but over the next seven years he added three Codicils, the last of which throws an interesting light on some developments in the countryside at that period. His original intention had been that his executors should offer some of his property to his brother, John 5th Lord Berkeley of Stratton, at the same price as he had paid for it and the money used for the benefit of his two daughters. He did, however, reconsider: "Since the time of making my Will I have with much care and Expense made considerable improvements upon my fffarms of Copplesberries and Horseley and the Grounds called Wiltons

Grounds." He decided that he should increase the price by £1,000, making a total of £5,500, "in Justice to my daughters and without injustice to my Brother." His actions on his estate may suggest that he was one of the progressive landowners of the eighteenth century who did so much to stimulate the Agricultural Revolution of that period.

The death of a Master meant that an apprentice could be viewed as a transferable commodity. In January 1717 the Churchwardens and Overseers of Shepton Montague apprenticed James Andrews, described as "a poor Boy", to William Dampier of Blackford. By April 1720 the latter was dead and so his executors arranged to tranfer the Apprenticeship Indenture to William Penny of Yarlington so that the "sd Boy should be taught & instructed in ye Art & Mysterie of Husbandry to which he was bound, whereby he may for ye future get a Livelyhood."

Finally, at different periods two unusual items were bequeathed: the first was in 1579 when Sir Maurice Berkeley willed, "that my three youngest sonnes ffrances Barkeley, Robert and John Barkeley shall have my cheyne equally devided betweene theme wch weigheth fortie twoe ounces of fine gould." As Sir Maurice had been a prominent courtier and had held a number of official offices this chain was presumably as a result of one of those. So that his four daughters would also benefit he gave them £20 "a peece to buye them cheynes withal." The second item was bequeathed in 1821 and indicated what was considered moveable at that period as Seth Smith gave his wife Edith "my kitchen grate."

14

THE WORLDLY
CONSEQUENCES
OF DEATH: HUMAN

For the bereaved the immediate consequence of death was grief and that manifested itself in many different ways: tears, distress, depression, a burst of activity as a distraction and even denial. Some sought comfort in committing their grief and thoughts to paper as they corresponded with family and friends. On the death of her husband in 1667 Lady Godolphin wrote to her sister-in-law Lady Fitzharding at Bruton, " Next my selfe and my poore fatherless children, I know nobody could have so great a share of affliction for our most grievous lose as your Ladyship..... this deare person was the worthiest husband and the tenderest father so he was the kindest brother that ever I knew."

When a younger son of John, 1st Lord Berkeley of Stratton died in January 1676, one year before his own death, Berkeley was clearly distraught, "I have lost one of my greatest delights in this world my 3rd sonne Maurice, which has sufficiently weaned me from the world: God grant me the spirit of patience that I may beare it as I ought to doe." On the death of his eldest daughter Jane who had managed the household at Bruton after the death of his wife, William, 4th Lord Berkeley of Stratton wrote to Lord Strafford, "The loss of one who did the part of mother to mine so many years has nearly touched me in this remote corner. Her company will be missed, though for my own particular, London would be a solitude when most of my acquaintances are gone, and the time past for making new." (17)

Before the Reformation the overwhelming majority of those who were bereaved derived substantial comfort from the prospect of ultimate reunion and that the prayers of the living would aid the souls of the dead. Through the centuries many of the living clung to the belief that the deceased had passed from a world of misery to a much better one. Even though obits for the dead ceased at the Reformation, a large number of the bereaved continued to remember special times of the year, such as a birthday or the anniversary of the day of death. But no matter how deep the grief may have been, life had to continue.

The first task for many of the bereaved was to make the arrangements for the funeral but there were a host of other administrative matters which had to be undertaken. News of the death had to be spread, often on market day, so that both creditors and debtors could come forward and all debts settled. Some of the debts were bonds which had been arranged years before but there could be more immediate ones, such as for Thomas Albin in 1641. He had clearly been taken ill or met with an accident away from home as his widow paid 10s to John Ames of Prestie "for lodgeing and diet of the said deceased when hee lay sick and brused in the said Ames howse." She also paid 5s "unto one Callowshall Chiourgion (*surgeon*) for his medicinces and paines about the said deceased."

There could be more pressing problems as the widow of John Dicer discovered in August 1588 when she had to spend 20s "in charges for the keeping of iiij of his Children and on of his servants in their sickness sinc the decease of hir sd husband." Additional money was spent "for apparell and other necessarie charges in keeping the forsd Children." The one piece of good news for the family was that although the death rate was very high in that year, with some seventy-six burials being recorded, the names of no other Dicer family members were listed. In 1598 the widow of Edward Collins had to pay immediately 2s 6d "for rent due to the landlord at the feast of the Annunciation of our Ladye St Marie the Virgin now next comyng." Widow Ann March had to pay 10s "for a mortuary due uppon the death of deceased unto the ffarmer of the Rectory of Bruton." In addition she claimed in her Account £3, "the price of one horsebeast prized in the aforesaid Inventory ....which was taken for a herriott upon the death of the said Deceaed."

By the Tudor and Stuart periods the majority of the Wills seem to have been proved in Wells and so it was there that the bereaved had to travel. This often entailed not only claims for money for sustenance but also the need to hire a horse to travel: Tabitha Albin spent 5s in 1641 "For travelling from Bruton to Wells to pass this account"; John Dicer's widow spent 16s on going to Wells and on various necesssary adminstrative expences; and the wife of Edward Collins claimed 15d in 1598 "for the charges disbursed by her for the hier of two horsses when she travelled to Wells."

Unfortunately, on occasions, sorting out the affairs of the deceased caused problems for the bereaved relatives. In 1598 the widow of Edward Collins found that she could not take possession of all of his goods which may imply that there was some dispute in progress. She entered a claim of 54s 4d "for the price of a Cowe in the hands & custodie of John Andrewes of Brewton pcell of the goods & chattells of the sd Edward Collins deceased wch shee cannott come by." It appears that Andrews also had some other goods and cash which had been delivered to him by John Walter, a servant of Edward Collins. Just over twenty years later in 1621 the widow of Edward Knewstubb was forced to make a claim when she discovered that some of his goods disappeared and she did not know "who hath them, nor whom to sue for them." It would appear that some degree of dishonesty was evident on occasions at the time of death.

On rare occasions there was the problem of knowing what and where an inheritance might be. In December 1789, for example, James Meaden of Brewham requested information about the place where Edward Meaden, surgeon, was interred and where his effects were after he had died about 1764. James believed that the property involved was of such value that he was prepared to offer a reward of £1,000 to obtain it.

For some of the bereaved death meant that they could expect to inherit and in some cases the inheritance was substantial. For generation after generation, for example, the Bruton Abbey estate passed down to the eldest son of the Berkeley family. Wills throughout the period under consideration indicated that where there was a male heir he could expect to receive the majority of what his father had to leave, even though in many instances he had to wait until after the death of his mother. If there was no male heir then whatever estate there was could be expected by a daughter, although according to the law as it existed until the late nineteenth century and the Married Women's Property Act of 1882, that was most likely to pass to her husband.

On the occasions when the direct line ended there could be a more unexpected inheritance, for example, both John and James the sons of Sir John Fitzjames of Redlynch predeceased their father and although John was already married he had produced no heir of his own. In this instance the estate was bequeathed to the nearest male heir, a first cousin, Nicholas Fitzjames. Similarly when the last Lord Berkeley of Stratton died childless in 1773 his vast estate passed to a number of people, especially members of the Egerton family, although the majority went to Earl Berkeley of Berkeley Castle. How far the terms of his Will were known before his death is impossible to deduce but certainly some of the beneficiaries, especially his Lordship's servants, may have been surprised by the amounts they received.

For some beneficiaries their inheritance must have been much more unexpected, for example, Sir John Fitzjames left the residue of his estate "to be distributed among my por kynnesmen and women that have much nede and little helpe." In 1619 Hugh Sexey left a similar instruction when he ordered £500 to be divided amongst any kindred he had not identified by name. For the distant relations of Robert Pavy there must have been an even greater surprise after his death as he left £200 each to the first cousins of his father and mother and £2,000 to be divided among the children of these cousins. There was so little information about exactly who they were that advertisements had to be placed in newspapers early in 1800 requesting them to come forward, "within one year of his decease but not afterward…with their pedigrees." In February 1880 solicitors Dyne and Muller of Bruton advertised for the heir or next of kin of George Shepherd formerly of Lamyatt to come forward for, although he had died in the Union Workhouse in Newport in South Wales, there was a small freehold property and some money available.

Even the aristocracy could be surprised at a bequest, for example, William, 4th Lord Berkeley of Stratton was remembered in the Will of Lady Belasyse of Oxgodby, possibly to the extent of £10,000, and was made one of her executors. In March 1713 Berkeley commented in a letter, "My Lady Belasyse was ever the most obliging to me in the world but

I never knew I had half one share of her favour that she hath expres't in her will, where she hath left me joint executor with her nephew, Sir John Wodehouse, which is likely to prove a considerable advantage to me and will help to portion my daughters." In a subsequent letter he added, "executorship proves very considerable and was so very little expected that it is in a manner fallen from heaven."

Berkeley tended to worry about money especially when John, Lord Fitzharding made him one of the executors of his Will in 1712 and that had provided him with no money, except for £50 to buy a mourning ring. The Will appeared very straightforward as after a number of bequests to various individuals, including servants, the executors were instructed to sell as much property as was necessary to pay his debts, funeral expences and provide for his two daughters. Although provision was made for the executors "to reimburse and save themselves harmless from all Costs and charges occasioned in the Execution of this my Will", Berkeley experienced a great deal of trouble as he complained on one occasion, "I don't know how 'tis in other places but where I am concerned no tenants pay (*in Bruton*), and we must live upon air, though moist and unpleasant with continual rains." (18)

a) Widows and Widowers

Throughout the period under consideration there was a stark variation between the impact of death on the widows of wealthy men and on those of the poor. Time and again the Wills of wealthier widows showed that they had landed property, houses, personal possessions and cash to distribute to children and others as they saw fit. Many of them continued to enjoy a comfortable physical existence within their established community. The widows of the poor on the other hand were frequently left with nothing and faced an uncertain future with the prospect of hard toil and often destitution.

Even for wealthier widows it was not always possible to deduce their overall situation as so much of what they received was never discussed in Wills, covered instead by words such as 'the residue'. There were of course specific grants, for example, Nicholas Goldesbrough left his wife Judith £700 in cash to be paid within one month of his death but in addition she received a life interest in much of the rest of his property, the value of which was not specified.

In instances when a man had been in trade there could be some security for his widow. Susan Morgan was left the Blue Ball and Wellington Inns along with all their contents by her husband Daniel in 1853 although no indication of their value was given. For at least the next thirteen years she continued to run these establishments, receiving many favourable comments for her catering for large meetings and gatherings. Mary Clarke on the other hand had decided not to continue in business after the death of her husband James in 1832. She sold his Goods and Stock in Trade for just over £182 and the leases of two properties in the High Street to Robert Griffin Hole for £525, with a further £10 2s 6d for fixtures.

As well as a life interest and the residue of an estate, arrangements had sometimes been made in advance for a husband's death in the marriage settlement but these were virtually never repeated in Wills. Similarly it was customary for widows to receive one third of an estate but that too did not find a place in a Will.

On the other hand, even for wealthier widows there were almost insurmountable problems: time could hang very heavily upon them as in many cases their central role as wife and supporter of a husband in his occupation and social status ended. After the death of John 1st Lord Berkeley of Stratton, the diarist John Evelyn noted that his widow Lady Christina, then in her late thirties, became socially inactive and that this led her first to lease out the grounds of Berkeley House in London and then to find a tenant for the mansion itself. It was to be another twenty years before she joined her husband in their family vault in Twickenham Parish Church.

While many widows were granted a life interest in the family home, some found that they had to leave as it passed to the eldest son and his family. In addition, if they were over forty years of age national statistics indicated that they had little chance of remarriage. It has been estimated that by the 1880s some 30% of all women aged between fifty-five and sixty-four were widowed.

Young widows could be in a different position, for example, after the death of John, 3rd Lord Berkeley of Stratton, his widow Jane, who was to survive him by fifty-four years married William 1st Earl of Portland. When the Countess of Falmouth became a widow on the death of Charles, Earl of Falmouth in 1665 she was just twenty years of age, having been married for two years. Rumours abounded that after her period of mourning she was going to marry Henry Jermyn and it was even suggested that she might marry James, Duke of York after the death of his first wife but nothing happened. She did however become one of the mistresses of Charles II and eventually married Charles Sackville, 6th Earl of Dorset in June 1674 and died in 1679.

In the earlier part of the period the remarriage of a widow did not appear to have been an issue for those who made Wills as they usually gave their wife a life interest in all or part of the estate and then it passed to another named person, usually a male heir. As greater prosperity was achieved by some men, they found that they had larger estates to distribute and clearly became more concerned that property in particular might be diverted from their own family in the event of remarriage. Increasingly therefore provisions in the event of remarriage were included.

The first surviving Bruton Will that made specific reference to this issue was that of Robert Albin in 1643. Property granted to his wife Christian was for her natural life and then went to his son James but she was also to receive an annuity of £40 a year for life. This was to cease "if my said wife shall marry." In 1686 Peter Walter of Wyke Champflower left his two leasehold estates there to his wife Elizabeth "during her widdowhood", but that arrangement was to end on "her inter-marriage with any other Husband." Such provision became much more common in the eighteenth century and found expression in the Wills of men such as Robert Fry and Henry Sampson: a bequest would cease "the day of Marriage with any other after taken husband." In the nineteenth century in the Wills of men such as Thomas White and Daniel Morgan it was expressed as "so long as she shall remain my Widow."

It was not of course an issue which faced the widow of a poor man as for her remarriage could be essential, especially if there were children involved.

For prosperous widowers the situation was very different as they often remained financially secure with their house and property intact, possibly even enhanced if a wife had originally retained her own goods under a marriage settlement. In many cases they had an occupation or profession to continue and were much more likely to remarry, especially if they were under thirty years of age. It has been estimated that by 1850 about 14% of all males who married were widowers, compared with 9% of all females as widows, and by the 1880s about a similar % of men aged between fifty-five and sixty-four were widow-ers. One historian had commented, "There is ample evidence to show that widowers tended to marry again quite soon and usually to considerably younger women….Dying wives and their friends encouraged husbands to remarry in the interests of motherless children, and to satisfy the assumed male need for sympathy and support." (19)

The amount of documentary evidence from Bruton is far too limited for any definite conclusions to be drawn. The status of 'widower' or 'widow' was rarely recorded in the Parish Registers until 1817 and ages were generally not included until after October 1869, and even then those of widowers and widows appeared very infrequently. In the period 1817 to 1900 however there were 177 marriages involving either widowers or widows and of these 124 or 70% were widowers and 53 or 30% were widows, although in twenty-eight instances or 16% a widower married a widow. Clearly therefore in Bruton widowers were much more likely to remarry than widows and between 1840 and 1860 the re-marriage level for widows was almost identical with the national estimate, as out of 263 marriages twenty-five or 9.5% involved a widow. For widowers the Bruton figure was slightly above the national level with forty-five re-marriages or 17.1%.

In the extremely small sample where both the age of the widower and his bride was recorded sixteen out of seventeen men married a younger woman. In the one exception the bride was just one year older than her husband. The average age difference was 7.5 years, with the largest gap being a forty-six year old widower marrying a twenty-four year old woman, a gap of twenty-two years, and the second largest gap was twenty-one years between a fifty-seven year old widower and his thirty-six year old bride. In just two instances the ages of widows and their new husbands were recorded: one aged forty-seven and the other forty-five and in both cases they married men aged thirty-nine.

The prospects for widows appeared especially bleak at the beginning and end of the nineteenth century as between 1817 and 1830 only two widows were recorded as remarrying compared with fifteen widowers and between 1880 and 1900 some four widows compared with twenty-one widowers. Such statistics do assume of course that the Registers were accurately maintained.

Some remarriages by widowers appeared to have been quite rapid, for example, William Wallis buried his first wife Ann, whom he had married in October 1842, on 2nd July 1874 and married Sarah Fleetwood, some three years his junior, just over four months later on 17th November.

For poor widows and widowers alike the situation was radically different from that of the wealthier bereaved in the community for, as well as coming to terms with their grief, they often had nothing with which to rebuild their lives and many were driven deep into a life of poverty and despair. The state of the cottage of widow Mary Morris of Shepton Montague may be implied from, the Hearth Tax survey of 1664-1665 as she originally had two chimneys but one was recorded as having fallen down. For some the only recourse was to seek help from the Poor Law System as it existed after 1601 and the Accounts for the Overseers of the Poor for Bruton paint a vivid picture of their extent and their misery. (20)

In the year 1653 to 1654, which is the first year that the surviving Accounts cover, out of fifteen women who were on the 'Disbursements Ordinary' list, that is who received regular weekly payments from the Overseers, eleven or 73% were widows. There was of course some marked variation in their numbers, for example in 1656 seven out of eight women or 88% so relieved were widows whereas just over a decade later in 1669 only nine out of twenty-two or 41% were widows. Many of these widows were also aged, for example, the Overseers gave 8d, "To the wid Cooke being very olde."

In addition widows could receive small sums of money from the Overseers under 'Disbursements extraordinary', that is an ad hoc payment as particular needs and circumstances arose. Some widows required immediate help so, for example, in May 1741 the Overseers paid 10s 6d for "A Shroud Coffin & burying Thos Lumber Wantcatcher" (*a mole catcher*). The following month they gave his widow 1s 8d and in July 1s 6d. Some widows found that with the death of the main breadwinner they were no longer able to pay their rent and so faced losing the roof over their head unless the Overseers stepped in:

"1653	pd for Mary Hopkins rent after her husband's death	2	0
1668	for a monthly house rent for Wid Young	1	0
1679 Ap 20	Payd the Wid Stader her quarter's Rent	5	0."

Occasionally it was the rates on a house that caused the problem:

"1817 May 18   Widow Barnard to be exempted from paying the last years rates."

Widows were sometimes in need of specific items and so provision could be made for them. In 1679, for example, 2s was given to Widow Helliar for "faggotts"; in April 1689 1s 4d "To ffrances Carrier Wid to buy her an Apron", and in May of the same year 2s 6d "ffor a paire of Shoes for Eliz Moore Wid." In September 1790 Widow Carior received a blanket, as did Widow Gapper in October 1804.

Young widows could be left with children and that was often an additional burden. In April 1749 the Overseers gave the small sum of 1s "To Widow Inkpens Family in distress." There were individual grants to a child such as in October 1804 when Widow Cox's son received a "Jackett & Trousers." The presence of Sexey's Hospital, which from the early 1660s admitted boys to be educated before being apprenticed, did ease the burden for some widows and once again the Parish helped:

"1669   Item for a paire of Shoes for   2s   0d."
        the Widdow Coward's sonne when
        he went into the Hospitall

In many cases as widows faced general destitution an overall phrase such as "in want" was commonly used by the Overseers:

"1653   Given the Widd Hulett in want   2   0
 1669   To the Wid Wornall in want   1   0."

One solution in the early nineteenth century, especially if there were a number of children, was to encourage emigration so that after the initial expense the family did not become a burden on the poor rates for decades: "1831 Sept/Oct. Expences of Mary White & Seven Children to Bristol & their passage thence to America by the Ship Charlotte & landing Money on their arrival at New York."

While the Overseers tended to designate widows with that title they did not do the same for widowers so the extent of aid to that category of poor men cannot be determined. There were, however, instances, especially immediately after the death of a wife when relief was given, if only for the burial.

"1662   Item for bringing Peter   3   0
           Walters wife to Earth

           Item for bringing his Children   1   6
           to Earth

 1727 Aug William Chapman's wife in   1   0
           Sickness

| Dec | Cofin and buring Chapman's wife | 8 | 6 |
| 1741 Oct/Nov | A Coffin & Shroud for Wm Davidge's wife 7s bury her and her two children 5   6 | 12 | 6." |

The devastating consequences for a family with the death of the breadwinner may be glimpsed briefly through entries such as the following:

"1730 Sept	Ryals family in want	5	0
Nov	Ryals Shroud and for Burying him	7	0
1731 Jan	Ryal in childbed	1	0
Mar	Ryals family in want	1	6."

In these four entries alone a family's six months of misery was vividly portrayed.

In the nineteenth century when the poor relief system changed with the introduction in 1834 of the Poor Law Amendment Act, widows continued to receive help. In the 1851 Census there were some ninety-four widows in Bruton and of these twenty-six or 28% were classed as paupers. When the Wincanton Poor Law Union was formed widows constituted up to 10% of all those who received Outdoor Relief, that is relief payments in their own home. Outdoor Relief Books indicate that in the early 1870s and 1890s between 7% and 15% of all females who received such relief in Bruton were widows. There were those within the Poor Law System who considered that widows were treated too generously as they argued that many were capable of work. As early as 1838 Inspector Weale commented, "Widows are still too much objects of sympathy." (21) Once again widowers were not mentioned as it was taken for granted that such men would continue to work.

One category of poor widows who were particularly badly affected by the Poor Law System were those whose husband died while they were not resident in their place of Settlement, which was usually defined as the parish in which the man had been born or possibly served an apprenticeship. Parish officials were extremely keen to remove widows from their parish especially if they had dependent children, as they could become a financial burden upon the parish. In a batch of Removal Orders from Bruton preserved in the parish records out of seventy-nine women who were removed to other places between 1688 and 1842, some twenty or 25% were widows and with them went at least twenty-six children.

In the period from 1691 to 1846 out of fifty-one women who were removed from other parishes to Bruton, twelve or 24% were widows with a total of thirteen children, one of whom was just seventeen weeks old. These statistics are not complete as there were other removals both from and to Bruton which were ordered by the Quarter Sessions and for which the Orders have not survived in the parochial deposit. In addition payments for removals were recorded in the Overseers' Accounts and for which there is no other surviving documentary evidence providing details.

Widows and widowers in Bruton were of course fortunate that provision was made for them in Sexey's Hospital and through small grants of money from the Visitors in their own homes. In May 1694, for example, the Visitors ordered, "that 20s be given to the Widow Rawlins…. And £3 to Mtrs Lamphew a poor widow. And that £3 be given to the Widow Sley to bind out her son an Apprentice." (22) The 1851 Census showed that of the thirteen elderly women in the Hospital seven were widows but of twelve elderly men no less than eleven were widowers. This statistic in itself may imply that widowers were less able to manage on their own, presumably after a long period of being looked after by a wife. It may also be that elderly widows more readily found a place within the family of adult children where they could continue to play a useful role.

Preserved amongst the records of Sexey's Hospital, probably by chance, is a small collection of petitions presented to the Visitors requesting assistance. One batch of eighty-seven of these petitions date predominantly from the early to mid-1660s and were sent mainly from Bruton inhabitants, with a few derived from other parts of the Visitors' estates. Although they seem to have been largely written by a scribe and were designed to illicit sympathy, they highlight dramatically the plight of the poor, including widows and widowers, at this period. Unfortunately, as in the Overseers' Accounts, elderly men were rarely designated as widowers.

Time and again widows were indicated facing the same problems. The death of a husband could leave his widow with small children: Margaret Drew found that her husband Aristotle's death left her with nothing "but the unsupportable Burden of extreme indigency & Misery, many small, feeble & Sickly Children; of wch two are disposed to the Kings Evill, and in great danger of blindness." Elizabeth Stroud was left with "two small children without support of maytenance" and Grace Penny found herself in "extreme penury and necessity; having six children, and the younger very feeble and sickly."

One widow, Anstice Leversuch als Jeffery had "pauned all that once I have and I am in a very sad condition." Nursing a sick husband before his death caused debt as Mary Creed stated that her husband "had a long tedious wearing Sickness before his death, by Meanes whereof yor pet became much indebted and was never able since that time to recover herselfe to be able to pay the same."

It was however in old age that poverty had its greatest effect upon widows as was reflected in petition after petition.

Joan Young referred to herself as "very aged and almost blinde in extreme want and necessity", and Joane Tice stated that she was "a poore blinde woman, and is neere about fower score and nine yeares of age and can doe nothing att all towards the getting of her maintenance." Christian Mitchell considered herself "a poor weake lame woman and neere fower score yeares of age." Elizabeth Hardin was younger at sixty-six but "now through age growen almost blinde & greviously lame under cure & cannot bee healed is fallen into gret poverty & want of all things not any wise able to Subsist."

The very small number of petitions that were clearly from widowers present a similar picture. Edward Carrier was left with three small children when his wife died, was unable to get work as a weaver and had fallen behind with his rent. Richard Edwardes who claimed to have "binn a very laborious person" found himself in "a very poor condition", partly as a result of "the hardness of this time" and partly as "his wiffee lay sick a long time on his handes before her desese." Robert Hore the elder "is now in his old age brought to great povertie, and is not able to labour as formerly he hath done." (23)

Nearly 30% of these documents specifically referred to the petitioner as being a widow or widower and a number of others, particularly from males, probably fell into that category as well. These petitions, together with the evidence from the Overseers' Accounts, indicated that for many widows and widowers from the poorer part of the community, life was very hard after the death of their spouse.

b) Children

Once again, as with widows and widowers, death could have a very different impact upon the children of the wealthy compared with those of the poor. For the former Wills indicated that provision was often made, including arrangements until a child reached a designated age while for the latter it could make a hard life even harder and often led them to sink further into poverty. In the bleakest situation, death could deprive a child of both parents, in which case he or she faced the possibility of years as a parish orphan.

i) For the wealthy.

In the earlier part of the period it was often essential first of all to establish beyond doubt who was the actual heir and the appropriate details, such as age. This was achieved through an Inquisition Post Mortem and one in 1410, for example, established that after the death of Ela, the widow of Sir Richard de Sancto Mauro, her heir was her granddaughter, Alice aged just twenty-eight weeks.

In such circumstances a landed estate was administered in the name of the monarch and could be leased or the right to it sold until the heir came of age. When Leonard Bosgrove of Godminster died his son Nicholas was a minor and so in March 1559 the whole estate, with its annual rental value of £10 2s 4d, was leased to John Arundell for a consideration of £12 to Queen Elizabeth. The Berkeleys' estate was much more extensive and hence much more valuable so that it was unfortunate from their perspective that when the second Sir Maurice died in 1617 his son Charles was a minor, aged seventeen years, four months and seventeen days. The estate was valued for rental purposes as £106 8s 5d, of which James I received £35 9s 5d and the rights were then sold for £800 to Charles's mother Dame Elizabeth and Sir William Killigrew, who was his grandfather. Various parts of a minor's inheritance could of course be sub-let and so, for example, in 1431 William Carpyntere of Bruton paid 12d to the Lord of Dunster for the right to occupy a watermill called Wykemylle at Wyke Champflower during the minority of John, son and heir of James Fitzjames. (24)

From the Tudor period onwards it was common when no extensive landed property and much smaller sums of money were involved, for the dying in their Wills to request their Executors to ensure that any provisions made for their children who were minors were fulfilled. In 1589 Edward Spicer left £10 to Henry Elliott with the instruction to his wife who was the sole executrix that it "be putt forthe to his use untill he be of yeares of discreation to use it himselfe." Thomas Mogg made a similar arrangement in 1656 when he gave £20 each to his sons James and Thomas that they were to receive at the age of twenty-one. For the latter there was also the request directed to his executor, his eldest son John, that he "shall Educate and bring him upp in learneinge, and then binde him Apprentice to some convenient Trade."

In the eighteenth and nineteenth centuries a further method of ensuring that the interests of minors were protected was to establish a Trust with two or more Trustees who were charged to implement the terms of a Will. In 1767 John Goldesbrough placed all his estate into a Trust to be administered by Walter Burton, clerk, and John Dampier, mercer, and there followed in his Will extensive arrangements for its administration for the benefit of his wife and sons. In 1816 Thomas White established a Trust managed by his two brothers, Lawrence and George, for the benefit of his wife during her natural life, or until such time as she remarried, and his children, with the particular request that it should be devoted "towards the Maintenance and Education of My Dear Children." This may well have been a very astute move on his part as when he died in August 1824 he left a widow and nine young children. The Trust established by Daniel Morgan in 1853 was also designed to benefit his two children: that his son should enter the appropriate profession, trade or calling and that his daughter should receive money on marriage.

Faced with the prospect that her children would be orphans, widow Elizabeth Meachem made her Will in September 1813. In this she left all her estate to her three children, John, Robert and Mary, and arranged for their uncles, her two brothers William and Robert Griffin Hole, to be their guardians.

The range of areas that could be adminstered during a minority was very large. In April 1765 Revd. Woodforde was requested by Parson Penny, his father's curate at Castle Cary, to officiate at a funeral one afternoon as he was being presented to the Living of Evercreech "to hold it for a Minor (Justice Rodbard's Son of 12 years old.)."

Not all arrangements during minorities were implemented in the manner intended. On one occasion Charles Pagett, who described himself as one of the ordinary Yeomen of the Queen's Chamber, petitioned Queen Elizabeth for redress. He explained that some seventeen years earlier he had married Margaret Ansly, the widow of Edmond Ansly who had two sons, Henry and Francis. Edmond Ansly had arranged that for their support they should have the copyhold of "a common Inn or hostery in Brewton in the Countie of Somst and called the sign of the George." With the money generated from this source Pagett undertook to provide for their education during their minority but in return for £80 leased the Inn to William Purdewe, a bellfounder. Pagett alleged that Purdewe only paid him half of the agreed sum and to avoid paying the rest persuaded Henry Ansley to occupy the Inn. Pagett described Henry as "a wilde youth and under age of one and twenty yeeres having carelessly and unthriftily spent his tyme in ill companie." (25)

ii) For the poor.

The position of a poor child who lost one or both parents through death could not have been more different. If a widow could find or retain employment, did not have too many dependent children or was able to remarry, then the situation was manageable. If not, it was often the case that the Overseers of the Poor had to be contacted and asked for assistance. As has already been seen it was not uncommon for them to grant a specific item, often clothing, to the child of a widow. There could also be assistance when the child of a widow was elected to Sexey's Hospital, just as, for example, "Widdow Coward's sonne" received a pair of shoes in 1669. In April 1747 the Overseers paid 2s for, "A pr of Breeches for Dame Wake's Boy of Week going into the Hospital." It was a very small outlay when the parish was to be relieved of the burden of any future support in childhood.

A small number of children who lost one or both parents might find refuge with other relatives, such as grandparents. On occasions the Overseers would provide assistance, as in the case of Richard Edwards who at various times in 1658 received 1s 6d "toward ye keeping his 2 grandchildren."

The group of children which the ratepayers in the parish wished to minimize was orphans as they had the potential to be a drain on finances for years, at least until they could be apprenticed. Amongst other things the Overseers had to provide the parish children with clothes, for example, in 1715 they paid Mr Ludwell £1 1s 5d "for clothes for Randals daughter and other parish children."

At times it was expedient, although not always in keeping with the concepts of Christian charity, to remove orphans to their parish of settlement. In January 1742, for example, Bruton officials were successful in persuading the Justices of the Peace at the Quarter Sessions to confirm the removal of Sarah

Collins and her four brothers and sisters back to South Brewham. At least in this instance two of these children were already nineteen and sixteen, so possibly able to find some kind of employment there.

Once the Bruton Poorhouse was opened in June 1734 orphans could be housed in this building in Silver Street. Unfortunately it is not possible to ascertain the exact number of orphans in the institution at any one time as, although there were monthly totals of inmates for over a hundred years, they did not differentiate the various categories but just presented the overall number. That children were in the House was clear from various entries in the Overseers' Accounts, such as in August 1738 they paid 6d for "A Combe for the Children" and in November 1744 Stephen Coles was paid 5s, "for 2 Boys coats & 2 Maids Gowns." When the Poorhouse was inspected early in 1836, prior to the removal of the inmates to the new Union Workhouse in Wincanton, there were "found 10 aged and infirm inmates together with 3 boys and three Girls." (26)

The principal aim of the Overseers was to apprentice the orphan children, especially the boys, as soon as possible and surviving Indentures indicate that many of them were already apprenticed by the time that they were ten years old. Such was the lack of interest in the boys that their names were virtually never recorded in their Accounts. In 1669, for example, Thomas Horsay was paid £2 10s 0d "wth the boy being bound for 8 yeares" and in June 1733 William Williams received £1 "with a poor Boy Apprentice", with a further 2s 6d being paid "to bind the sd Boy." In June 1843 £4 12s 6d was "Pd for the Two Boys put Apprentice."

Similar anonymity was to be found when it came to purchasing clothes for the apprentices, for example, in 1658 the Overseers paid £2 14s 3d "for 15 yds & ½ of Cloth att

3 6 p yard to make ye Apprentices cloths" and in 1669 it cost 2s "for a hatt for Thos Horsey's apprentice." In 1742 the Overseers paid 5s 6d for "4 pr of leather Breeches for the Boys that left the House." While apprentices were generally male, female parish children were sent out to service, for example, in May 1733 the Overseers spent 1s 6d "for a Warrant in order to send the wenches of ye Parish to service."

The apprenticeship system received a financial boost when in their Wills both John Yeadle and Lucy Temple left money to bind out apprentices but it was not clear if these were to be orphans or any boys from within the parish. At the other extreme not all apprentices were well treated by their masters as a case was heard in the Quarter Sessions in 1654 when yeoman William Morris of Bruton attempted to rid himself of an apprentice, Robert Redwood, described as "a poore father-less child", by putting "the said apprentice out of his service and endeavouring to have transported him to ye Barbados." No reason was given for this action, which was not uncommon at that period, and the Sessions supported Redwood. (27)

Once the New Poor Law was in operation after 1834, responsibility for orphans passed to the Boards of Guardians. Returns in the early 1870s and 1890s indicated that one orphan was receiving Outdoor Relief in Bruton and that in the early 1890s there were two orphans from the town resident in the Wincanton Workhouse. They were in fact the only category of inmate that could not leave that institution at their own request and so were kept there until the Guardians decided on a course of action, which might be apprenticeship or employment as a servant or very late in the century to be fostered.

The other avenue of help for boys who had lost one or both parents was Sexey's Hospital that from the early 1660s educated twelve boys and then apprenticed four of them each year. Even before that decade the Visitors had been making grants to orphan children such as 10s in 1628 to those of Mtrs Rog'son, "Given after her death towarde the releife of her ffive Children." (28)

Evidence from the petitions to the Visitors showed that attempts were made to get orphans and the children of widows into the Hospital. In 1664 Roger Burges and James fflinger petitioned the Visitors to inform them that fflorance Collens "about a fortnight since dyed possessed of very little left two boyes behind her and now ud. yor. petionrs. custody, one of them about 7 yeares of age & thother 6." They asked the Visitors to "butt keepe one of them until they shalbee of a little better abilitie to be disposed of." Although this petition was endorsed by the Minister, Overseers, Churchwardens and Constables, no action was recorded.

A second undated petition was presented by "ye Widdow Mitchell who now liveth In the Parish of Widcombe", which was part of the Visitors' estates. She claimed that she was "hardly able to Subsist" and asked the Visitors "to admit her Sonn Into the Hospitall." In this instance they agreed that one of her sons, John, should be admitted and that another, William, should be bound apprentice to Simon Bush, a Merchant Taylor of Bath. (29)

The treatment of the children of widows and orphans reflected very much the social division that existed in society at various times in the past. For the children of the wealthy there was a period of bereavement, followed usually by some provision having been made for them. For the poor it was a different matter and many were condemned to an early life of uncertainty, hard work and little affection. It has in fact sometimes been argued that as so many very young boys were apprenticed and did not grow up in a normal affectionate family situation, in later life they became more distant and even cruel, which may go some way to explain their involvement for centuries in a range of violent sports and leisure activities.

No matter what their social background, however, the overwhelming majority of the bereaved faced the same human consequences of death: the sense of loss, grief, and concern for the future. How long each of these would persist depended very much upon the nature of the individual, their place within the community and the support network which surrounded him or her. For many through the centuries their faith was of significant importance, despite all the changes that occurred in religious beliefs and practices. The sense of reassurance and comfort which was derived is impossible to quantify.

15

WORLDLY CONSEQUENCES OF DEATH: MOURNING

For poorer families a designated period of mourning was out of the question as it was generally essential that the surviving partner continued to work. They had no financial reserves to see them through a period of inactivity and so faced the prospect with no money being earned of homelessness and starvation. For wealthier families on the other hand a period of mourning became increasingly an integral part of the grieving process.

Prior to the Reformation the belief that the prayers of the living could aid the prospect of reunion meant that such grieving was unnecessary. Changes during the Reformation period that swept away many of these older beliefs, led to a greater tendency to mark anniversaries and increasingly some kind of mourning attire, usually black, became a mark of respect and personal sense of loss. Black in fact was reserved not just for clothes as the interior of churches could be drapped in black cloth as well. In June 1552, for example, when Henry Machyn attended the funeral in St Giles Church in Cripplegate in London of Baptyst Borow, a well-known "melener", he noted that there were "many mornars in blake......and ys place was hangyd with blake."

If a person was attired in mourning clothes they became readily identifiable so that when Samuel Pepys saw the Countess of Falmouth, the widow of Charles, the Earl of Falmouth who was killed at sea in 1665, he noted somewhat vaguely in his Diary on 24th June 1666 that, "she was now in her second or third (*year of*) mourning." He did however add characteristically that she was still "a pretty woman.... and pretty pleasant in her looks."

By the eighteenth century set periods of mourning had become established for the wealthier members of the community, for example, usually one year for a husband or wife, six months for parents or a child and three months for a brother or sister. By 1850 the last two had generally doubled to one year and six months respectively. It was rare for mourning to last more than a couple of years but there were exceptions, such as Queen Victoria who mourned for over thirty years. In these instances chronic grief often led to severe depression.

Some of the bereaved derived considerable comfort from receiving a bequest of a personal item or items from the deceased. Its exact nature or value was not important, as what mattered was that it had been special enough to the deceased for him or her to identify it for legacy purposes and it therefore had emotional importance. One item that became prominent and figured in a number of Bruton Wills was a ring. One historian had commented that in the broader perspective, "The gap left by the abolition of Catholic intercessory rites and the inadequacy of mourning dress as a means of expressing a personal sense of loss help to explain the growth of private rites of commemoration and the increasing popularity of personal mementoes of the dead such as rings and lockets." (30)

The earliest surviving reference to a type of mourning ring appeared in the Will of Sir Maurice Berkeley in 1580 when he appointed three of his nephews as overseers of that Will,

"And for theire paines taken herein doe geve to everie of theyme a ringe of goulde, weyghinge one ounce with a deademannes head graven in it." The last few words reflected very much the fashion in the sixteenth century to give rings with a skull and crossbones engraved upon them. In 1617 his grandson, the second Sir Maurice, also gave rings to his four overseers but in this case, "I give unto each of them Thirtie shillings to make each of them a Ringe."

In the seventeenth and eighteenth century it had become the practice to leave mourning rings to family and friends, for example, in 1636 William Swanton left 20s each to his son and daughter-in-law to buy such a ring and in 1700 Sarah Dring gave her son and daughter 10s each to buy a mourning ring. Robert Albin of course had used a slightly different approach in 1643 when he gave his son his own gold ring that had his name engraved upon it so that it could "be kepte and worne by him in rememberance of me."

In 1676 Sir William Berkeley generously gave £10 to his friend Mrs Sarah Kirkman "to buy her a ring" and in 1695 Catherine Drew left mourning rings valued at 15s to two of her friends, Mrs Philadelphia Perkins, "a servant to my Lady ffitzharding", and to Mary Ludwell, the niece of Thomas Ludwell her executor. When he made his Will in 1712 John, Lord Fitzharding gave £50 each to his two executors "to buy them Rings in remembrance of me." In 1738 Nicholas Goldesbrough left a total of eight mourning rings, each valued at 20s, to various members of his family and friends. By this period many of the gold rings were inset with enamel or ivory which has been seen as a way of masking the reality of death as no pronounced symbols were visible any longer.

Gifts of mourning rings continued into the nineteenth century, for example, in 1833 Mary Clarke gave her granddaughter, Elizabeth Creighton, amongst other things "two maurning Rings", presumably ones which she had received in her lifetime. As late as 1885 in a very generous gesture Alfred Whalley of Cliff House gave each of his two stepsons, "one hundred pounds to buy a mourning ring."

In the nineteenth century other commemorative jewellery was also worn such as brooches and lockets, the latter often with a small lock of hair from the deceased contained inside. Memory was kept alive with death masks, busts, paintings, drawings and from the middle of the century by photographs, as has already been seen in the case of the children of Josiah Jackson.

The Victorian era, more than any other period, seemed to have been one in which the memory of the deceased was seen as central to the mourning process. This practice was closely linked to the belief that in the not too distant future they would all be reunited. As well as writing lengthy letters of condolence there was the need to talk through in detail memories of the deceased, possibly some-what idealized. The Quakers in particular were keen on this aspect of talking as they did not have any other external forms of grief. "If you wish to honour a good man who has departed this life, let all his good actions live in your memory."

It was perfectly permissible for friends to call upon a widow to express their sympathy and to talk about the deceased. Once again in the nineteenth century this practice was governed by very strict etiquette. It was, for example, suggested that a man should always ensure that he possessed a clean pocket handkerchief on these occasions, "Can a man of any feeling call on a disconsolate widow, for instance, and listen to her woes without at least pulling out that expressive appendage? .... We are bound to weep with them, and we are bound to weep elegantly." (31)

As well as jewellery there was the complex business of mourning dress, which became more widespread and highly organised during the eighteenth century. The dress code was applied most rigorously to widows who were expected to wear full black mourning for two years. In the first year when they were in deepest mourning they wore non-reflective black paramatta and crape. The former was a fabric that combined silk and wool or cotton, and the latter a black silk fabric with a crimped appearance produced by heat. For the next nine months a dull black silk, heavily trimmed with crape was worn and the same for the following three months with the crape discarded. (32)

Men on the other hand were expected to wear a sombre suit with a black mourning cloak. In the mid-nineteenth century the latter tended to be replaced by black gloves, hatband and cravats. Wearing such apparel clearly identified the mourners of either sex, matched the sombre mood of the occasion and did elicit sympathy from bystanders who, along with the mourners, could show respect for the deceased.

The pronounced difference between the expectations for male and female mourners did suggest the generally submissive role of the wife and there can be little doubt that such a long period of imposed mourning could have led to social isolation, possibly at the very time when increased human contact might have been most beneficial. On the other hand wearing mourning dress did free a widow from many social obligations, such as visiting and attendance at public functions that could have become burdensome.

Evidence of mourning dress from Bruton is very sparse, especially as it was not a topic that found coverage in the local press although there were occasional references in Wills. In 1708 Samuel Brodripp bequeathed "unto my father mother & sister Grace the sum of ten pounds to be paid by my brot John Broadripp out of my Estate to buy them mourning." In 1713 Robert ffry gave Mrs Alice Grey, "Tenn pounds for

Mourning" and in 1763 William Pavy bequeathed one hundred pounds to each of his parents "and also such Mourning as they shall want." In these two instances it was presumably to purchase mourning dress. Robert Pavy was much more specific in 1796 when he gave his servant Sarah Andrews £20 "and a suit of Mourning" and the same to another servant Mary Lappin along with £40.

The most extensive arrangements for mourning were made in the Will of John, Lord Fitzharding in 1712. He gave money to at least seven named individuals "for mourning" and then "to each of my servants living with me at the time of my death Eight pounds apiece to buy them Mourning."

The impression created by the items associated with mourning and all the various rituals that developed at different periods, was that it was essentially the business of the wealthier members of the community. They had the necessary money to purchase the required clothes or the particular items fashionable at a given time. It was an outward manifestation of grief and must have been beneficial to some, if not all, of the bereaved. For the poor it was a different matter as they did not have the financial resources to have a period of time away from their employment or to buy different clothes or mourning items. Along with their family, the strength and support of their social grouping may have been their greatest comfort. In the last analysis mourning was a very personal matter and no one could prescribe its intensity or length of time.

16

WORLDLY CONSEQUENCES OF DEATH: MONUMENTS

Lifes book shuts here its pages if lost
With them & all its busy claims
The poor are from its memory crost
The rich have nothing but there names.
(Thoughts in a Churchyard, by John Clare, 1835)

Monuments were generally set up by other members of the family and often served as a focus for personal grief, affection and even gratitude, while some were erected out of a sense of duty. At a very basic level they could be used to mark the site of a burial. For particular families it was important that they reminded local inhabitants not only of the person's standing in the community but also the status of the family. In later centuries, monuments indicated the rise in prosperity of many local families as they felt that they were in a position to spend money on such items. Finally the prevalence of monuments of all kinds reflected the increased literacy of the population as a whole as if people could not read there was no point in providing information on a gravestone.

Until the end of the seventeenth century monuments and tombstones were rare, except for the wealthy, and so churchyards remained predominantly open spaces. In the medieval period wealthy clerics might leave instructions for a tomb to be built within a church such as Richard Bruton whose Will contained details for his tomb in the chancel of Bruton Church: he wished for, "a marble tombstone over my body with the image of a priest carved on the top." For others such as the family of Prior Henton there was a chantry or a place in front of a particular altar.

From the reign of Queen Elizabeth I until the end of the nineteenth century and beyond, private vaults such as that of the Berkeleys were popular with the wealthy. Others inhabitants judged that as the church itself was becoming crowded with burials, a tomb-chest outside would be a more fitting monument and a few of these remain in Bruton churchyard, mainly to the west of the Church.

From the late seventeenth century, and throughout the eighteenth, much greater emphasis was placed upon an inscription on a monument. For the very wealthy or those who were patrons of a Church, along with relatives and close friends, there could be an ornate hanging monument in the chancel. For the less wealthy there were simpler ones with a brief memorial, usually on slabs of stone set into the floor of the main part of the Church.

The earliest monuments tended to be designed either to give comfort to the family or to provide more of a record. For the wealthy of course they could be more fulsome such as the monument on the south wall of the chancel of Bruton Church in black marble with an oval panel in which is the bust of a man with a sash across his chest and is dedicated to William Godolphin who died in 1636, "who after he had liv'd to be a chiefe ornament to his family, & comfort to his friends, by his many vertues & good life, piously resign'd his spirit to Almighty God, in the yeare of his age the 25th." In this instance, however, the description was followed by ten lines in Latin extolling his virtues. (See Appendix 4a) Similarly the monument in South Brewham church to Revd. Edward Bennet dating from 1673 dwelt upon his character. (See Appendix 4b)

What is perhaps unusual about the chancel in Bruton Church is that, apart from the monument to the first Sir Maurice Berkeley and his two wives, there are no other Berkeley monuments of any kind there which date from before the eighteenth century. Elsewhere however the whole life history of John, 1st Lord Berkeley of Stratton, the youngest son of the second Sir Maurice Berkeley of Bruton, was included on his large monument in Twickenham Church in Middlesex. While there is no documentary evidence to indicate that any more Berkeley monuments existed in Bruton Church it is possible that if they had done so they were removed from the chancel when it was rebuilt in 1743.

The monument of the first Sir Maurice is typical of the later Tudor period and being carved in Bath stone allowed for a great deal of detail. In one respect it looked back to the medieval period as Sir Maurice is portrayed in the armour of a medieval knight while his two wives are in fashionable Elizabethan dress. Each is shown recumbent with hands clasped together in prayer. Carved on the spandrels are two small figures which appear to be casting off their shrouds and being resurrected, a powerful message at that period.

In the main body of Bruton Church the slabs that once covered the bodies of those who were less wealthy such as John and Alice Russ who died in 1685 and 1705 respectively, simply recorded the dates of their deaths and in the case of Alice her age. That of Charles Brawn, gent, buried on 5th September 1702 was also very plain as it read, "Hic jacet Carolus Brawn, ob. Sept. 3 1702." (*Here lies Charles Brawn, died Sept 3 1702*).

By the middle of the eighteenth century for the very wealthy there was a pronounced change as most of their monuments began to focus on both public and private virtues, personal achievements and even physical appearance. This information was usually written in prose but sometimes in verse. The memorial for John Donne in the chancel of Bruton Church used poetic form:

"Where rests in hope, beneath a peaceful sod,
What Pope has call'd, 'the noblest work of God'.
However, he surpass'd the poet's plan,
A real Christian was this honest man."

The memorial to Captain William Berkeley, which was erected in the chancel by his brother John, 5th Lord Berkeley of Stratton in 1749, some sixteen years after William was buried at sea, is much more ornate in white and grey marble with trophies and military ensigns surmounted by a fluted urn. Having given details of his death the memorial continues:

"Just, Generous, Steady, Intrepid, Gentle,
Loved, honoured, and Lamented by his Friends,
Eminently distinguished in his profession,
Still serving his Country by his Example."

In the nave of the Church was a flat stone with similar sentiments dedicated to the memory of Mrs Ann Fenn, who died 4th March 1748, aged sixty-five:

"a woman of exemplary piety and goodness, of a mild and affable temper, whose manly sense and sweet conversation engaged the admiration of the wise and great; whose wise submission to her Maker's will in every trial of her virtues; whose chearfulness and affection for her friends in her painful and severe distemper, were instances of uncommon constancy."

For the less wealthy there was still the tendency to record just the basic details of death and age on flat stones in the nave and aisles, such as Robert and Thomas Albyn who both died in 1755 aged seventy-five and seventy-two respectively. A few other families began to invest in small brass plates, such as Thomas and Robert Cheeke, William and Mary Pavey. An exception was the Young family who included a verse, with a possible pun, in 1764:

"Beneath this stone the aged and the young both lie,
In hopes for their souls to be received on high,
Join'd in Christ's kingdom ever to reign,
To sing and glorify his Holy name." (33)

The erection of memorials within the Church continued in the nineteenth century, for example, Captain Colby placed a small marble tablet dedicated to his wife and son in the chancel and in the centre of the nave was a flat stone under which were "the remains of Thomas Goldesbrough, Rear-Admiral of the White", who died in 1828 aged eighty-one. In fact the only flat memorial stone that is still legible and that for some unknown reason seems to have survived the Victorian era with its extensive restoration, is that of Laetitia Goldesbrough, his widow who died in November 1834 aged eighty. It is now under one of the arches of the south aisle, opposite the south door.

A few of the nineteenth century memorials became more ornate, possibly indicative of an increase in prosperity in some families, for example, George Prince who died in August 1817 aged sixty-seven, had a wall-mounted monument with a draped urn and the lines:

Here lies a man by all the good esteem'd,
Because they prov'd him really what he seem'd."

This monument was apparently carved by "Rawlings John of Bruton."

As the nineteenth century progressed there was an increasing tendency to carve some sort of epitaph on tombstones. Some of these epitaphs were religious in origin, such as, "Verily there is a Reward for the Righteous", while others were much more sentimental:

"My husband dear my time is past
So long to me your love did last.
But now for me no trouble take
Only love your Children for my sake."

(For a selection of epitaphs from Bruton churchyard see Appendix 6a)

The Victorians took great care in their choice of gravestones and in particular the carvings and inscriptions on them. In a few cases no doubt this was intended to impress other people but in most instances they wanted their choices to be appropriate for them. Visiting these graves with their well-kept stones, cut grass, flowers, possibly shrubs and painted railings, was for them an important part of the grieving process. Many of the bereaved wanted it to be a pleasant place for remembrance and contemplation, particularly easy in the very rural churchyards in villages such as Pitcombe and Shepton Montague.

One development in the eighteenth century that aided the spread of information about a dead person and their monuments was the expansion in the availability of local newspapers. While writing a favourable comment about a deceased man or woman had long occurred, those who read it constituted a very small number, for example, on the death of Sir Maurice Berkeley in 1617, George, Lord Carew wrote in a letter to Sir Thomas Roe, "Sir Morice Barkeley is latelye dead, who was a gentleman, as you know, of many good parts." (34) One of the longest tributes must have been the entry which appeared in the 'Salisbury and Winchester Journal' on the death of the last Lord Berkeley of Stratton in 1773. It was written in poetic form and covered forty-one lines, most of which dealt with his virtues and qualities rather than any activities. (A copy is included in Appendix 4c)

His father, Lord William, had received a much briefer tribute in 1741, "This noble lord was great by Birth, Nature and Education. He was greatly learned; he understood religion and practised it." It was also mentioned that he had been Chancellor of the Duchy of Lancashire under Queen Anne and then under George I First Commissioner of the Board of Trade. (35)

In the latter part of the eighteenth century a range of different comments appeared in local newspapers which gave some indication of the nature of the deceased and his or her virtues and in so doing provided some degree of comfort to the bereaved. When John Prince, "an eminent shoe-maker and clerk of that parish", died in August 1771 it was stated that his "natural genius for music was so great, that by his own appreciation he acquired such a proficiency in that Science as to be able to play with great judgment on the harpsichord, violin &c. He has left a widow and seven children; by whom his loss will be severely felt, as he was in a true sense of the words 'an industrious, honest man.'" Such was Prince's musical ability that in 1764 Revd. Woodeforde confided to his Diary that he had requested Prince to visit him to measure him for a pair of shoes, but added, "This Prince being a musical Man, I desired him to tune my Spinnett for me, which he did and pretty well but would have nothing for it." Then came the confession, "NB My Chief Intent for sending for him was to tune my Spinnett for I have at present Shoes sufficient." (36)

When Dr. John Robertson died at Pitcombe in May 1761 he was referred to as "A Gentleman eminent in his Profession, and well known to the Literary World, for many excellent

Compositions." In January 1790 the wife of the Revd. Dalton who died at Pitcombe House was described as "greatly loved by all who knew her", and when he followed her to the grave some eighteen years later it was said "the poor have lost a worthy and generous benefactor, and numerous aquaintances a sincere friend." In fact, Revd. Woodeforde recorded that when he was staying with his sister Jane in Cole it was not unusual for Revd. Dalton to call and bring a gift of a brace of pheasants: "old Mr. Dalton called on us with two fine Pheasants in his Pocket as a present to us."

Of the Revd. Michell, the Master of the Free School who died in June 1799 it was said, "He was honest, humane, and charitable; an affectionate husband, tender father, a faithful minister of the gospel, and a scholar." The same process continued into the nineteenth century as on her death in 1801 the wife of Lieutenant Agnew was reported to be "a sincere Christian, an affectionate wife, and mother of fourteen children." When James Harding of Henley Grove died in 1816 aged eighty-two a local newspaper commented, "By this event eleven children have to deplore the loss of one of the best of fathers; an extended circle of friends, a cheerful companion; the poor, a kind master and benefactor; and society, a valuable member." The following year, however, the reference to ninety-eight-year old Mrs Lloyd was much simpler, "a respectable widow lady." At the other extreme the death of a young person could elicit some appropriate sentiments, as was the case on the death of fifteen-year old Thomas Mostyn in October 1839. "He was a youth of much promise, and endeared to all by his amiable and affectionate disposition." (37)

Throughout the Victorian era the deaths of many of the most prominent inhabitants of the town also attracted passages of varying lengths in the local press. In 1859, for example, the death of Daniel Ward elicited the following, "The circumstance has cast a melancholy gloom over Bruton and its neighbourhood, for never was a man more beloved of all classes than Mr Ward: to the higher ranks he was always a good and kind hearted companion, and to the poor he was always a benevolent, generous and liberal friend. We do not hesitate to say that by his death the poor have lost a very great friend indeed." There were similar sentiments expressed on the death of J.R. White in 1874, "a gentleman well known in Bruton and the neighbourhood for his kindness to the poor and his general efforts for the welfare of the town and its inhabitants." (38)

While it had long been the practice to leave a bequest to servants in the Wills of the wealthy, an interesting development in the nineteenth century was the inclusion of comments in the local press on the death of long-serving family servants. While there can be little doubt that these men and women were highly regarded within some families and a very strong bond existed, it may also be a reflection of the changed nature of society. A rigid social structure had developed, particularly from the middle of the previous century, one in which every person was expected to know their station in life. The nature of the comments made in the local newspapers were one way in which this hierarchical society could be emphasised and the appropriate messages of reliablity, faithfulness and duty could be stressed.

When seventy-nine-year-old Mrs Longford died at Redlynch in November 1835 she was the housekeeper of the Earl of Ilchester "in whose family she had lived for more than 60 years a faithful and valued servant." The Dampiers at Colinshayes tended to record the death of their servants so that when Mrs Christian Bricknell died in March 1834 she had "for nearly 48 years lived in the families of the Hon. Mrs Charles Digby and the Rev. John Dampier, beloved and respected in both, in the twofold character of a devoted friend and truly faithful servant." Three years later John Herbert, aged seventy-five died, "having lived nearly thirty years in the capacity of butler in the family of the Rev. John Dampier, by every member of which he was most sincerely beloved, and died as he had lived, highly and deservedly respected." In December 1849 the Dampiers lost another old retainer, Richard Cox, aged seventy-two, "universally respected, a truly honest faithful servant." The following year the Master of the Free School was deprived at the early age of forty-one of Edith Williams, "for upwards of twenty-three years the truly faithful servant and housekeeper of the Rev. J. Hoskyns Abrahall." (39)

The final and most striking and visual form of monument that was beloved of the Victorians was the stained glass window. Here was a commemorative object that was highly visible to all, beneficial to the Church and so the community as a whole and was aesthetically pleasing. The Victorians were of course reviving an old medieval practice that had largely been destroyed at the time of the Reformation. Before the Victorian era, a small amount of painted glass may have been added by the Berkeleys at various times to display their shields in the chancel. One suggestion is that the painting of two of these shields is late sixteenth century work, one in the westernmost window on the north side of the chancel and the other in the east window in the vestry. Two shields on the south side of the chancel and the eastern most shield on the north side may be seventeenth century. (40)

The Victorians gave Bruton Church its most highly decorated stained glass windows as memorials: the earliest was dedicated to Edward and Fanny Dyne in the 1850s and is the second from the east in the south aisle wall. The window next to it on the eastern side was erected in the 1890s by Susanna Dyne in memory of her husband, Henry, along with her father, mother and brother, Frederick, Susanna and William Muller. In 1899 parishioners decided to commission a window in memory of their late Vicar, Revd. H.T. Ridley. A design with the subject of 'The Good Shepherd' was accepted from Messrs. Bell and Son of Bristol at a cost of £120 and the window was dedicated at the west end of the north aisle in October 1899. A memorial window to the Longman family is to the west of the south door and was added in 1905 and a year later one to James Pearce, a former organist in the Church. In 1888 the great west window was filled with stained glass by Clayton and Bell as a memorial to the Bennett family.

One stained glass window was constructed very belatedly as a memorial and that is the one at the west end of the south aisle and is dedicated to two brothers, John and William Ames, who emigrated to America in the 1630s. They established a very successful dynasty and it was one of their descendants, Frederick L. Ames, who commissioned the window from the Royal Stained Glass Company in 1888 and when unveiled was referred to as "a most beautiful piece of workmanship." (41)

Carved, written or visual, these monuments were designed not only to aid the grieving process but also to make a statement that would be seen by the rest of the community and which might bear witness for generations to come.

> Remember me when I am gone away,
> Gone far away into the silent land.
> (Remember by Christina Rossetti)

17

CONCLUSION

Between 1400 and 1900 some of the aspects surrounding the topic of death had changed significantly. The Plague had generally disappeared from this country and smallpox was well on its way to eradication as a major killer. Improvements in factors such as medicine, public health, the availability of food and a rise in the overall standard of living meant that some of the traditional causes of death were being dramatically decreased. Such a situation was in turn to have a marked impact upon life expectancy so that by the end of the Victorian period death in old age became the expected norm and not in childhood, especially before the age of five years.

The passing of the centuries marked a profound change in attitudes towards death. Throughout the medieval period there had been a much closer relationship between the dead and the living as the latter were expected to aid the deceased in their passage through purgatory. The result was that the whole burial process was much longer with masses, prayers and some other services taking place over days, weeks, months and, for some of the very wealthy, years

The concept of purgatory was abolished at the time of the Reformation and so led some people to believe that the Soul would be judged immediately while others placed greater emphasis upon a wait until the Day of Judgement when the souls of the dead would be re-united. It was left to the Victorians to develop the idea even further when they increasingly expressed a belief in their 'heavenly home'.

These changes in attitude relating to death also had the effect of separating the living much more from the dead and so the idea of burial within a sacred space, such as a monastery or a church, became less prevalent: a practice which was occurring anyway particularly fostered by growing concerns about the health implications of these intra-mural interments. The result was that such burials although continuing for a small number, usually the wealthier members of the community, decreased markedly for the mass of the population. While the churchyard had always had a prominent role as a community space, it became more and more the location for the burial of the dead.

Another change in the period under consideration was a different approach to remembrance. For the wealthy in the medieval period it had been important that their names should be remembered, mainly so that they would be included in masses and prayers to help them in purgatory, but also to emphasise their status within the community. For this privilege of remembrance they were prepared to spend very large sums of money, a fact which might not always have impressed some of their heirs. Increasingly there was a trend for a wider range of families to want some kind of physical remembrance of the departed. For some it was a monument, large or small, on the wall inside a church, a gravestone which recorded their details and possibly virtues, a designated plot in a churchyard which might have been surrounded by a kerbstone or painted iron railings. It was a place that the bereaved could visit, keep tidy and leave or plant flowers. For a very small number an ornate stained-glass window was prized in some country churches.

The progress of time meant that the increased prosperity of the nation as a whole became discernible at death as more and more men and women wrote a Will, although they remained a small minority of the population overall. They actually had something to leave to the next generation: land, houses, money, household goods, a treasured or prized item. To a modern-day reader the emphasis placed upon beds by wealthier families must seem one of the more unusual bequests. In the eighteenth and nineteenth centuries in particular some of these Wills became increasingly complex and they established Trusts which in a few cases they believed would endure for ever.

There were also of course areas of continuity. In the first place the vast majority of people died at home, usually nursed by a family member as the poor certainly could not afford much in the way of medical aid. Most wished for a decent burial in consecrated ground: an idea which found expression in many of the Wills of the wealthier members of the community, while some of the poor would try and save money for such a burial, aided from the late eighteenth century by small payments to a Friendly Society. For them 'decent' meant not the cheapest form of burial, 'the 'pauper's funeral', although how far this was a concern of the Victorian middle class which they tried to instil in the labouring classes and how far it actually mattered to the really destitute is impossible to determine.

It remained an undeniable and sad fact that in death as in life there was a profound gulf between the rich and the poor in every generation. The wealthy could arrange or expect an elaborate funeral with a coffin, extensive prayers, candles, torches, a sermon, possibly with a procession through the town, and a suitable monument, often in white marble. For the poor it was a much simpler, cheaper affair with originally just a shroud and in the end a grass mound for a while, with possibly a wooden cross, if the spot was marked at all.

The death of a loved one continued to cause grief for the bereaved through all the generations and that did not change. For some it was to manifest itself in tears, withdrawal and depression and in others in increasingly complex forms of mourning rituals. But the vast majority of the population could not afford the luxury of such emotion or time and money as they had to continue to work to survive.

Above all, one fact did not change for an overwhelming number of people: death was feared. Despite all the promises of religion and the deep faith which so many of the population professed, including ideas of peace, rest and everlasting happiness in the presence of God, the vast majority of people clung to life for as long as possible. Medical men and traditional herbal and other remedies remained in great demand throughout the period. Death after all was felt to destroy everything that was unique about an individual.

No matter how much misery death had brought through the centuries, nothing had prepared the country as a whole for the slaughter which was generated in the Great War, 1914-1918. Unimaginable numbers of soldiers were killed almost simultaneously in the most horrific of ways. At a stroke the traditional process of burial and mourning was destroyed for many families: their young men were buried in graves that their families could not visit and see as they were far from home, that is if they had a grave at all. The whole concept which the Christian Church had believed for centuries relating to a good death leading to the hope of eternal life, was shattered. Not only was a whole generation lost but also those who were left behind to grieve saw death in a very different way.

18

AND FINALLY OR NOT?

Throughout the period under consideration there were always people who were absolutely convinced that after death they would be reunited with family and friends in another place. Some Victorians, as has been discussed, especially in the second half of the nineteenth century, were determined to establish that death was not the end. The result was their interest in the séance and spiritualism that did seem to have found a ready audience in Bruton.

Throughout the centuries in many parts of Somerset there was the widespread belief amongst the rural population that it was possible to see spirits at certain times. The most common occasion was April 24th, St Mark's Eve, when it was claimed that if a man stood in the church porch between eleven o'clock in the evening and one o'clock in the morning he would see the spirits of all those who were to die in the parish during the ensuing year. Such a belief even found expression in poetic form:

> How, when the midnight signal tolls,
> Along the churchyard green,
> A mournful train of sentenced souls
> In winding sheets are seen!

The ghosts of all whose death shall doom
Within the coming year,
In pale procession walk the gloom
Amid the silence drear. (1)

Considering the age of the town and the love of folk tales and superstitions that has always been prevalent in such rural areas, the number of accounts that include the supernatural is remarkably few. One well-documented example came from the eighteenth century and related to the time of the death of Revd. John Goldesbrough, the Minister of the Parish Church and Master of the Free School. One of his sons, Thomas who rose to be the Admiral, had already started his career at sea when his father died.

On his death bed the Revd Goldesbrough was supposed to have said to his wife " 'Anne, I have a great wish to see Tom', whereupon the old man fell asleep. On awaking, he exclaimed 'Well! I have seen Tom, and can now die content,' shortly after expiring. His son, the aforesaid Tom, was at the time lying so ill on board his vessel, that the lieutenant of the ship sat by his bedside watching him. Whilst Tom slept, his companion was startled by the figure of an old man bending over the ailing youth, and on his awaking asked him what kind of looking man his father was. On receiving the description, his friend said 'Then he has been looking upon you,' and Tom acknowledged that he had appeared to him in his sleep, saying that he (the father) must very shortly die, but that his son would soon be better. The incident made so deep an impression on the two friends that they entered it immediately in the log book of the ship. On arriving in England, Tom was scarcely surprised to find that the death of his father exactly corresponded with the date of the apparition." (2)

Apparitions have been reported in local country houses in the early twentieth century. One was when a builder was undertaking some alterations in Redlynch House and in the days when the area around the Lake was frequented by courting couples, several people reported seeing the figure of a man pass by, but added that they could see right through him. As has already been discussed, at least one suicide had occurred in the grounds of the Mansion which of course gave rise to speculation about a restless soul. The other location was Godminster Manor where domestic staff were convinced that they saw a monk wandering about in one of the rooms and that he disappeared into a cupboard. The then owner of the house refused to believe the story but for some reason she always kept this cupboard locked. This may be the bedroom in which her brother was meant to sleep but in the end he spent the night in the dressing room and refused to sleep in that bedroom again. After a subsequent owner undertook some repairs and alterations in the mid-twentieth century several people reported that they saw a black shadow pass across the floor, giving rise to speculation that the monk had been disturbed.

On another occasion when the former owner was in bed she heard her dog bark and when she got up and looked out of the window she saw the white spectacle of a carriage and horses approaching from the pond area, which had originally been a turning circle, then drive slowly around the courtyard and finally disappear down the road. A horse and carriage has also apparently been sighted on Hardway.

Perhaps not unsurprisingly as a result of its importance through the centuries and its remoteness, the Creech Hill area has produced a number of supernatural stories. In the middle of the nineteenth century it was noted that, "many are the legendary tales in circulation, connected with this spot, of ghosts, and other supernatural appearances." (3) Most recent stories seem to relate to black figures: one farmer returning from market saw something lying in the middle of the road and when he went to see if he could help, a black figure rose up with a loud scream which sent the farmer running. His family went to his aid and they too saw a black figure bounding over the Hill, shrieking with laughter. Another local resident, this time armed with a lantern and thick stick, was also confronted by a black figure. He attempted to strike it but his stick went straight through it. Once again he heard loud laughter. Both of these stories seem to date from the late nineteenth or early twentieth centuries. It is of course interesting to note that not only has at least one murder occurred in this area but also that a number of skeletons have been unearthed there.

There have been two reputed sightings in the town itself which have led to an exorcism being performed. One ghost was seen at the bottom of Dyne's garden and taken so seriously that an exorcism was conducted by a clergyman and this seemed to lay the ghost to rest. The location is unclear as it may have been either the garden of the part of The Priory in the High Street which was for many years the offices of Solicitors, Dyne, Hughes and Archer or in the garden of Berkeley House (now Priory House) which was purchased by Edward Dyne in the mid-nineteenth century. In the twentieth century an evil presence was reported as being felt in the churchyard by the vicar's wife. An exorcism was performed but the spirit apparently moved to Bow Bridge where a second exorcism was performed, this time with success.

A rather different story linked two types of spirits. In the late nineteenth and early twentieth centuries there was a man in Bruton who was frequently drunk, possibly by the name of Balch. (4) A horse-drawn hearse carrying a coffin stopped in the town to water the horses at a well. For their own amusement a group of local men lifted the drunk into the back of the hearse where he promptly fell asleep.

The hearse drove off and when it was heading along the road to Frome near Marston Park where the road was narrow and dark as a result of overhanging trees, the drunk woke up and all the driver heard was, "All in the dark and nothing to drink." It was reported that he reached Frome in a remarkably quick time.

APPENDICES

APPENDIX 1

RELATIVE VALUE OF MONEY

This list gives the approximate purchasing power of £1 in the years indicated compared with 2010.

Year		£
1420		629
1450		633
1500		649
1550		299
1600		174
1650		108
1700		117
1750		123
1800		63
1850		83
1900		84

For £10 the above figures would need to be multiplied by 10, for £50 by 50 etc.

APPENDIX 2

LIST OF WILLS CONSULTED

Date		Name	Location
1414	November	Countess of Salisbury	Canterbury and York Society, 42, 1937, p. 15
1415	December	John Venables	SRS, 16, 1901, p. 71
1417	October	Richard Bruton	SRS, 16, 1901, p. 90
1429	October	John Gregory	SRO DD/WHh/624-5
1457	April	Amice Gregory	SRS, 16, 1901, p. 171
1471	September	Richard Dekyn	SRS, 16, 1901, p. 221
1493	September	Margery Moleyns	PRO PROB 11/10/151
1496	February	Alianora Ede	PRO PROB 11/11/148
1496	February	Richard Grene	SRS, 16, 1901, p. 349
1498	November	Richard Vowell	SRS, 16, 1901, p. 369
1500	January	John Vynyng alias Dyer	SRS, 16, 1901, p. 396
1500	April	Henry Sutton	SRS, 19, 1903, p. 4
1501	July	William Knoyell	SRS, 19, 1903, p. 19
1503	December	William Samford	SRS, 19, 1903, p. 50
1504	October	William Bysshop	SRS, 19, 1903, p. 75
1506	March	Symon Grene	PRO PROB 11/16/290
1509	May	John Harman	SRS, 19, 1903, p. 129

Date		Name	Location
1509	October	Richard Philippys	PRO PROB 11/16/558
1510	February	John Jeffreys als Cockes	SRS, 19, 1903, p. 148
1510	October	John Fitzjames, senior	SRS, 19, 1903, p. 143
1512	May	John Tyler of Wells	SRS, 19, 1903, p. 159
1515	November	William Baily als Rawlyns	SRS, 19, 1903, p. 182
1516	April	William Carent the elder	SRS, 19, 1903, p. 186
1517	February	Alice Brymmore	PRO PROB 11/19/473
1518	April	Richard Fitzjames	SANHSP, 24/5, 1878-9, pt. II, p. 35
1520	August	Richard Holmede	PRO PROB 11/19/348
1524	August	John Brent	SRS, 19, 1903, p. 229
1526	February	Isabel Fitzjames	SRS, 19, 1903, p. 251
1526	July	John Chaper als Nicolls	SRS, 19, 1903, p. 254
1526	August	William Burges	SRS, 19, 1903, p. 256
1527	May	Joane Serne	SRS, 19, 1903, p. 261
1532	July	John Hadley	SRS, 21, 1905, p. 14
1538	October	Sir John Fitzjames	SRS, 21, 1905, p. 48
1539	August	George George	SRS, 21, 1905, p. 54
1539	December	James Wicks of Brewham	SANHSP, 61, 1915, p. 95
1540	November	Alice Marshall	SANHSP, 61, 1915, p. 72
1540	January	George Wylton	SRO DD/SAS C795 SW5
1542	July	Robert Chyke	PRO PROB 11/29/133
1542		John Exhall of Brewham	SRS, 21, 1905, p. 74
1543	July	John Hoper alias Smyth	SRS, 40, 1925, p. 21

Date		Name	Location
1544	January	Thomas Walter	SRS, 40, 1925, p. 17
1544	January	Roger Ames of Wyke	SRS, 40, 1925, p. 31
1544	January	John Stevys	SRS, 40, 1925, pp. 56-7
1544	January	William Gane	SRS, 40, 1925, p. 23
1544	January	John Togood of Brewham	SRS, 40, 1925, p. 19
1544	October	Thomas Toar	SRS, 40, 1925, p. 62
1544	October	Stevyn Broke	SRS, 40, 1925, p. 57
1544	November	William Borne	SRS, 40, 1925, p. 53
1545	March	Jone Hardwell of Wyke	SRS, 40, 1925, p. 80
1545	September	Robert Bartlet	SRS, 40, 1925, p. 206
1545	November	Dame Elizabeth Fitzjames	SRS, 21, 1905, pp. 86-87
1545	November	John Turges of Redlinch	SRS, 40, 1925, p. 207
1546	February	William Cleves	SRS, 40, 1925, p. 159
1546	February	William Walter	SRS, 40, 1925, p. 159
1546	April	John Langyer	SRS, 40, 1925, p. 136
1550	September	Elizabeth Fitzjames	SANHSP, 25, 1878, pt. II, p. 37
1554	April	Henry Ottis alias Calowe	SRS, 40, 1925, p. 54
1554	July	John Ottlye of Redlinch	SRS, 40, 1925, p. 95
1554	August	Johan Peter	SRS, 40, 1925, p. 95
1554	August	Roger Hurman	SRS, 40, 1925, pp.240-1
1554	September	John Plimpton	SRS, 40, 1925, p. 165
1555	December	Isabell Blackmore	SRS, 40, 1925, p. 237
1556	January	John Yonge	SRS, 40, 1925, p. 240

Date		Name	Location
1557	August	John fflenger	SRO DD/SAS C795 PR 40
1557	September	Richard Bower	SRO DD/SAS C795 PR 40
1557	September	William Aunswell	SRO DD/SAS C795 PR 40
1560	May	Agnes Plumley	PRO PROB 11/43/418
1566	June	Nicholas Gilbert	PRO PROB 11/48/545
1567	December	Walter Tynbury of South B	SRO DD/SF/11/1/12
1573	August	George Stevens	PRO PROB 11/55/329
1577		Matthew Grene of Milton C	SRO A/ABS/1
1578		John Fraunces of Alford	Castle Cary Visitor, vol. 4, 1902-3, p. 125
1580	February	Sir Maurice Berkeley	PRO PROB 11/63/488
1584	November	Lady Elizabeth Berkeley	F.Brown, Som. Wills, 6, p. 103
1588	September	John ffrye	PRO PROB 11/73/376
1589	April	Edward Spicer	PRO PROB 11/73/453
1589	June	Petronell als Purnell Spicer	PRO PROB 11/74/162
1597	March	Francis Poole	PRO PROB 11/89/469
1597	August	Sir James Fitzjames	SANHSP, 25, 1878, pt. II, pp. 38-9
1600	May	Sir Henry Berkeley	SRO DD/WR/2
1603	January	Thomas Albin	PRO PROB 11/101/673
1612	June	Roger Popley of Discove	F. Brown, Som. Wills, I, p. 27
1613	January	James Plympton	PRO PROB 11/125/666

Date		Name	Location
1616		Joseph Killigrew of London	F. Brown, Som. Wills, 5, p. 18
1617	February	Dame Margaret Berkeley	SRO DD/WR/2
1617	April	Sir Maurice Berkeley	PRO PROB 11/130/1
1619	August	Hugh Sexey	SRO DD/SE/38/1
1623	December	Benjamin Ellis	SRO DD/X/BTTN
1624		Humphrey Wootton	SRO A/ABS/1
1624	October	William Hellier	PRO PROB 11/145/11
1626	April	Dame Elizabeth Berkeley	PRO PROB 11/149/156
1629	February	John Mogg	PRO PROB 11/156/238
1630	October	John French	PRO PROB 11/158/289
1633	January	Agnes Morris	PRO PROB 11/163/535
1635	February	Ursula Sammes (Sexey)	PRO PROB 11/168/185
1637	May	William Swanton	PRO PROB 11/189/121
1638	May	Lawrence Goolde	PRO PROB 11/177/270
1639	April	Thomas Wilton	PRO PROB 11/180/255
1640		James Hodges of Milton C	SRO A/ABS/1
1640	February	John Swanton	PRO PROB 11/182/474
1640	June	Alice Hill	PRO PROB 11/184/352
1643	November	Robert Albin	PRO PROB 11/196/16834
1647	July	Peter Tinnie	PRO PROB 11/202/543
1648	September	Joane Sampson	PRO PROB 11/208/448
1650		Thomas Coles	Castle Cary Visitor, vol. 6, 1906-7, p. 148
1650	March	John Albin	PRO PROB 11/216/80

Date		Name	Location
1650	July	Christian Albin	PRO PROB 11/220/224
1652	February	John Hodges	PRO PROB 11/221/407
1652	December	Susanna Gatehouse	PRO PROB 11/228/353
1653	November	William Ewens of Hadspen	SRO DD/SAS/H202/7b
1654	February	William Wilton	PRO PROB 11/242/583
1656	February	Thomas Mogg	PRO PROB 11/265/554
1657	May	Robert Jeanes	Records of the Jeanes-Janes Family
1660	January	Edward Norton	PRO PROB 11/298/65
1666	December	Charles, 2nd Lord Fitzharding	PRO PROB 11/382/2
1667	August	William Morris	PRO PROB 11/325/221
1673	April	Robert Ludwell	PRO PROB 11/343/306
1676	February	Richard Dimond	PRO PROB 11/350/516
1676	May	Sir William Berkeley	W. Kavengh, ed. Foundations of Colonia America, III, p. 2563
1676	November	Thomas Ludwell	N. Currer-Briggs, English Adventurers and Virginian Settlers, vol. II, p. 371
1678	September	William Day	PRO PROB 11/361/379
1678	November	Robert Ludwell	New Eng. Hist. Review, 47, 1893, p. 278
1681	August	John Kenniston	SRS, 94, 2008, p. 243
1683	November	Thomas Tice als Rogers	PRO PROB 11/374/434
1686	January	Peter Walter of Wyke C.	SRO DD/SAS/C127/8
1687	February	William Tice	PRO PROB 11/391/801
1688	May	John Yeadle	PRO PROB 11/393/262

Date		Name	Location
1690	April	Maurice, 3rd Lord Fitzharding	PRO PROB 11/402/493
1690	November	Thomas Whitehead	PRO PROB 10/1220
1691	April	Christian Ludwell	New. Eng. Hist. Review, 47, 1893, p. 278
1695	September	Catherine Drew	PRO PROB 11/430/65
1696	August	Mary Allen	F. Brown, Som Wills, 4, p. 93
1696	November	Thomas Warner	PRO PROB 11/457/234
1696	December	Thomas Cornish als Allen	PRO PROB 11/439/1677
1697	June	Joane Pride of Knowle	SRO DD/X/AR/1/16
1697	December	Sarah Dring	SRO D/P/mil.c. 23/4
1699	February	John Webb	F. Brown, Som. Wills, 4, p.101
1701	March	Thomas Morren	SRO D/P/brut 23/1
1704		John Baynard of Wanstrow	SRO A/ABS/1
1708	February	Samuel Brodripp	SRO DD/SE 83
1711	January	Robert ffry	PRO PROB 11/519/243
1712	June	John, 4th Lord Fitzharding	PRO PROB 11/531/84
1713	January	Robert Fry	PRO PROB 11/531/72
1713	August	James Bisse of Batcombe	F. Brown, Som Wills, 2, p. 6
1714	March	John Whitehead	PRO PROB 10/1512
1718	February	William Mogg of Shepton M	SRO DD/FS/1/16
1718	October	Henry Sampson	PRO PROB 11/566/172
1719	February	George King	SRO A/ADG
1719	May	William Russ	SRO DD/FC/14

Date		Name	Location
1722	November	Mary Griffen	SRO D/P/brut 23/1
1726	June	John Ludwell	PRO PROB 11/612/318
1733	May	William Dibben of Shepton M	SRO DD/FS/24/5/2
1733	September	Lucy Temple	PRO PROB 11/662/423
1738	June	Nicholas Goldesbrough	PRO PROB 11/690/329
1740	September	Amey Gibbs	SRO DD/JO/26
1744	January	Richard Creed	DRO DD/FFO 18/73
1747	February	John Hartgill	SRO DD/BT/2/2/6
1748	May	Peter Ames	SRO DD/BR/wh
1757	October	Austin Goldesbrough	PRO PROB 11/838/20
1757	November	Hon. Charles Berkeley	PRO PROB 11/911/354
1757	November	Ann Creed	DRO DD/FFO 18/73
1758	January	John Thomas	DRO D/FSI Box 244A
1763	January	Robert Smart	SRO D/P/brut 4/1/1
1763	February	William Pavy	PRO PROB 11/885/513
1764	May	Anne Pitney of Lamyatt	SRO DD/FS/24/17/1
1767	October	John Goldesbrough	PRO PROB 11/948/172
1769	September	Ellis Paine	SRO DD/JO/26
1772	May	John, 5th Lord Berkeley	PRO PROB 11/987/326
1775	January	Susannah Hunt of Pitcombe	SRO DD/FS/4/2/3
1796	November	Robert Pavy	SRO DD/DN/13
1797	February	Nicholas Everatt	PRO PROB 11/1335/139
1804	October	William Saunders	PRO PROB 11/1621/368
1805	October	William Meachem	SRS, 94, 2008, p. 243

Date		Name	Location
1806	October	Mary Talbot	PRO PROB 11/1514/352
1810	December	Mary Coles	SRO DD/JO/1
1813	June	John Dalton of Pitcombe	SRO DD/BR/mmd/3
1813	September	Elizabeth Meachem	SRS, 94, 2008, p. 243
1816	October	Thomas White	SRO T/PH/whe 1
1817	January	William James	PRO PROB 11/1615/209
1817	June	Ann Hallett	SRO D/P/mil.c. 17/1/1
1821	August	Seth Smith	SRO DD/SAS/C795/SW17
1822	October	Richard Amor of Pitcombe	SRO DD/X/BONE/1
1823	June	Harry Sims of Shepton M	SRO DD/SAS/C795/SW/21 p. 70
1823	September	Richard Biggs	PRO PROB 11/1676/49
1827	May	Samuel Mead of South B	SRO DD/SAS/C795/SW/21 p. 70
1827	September	Patience Hicks of Shepton M	SRO DD/SAS/C795/SW/21 p. 70
1827	September	Mary Mead of South Bruham	SRO DD/SAS/C795/SW/21 p. 70
1831	April	Lucy Lloyd	PRO PROB 11/1851/2
1830	April	John Mills	SRS, 94, 2008, p. 245
1833	April	Mary Clarke	SRO DD/BT 2/2/5
1849	November	Edward Dyne	SRO DD/JO/4
1851	September	Stephen Penny	SRO A/ANZ/1
1853	April	Daniel Morgan	PRO PROB 11/217B
1855	October	Richard Sly of Shepton M	SRO DD/SAS/C795/SW21 p. 39
1856	January	William Greenstock of Pit.	SRO DD/BT/18/2
1857	April	Charles Oram	PRO PROB 11/2256/362

Date		Name	Location
1878	December	Elizabeth Pickford of Shepton Montague	SRO DD/X/SS/1/2
1885	August	Alfred H. Whalley	SRO DD/Br/vi/46
1902	December	Ann Bowring	SRO DD/JO/37

APPENDIX 3

CAUSES OF DEATH IN WINCANTON SANITARY DISTRICT: FOR 13 YEARS BETWEEN 1878 AND 1897

	Children under 5	Children over 5
Measles	17	5
Scarlatina (Scarlet fever)	27	15
Diphtheria	9	22
Croup	14	4
Whooping Cough	33	12
Typhus	0	8
Enteric Fever or Typhoid	1	20
Diarrhoea or Dysentery	39	39
Rheumatic Fever	2	4
Erysipelas	2	5
Phthisis	11	287
Bronchitis, Pneumonia & Pleurisy	255	448
Heart Disease	6	297
Injuries	17	72

	Children under 5	Children over 5
Puerperal Fever	0	5
Influenza	1	0
Other Diseases	658	1938
Total	1092	3180

For these children 60.3% and 60.9% respectively were categorised as dying from 'Other Diseases' Out of a total of 4272 deaths 25.6% occurred in children under 5 and 74.4% in those over 5.

APPENDIX 4

MONUMENTS AND MEMORIALS

a) William Godolphin in the Chancel of Bruton Church

At non infleti iacebitis Charissimi cineres, nec animis nostris unquam excidet amantissimi fratris suauissima simul et acerba memoria: habebimus semper ante oculos modestissimi vultus Imaginem, manebunt infixi cordibus mores, Iudicu ultra annos maturum, tranquilly pectoris fortitudo verborum certissima fides, totius vitae lenitas, simul et severitas, nulli unquam gravis erat, nulli non ambilis, supra turpitudinem qualemeunqz elatus, et quamuis Iuvenis, reverential, ubiqz except', nobis autem intimis affectibus prosequendis, quamdiu hic manebinus:
Haec, meritissimo fratri, moestissimi fraters et soror Posuimus.

[One translation of the above may be:
But not unmourned your most blessed body lying dead, not only is our most loving and wisest brother not banished from our thoughts but also at the same time nor is the sad memory: we have always before our eyes the picture of the most modest appearance, his character remaining imprinted on our mind, He was wise beyond his mature years, calm of spirit true to his word, the whole of his life tender, and at the same time serious, not at all at any time overbearing, but loveable, raised high

about disreputable behaviour of any kind, and although a young man, respected everywhere without exception. Indeed we have remained his most affectionate loyal friends right up to the present:

This we set up to the most worthy of brothers, by his most dutiful brothers and sister.]

b)

Under This Marble
Lyes the renowned Ashes of the Right Honorable
The Ld JOHN BERKELEY Baron of STRATTON youngest son
of Sr MAURICE BERKELEY of BRUTON in
SOMERSETSHIRE.
In the Civill Warres
In the dayes of CHARLES ye 1st (for his Singulr Valour &
Conduct
In recovering ye Citey of EXCESTER out of the hands of ye
Rebells.)
He was made Governr thereof & one of his Majtes Generls in
ye west
Those Unhappy Warres ended
He served many Campaenes in FLANDERS
Both in the FRENCH and SPANISH Armyes
According to their Alliances wth ENGLAND engaged him
After the happy restauration of CHARES ye 2
He was made Privy Counsellour Governour of CONAUGHT
And after Ld Lieuten of IRELAND Sent twice Extraordry
Embassaor
First into France 2^{ndly} to the Treaty of NIMEGVEN
His other Felicityes were Crownd
By his happy Marriage to CHRISTINA Daughtr of Sr ANDREW
RICCARD.
A young Lady of a Large Dowry & yet larger Graces and Vartues
Who also Enricht him with a most hopefull Progeny
He deceased
Aug ye: 26: 1678 in ye 72 yeare of his Age.
Though sprung from Danish Kings of Brightest fame
Whose Blood and High Exploits Exalt their name,
Berkeley's oune virtues most his Tombe doe grace
Adde Glory To, not borrow, from his Race.

(Memorial to John, 1st Lord Berkeley of Stratton in Twickenham
Parish Church, Middlesex.)

419

[*The Berkeleys claimed descent from Fitz Harding who was a younger son of a King of Denmark. After the Restoration of Charles II, Charles Berkeley one of Lord John's nephews in Bruton was rewarded with a series of titles, one of which was Lord Fitz-harding.*]

To the ever living memory of the Reverend Edward Bennet MA Minister of the Gospel who by a suddain surprize fell asleep in Christ the 8th day of November Anno Dom 1673 Aetatis sua 56

> Would'st thou him know whose dust lies here below,
> Then heare what truth doth say to Freind, and Foe,
> He was no mock-Priest but what he did preach,
> By his Example also did he teach
> Error and Vice in Pulpit, and in Field,
> He fought a gainst and would to neither yield
> In bad times he was good, true to his God:
> No turn Coat under Persecutor's rod
> His Worke, His Crosse, His Life, end, all in Rest,
> With God in Heaven, where he's ever blest
> But still he cries, watch, for this shining light
> Was in a moment, taken out of sight.

(*alongside the lines are a winged hourglass and skull and cross bones.*)

And Mary his wife who also by a Suddain Surprise fell asleep in Christ February ye 26th 1694 An Aetate 79.
(*This second brass plaque is signed in copperplate lettering 'Guliet Cockney de Wincanto' and is reputed to be the only such brass to be found in Somerset.*)

(Memorial to the Revd. Edward Bennet and Mary his wife in South Brewham Church)

----

c)
    "Yesterday sennight were interred, at Bruton, Somerset, the remains of the Right Hon. John Lord Berkeley, of Stratton.

A Nobleman
Whose many accomplishments and virtues
Added lustre to an exalted station.
In his person manly and engaging:
To look at him was to admire him.
Of old British Hospitality,
Of manners gentle and thoroughly polished.
An instructive and entertaining companion,
Replete with science and true wit.
His excellent understanding and judgment
Were constantly refined and improved
By reading the best authors in most languages.
His goodness of heart
Diffused a most wonderful cheerfulness
Over his whole deportment,
At the age of seventy-six.
With his equals
Free and unreserved;
Easy to access and condescending
To his inferiors;
Beloved and revered by all.
A true lover of his country;
A faithful servant to his prince:
A courtier that never deceived.
An exemplary and humane master;
An affable and heart-cheering neighbour:
A steady friend.
The special patron of the poor,
For whom he wisely considered himself
As the steward of their common Lord.
His tender heart
Felt every kind of distress,

And relieved it.
To make all around him happy,
Was the only luxury
In which he indulged himself,
Of benevolence universal.
On the public worship of his God
A constant and devout attendant;
Of genuine unaffected piety;
And an honour to human nature.

(Printed in the 'Salisbury and Winchester Journal,' 10th May 1773 on the death of John 5th Lord Berkeley of Stratton.)

----

d) In Pitcombe Church

"To the memory of Mrs Elizabeth Millard, this marble is inscribed by her nephew William Hunt Prinn, on whom, for six and forty years, her face was never turned but with an expression of kindness and affection. She died August the 24th, A.D. 1818, aged 78."

(On an open scroll under a weeping willow in white marble on the north wall of the nave. Recorded by Phelps in 1836.)

"Let this marble perpetuate the remembrance and recommend the example of Sarah Hobhouse, only daughter of Henry Hobhouse, late of Hadspen House, Esq. whose vigorous mind was applied to the acquirement of all useful and elegant knowledge, but most ardently to the study and practice of the Christian religion, which taught her to possess her soul in patience under the severest bodily pains for many years, and to resign it to God with perfect tranquillity, on the fifth day of July, 1810, at the age of thirty three years."

(On a monument representing a sarcophagus in white marble with a black backgound. Recorded by Phelps in 1836 as being on the south side of the east window in the chancel but now on south side of window at east end of north aisle. The location given by Phelps was either an error or the monument was moved during the Victorian restoration.)

"Nathaniel Jekyll d. 1826 aged 51 and Sarah Charlotte Campbell Jekyll died 1853 aged 76."

(Details recorded on an open wavy scroll of white marble with a tree on the left hand side and with its branches/leaves draped over the top and down part of the right hand side. On the south wall under the Tower in 2013.

----

e) In Brewham Church

Here lyeth buried Neere unto this place, the bodie of Francis Lynewraye, the elder, who having lived heere steward of this manor of South Brewham for 44 yeares, departed out of this wretched world, in the true faith of Christ Jesus, the 30 daye of September, anno Dom. 1596, et R. R'ne Eliz. 38.
(under these words is a recumbant skeleton lying on its face with head slightly turned to the left, the left hand raised to the mouth and legs crossed. Then)
            Sic sum, et sic eris tu."

(On a brass plate in the nave. Recorded by Phelps in 1836.)

----

f) In Bruton Church

To the glory of God and in loving memory of John Jelley, who was born on the 17th April 1808, fell asleep 17th Febr. 1888 and for nearly 50 years was a wise and successful Schoolmaster. This Tablet is erected by some of his old pupils in acknowledgement of his worth and their obligations. His Body rests in God's Acre around these walls.

"My Hope through Christ is full of immortality."

----

g) In Wyke Champflower Church

"Here under lyeth the body of Henry Southworth, esq., lord of this mannor of Wyke, who at his owne Charge builte and adorned this chappell, and departed this life the 23rd of May, 1625."

(In the Chancel on a Classical style monument of black and white marble, with colouring, and Corinthian columns.)

APPENDIX 5

INVENTORIES

A true & pfect Inventory of all & singular ye goods Chattells & debts of Thomas Tice als Rogers of Bruton in ye County of Somerset Batchelor deced as followeth

Item	due to ye deced on Bonds	DCCxxxiij li
Item	due in Shipping	CCCxlvj li
Item	Left by him at his (House?)	xxxvij li xiijs
Item	Chatale & other Goods	xxx li
Item	wearing Apparrell	xij li
	Summa totalis hujus Inveny (£1158 13s 0d)	mclviij li xiijs

Taken by Richard Martin 19th October 1685.

(PRO PROB 4/11910)

An Inventory of the goods & Chattels of Peter Walter of Weeke Champflower ...taken the 18 day of November 1690

	£	s	d
Imp(*rimus*) His wearing Apparrell	8	0	0
Item Two Cattle Leases	69	0	0
Item two Kine	3	0	0
Item Two Young beast	3	0	0
Item One horse beast	2	0	0
Item two Hogys	2	0	0
Item two Mows of Wheate	10	0	0
Item Corne & hay in the Barne	5	0	0
Item three hay reeks	15	0	0
Item three score sheepe	10	0	0
Item one Mow saddle		10	0
Item one Wayne & wheeles Putt wt some other Plough Tackle	3	0	0
Item in the Seller Chamber two ffeather beds & theire furniture	10	0	0
Item in the Hall Chamber one ffeather Bed & other goods	8	0	0
Item in Cheese	4	0	0
Item in the Parlour two Table boards & other furniture	2	0	0
Item in the Hall one Table board & Cubbord wth pewter and brass & other goods	10	0	0
Item Goods in the Milkehouse	1	0	0
Item goods in the Kitchen	2	0	0
Item goods in the Seller	4	0	0
Item in Linnen	10	0	0

Item Plate	8	0	0
Item Six Acres of Wheate	10	0	0
Item Small lumber goods	1	0	0
Sume Totall	200	10	0

Apprised by us   Thomas Walter, Robert ffry

(SRO DD/SAS/C127/8)

Inventory of Thomas Whitehead's estate taken 19th May 1691.

Imprimus the said Deceased wearing apparel	£15
Item Six feather beds & Six bedsteads with their furniture thereunto belonging	£30
Item three flock beds & three bedsteads with ye furniture thereunto belonging	£3
Item twenty four pair of sheets seven dozen of table napkins fifteen palliasses & four suites of table linen	£30

In the Parlour Chamber

Item One cabinet 18 chairs Mirror or glass & one trunk	£7

In ye Middle Chamber

Item One press and Cabinet & Stand one Mirror or glass & one little looking glass £2	10 0

In one of the Garrets

Item three boxes & one chair	5 0

In ye other Garret

Item one chest and one trunk	15 0
Item one Clock	£3

427

In ye Parlour

Item	£	s	d
Item one Oval board one sideboard 18 chairs one glass case & one looking glass	£6		

In ye Hall

Item one Cupboard Six chairs one tableboard Six joint stools & one strainer	£4		

In ye Kitchen

Item	£	s	d
Item in pewter plates and large dishes	£5		
Item in Brass, four brass pots three brass kettles & other small brass	£5	10	0
Item two table boards one settle five chairs three joint stools & one Rack	£2		
Item one Jack 3 Spitts with fire irons and Iron Rack And other Irons thereunto belonging	£2		

In ye Brew house

Item	£	s	d
Item one Furnace Six tubs trundells & other timber vessels	£4		
Item in silver plate, one Silver Tankard, one Silver Salt seller two Silver Cups one silver Taster & six silver spoons	£15	10	0
Item two pair of iron grates & three pair of Andirons	£2		
Item in wood & Hay in the back Side	£2	10	0
Item in Mault in ye house & one strainer	£10		
Item one leaden Plumb & three stone cisterns and one lead cistern valued at	£5		
Item in wool yarn cloth & one horse, Dye stuff & Oyle	£3	11	6
Item in Book debts such as are accounted good	£800		
Item in doubtful debts	£400		

Item in desperate debts	£400
Item in bonds Bills and Mortgages the sum of	£500
Item in terms of a Lease yet to come & unexpired in the deceased dwelling house and also a Term of a lease years to come on a Close called	
Tbury Corner	£200
Item one Chattel lease of a Dye house valued at	£10
Item a Shop of tools for shearing and dressing of cloth with a Rack & press valued at ye sum of	£50
Item One Dye Cistern and one Stew Pot	£15
Item two mares & one pig at	£9
Item ready money in ye house at the time of ye said deceased death the sum of	£12
Item one Oaken piece of Timber with all other the timber belonging to ye house before forgotten & not appraised	

Sum Total £6,806   16   6

(PRO PROB 10/1220)

Inventory of the Goods & Chattles of William Wilton late of Brewton Stocken Maker deceased taken by Thomas Sampson Clothier and John Robins Stocken Maker 1736

And first a Leasehold Estate Valued and Appraised at	240	0	0
And wearing Apparrel	1	10	0
Parlour Chamber			
Six old Pictures		3	0
One Bed Bolsster & Pillows & Bedstead and Curtains at	2	10	0
about three dozen Glass Bottles		3	0
six old Leather Chairs and 7 Rush Chairs		7	0
Kitchen Chamber			
One old flock Bed Bedstead and Appurtences		15	0
One old Press Chest		3	6
One Small Looking Glass and a few old Books		2	6
In the Garrett			
Bed Linnen & Table Linnen		14	0
In the Parlour			
One old Clock & Case		21	0
Fourteen old pictures		7	0
Window Curtains and Rods		2	0
In the Kitchen			
Nine Pictures and other Toys		7	0
24 pounds of pewter		12	0
Two Little Table Boards six old Chairs		5	0
In the Buttery			
One dripping Pan frying pan Cullinder & cover		3	0

Item	£	s	d
One Iron Pott Brass Kettle and Possnett		4	0
One other Brass Kettle and a pair of Tongs		5	0
One half hogshead 2 Quarter Barrels & two small firkins		8	0
In the Wash house			
One furnace & grate Washing Poll & Wringer	3	0	0
In the Wool Loft			
Fifty seven pounds of Colourd Pinions (*wool on spindles*)	1	8	6
Thirty eight pounds of White Pinions		12	8
Eighteen pounds of blue Slivered Wool (*loose wool which has been combed*)		18	0
Twenty two pounds of white Slivered Wool		14	8
One hundred thirty eight pounds of Combing wool	4	0	6
In the Combshopp			
Two pair of Old Combe		4	0
Charcoal		7	0
In the yarn shop			
Four dozen and 3 stockens at 24s ye dozen	5	2	0
One dozen & half at same		5	0
Small scales and weights		2	6
24 pounds of scoured worsted	2	10	0
Thirteen pounds of greasy worsted	1	6	0
47 Pounds of Lead Weights		6	0
Thirty two pounds of Worsted in Knitters hands	3	10	0
In ready money	1	0	0
Total	275	9	4

And to the Saxton for burying her husband		11	0
And for a Coffin		17	0
And for removing his Tombstone		4	6
And for £5 due to Tho Horsey for Sope and Candles	5	0	0

(SRO D/D/cta W46)

Ann Hebditch late of the Parish of Pitcombe died 2 June 1799, exhibited by Thomas Hebditch, labourer, surviving executor.

Payments Out

Probate	3	10	0
Funeral Expences	5	0	6
Debts	38	15	10
	47	6	4

Value of Property

Estimated value of the House bequeathed to George & Thomas Hebditch, sons of the deceased – the former of whom is dead	70	0	0
Household goods	5	16	1
Balance	28	9	9

James Garland of Bruton, Cordwainer, died 20 Aug 1825, exhibited by Stephen Penny.

Cash in house	4	10	0
Household goods	13	12	0
	18	2	0
Probate	3	3	0
Funeral Expences	10	1	0
Executorship Ex.	1	1	0
	14	5	0
Balance in Cash	3	17	0

Leasehold estates	84	0	0
Rents due	10	10	0
Wearing Apparel	2	0	0
	100	7	0

Due in Stamp Duty	1	0	0

Susannah Cox of Bruton, Spinster, died 5 July 1826, exhibited by Frances Evet, wife of Wm.

Cash in House	7	10	0
Household Goods and Furniture	39	10	0
Wearing Apparel	10	0	0
Jewels, Trinkets, Ornaments of the Person	1	0	0
	58	0	0
Principal on Bonds etc.	100	0	0
Interest		15	0
	158	15	0

Probate	4	10	0
Funeral Expences	19	17	$5^{1}/_{2}$
Executorship Ex	12	0	0
Debts	8	1	0
9 Legacies of £5 each	45	0	0
	89	8	$5^{1}/_{2}$

Balance in Cash	69	6	$6^{1}/_{2}$
To pay at £3 per cent	2	1	7

(Stamp Duty Receipts, SRO DD/BT/12)

APPENDIX 6

a) Epitaphs from Bruton Churchyard

> My Husband dear by time is past
> So long to me your love did last.
> But now for me no trouble take
> Only love your Children for my sake.

(Hannah wife of Samuel Green who died 1st Dec. 1804, aged 59 years)

> My Dearest Wife, my time is past
> And now to you I come at last,
> Here we shall lay and take our rest
> Till we are call'd to join the Blest.

(1811, printed in A.S. MacMillan, Somerset Epitaphs, Somerset Folk Series, 18, 1924, p. 104)

> My long afflicted Father dear,
> Whose gross material Part lies here,
> At length has ta'en his flight
> In Christ redeem'd whose Spirit's Pow'r
> Hath saved him in the trying hour
> Into a World of Light.

(1827, A.S. MacMillan, op.cit., p. 86)

Verily there is a Reward for the Righteous.

(John Clarke who died 15th May 1847, aged 73 years)

The ransomed of the lord shall return, and come to Zion with songs and everlasting joy upon their heads; they shall obtain joy and gladness, and sorrow and sighing shall flee away.

(John Ackerman who died 31st October 1848, aged 55 years)

The sweet remembrance of the just
Shall flourish when they sleep in dust.

(Richard Cox who died 24th October 1849, aged 72 years and Patience Read his wife who died 29 May 1859, aged 84 years.)

Affliction long time I bore.
Physicians were in vain
Till God did please death should so(?)er
And cure me of my pain.

(Thomas White who died 6th November 1862, aged 78 years)

Our parents beloved no longer nigh
In Jesus name we shall meet again.

(Thomas Shore who died 18th July 1878 and Hester Shore who died 15th April 1900)

Earth to earth and dust to dust
Calmly now the words we say
Leaving them to sleep in trust
Till the Resurrection day
Father in thy Gracious keeping
Leave we now thy servant sleeping.

(Joseph Mills who died 29th January 1885, aged 73 years)

Angel hands have borne our dear ones
From us tenderly away
Even though our hearts so loved them
Yet we could not bid them stay.

(Lizzie Marshall who died 2nd February 1885, aged 18 years)

Their not gone from memory, not from love,
But gone to their father's home above.

(Susanna Kate Jeffery who died 5th February 1890, aged 2 years 4 months)

We cannot Lord thy purpose see
But all is well that's done by thee.

(Florence Jane James who died 18th June 1891, aged 28 years)

Holy Father Gracious Lord
By thy Holy Name adored
Praise to thee be always given
By all on earth and all in heaven

(Nathaniel White who died 4th February 1892, aged 69 years)

Of such is the Kingdom of Heaven.

(Elizabeth Dorothy May Jackson who died 27th March 1895, aged 1 year 8 months)

Jesus called a little child unto Him.

(Henry Franklyn Jackson who died 26th April 1895, aged 3 years and 4 months)

Is it well with the Child? It is well.

(Albert Joseph Stuart Jackson who died 13th May 1895, aged 5 years and 11 months)

Into Thine Hand, I commit my spirit.

(Anne Elizabeth Jackson who died 12 June 1901, aged 46)
and
Be ye therefore Ready also

(Josiah Jackson who died 29th September 1904, aged 52)

Nothing in my hands I bring
Simply to thy cross I cling.

(Charles James Clarke, who died 17th November 1895, aged 24 years)

And God said Let there be light, and there was light.

(Chandos Swain who died 17th February 1898, aged 2 years)

How little did I think that thou,
Should'st first the summit gain,
And leave me thus so far behind,
Slow journeying o'er the plain,
But so it was our Father's will
And his lov'd voice is 'Peace be still.'

(Frank White who died 24th October 1901, aged 52 years)

Home at last thy labour done,
Safe and blest the victory won
Suffering o'er from pain set free
Christ has now received thee.

(Elizabeth Davis who died 20th May 1904, aged 77 years)

Light after darkness, gain after loss,
Strength after weakness, crown after cross,
After long agony, rapture of bliss,
Right was the pathway leading to this.

(George White who died 20th September 1904, aged 70 years)

Watch therefore: for ye know not what hour your Lord doth come.

(James Sutcliffe, who died 6th September 1885, aged 64.

----

b) Epitaphs and Memorials from local Churches and Churchyards.

From Pitcombe Churchyard

Com'st thou to gaze upon my tombe
And leave a fruitless sign
Or Com'st thou in youth's purple bloom
To learn that thou must die
Death may be hov'ring o're thine head
Awake believe and pray
The Saviour who on Calvary bled
To wash my sins away.

(John Cook who died 14th November 1827, aged 57 years)

This peaceful grave doth now contain
A wife and child together laid
A loving wife, a friend most dear
Such was she who now lies here,
O cruel Death that could not be Denied,
That broke the Bond of Love so lately tied.

(1820, copied by G. Sweetman in 1896, in A.S. MacMillan, op.cit., p. 86)

A loyal loving virtuous wife moste dear,
With her sweet babe doth lie interred here,
Whose souls sit around in that heavenly Quire
Of endless joy, filled with celestial fire.

(1733, copied by G. Sweetman in 1896, in A.S. MacMillan, op.cit., p. 86)

Grieve not for us our parents dear we pray,
'Twas our blest Saviour called us hence away,
Come all ye blessed babes come unto me
Where bliss & Glory will for ever be.

(1776, copied by G. Sweetman in 1896, in A.S. MacMillan, op.cit., p. 123)

From Shepton Montague Churchyard

(*On a Tablet inside the Church*)
Here I lie till trump doth sound
And Christ for me doth call
Then shall I rise and live again
And die no more at all

(John Mogg of Castle Cary, died May 30 1695. *Also included are William Mogg and Rebecca his wife along with Mary their daughter and Thomas Woolmington her husband.*)
(Copied by G. Sweetman in 1913 in SRO DD/SAS/C795/ SW/15)

Here lies a piece of Christ, a star in dust
A grain of gold, a china dish that must
Appear in Heaven when Christ doth feast the just.

(Mogg family gravestone, collected by Bishop Hobhouse in 1840/50s but no longer in the churchyard when he re-visted in May 1890)

Dear Husband
Mourn not for me but let your sorrow cease
And pray to God through Jesus Christ for peace
Enjoin the truest source, to have our sins forgiven
That we may meet a Future Day in Heaven

(Elizabeth wife of Robert Sharp who died 17th November 1821, aged 56 years)

Here I lye till trumpe doth sound
And Christ for me doth call
Then shall I rise to life again
And die no more at all.

(1695)

Death in my prime gave me a fall
From my wife and 4 children small,
I hope in Christ he will them bless,
And send them to eternal rest.

(William Mogg, died 8 October 1766, aged 35. Copied by G. Sweetman in May 1884, in A.S. MacMillan, op.cit., p. 23)

As Life's short span with mutual love was passed,
Let this same grave receive our souls at last,
My consort dear in hopes we both shall rise
To boundless joys and love that never dies.

(Copied by G. Sweetman in 1896 by which time names and dates were no longer visible. Sweetman Papers in SRO DD/ SAS/C795/SW/15 – hereafter Sweetman 1896)

Meek was her temper, Sober was her life
A Tender Mother, and a virtuous wife.

(Elizabeth Fiander who died 20th April 1787, aged 67.
Also found by Sweetman in 1896 on the gravestone of Johanna,
wife of John Mogg, who died 12th October 1785, aged 75.)

With patience to the last he did submit
And murmered not at what the Lord thought fit
He with a Christian courage did resign
His soul to God at the appropriate time.

And as we have borne the image of the Earthly we shall also
bear the image of the heavenly.
(John Fiander, husband of the above, who died 10 June 1797
aged 66. Sweetman 1896)

Behold, He Taketh Away; who
Can hinder Him? Who will say
Unto Him What Doest Thou?   Job ix 12

(Martha, wife of Edwin Sims, who died 1st December 1868,
aged 63)

By sudden death I'm snatched away
Death scarcely left me time to say
The Lord have mercy on my Soul
So absolute is His controul
Reflect when thou my grave doth see
The next that's made may be for thee.

(Richard Jukes who died 10th September 1812, aged 52 years.
Sweetman 1896)

Affliction sore,
Long time I bore,
Physicians were in vain
Till God was pleased
Death should me seize
And ease me of my pain.

(William Jukes, son of Richard above, who died 27 February 1814, aged 32 years. Sweetman 1896)

Much have I been with pain opprest
That wore my strength away
Which made me long for endless Rest
That never will decay.

(Mary Jukes, daughter of Richard above, who died 31st May 1824, aged 21 years.
Also on gravestone of Mary Moger who died 15 December 1845, aged 91. Sweetman 1896)

This world I did freely leave
And begged of God me to receive
To my dear mother I did say
I'll haste to God and make no stay.

(William Jukes, son of George and Betty, who died 10 June 1771, aged 27. Sweetman 1896)

Our Life hangs by a slender thread
Which soon is cut and we are dead
Then reader boast not of thy might
We're here at noon and gone at night.

(George Moger who died 13 November 1827, aged 64.
Sweetman 1896)

Let angels guard thy sleeping dust
Till Christ shall come to raise the just
Then may'st thou wake with sweet surprise
And in thy Saviour's image rise.

(Catherine Sophia Moger who died 2 November 1855, aged
66. Sweetman 1896)

From Lamyatt Church

Grive not for us our Parents dear
We are not lost but sleepeth here
For in our Prime we'r Snatched away
And for our children take Care I pray.

(Joseph Andrews and his wife – collected by Edmund Rack in
1780s)

My loving wife my time is past,
So long to me your love did last,
But now for me no trouble take,
And love our children for my sake.

(1782, in A.S. Macmillan, op.cit., p. 24)

He shall gather the Lambs with his arm
And carry them in his bosom.

(Ernest Edward Rex who died 18th March 1885, aged 9 months.)

From Wyke Champflower.

Gone unto God,
Gone to the Father, In his House To Dwell
Gone through the Shadowed Vale that Jesus trod
Beloved, it is well.

John Whitehead, who died 27th February 1894, aged 84)

From South Brewham

Weep not for me my husband dear,
Pray think on me but shed no tear,
See I am here return'd to dust,
Prepare to come, for come you must.

(1838, A.S. MacMillan, op.cit.. p. 50)

To her children ever loving,
Kind and faithful to her mate,
Ever all that's good approving
All that's evil prone to hate.

(1754, A.S. MacMillan, op.cit., p. 54)

Pale Death can hardly find another
So good a Wife and tender Mother,
In all her Actions well inclin'd
She never will be out of mind
Why should we grieve
For what we must approve,
The Joys of Heaven
Surpass our fondest Love.

(1801, A.S. MacMillan, op.cit., p. 63)

Farewell my Husband & children dear that are behind,
Pray think on me and call to mind,
Make Christ your friend while time do last,
Twill be too late when time is past.

(Copied by E.W. Swanton in 1897, in A.S. MacMillan, op.cit.,
p. 76)

These Forty Years of Mortal life,
They were a happy Man and wife;
And being so by Nature tied,
When one fell Sick the other Died,
And both together laid in Dust
To wait the Raising of the Just.

(1810/11 on gravestone of Thomas King and his wife Mary, in
A.S. MacMillan, op.cit., p. 97)

Behold the Husband and the Wife,
Now join'd in death as once in life,
Whose Souls are now at rest we trust
In the blest manions of the just.

(1778-1795, A.S. MacMillan, op.cit., p. 98. This was a popular verse and was also found on gravestones in Pitcombe from the period 1750-1786 and in Shepton Montague in 1805)

Here lies a darling sweet asleep
Left us behind to mourn and weep,
Weep not for me my Mother dear,
I am not dead but sleepeth here.
In love he lived in peace he died
Life was desir'd but God Denied.

(1804 for a man aged 27, copied by E.W. Swanton in 1896, in A.S. MacMillan, op.cit., p. 118)

Sister farewell, in Peaceful slumber rest,
Secure of thy reward amongst the Blest,
Thy greatest Treasure in thy Life we see,
And sweet and blest are they that follow thee.

(1795, copied by E.W. Swanton in 1897, in A.S. MacMillan, op.cit, p. 137)

Though gone from sight to Memory Dear.

(John Balch, who died 28th January 1890, aged 55)

I shall go to him but he shall not return to me.

(Hugh Russell Cannon, who died 28th March 1899, aged 53)

Milton Clevedon Churchyard

The Lord gave and the Lord hath taken away
Blessed be the name of the Lord.

(Ann, wife of James Harding, who died 23rd June 1840,
aged 66)

Jesus loves his little children
Once he took them on his knee
Gently laid his arms around them
And said let them "Come to Me".

(Isabel Audrey Percy of Spargrove, who died 6th September
1906, aged 51/2)

APPENDIX 7

a) Victorian Hymns

> Brief life is here our portion,
> Brief sorrow, short-lived care;
> The Life that knows no ending,
> The tearless life, is there,
> O happy retribution!
> Short toil, eternal rest;
> For mortals and for sinners,
> A mansion for the blest!
>
> Strive, man, to win that glory;
> Toil, man, to gain that light;
> Send hope before to grasp it,
> Till hope be lost in sight.
> Exult, O dust and ashes;
> The Lord shall be thy part:
> His only, His for ever
> Thou shalt be, and thou art.

Originally written by Bernard of Cluny in C12th and then translated by J.M. Neale (1818-1866)

When the day of toil is done,
When the race of Life is run,
Father, grant Thy wearied one
Rest for evermore.

When the breath of life is flown,
When the grave must claim its own,
Lord of Life, be ours Thy crown –
Life for evermore.

J. Ellerton (1826-1893)

Now the labourer's task is o'er,
Now the battle-day is past;
Now upon the farther shore
Lands the voyager at last.

There the penitents who turn
To the Cross their dying eyes
All the love of Jesus learn
At his feet in paradise.

J. Ellerton (1826-1893)

There is a blessed home
Beyond this land of woes,
Where trials never come,
Nor tears of sorrow flow;
Where faith is lost in sight,
And patient hope is crown'd
And everlasting light
Its glory throws around.

H.W. Baker (1821-1877)

Shall we gather at the river,
Where bright angel feet have trod,
With its crystal tide forever
Flowing by the throne of God?

Chorus

Yes, we'll gather at the river,
The beautiful, the beautiful river,
Gather with the saints at the river
That flows by the throne of God.

R. Lowry, 1864

When the trumpet of the Lord shall sound, and time shall be
no more,
And the morning breaks eternal bright and fair,
When the saints on earth shall gather over on the other shore,
And the roll is called up yonder I'll be there.

J.M. Black, 1893

The following two examples were specifically written for children:

There's a home for little children
Above the bright blue sky,
Where Jesus reigns in glory,
A home of peace and joy.
No home on earth is like it,
Or can with it compare;
For every one is happy,
Nor could be happier, there.

A. Midlane (1825-1909)

Let my sins be all forgiven;
Bless the friends I love so well;
Take me, when I die, to heaven,
Happy there with thee to dwell.

Mary Duncan (1814-1840)

------

b) Victorian popular songs

Down yonder green valley where streamlets meander,
When twilight is fading I pensively rove;
Or at the bright noontide in solitude wander
Amid the dark shades of the lonely Ash Grove;
'Twas there, while the blackbird was singing,
I first met that dear one – the joy of my heart!
Around us for gladness the bluebells were ringing,
Ah! Then little thought I how soon we should part.

Still glows the bright sunshine o'er valley and mountain,
Still warbles the blackbird its note from the tree;
Still trembles the moonbeam on streamlet and fountain,
But what are the beauties of Nature to me?
With sorrow, deep sorrow, my bosom is laden,
All day I go mourning in search of my love!
Ye echoes! Oh, tell me, where is the sweet maiden?
"She sleeps 'neath the green turf down by the Ash Grove."

The Ash Grove,   Thomas Oliphant

Sleep, my love, and peace attend thee
    All thro' the night;
Guardian angels God will lend thee
    All thro' the night.
Soft the drowsy hours are creeping,

Hill and vale in slumber sleeping;
Love alone his watch is keeping
    All thro' the night.

Hark! A solemn bell is ringing,
    Clear thro' the night;
Thou, my love, art heav'nward winging
    Home thro' the night.
Earthly dust from off thee shaken,
Soul immortal, thou shalt waken
With thy last dim journey taken
    Home thro' the night.
            All thro' the Night,   Walter Maynard

Could you come back to me, Douglas, Douglas,
In the old likeness that I knew,
I would be so faithful, so loving, Douglas,
Douglas, Douglas, tender and true

O to call back to the days that are not!
My eyes were blinded, your words were few:
Do you know the truth now up in heaven,
Douglas, Douglas, tender and true?
Stretch out your hand to me, Douglas, Douglas,
Drop forgiveness from heaven like dew:
As I lay my heart on your dead heart, Douglas,
Douglas, Douglas, tender and true.
            Too Late,   Dinah M.M. Craik.

We shall meet, but we shall miss him
There will be one vacant chair
We shall linger to caress him
While we breathe our evening prayer;

453

When a year ago we gathered
Joy was in his mild blue eye
But a golden cord is severed
And our hopes in ruin lie.

True, they tell us wreaths of glory
Evermore will deck his brow,
But this soothes the anguish only
Sweeping o'er our heartstrings now.
Sleep today, Oh early fallen,
In thy green and narrow bed,
Dirges from the pine and cypress,
Mingle with the tears we shed.

The Vacant Chair,   Henry Washburn.

When I'm dead and gone from you darling,
When I'm laid away in my grave,
When my spirit has gone to heaven above,
To Him who my soul will save;

When you are happy and gay once more,
Thinking of days that have been;
This one little wish I ask of you,
See that my grave's kept green.

Oh the day will come to you darling,
When on earth no more I'll be seen;
One sweet little wish darling grant me,
See that my grave's kept green.

See that my grave's kept green,   Gus Williams

The popularity for sentimental songs relating to death continued into the twentieth century and was given an added impetus
by the impact of the First World War. As a result of the death
of his son in France in December 1916 the Musical Hall
performer Harry Lauder wrote 'The End of the Road.'

Chorus

> Keep right on to the end of the road
> Keep right on to the end
> If the way be long, let your heart be strong
> Keep right on round the bend
> If you're tired and weary still journey on,
> Till you come to your happy abode
> Where all you love, and you're dreaming of
> Will be there, at the end of the road.

APPENDIX 8

DIALECT POETRY

In our Churchyard

E' es wife, 'Twas here we laid or darlin' bwoy
The merry vour year wold we prized so dear,
'Twer here we stod, thik day, when all the joy
Sim'd drove from out our hearts, and life wer drear.

The vriends a-standen' round an' looken' on
The little coffin wi' its wreath of flowers,
The last look 'fore we left 'un theer alon,
The aching heart an' anguish that wer' ours.

Volks zay the spirits o' the dead d'rise
An' hover auver us as we d'walk,
An' though we cannot zee 'em wi' our eyes,
They can zee us, an' hear us when we talk.

Well, well. Theer lies a little heap o'dirt,
Wi grass growed auver. Tidden much to see,
Wi' two or dree fresh flowers drowed athirt.
It idden much, but dear it is to we.

(Poems in Dialect by R.R.C. Gregory, Somerset Folk Series,
No. 5, London, 1922, pp. 22-3)

When I Die

Don't let no tears o' grief be shed vor I
When, zoon as must, my turn do come to die,
Life's journey's getten nearer to the west,
An' I can hear the call to hwome an' rest.

Don't let there be no fuss, n'eet vulgar show
When up to God's green eacre I do go;
Let friends that have a-bin both firm an' fast
Stan' by thik earthen bedzide at the last.

Put but a simple rough-hewed stwone to show
The spot where theage wold bwones do rest below;
An' let no nonsense on the stwone be put,
But jist the neame an' date, rough chisel cut.

Life ha' bin zweet intheaze feair sunny land,
Framed wi' sich beauty by the Measter's hand;
Zoon by God's love an' mercy I shall zee
What vurder wonders be prepared vor we.

(Dialect Poems and a Play by J. Mackie, Somerset Folk Series,
No. 23, London, 1925, pp. 74-5)

APPENDIX 9

PRINCIPAL MEMBERS
OF THE BERKELEY FAMILY
BETWEEN 1545 AND 1773

Sir Maurice *(who purchased Bruton Abbey)*

Sir Henry

Sir Maurice

Sir Charles ------------------ Sir William ------------------ Sir John
2nd *Lord Fitzharding*   *Governor of Virginia*   1st *Lord Berkeley*
                                                                             of Stratton

Maurice -------------- Charles --------------- John
3rd *Lord Fitzharding*   1st *Lord Fitzharding*   4th *Lord Fitzharding*
d. childless   *& Earl of Falmouth* *d. childless*
                     d. childless

Charles   John   William
2nd *Lord Berkeley*   3rd *Lord Berkeley*   4th *Lord Berkeley*
of Stratton   *of Stratton*   *of Stratton*
d. childless   *d. childless*   *(repurchased Bruton Abbey)*

                                                                          John
                                                                      5th *Lord Berkeley*
                                                                      of Stratton
                                                                        d. childless

NOTES AND REFERENCES

DRO   Dorset Record Office
PRO   National Archives
SANHSP   Somerset Archaeological and Natural History Society
          Proceedings
SRO   Somerset Heritage Centre
SRS   Somerset Record Society
WRO   Wiltshire Heritage Centre.

Introduction

1. A similar failure to complete the Registers may also be found in the Baptism and Marriage Registers. In some, but by no means all, of the gaps of months and years identified in the Burial Registers there were the same sort of omissions in the other Registers: for example, there were just 4 baptisms recorded between January 1577 and April 1578, with all these in September and October; there were 3 baptisms between March 1581 and August 1582; and none at all between June 1767 and March 1768. Just 2 weddings were recorded between October 1583 and May 1585 and none at all between January 1576 and July 1578, February and June 1616, December 1742 and September 1743.

Chapter 1 Setting the Scene

1. M. McDermott & S. Berry, ed., Edmund Rack's Survey of Somerset, SANHS, 2011, p. 61.
2. WRO Hoare Papers 383/142, Return to Querys of the Society of Antiquaries, pt. I, No. 30. (hereafter Querys).
3. J. Leland, Itinerary, vol. II, London, 1710, p. 74; J. Vanes, ed., The Ledger of John Smythe 1538-1550, Historical Manuscripts

Commission, J.P.19, London, 1994, pp. 4, 82-3, 166-7, 201; Querys, op.cit., pt. I, No. 43; Report of the Select Committee on the Silk Trade, 1832, PP 1831-2 XIX, Minutes of Evidence of John S. Ward, p. 209.

4. In 1805 Edward Dyne signed an agreement with mason Edward Read "to take down the old House at Coombe Farm & to clear the Stones at £10 - & to dig cellar at 4d per yard & to build a new House at 23d a Perch." A list of expenses between March 1805 and May 3 1806 when it suddenly stopped showed that over £200 had been paid out. SRO DD/JO/7, Account Book of Mr Dyne.

5. Rev. D.L. Hayward, ed., The Registers of Bruton, Co. Somerset, vols. I and 2, 1554-1812, London, 1911. Typed transcript of subsequent years in possession of the author.

6. M. Havinden, The Somerset Landscape, London, 1981, p. 7; R. Houlbrooke, Death, Religion and the Family in England 1480-1750, Oxford, 1998, pp. 4-5; A.E. Nash, 'The mortality pattern of the Wiltshire lords of the manor 1242-1377' in Southern History, vol. 2, 1980, p. 35.

7. PRO E179/170/202a and 216, 37 Henry VIII; PRO E179/256/1, 18 Eliz.; E. Green, 'On the Poor and some attempts to Lower the Price of Corn in Somerset, 1548-1638', in Proceedings of the Bath Natural History and Antiquarian Field Club, vol. IV, 1881, p. 32; J. Collinson, History and Antiquities of the County of Somerset, Bath, 1791, vol. I, p. 218.

8. The Census figures may be found in W. Page, ed., The Victoria History of the Counties of England: Somerset, London, 1911, vol. II, pp. 341-2. They included the total for the hamlets of Redlynch, Wyke Champflower and part of Discove. Throughout the nineteenth century the combined populations of these hamlets ranged between 189 and 224 so on average the population figures for the town of Bruton itself were about 200 lower. Queries, pt. I, No. 4; The Reports of the Medical Officers of Health may be found in PRO MH/12 10567-10583.

Chapter 2   Causes of Death.

1. 'Western Flying Post', 16 February 1829; Notes and Queries for Somerset and Dorset, vol XXXVII, September 2012, p. 144; 'Sherborne Mercury', 21 September 1789; 'Taunton Courier', 19 March 1828.

2. Eulogium Historiarum sive Temporis, Rolls Series, 1858-1863, vol. III, pp. 213-4; Register of Bishop Ralph of Shrewsbury, SRS, vol. X, 1896, pp. 555-6; Wilkes Concilia, vol. ii, pp. 735-6, cited in P. Ziegler, The Black Death, London, 1997, pp. 102-3. (Little did he know that one day there would be women priests, although not yet in the Catholic Church!).

3. Bruton and Montacute Cartularies, SRS, vol. VIII, 1894, No. 363, p. 94.

4. W. Murphy, ed., 'The Earl of Hertford's Lieutenancy Papers, 1603-1612', in Wiltshire Record Society, vol. XXIII, 1967, pp. 160, 174; Manuscripts of the Duke of Somerset, Historical Manuscripts Commission, vol. 43, London, 1898, p. 87.

5. SRO DD/SE 43/17, Account of Robert Ludwell 1666-1676; SRO D/P/brut 13/2/1, Bruton Overseers' Accounts 1653-1669, and 13/2/2 Accounts 1669-1678.

6. Years when smallpox was definitely present in Bruton: 1675, 1682-4, 1689, 1690, 1693, 1721, 1722, 1727-9, 1736-8, 1742, 1743, 1746, 1747, 1753, 1754, 1757, 1764, 1765, 1770-1773, 1784, 1785.

7. Details of payments to individuals and families may be found in the appropriate volumes of the Accounts of the Overseers of the Poor, SRO D/P/brut 13/2/1-13/2/8 and 13/2/14 which contains monthly accounts 1705-1730; J. Beresford, ed., The Diary of a Country Parson: the Reverend James Woodforde, vol. I, p. 80 (hereafter J. Beresford, Diary); R.L. Winstanley, ed., The Ansford Diary of James Woodforde, vol. 2, 1764-1765, Parson Woodforde Society, 1979, p. 101 (hereafter R.L. Winstanley, Ansford Diary); SRO Q/SR 325/2/25, Letter concerning smallpox in 1757.

8. SRO D/P/brut 9/1/1, Bruton Select Vestry Minute Book for the Administration of the Poor 1790-1806; SRO D/G WN 8a/3,

Minute Book 13 January 1840; 'Western Flying Post', 21 September 1840; PRO MH12/10572, 60828/69, Letter from Clerk of Wincanton Board of Guardians to Poor Law Board, 23 December 1869; PRO MH 12/10580, 14716/91 and 17523/92, Reports of the Medical Officer of Health.

9. J. Martin, Wives and Daughters: Women and Children in a Georgian Country House, London, 2004, pp. 210-211; 'Western Gazette', 31 October 1863, 13 June 1879; British Library Add MSS 51766, fol. 106, Holland House Papers, Letter from 4th Lord Holland to his mother, 25 December 1841; 'Western Gazette', 1 April 1887; SRO D/G WN 8a/15, Minute Book, 16 and 23 January, 13 March, 29 May, 3 and 10 July 1889.

10. SRO Q/SR 322/1/7, Coroner's Inquisition 23 October 1753; 'The Bath Journal', 13 August 1810; 'Western Flying Post', 23 November 1852, 10 March 1852; 'Shepton Mallet Journal', 22 February 1867, 9 July 1858.

11. 'Shepton Mallet Journal', 11 September 1885; 'Western Gazette', 2 March 1888.

12. 'Western Gazette', 13 February 1885; L. Stephens, ed., Dictionary of National Biography, vol. IV, London, 1885, John, 3rd Baron Berkeley of Stratton; 'Bristol Mercury', 18 November 1843; 'Shepton Mallet Journal', 18 March 1874, 28 July 1876; 'Western Gazette', 6 April 1881, 6 February 1891, 13 February 1885, 7 December 1888, 11 May 1883, 12 July 1889; 'Shepton Mallet Journal', 29 August 1862, 19 January 1866, 14 January 1876; 'Bath Chronicle and Weekly Gazette', 16 February 1769; 'Western Flying Post, 6 March 1769; 'Shepton Mallet Journal', 11 July 1873, 7 May 1875; 'Oxford Journal', 3 February 1787; 'Western Flying Post', 18 February 1843.

13. B. Falk, The Berkeleys of Berkeley Square, London, 1944, pp. 90-2; Longleat House, Coventry Papers, vol. XXXIII, 1664-1677, pp. 189-190, Letter from Lord Berkeley to Lord Coventry, 7 December 1775; 'The Diary of Dr Edward Lake', in The Camden Miscellany, vol. I, Camden Society, vol. 39, 1846, p. 16; 'The Scots Magazine', 1 April 1773; 'Western Flying Post', 7 June 1790; Castle Cary Visitor, vol. III, 1900-1, p. 170; 'Wells

Journal', 27 May 1854; 'Western Flying Post', 2 January 1855; 'Shepton Mallet Journal', 17 October 1862; 'Western Daily Press', 11 October 1871; 'Oxford Journal', 5 October 1776.

14. Castle Cary Visitor, vol. V, 1904-5, p. 168; 'Shepton Mallet Journal', 15 April 1864; 'Wells Journal', 7 October 1865; 'Western Gazette', 7 April 1882; 'Shepton Mallet Journal', 21 June 1867, 17 April 1874.

15. WRO Hoare Papers 383/331, Bruton Court Leet and Court Baron Presentments 1787-1802; PRO MH12/10573, 46832/71, Letter from A.D. Gill to Sanitary Commissioners, 15 October 1871, 47479/71, Letter from Henry Dyne to Local Government Board, 28 October 1871, 44404/72, Report of the Subcommittee appointed by the Sewers Authority, January 1872, 21327/72 Report of Dr Homes on Enteric Fever in the Union of Wincanton, February 1872; McDermott & Berry op.cit., p.61; PRO MH12/10577, 18162/85, Report of Dr Parsons 1886. For details of public health problems in Bruton and actions proposed, see P.W. Randell, 'Public Health in Bruton, 1872-1898' in Notes and Queries for Somerset and Dorset, vol. XXXIII, September 1992, pp.157-164.

16. 'Western Flying Post', 29 March 1853, 11 October 1853; Report of Dr. Homes, op.cit.; PRO MH12/10576, 24677/78, Report of Medical Officer of Health for 1877.

17. C. Clarke, ed., The Diary of a Wessex Farmer, Josiah Jackson 1882-1904, 24 and 27 March 1895, p. 153, 26 April and 3 May 1895, p. 155, 28 and 29 May 1895, p. 156. (hereafter C. Clark, Diary)

18. The 1861 Census showed that the total population of the Cats Lane-Tolbury area, excluding Tolbury House was 167. Joshua Smith was recorded as living at Tolpenny or Tolbury with a wife and 4 sons aged from 8 to 21years and 4 daughters aged from 6 months to 17 years. SRO D/G/WN 8a/5, Letter from Dr. Crouch to the Wincanton Board of Guardians, 7 February 1844; PRO MH12/10576, 24677/78, Report of Medical Officer of Health, March 1878; 'Bath Chronicle and Weekly Gazette', 28 April 1853, 19 January 1865; 'Western Gazette', 4 April 1884;

'Bath Chronicle and Weekly Gazette', 17 June 1841; 'Salisbury and Winchester Journal,' 10 January 1857.

19. Letters relating to the Suppression of the Monasteries, Camden Society, vol. 26, 1844, Letter from Dr. Layton to Thomas Cromwell, pp. 58-9; P. Matheson, Reformation Christianity, London, 2010, p. 104; D.M. McCallam, 'Age at Baptism: Further Evidence', in Local Population Studies, vol. 24, 1980, p. 49.

20. This is probably the same Mrs Threadgold who was buried on 11th May 1767. Although her Christian name was never specified, she may well have been the Eleanor Tice als Rogers who married Thomas Thridgould on 1st November 1737.

21. PRO MH 12/10569, 11123/56, Letter from Dr. Crouch to Poor Law Board 9 April 1856; MH12/10569, 20073/56, Report of Investigation by Inspector E. Gulson 10 June 1856.

22. WRO 383/72 Hoare Papers, Stourhead Account Book containing a note of a reply in 1813 by Lady Wodehouse in response to 'Quere'; 'Bath Chronicle and Weekly Gazette', 24 February 1853; 'Dorset County Chronicle and Somersetshire Gazette', 16 March 1865; 'Western Gazette', 13 June 1873, 31 January 1873, 7 March 1879.

23. C. Clark, Diary, op.cit., 23 May 1901 p. 260, 12 June 1901 p, 261.

24. 'Shepton Mallet Journal' 30 December 1859; 'Western Gazette', 24 February 1882; 'Wells Journal', 30 November 1861; 'Western Gazette', 9 September 1898.

25. J.A. Giles, trans. Matthew Paris's English History from 1235-1273, vol. III, London, 1854, pp. 266, 280, 283.

26. Wiltshire Record Society, vol. XXIII, op.cit., p. 153, Letter from Deputy Lieutenants 29 June 1609; op.cit., p. 174 12 August 1611; "The Potato Famine in the West of England", in 'Morning Chronicle', 5, 6 and 8 December 1845; D.Defoe, 'The Storm', in L.A. Curtis, ed., The Versatile Defoe, London, 1979, p. 293; 'Bath Chronicle and Weekly Gazette', 10 July 1845; 'Western Gazette', 1 July 1881; 'Derby Mercury', 24 June 1790.

27. For details of crimes of violence in Bruton see P.W. Randell, Crime, Law and Order in a Somersetshire Market town: Bruton

c1500-c1900, Brighton, 2011, esp. pp. 48-61; Somerset Pleas, S.R.S. vol. 11, 1897, pp. 52, 53, 267, 269, 272. The case of 1532 cited in Castle Cary Visitor, vol. VII, 1908-9, p. 177; Copy of pardon of John Whyt published in the 'Somerset County Gazette', 10 January 1931; Calendar of Patent Rolls, Elizabeth I, vol. IX, 1580-1582, London, 1986, p. 100.

28. J. Walker, An Account of the Number and Sufferings of the Clergy in the late times of the Great Rebellion, London, 1714, p. 422. In 1640 a Robert Bolsom was the curate of Upton Noble and is probably the same clergyman. If so, he was already deeply in trouble with the Church authorities as a result of some of the comments he was alleged to have made. On 23rd June 1640 he was brought in front of a Church Court where the serious charge was laid against him that he had declared that, "anie minister had as much authoritie as anie Buishopp in the Church." He went on to claim that any minister could ordain another priest and it did not require a Bishop. (SRO D/D/Ca 326.) If he continued to be that outspoken during the years of the Civil War he would undoubtedly have alienated many supporters of the Royalist cause.

On 13th February 1604 Alexander, son of Richard Randall was baptised in Shepton Montague Church so this may be the same person.

29. 'Salisbury Journal' 16 September 1765.

30. Acts of the Privy Council, New Series, vol. VI, 1556-1558, London, 1893, p. 72; J.C. Jeaffreson, ed., Middlesex County Records, vol. IV: Session Rolls, p. 234; Calendar of State Papers, Domestic, May 1684-February 1685, London, 1938, p. 13.

31. Case of Francis and Wilmot cited in Castle Cary Visitor, vol. X, 1914-15, p. 138; 'Bath Chronicle and Weekly Gazette', 27 May 1790; 'Western Flying Post', 6 April 1852; 'Shepton Mallet Journal', 18 August 1865, 11 August 1871; 'Western Gazette', 24 October 1890.

32. J. Beresford, Diary, op.cit., vol. I, pp. 52-3; 'Shepton Mallet Journal', 27 May 1870. When some redecoration was taking place in a house in Cats Lane (St Catherine's Hill) some fifty years

ago, the householder removed some of the plaster on a wall to discover the bones of an infant concealed behind it. The cause of death and the reason for concealment was never ascertained. I am indebted to Dr. Colin Clark for reminding me of this event.

33. 'Bath Chronicle and Weekly Gazette', 13 August 1857; Castle Cary Visitor, vol. V, 1904-5, pp. 150, 156.

34. Calendar of Patent Rolls, Henry IV, 1405-1408, London, 1907, p. 169; W. Shakespeare, 'Hamlet', Act III, Scene I, lines 80-86; Legal prescription cited in P. Jalland, Death in the Victorian Family, Oxford, 1999, p. 72; 'Bath Chronicle and Weekly Gazette', 4 March 1762; Castle Cary Visitor, vol. IV, 1902-3, p. 130, vol. V, 1904-5, p. 84; 'Salisbury and Winchester Journal', 20 November 1815.

35. 'The Lancet', 20 September and 4 October 1884.

36. 'Western Flying Post', 23 November 1772; 'Bath Chronicle and Weekly Gazette', 1 May 1800; 18 July 1822; 'Sherborne Mercury', 10 November 1857; 'Western Gazette', 24 November 1884; C. Clark, Diary, op.cit., 3 April 1898, p. 211; 'Bath Chronicle and Weekly Gazette'. 16 February 1843; Castle Cary Visitor, vol. VI, 1906-7, p. 7, vol. V, 1904-5, p. 98, vol. IX, 1912-13, Recollections of W.E. Cooper on Hadspen Cricket Club, pp. 22, 26.

37. Castle Cary Visitor, vol. VI, 1906-7, p. 128; 'Shepton Mallet Journal', 28 November 1862. Details of the suicide by poisoning at Wyke appeared in both the 'Somerset and Wilts Journal', 3 April 1858 and 'Bath Chronicle and Weekly Gazette', 8 April 1858. Their accounts are similar except that the former referred to the deceased as Mrs Everett and the latter as Louisa Hicks.

38. 'Western Gazette', 17 June 1887, Castle Cary Visitor, vol. III, 1900-1, p. 31 and 'Western Daily Press', 5 March 1900; 'Shepton Mallet Journal', 8 November 1861, 29 August 1862.

39. Quarter Sessions Records: Commonwealth, SRS, vol. 28, 1912, p. 287; 'Shepton Mallet Journal', 15 and 29 September 1871; 'Western Gazette', 3 May 1889; 'Shepton Mallet Journal', 18 April 1873; 'Taunton Courier & Western Advertiser', 26 August 1868; 'The Annual Register', vol. 8, 5 August 1765, p. 171; W.R. Ward & R. Heitzenrater, ed., The Works of John

Wesley, vol. 22: Journal and Diaries V, 1765-1775, entry for 14 October 1765, p. 24.

40. SRO Q/SR 66/135, Petition of Walter Cleeves, 1631. For those from Bruton who were discharged from the military in the late eighteenth and early nineteenth centuries see, for example, War Office and Admiralty Papers, PRO WO 97-121 and PRO ADM 29. Manuscripts of R.R. Hastings, vol. II, H.M.C. vol. 78, London, 1930, p. 147, Letter from Thomas Salisbury to Earl of Huntingdon; M. Bright, The Diary of Samuel Pepys, London, 1906, vol. II, 15 January 1665, pp. 83-4, vol. I, 15 December 1662, p. 327; Earl of Clarendon, The Life of Edward, Earl of Clarendon with a continuation of his History of the Great Rebellion, written by himself, London 1668, vol. I, p. 331; J.H. Jesse, The Court of England under the Stuarts, London, 1840, vol. II, p. 457; Bishop Burnet, History of His Own Time, London 1823, vol. I, p. 137; The Diary of Samuel Pepys, 9 June 1665, 8 June 1665, www.pepysdiary.com; Calendar of State Papers, Domestic, 1664-5, London, 1863, Letter from Duke of York to Lord Arlington, 4 June 1665, p. 407, Letter from Earl of Sandwich to Lord Arlington 21 June 1665, p. 421; Clarendon, op.cit., vol.1. p. 269; F.R. Harris, Life of Edward Montague, 1st Earl of Sandwich, London, 1912, vol. I, p. 310.

"Falmouth was there, I know not what to act;
Some say, 'twas to grow Duke too by contact.
An untaught Bullet in its wanton Scope,
Dashes him all to pieces, and his Hope;
Such was his rise, such was his fall unprais'd;
A Chance-shot sooner took him, than Chance rais'd.
His shattered Head the fearless Duke distains,
And gave the last first proof, that he had Brains."
Sir John Denham, 'Directions to a painter concerning the Dutch War', in Poems on State Affairs, 1667, vol. I, p. 26.

41. B. Falk, op.cit., p. 58; Sir John Denham, op.cit. p.26, J. Marvell, 'The Third Advice to a Painter', in Poems on State Affairs, 1667, vol. I, p. 76. No monument or gravestone has survived in Westminster Abbey for either of the Berkeley brothers.

42. Somersetshire Pleas, SRS, vol. 11, 1897, p. 268; 'Bath Chronicle and Weekly Gazette', 4 April 1774; 'Bath Journal', 27 August 1810; 'Western Flying Post', 17 April 1815; 'Bristol Mercury', 13 October 1849; 'Shepton Mallet Journal', 16 April 1869, 14 January 1859, 9 May 1879; 'Oxford Journal', 28 December 1799; R.L. Winstanley, Ansford Diary, op.cit., p. 127.

43. 'Bristol Mercury', 29 September 1823, 21 September 1830; Castle Cary Visitor, Vol. VI, 1906-7, Local Inquests, p. 128; 'Wells Journal', 16 May 1857; 'Western Gazette', 5 April 1878; 'Salisbury and Winchester Journal', 10 August 1852; 'Wells Journal', 9 July 1859; 'Shepton Mallet Journal', 3 May 1861, 8 March 1872, 9 August 1861; Castle Cary Visitor, vol. III, 1900-1, p. 85.

44. 'Shepton Mallet Journal', 20 July 1858; 'Western Daily Press', 22 and 23 December 1899; Railway Accident: Board of Trade Report of Col. Yolland, 22 July 1865; 'Shepton Mallet Journal', 18 August 1865.

45. 'Wells Journal', 27 September 1851; 'Shepton Mallet Journal', 19 March 1886. This was not the only incident involving Solicitor Balch as he also appeared in Court facing debt charges and was involved in a quarrel that led to a fight in the Blue Ball Inn.

46. Somersetshire Pleas, op.cit., p. 269; 'Bristol Mercury', 11 October 1824; Castle Cary Visitor, vol. III, 1900-1, Local Inquests, pp. 181, 185; 'Bath Chronicle and Weekly Gazette', 16 February 1843; ibid., 28 November 1873, 4 April 1884; 'Shepton Mallet Journal', 8 February 1867; 'Bath Chronicle and Weekly Gazette,' 8 May 1851, 6 August 1857.

47. 'Western Flying Post', 27 June 1768; Castle Cary Visitor, III, Local Inquests, op.cit.; 'Bath Chronicle and Weekly Gazette', 9 August 1849 – the only burial of a boy in Bruton at this time was Frederick Curtis on 29 July; 'Shepton Mallet Journal', 9 August 1861, 21 July 1876; C. Clark, Diary, op.cit., 23 May 1895, p. 156; 'Shepton Mallet Journal', 30 December 1859 and it was also reported in the 'Somerset and Wilts Journal' the

following day; 'Western Flying Post', 11 May 1767. It is not possible to trace these three deaths in the Burial Register as no entries were made between 11 May and 3 August; they ceased again on 6 November and did not resume until 3 June 1768 when the Parish Clerk, John Biggs, was replaced by John Prince. 'Bath Chronicle and Weekly Gazette', 15 October 1896.

48. 'Western Flying Post', 16 January 1766; 'Somerset and Wilts Journal', 31 December 1859; Castle Cary Visitor, vol. VIII, 1910-11, p. 172; 'Shepton Mallet Journal', 3 October 1862; 'Bristol Mercury', 13 July 1822; 'Shepton Mallet Journal', 30 August 1872; 'Western Flying Post', 30 May 1874; 'Salisbury and Winchester Journal', 17 November 1828; 'Western Gazette', 11 November 1870; 'Bath Chronicle and Weekly Gazette', 6 September 1821; 'Sherborne Mercury', 2 February 1864, 23 March 1858; 'Western Gazette', 16 January 1885; 'Hampshire Chronicle', 22 February 1819; 'Somerset Gazette', 10 May 1837; 'Shepton Mallet Journal', 7 November 1873; 'Western Gazette', 28 August 1896; ibid., 10 November 1876; 'Shepton Mallet Journal', 26 January 1866.

49. Calendar of State Papers, Domestic, 1671, London, 1895, p. 8, Letter dated June 6th 1671; Moody, Martin and Byrne, ed., A New History of Ireland, vol. III: Early Modern Ireland 1534-1691, Oxford, 1991, p. 451.

Chapter 3 Death for Young and Old.

1. A.S. MacMillan, Somerset Epitaphs, Somerset Folk Series, No. 18, London, 1924, p. 128.

2. Somerset Wills from Wells, SRS, vol. 40, 1925, p. 136. A very detailed analysis of the Bruton Parish Registers may provide some other instances of this practice. The complicating factor, however, was that families adopted the same Christian names for generations so for example two brothers who had been given the name of their father and grandfather might then give their own two sons the same names, so in 4 generations in the family 8 men shared the same 2 names.

3. 'Bath Chronicle and Weekly Gazette', 17 July 1784; 'Bristol Mercury', 3 March 1838; 'Sherborne Mercury', 13 March 1860.
4. C. Gittings, Death, Burial and the Individual in Early Modern England, London, 1984, p. 7. For a detailed account of Sexey's Hospital and its care of the elderly, see P.W. Randell, Stones We Cannot Eat: Poverty, the Poor Law, Philanthropy and Self Help in Bruton, Somerset, c1500-c1900, Brighton, 2009, esp. pp. 230-243.
5. See P.W. Randell, Life in a Rural Workhouse: Wincanton Workhouse, Somerset, 1834-1900, Brighton, 2010, esp. pp. 51-57.

Chapter 4 Attitudes to Death.

1. The idea of not dying alone was in fact still to be found in Bruton in the mid-twentieth century. A common sight at that period was an elderly nurse, Nurse Street, as she peddled around the town on her old black bicycle which had a basket attached to the front handlebars in which was her nurse's bag. She would sit with the very sick and the dying throughout the night and give some respite to the family.
2. PRO PROB 11/19348, Will of Richard Holmede 1520; PRO PROB 11/10/151, Will of Margery Moleyns September 1493. Hereafter all Wills referred to may be found listed in chronological order in Appendix 2.
3. Jesus, lord, welcome thou be
   In form of bread, as I thee see,
   Jesu! For thy Holy Name
   Shield me today from sin and shame,
   Confession & absolution, lord, thou grant me both,
   Before that I shall go hence,
   And very contrite of my sin,
   That I lord never die therein.
   Letters of Sir Francis Hastings 1574-1609, SRS, vol. 69, 1969, p. 66; J. Beresford, Diary, op.cit., vol. I, p. 54.
4. E. Duffy, The Stripping of the Altars, Yale, 2nd ed. 2005, p. 303.

5. Bruton and Montacute Cartularies, op.cit., see for example Nos. 8, 69, 72.

6. SRO DD/L/P1/17/1, Summary Account of Robert Rivers 1430-1431.

7. Register of Bishop Bekynton, SRS, vol. 49, 1934, pp. 323-5. This document in Latin may also be found printed in Notes and Queries for Somerset and Dorset, vol. 3, pp. 88-90.

8. It is no coincidence that the results of an analysis of and dendrodating of various properties in the High Street also suggest early- to mid-fifteenth century dates for construction, see, for example, M. McDermott, 'Somerset Dendochronology Project Phases 5 and 6', in SANHSP, vol. 149, 2006, p. 91, and also J. and J. Penoyre, 'Some Bruton Town Houses', in SANHSP, vol. 140, 1997, pp. 121-131.

9. Exactly how Richard Bruton became so wealthy is not clear but the suggestion has been made that he was none too honest, see, for example, R. Dunning, 'Clerical Crook', in Somerset Magazine, vol. 6, February 1996, p. 31. His preferments included: Vicar of Minehead, Rector of High Ham, Canon and Chancellor of Wells Cathedral and Prebendary of Ashill.

10. This gift of £400 was a remarkable one as today it would have a value of at least a quarter of a million pounds. John Henton, senior, was clearly a very successful and wealthy mercer, one who was undoubtedly able to influence his son's election as Prior.
Feet of Fines, Edward III to Richard II, SRS, vol. 17, 1902, p. 16.

11. Calendar of Patent Rolls, Edward III, 1361-1364, London, 1912, p. 221; Calendar of Patent Rolls, Richard II, 1381-1385, London, 1897, p. 433; W. K. Jordan, 'The Forming of the Charitable Institutions of the West of England, 1480-1660', in Transactions of the American Philosophical Society, New Series, 50, pt. 8, 1960, pp. 68-9.

12. R. Dyboski, ed., Songs, Carols and other Miscellaneous Poems.... From Richard Hill's Commonplace Book, Early Text Society, 1908, p. 141.

13. Bridges were deeply symbolic as emblems of Christian life and of communication. It was no coincidence that the Pope and each

bishop was a 'pontifex', that is, a bridge-builder. It was not uncommon for bridges to have a hermitage or small chapel built on or near them, As there were a number of references to a chapel of St George in Patwell Street, this may well have been located very close to the old Church Bridge.

14. SRO D/D/Ca 22, Comperta 1554; SRO D/D/Ca 27, Bishop's Visitation 1557; Commission February 1549, The Surtees Society, 1896, pt II, vol. 97, p. xii.

15. 1547 Nov 1 Lettre from the king's Majesties Commissioners, Calendar of the Manuscripts of the Dean and Chapter of Wells, vol. II, Historical Manuscripts Commission, 13, London 1914, pp. 264-5. For some consideration of the continued use of bells in Bruton, see P.W. Randell, Alcohol, Violence, Feasts and Fairs: Leisure Pursuits in Bruton, Somersetshire, c1500-c1900, Brighton, 2012, pp. 20-25.

16. SRO D/P/brut 4/1/1 and 4/2/2, Bruton Churchwardens' Accounts 1735-1831.

17. 'Western Flying Post', 26 February 1838 and 15 February 1859; P. Jalland, Death in the Victorian Family, Oxford, 1999, p. 2.

18. G. Best, 'Evangelicalism and the Victorians', in A. Symondson, ed., The Victorian Crisis of Faith, London, 1970, pp. 54-5.

19. W. Blake, Vide Sola Pinto, London, 1965, p. 151; F. Engels, The Condition of the Working Class in England, with Introduction by E.J. Hobsbawn, London, 1969, p. 86.

20. Boyd Hilton, The Age of Atonement: The Influence of Evangelicalism on Social and Economic Thought, 1795-1865, Oxford, 1988, pp. 335-6.

21. 'Western Gazette', 29 July 1881, 12 April 1889.

22. 'Wells Journal', 15 November 1851; 'Bath Chronicle and Weekly Gazette', 17 January 1850; 'Wells Journal', 23 July 1853; 'Western Gazette', 24 January 1888. See also Appendix 4f for details on brass plaque erected to John Jelley in St. Mary's Church.

23. 'Salisbury and Winchester Journal', 10 February 1849; 'Wells Journal', 15 November 1851; 'Western Daily Press', 16 February 1899. Comment by Florence Nightingale cited in B. Abel Smith, A History of the Nursing Profession, London, 1982, p. 5.

Chapter 5 The Role of the Parish Church and Churchyard.

1. Register of Bishop John de Drokensford, SRS, vol. I, 1887, p. 143; G. Grigson, ed., Faber Book of Epigrams and Epitaphs, London, 1977, p. 170.
2. H. Spelman, 'De Sepultura', in The English Works of Sir Henry Spelman, London, 1727, pp. 173-190.
3. SRO DD/JO/26, Parish Accounts: Overseers' Accounts 1735-84, pp. 193, 203-4.
4. W. Phelps, The History and Antiquities of Somersetshire, London, 1836, pp. 238-241.
5. D. Dymond, 'God's Disputed Acre', in Journal of Ecclesiastical History, vol. 50, 1999, p. 467.
6. For details of markets, feasts and fairs, see P.W. Randell, Alcohol, Violence, Feasts and Fairs, op. cit., pp. 25-50.
7. Register of Bishop John Drokensford, op.cit., p. 45; SRO D/D/Ca Metropolitan Visitation 1605; SRO D/D/ Ca 81 Ex-Officio 1587-1592; McDermott & Berry, op.cit., p. 346; 'Bath Chronicle and Weekly Gazette', 14 August 1851.
8. 'Gibbis ' or 'gibbons' usually meant hunchback so this may be a reference to the grave of a well-known Bruton inhabitant.
9. The original Latin inscription reads:

Pulvis et ossa Sumus
    Cadavera antehac jacentium
    In ossuario
    Sub Adytu
    Hujusce Ecclesiae
  Sub hoc marmore Condita
  Jussu Honorabilis C. Berkley
    Anno 1743.

A literal translation is given here but more liberal ones have appeared:
the first line has been translated as 'We are the dust and ashes';
'ossuario' called an ossuary or even crypt;
'Adyto' has been referred to as the Chancel;
'marmore' translated as marble or tablet.

An Account of Berkeley's action was given in the mid 1750s: "There is but one monument that has anything remarkable, and that is a monument of Bones, the story of which is this. When Mr Berkeley in the year 174 rebuilt the Chancel he found the Bodies of his Ancestors crammed in a corner under the Altar and the rest of the Vault partly in rubbish and partly full of dead mens bones, he cleansed it, and because he would give no offence nor occasion to say that he disturbed the Ashes of the Dead, he ordered them to be with care collected and decently put under ground on the south side of the Church, over which he raised a kind of Tumulus, and on that built a monument of Stone with an Urn and an inscription on a plate of Marble," Querys, op.cit., pt. I, No. 18.

10. 'Bath Chronicle and Weekly Gazette', 5 March 1772; Notes and Queries for Somerset and.
Dorset, vol. XXXIV, March 1999, p. 291.
Although Atkin's Hill does contain some relatively flat areas there is no documentary evidence that any buildings were ever erected there. Given the steep sides of the valley where building has taken place this is perhaps surprising. It is possible that the hill had some significance in Pre-historic and Roman times as it provides a clear view of Creech Hill with its Iron Age encampment and Roman Temple. This particular burial may of course be pre-Christian.
R. Leech, 'The Excavation of a Romano-Celtic Temple and a later Cemetary on Lamyatt Beacon, Somerset', in Britannia, vol. 17, 1986, pp. 272, 326, 328; 'Bath Chronicle and Weekly Gazette', 6 December 1849.

11. SRO D/D/Ca 236, Comperta 1623; SRO D/D/Ca 22 Comperta 1554; SRO D/P/brut 4/1/2, Churchwardens' Accounts, entry 26th May 1827.

12 The United Counties Miscellany: Somerset, Dorset and Devon, vol. I, 1849-50, p. 252.

13. An unusual story circulated in the mid-twentieth century concerning one family vault. It was claimed that when a member of the family was laid to rest the coffin was placed on the top

shelf, which was more than the width of the coffin, but when the vault was re-opened at a later time for another member of the family, it was on the bottom shelf. Leaving aside supernatural explanations, the presence of water may have played a part as the extension of the churchyard along with alterations to the Abbey Field may have significantly affected the sophisticated medieval drainage system of the monastery. There clearly were drainage issues as the Churchwardens' Accounts do contain many references to drainage and the installation of drainage pipes. Flooding by the River Brue may have played a part as well as for example in 1917 the flood waters almost reached the West Door. There have even been claims that at times the coffins in the Crypt could be heard banging together.

14. 'Shepton Mallet Journal', 25 January 1867, 17 December 1869, 11 June 1870; SRO D/D/cf/1884/3, Consistorial Episcopal Court of Wells, Petition of Emily Melita Dickens, 24 January 1884.

15. C. Clark, Diary, op.cit., 12 December 1895, p. 166, 18 January 1896, p. 168.

Chapter 6 Burial of the dead: general.

1. One of the earliest men to be specifically referred to as an undertaker in Bruton was John Evans in 1832, see SRO DD/BT/18/4.

2. J. Beresford, Diary, op.cit., vol. I, p. 109.
   Another example of a delay in final burial may be found in the case of Ralph Hopton, 1st Baron Hopton of Stratton who lived at Witham Friary. He was a Royalist commander during the Civil War in the 1640s and on the defeat of Charles I went into exile in Bruges. There he died of fever, probably malaria, in 1652. His body was embalmed and finally brought back to England nine years later and buried in Witham Parish Church in 1661.
   R.L. Winstanley, ed, The Diary of the Revd. James Woodforde, vol. II, 1763-1765, Parson Woodforde Society, 1996, pp. 179-180 (hereafter R.L. Winstanley, Diary); J. Beresford, Diary, op.cit., vol. I, pp. 114-5.

3. E.S. de Beer, ed., The Diary of John Evelyn, London, 1959, p. 658, 16 September 1678; J.V. Kitto, ed., St Martin's-in-the-Fields. The accounts of the churchwardens, 1525-1603, London, 1901.

4. B. Raphael, The Anatomy of Bereavement, London, 1984, p. 37.

5. The Works of Alexander Pope, vol. III, Moral Essays, London, 1751, pp. 124-5.

6. SRO D/P/brut 2/4/1, Order to Churchwardens and Overseers 22 September 1692; SRO D/P/brut 13/10/2, Instruction to Constable of Brewton 30 May 1695.

7. For details of the Wincanton Union Workhouse, see P.W. Randell, Life in a Rural Workhouse, op. cit., esp. pp. 140-1.

8. 'Somerset and Wilts Journal', 26 February 1859; 'Shepton Mallet Journal', 10 July 1868; 'Western Gazette', 13 June 1879, 1 March 1878, 24 June 1892.

9. P.L. Couzens, Bruton in Selwood, Sherborne 1968, p. 93; G.de Y. Aldridge, 'The Church Bells of Somerset', in SANHSP, vol. LX, 1914, p. 68; 'Western Gazette', 11 January 1889.

10. ibid., 1 September 1899; ed. R.L. Winstanley, Ansford Diary, op.cit., p.133.

11. ibid. p. 101. For details of pauper deaths and burials see P.W. Randell, Life in a Rural Workhouse, op.cit., esp. pp. 138-144.

12. SRO D/D/Cta W36, C59, M10, A18, Executors' Accounts.

13. SRO DD/BRU 1/2/1, Governors' Register 1554-1700; SRO DD/SE/43/2, The Accompte of Richard Illing of Brewton 1649-1652; SE/43/15, Mr Cheeke's Accompt 1656-1662; SRO DD/BT/18/4, Estate of James Clarke 1832-3.

14. C. Gittings, Death, Burial and the Individual, op.cit., p. 238; SRO D/D/Cta D33 and M10; The Diary of John Evelyn, op.cit., p. 658. The Berkeleys and the Godolphins were linked through various marriage alliances, for example, Sir Charles Berkeley married Penelope the daughter of Sir William Godolphin and her brother Sir Francis married Dorothy, the daughter of Sir Henry Berkeley of Yarlington, a union which produced 16 children, some 13 of whom were still surviving in 1668 when Lady Godolphin made her Will.

15. SRO DD/BT/12, Stamp Duty Recepits; SRO/DD/BT/18/4, Estate of James Clarke, op.cit.

16. The Vestry Meeting in 1840 ordered that the list should be published and "placed in the Bellfry for the use of the Parishioners." A slightly different version of the List dated November 1840 may be found on display in Bruton Museum.

Chapter 7 Burial of the Wealthy.

1. R.W. Dunning, 'The Wells Consistory Court in the Fifteenth Century', in SANHSP, vol. 106, 1962, p. 61; R.W. Dunning, 'Clerical Crook', op.cit., p. 31.

2. R. Leech, op.cit., pp. 272, 326.

3. D. Postles, 'Monastic Burials of Non-Patronal Lay Benefactors', in Journal of Ecclesiastical History, vol. 47, 1996, pp. 623-4; H.C. Maxwell, A History of Dunster, London, 1909, vol. I, pp. 30, 46, 113.

4. 'A Brief Summary of the Wardrobe Accounts of King Edward the Second', in Archaeologia, vol. XXVI, 1836, p. 339; Register of Bishop John de Drokensford, op.cit., p. 143; Sarum Charters and Documents, Rolls Series, vol. 97, London, 1891, pp. 225-6.

5. Calendar of the Manuscripts of the Dean and Chapter of Wells, vol. 2, London 1914, No. 684; Summary Accounts of Robert Rivers, op.cit.

6. J.G. Nichols, ed., 'The Diary of Henry Machyn, a citizen of London, 1550-1563', Camden Society, 1st Series, vol. 42, 1848, p. 227; E. Ironside, The History and Antiquities of Twickenham, London, 1797, p. 42. Sir William had returned to England after his fall from grace as a result, amongst other things, of some very severe actions he had taken after Bacon's Rebellion in the Colony. It was claimed that he had hanged as many as 22 of the rebels and even Charles II was supposed to have exclaimed, "That old fool has put to death more people in that naked country than I did here for the death of the father!"

7. Lady Elizabeth Egerton was incorrectly stated in the Burial Register and on the plate on her lead coffin to be the daughter of

the 1st Duke of Portland. Other members of the Berkeley family were probably interred in the vault as well but such details were not given in the Burial Registers. Alterations to the entrance to the crypt in the Victorian period meant that the removal of the lead coffins became impossible so that 7 remain, 5 adults and 2 children. The latter may well be the 2 children of the Hon. Charles Berkeley interred on the 9th May and 19th August 1757.

A possible translation of the Latin words on William Lord Berkeley's coffin may be, "A few admired, a few more despised."

8. J. Beresford, Dairy, op.cit., vol. I, pp. 54, 109; J. Winstanley, Diary, op.cit., vol. 3, p. 185; J. Beresford, Diary, op.cit., vol. I, p. 43.

9. C. Clark, Diary, op.cit., 18 June 1901, p. 262; J. Beresford, Diary, op.cit., pp. 155-6.

Chapter 8 Burial of the Poor.

1. Many of the examples in this section are taken from the Accounts of the Overseers of the Poor for Bruton 1653-1836, SRO D/P/brut 13/2/1-13/2/12, and from the Overseers' Monthly Accounts 1705-1730, SRO D/P/brut 13/2/14.

2. For more details of Sexey's Hospital, see P.W. Randell, Stones We Cannot Eat, op.cit., esp. pp. 205-282.

3. Accompt of Mr Cheeke, 1662, op.cit.; SRO DD/BT/7/2, Bruton Hospital Small Account Books, 1791-1835, vol. 7, 1819-1835.

4. The Accompte of Richard Illing, op.cit; SRO DD/SE/72, Visitors' Minute Book, 5 May 1892; SRO DD/BT 25/97, Sexey's Hospital Letter Book 1893-1896, 5 February 1895; Minute Book, op.cit., 6 May 1899; 'Western Flying Post', 24 January 1846; Castle Cary Visitor, vol. VII, 1908-9, p. 190.

5. Accompt of Mr Cheeke, 1662, op.cit.; SRO DD/SE/45/5, Mr Albyns Book of Disbursements 1652-5; SRO DD/SE/43/17, Accounts of Robert Ludwell, 1666-1676; Small Account Books, op.cit., vol. I, 1791-8; Further Report of the Commission to Inquire Concerning Charities, 1824, PP 1824 XIV, p. 376.

6. SRO DD/SE/47, A Schedule of Goods belonging to the Hospital of Brewton, 9 February 1703; Castle Cary Visitor, vol. VI, 1906-7, p. 159.
7. SRO A/DBR/10, Rules of the Bruton Friendly Society, p. 2; Rules of the Shepton Montague Friendly Society, p. 12; SRO Q/R Friendly Society Rules and Regulations: The North Brewham Society.
8. 'Western Flying Post', 20 January 1844.
9. 'Shepton Mallet Journal', 27 March 1874; Castle Cary Visitor, vol. VI, 1906-7, pp. 7, 142.

Chapter 9 Burial of Children

1. J. Beresford, Diary, op.cit., vol. I, pp. 74-5; R.L. Winstanley, Ansford Diary, op.cit., vol. 2, p. 141. Although Woodforde held curacies in Somerset early in his career and continued throughout his life to visit and enjoy lengthy stays with his sister Jane at Cole, his main Ministry was in Norfolk. There he had to bury children of the local Squire and he gave considerable detail in his Diary, such as on 15th November 1780. The parents did not attend the funeral service or burial and there was usually only one relative present. Inside a lead coffin, "The Corpse was brought in a Coach and four attended by two Servant maids in very deep mourning and long black Hoods.... The Driver and other Servants had hatbands and gloves." J. Beresford, Diary, op.cit., pp. 295-6.
2. C. Clark, Diary, op.cit., 27 March 1895 and passim p. 153, 26 April 1895 and passim p. 155, 13 May 1895 and passim p. 156.
3. Cited in C. Gittings, op.cit., p. 78.
4. 'Shepton Mallet Journal', 20 December 1872; C. Clark, Diary, op.cit., 19, 22, 23 March 1896, p. 172.

Chapter 10 Burial of Non Conformists.

1. SRO DD/SFR/8/1, A Record of the Sufferings for Truth in the County of Somerset 1654-1672, pp. 46-7, 58.
2. B. Montague, The Funerals of Quakers, London, 1840, pp. 55-7.
3. PRO PROB 10/1220, Will of Thomas Whitehead, 4 April 1691.

4. SRO, DD/SFR/8/2, A Record of Sufferings, 1659-1695, p. 283.

5. 'Shepton Mallet Journal', 25 February 1859.

Chapter 11 Burial of the Dead: miscellaneous

1. The practice of regular visits to graves over a prolonged period still occurred in the mid-twentieth century. For example, two elderly ladies, the Curtis sisters who lived in Coombe Street, made a weekly visit to family graves, especially that of their parents, which were located just to the south of the West Tower. On each occasion fresh flowers were brought and the grass trimmed around the headstone and the kerbstones, with these being washed and cleaned as necessary. They were always dressed in black and frequently attended local funerals. With them at the latter were other women, sometimes widows but often spinsters – some were from the generation which was left behind after the slaughter of the First World War.

2. 'Devises and Wiltshire Gazette', 3 March 1842.

Chapter 12 Prosperity at Death.

1. WRO Hoare Papers 383/148, Stourhead Account Book 1812.

2. R. Dunning, 'Clerical Crook', op.cit., p. 31.

3. SRO DD/SE/4/10.

4. SRO D/D/Cta D33, W36, C59, K2, W46, A18.; PRO PROB 4/11910, A true & pfect Inventory...of ye goods Chattells & debts of Thomas Tice als Rogers; PRO PROB 10/1220, Inventory of Thomas Whitehead's estate, 1691.

5. Although the younger sons received money that often allowed them to live comfortably, it was not always as much as they would have wished and so sometimes did encourage them to seek fame and fortune. William became a courtier and was in 1642 appointed Governor of Virginia, a position he held until the mid 1670s, with an interruption in the 1650s when he was removed by Cromwell. He was a noted Indian fighter and was the first Governor of the Colonies to proclaim the Restoration of Charles II. In fact the family had an older connection with the Colony as

William's father, Sir Maurice, had been a member of the Council of the Virginia Company. The activities of John, the youngest son, were even more crucial for the Berkeley family history as through his loyal support of and exile with Charles II and the Duke of York, he was richly rewarded with titles, honours, positions and land, including in London and what became the Berkeley Square/Bruton Street area. It was one of his younger sons, William, as the 4th Baron Berkeley of Stratton, who bought back the Bruton estate which had been mortgaged to pay the huge debts which his cousin Maurice Berkeley, 3rd Lord Fitzharding, had accumulated, and which became available for purchase after the death of John, 4th Lord Fitzharding without any male heirs. John, the 5th and last Lord Berkeley of Stratton bequeathed land, property and money valued at well over £150,000, worth at least £15m in modern terms.

6. Roper's Tenement is the name still used for a building behind the Pharmacy (No. 3) in the High Street. If this is in fact the same building then it implies a very different layout of property in the area at that earlier period, possibly relating to a market square. It would have been unlikely that a prosperous, prominent family such as the Ludwells would have lived in a house hidden behind another.

7. SRO D/D/cta W46, Inventory of the Goods & Chattles of William Wilton, 1734;

8. SRO DD/SE/39/4, Bill of Complaint of Sir Gerrard Sammes and his wife Dame Ursula 9 November 1624; SE/39/5 and SE/39/6, Answers of Trustees.

9. W.K. Jordan, Forming etc., op.cit., p. 48.

Chapters 13-16 Worldly Consequences.

1. Calendar of Inquisitions Post Mortem, vol. II, Edward I, London, 1906, p. 400; Calendar of Inquisitions Post Mortem, Henry VII, vol. I, London, 1898, p. 300; Calendar of Inqusitions Post Mortem, vol. III, Edward I, London 1912, p. 64; Calendar of Inquisitions Post Mortem, vol. VI, Edward II, London, 1910,

p. 142; Calendar of Inquisitions Post Mortem, vol. XVIII, 1-6 Henry IV, 1399-1405, London, 1987, p. 124; Calendar of Inquisitions Post Mortem, Henry VII, vol. I, London, 1898, p. 131; Calendar of Inquisitions Post Mortem, Miscellaneous, vol. I, 1219-1307, London, 1916, p. 36; Calendar of Inquisitions Post Mortem, vol. VIII, Edward III, London, 1913, p. 387; Calendar of Inquisitions Post Mortem, vol. XI, Edward III, London, 1838, pp. 49-50; SRO DD/SG/1, Inquisition Post Mortem of Nicholas Fitzjames, 1550; SRO DD/SE/38/3, Inquisition Post Mortem of Hugh Sexey 1620; SRS, Register of Ralph of Shrewsbury 1329-1363, vol. 9, 1896, p. 397.

2. Calendar of Inquisitions Post Mortem, vol. III, Edward III, London, 1937, pp. 298, 330; Calendar of Inquisitions Post Mortem, vol. XIX, 7-14 Henry IV, 1405-1413, London 1992, p. 254; Calendar of Inquisitions Post Mortem, Henry VII, op.cit.; SRO DD/WHh/648, Inq. Post Mortem of Sir William Weston 1594; SRO DD/L/P/25/1, Inq. Post Mortem of Henry Southworth, 24 November 1625.

3. Calendar of Inquisitions Post Mortem, Henry VII, vol. III, London, 1955, p. 250; Calendar of Inquisitions Post Mortem, vol. VII, 1399-1422, London, 1968, p. 333. The bronze vessel had passed to the king under the system of 'Deodand', which was originally 'Deo Dandum' that literally meant 'to be given to God'. Any object which caused a person's death became subject to forfeit. Such a requirement was finally abolished in 1846, mainly after a number of deaths caused by steam locomotives on the newly opened railways.

4. For details of the activities of Church Courts in Bruton, see P.W. Randell, Crime, Law and Order in a Somersetshire Market Town: Bruton c1500-c1900, Brighton, 2011, esp. pp. 80-114.

5. SRO D/D/Ca 204, Comperta 1617; SRO D/D/Ca 236, Comperta 1623.

6. WRO Hoare Papers 383/321, Manor Courts, Wilts, Dorset, Somerset, volume Second, pp. 115, 146, 194, 206; WRO Hoare Papers 383/327, A Survey of the Mannor of Brewton in the County of Somerset 1669; WRO Hoare Papers 383/96, A Survey

of Sir John Brownlow's Estates 1713; SRO DD/PH/149, Court Baron Shepton Montague.

7. SRO DD/SE/39/1, Bill of Complaint of Thos Banckes, DD/SE/39/2-3, Answers of Trustees.
8. SRO DD/SE/81, Deed of Trust, 14 June 1616.
9. 'Wandell' was probably a version of 'wennell' which means a newly weaned calf.
10. 'kyne' was often used as the plural of cow. 'Rother' meant bovine cattle, so in this context probably oxen.
11. For details of Hugh Sexey's charitable bequests see P.W. Randell, Stones We Cannot Eat, op.cit., esp. pp. 205-282. The arrangements for Dorothy Sexey's Charity are contained in a letter to Hugh Sexey, SRO DD/SE 35/2.
12. 'Western Gazette', 1 February 1878; SRO D/P/brut 4/1/1, Churchwardens' Accounts
13. W.P. Balsdon, 'Some Correspondence of the Maudes of Hollinghall 1594-1599', in Thoresby Society, vol. 24, 1919, pp. 110-112.
14. See P.W. Randell, Stones We Cannot Eat, op.cit., pp. 200-204 for details of Hospital.

    It is interesting to note that leprosy was still prevalent in Bruton in the nineteenth century as Thomas Sims and William Young were both discharged from Bath Hospital in October 1824 and August 1833 respectively when it was stated that they were "cleansed" of leprosy. 'Bath Chronicle and Weekly Gazette', 7 October 1824 and 1 August 1833.
15. P.W. Randell, Alcohol, Violence, Feasts and Fairs, op.cit., pp. 41-2.
16. Comment of Colley Cibber, who lived at the Bruton Street corner of Berkeley Square, on Anne Bracegirdle, cited in B. Falk, op.cit., p. 112. Lord Berkeley himself had pursued a career at sea and at various times in the late 1680s and through the 1690s served as a Rear Admiral, Vice Admiral and finally between 1696 and 1698 as an Admiral. For a list of his appointments see J. Ehrman, The Navy in the War of William III 1689-1697, Cambridge, 1953, pp. 647-648.

17. British Museum, Add. MSS 28,052, f.4, undated letter from Lady Godolpin to Lady Fitzharding; Longleat House, Coventry Papers, XXXIII, pp. 207-8, Letter from John, Ist Lord Berkeley of Stratton to Lord Coventry, 15 January 1676; Letter from William, 4th Lord Berkeley of Stratton to Lord Strafford quoted in B. Falk, op.cit, p. 115.

18. 'Bath Chronicle and Weekly Gazette', 17 December 1789; 'Western Flying Post', 10 and 17 February 1800; 'Western Gazette', 20 February 1880; B. Falk, op. cit., p. 116.
Both John, 4th Lord Fitzharding and his wife were buried in the north ambulatory of Westminster Abbey under simple gravestones:
"Here lyeth the body of John Lord Viscount Fitzharding of Bearehaven and Baron Berkeley of Rathdowne in the Kingdom of Ireland. He was one of the tellers of the Exchequer and Treasurer of ye Chamber to Her Majestie Queen Anne and Custos Rotulorum of Somersetshire who departed this life the 19th day of December 1712 in the 63rd year of his age."
"Here lyeth the body of Barbara Villiers, Viscountess Fitzharding, Governess to His late Royall Highness the Duke of Glocester, daughter to the Hon. Sr. Edward and the Hon. Lady Frances Villiers, who died September 19th 1708 in her 52nd year."

19. P. Jalland, Death in the Victorian Family, op.cit., p. 254.

20. R. Holworthy, ed, 'Hearth Tax for Somerset 1664-5' in Dwelly's National Records, vol. I, 1916, p. 91. As well as the Accounts of the Overseers of the Poor for Bruton from 1653-1836 previously cited, there are 2 volumes of the Bruton Select Vestry Minute Book for the Administration of the Poor from 1790-1820, SRO D/P/brut 9/1/1 and 9/1/2.

21. PRO MH32/85, Correspondence of R. Weale, 7 November 1838.

22. SRO DD/SE/44, Orders made by ye Visitors of ye Hospital of Brewton 10 May 1694.

23. SRO DD/SE/45/1, Petitions to the ffeoffees of Sexey's Hospital, No. 2 Margaret Drew, No. 20 Elizabeth Stroud, Nos. 41 and 75 Grace Penny, No. 13 Anstice Leversuch, No. 27 Mary Creed,

Nos. 5 and 7 Joan Young, No. 11 Joane Tice, No. 44 Christian Mitchell, No. 70 Elizabeth Hardin, No. 60 Edward Carrier, No. 17 Richard Edwardes, No. 26 Robert Hore the elder.

24. Calendar of Inquisitions Post Mortem, 7-14 Henry IV, op.cit, p. 254; Cornwall Record Office AR/1/943, Lease of Godmanston during Minority 9 March 1559; Sales of Wards in Somerset 1603-1641, SRS, vol. 67, 1965, pp. 85-6; Honour of Dunster, p. 191, in SRO DD/BRU 9/6.

25. R.L. Winstanley, Ansford Diary, op.cit., p. 110; PRO REQ 1, Court of Requests, 32 Bundle.

26. SRO D/G/WN/8a/1, Wincanton Board of Guardians' Minute Book, 27 April 1836.

27. Quarter Sessions Records: Commonwealth, SRS, vol. 28, 1913, p. 242.

28. SRO DD/SE/38/5, Accounts of Edward Wykes 1628.

29. SRO DD/SE/45/1, Petitions, op.cit., No. 86; SRO DD/SE/45/2, Petitions to the ffeoffees of Sexey's Hospital, No. 22.

30. R. Houlbrooke, Death, Religion, etc. op.cit., p. 254; J.G. Nichols, 'The Diary of Henry Machyn' op.cit., p. 21.

31. B. Montague, op.cit., pp. 56-7; C. Hartley, Gentleman's Book of Etiquette, and Manual of Politeness, London, 1873.

32. As an alternative for the final six months a widow could wear half colours, that is grey and lavender or black and white. The belief existed that it was unlucky to keep crape in the house and so women tended to renew mourning clothes on a number of occasions. That of course did no harm to the profits of Courtaulds who had a near monopoly on its manufacture from the1840s to the 1880s.

33. A few examples of memorials in Bruton Parish Church may be found in J. Collinson, The History and Antiquities, op.cit., vol. I, pp. 217-8. A further list was produced by W. Phelps in The History and Antiquities, op.cit., vol. I, pp. 239-241. The Young memorial verse was printed in Castle Cary Visitor, vol. VII, 1908-9, p. 87.

34. Letters of George Lord Carew to Sir Thomas Roe, Camden Society, vol. 76, 1860, p. 106.

35. 'Sherborne Mercury', 7 April 1741;

36. 'Bath Chronicle and Weekly Gazette', 8 August 1771; ed. R.L. Winstanley, Diary, op.cit., vol. 2, p. 167.

37. 'Bath Chronicle and Weekly Gazette', 14 May 1761, 21 January 1790; Salisbury and Winchester Journal, 11 January 1808; J. Beresford, Diary, op.cit., vol. IV, p.224; 'Bath Chronicle and Weekly Gazette', 6 June 1799; 'Western Flying Post', 20 July 1801, 21 October 1876, 26 May 1817; 'Taunton Courier and Western Advertiser, 30 October 1839.

38. 'Shepton Mallet and East Somerset Herald', 18 February 1859; 'Shepton Mallet Journal', 18 March '1874.

39. 'Salisbury and Winchester Journal', 9 November 1835, 24 March 1834, 13 February 1837; 'Bath Chronicle and Weekly Gazette', 7 November 1849, 30 May 1850.

40. C. Woodforde, Stained Glass in Somerset 1250-1830, Oxford, 1946, p. 221.

41. J. Bishton, St Mary the Virgin, Bruton: A brief history, privately printed, 2011, pp. 76-80; 'Western Gazette', 20 April 1888.

Chapter 18 And finally or not?

1. W.G. Willis Watson, Calendar of Customs, Superstitions, Somerset County Herald, 1920, pp.143-4.

2. This version of the Goldesbrough Apparition is taken from 'The Dolphin', Christmas 1924, p. 12, which was itself based upon one in 'Notes and Queries', 11 June 1870.

3. 'Bath Chronicle and Weekly Gazette', 28 February 1850.

4. This story may be a reference to a local solicitor John Balch who may have had a severe drink problem. On one occasion his behaviour in Court was deemed to be so outrageous that he was ordered to leave the room. At other times he himself was the defendant after he was alleged to have started a fight in the Blue Ball Inn and was also found guilty of failure to repay a debt.

9 781781 487020